TAKING SIDES

Clashing Views on Controversial

Issues in Marketing

Selected, Edited, and with Introductions by

Barton Macchiette
Plymouth State College

and

Abhijit Roy
Boston University

McGraw-Hill/Dushkin
A Division of The McGraw-Hill Companies

To our parents, with love and gratitude

Photo Acknowledgment
Cover image: © 2001 by PhotoDisc, Inc.

Cover Art Acknowledgment
Charles Vitelli

Manufactured in the United States of America

First Edition

123456789BAHBAH4321

Library of Congress Cataloging-in-Publication Data
Main entry under title:
Taking sides: clashing views on controversial issues in marketing/selected, edited, and with introductions by Barton Macchiette and Abhijit Roy.—1st ed.
Includes bibliographical references and index.
1. Marketing. I. Macchiette, Barton, *comp.* II. Roy, Abhijit, *comp.*
658.8
0-07-238449-2
ISSN: 1530-0773

Printed on Recycled Paper

Preface

Background Marketing is arguably the most inescapable aspect of our culture. It has a dramatic presence and pervasive influence on our daily lives, shaping our habits, lifestyles, and behaviors. People are exposed to thousands of promotional stimuli a day, and marketing is somehow embedded in the majority of activities and decisions in which we routinely engage.

Recent revolutionary changes in the marketing environment have directly modified our behavior in terms of what, where, who, how, and why we buy. Many of the basic precepts and paradigms of traditional marketing are undergoing dramatic changes. The emergence of information technology and communications is raising serious questions about the future of our most basic marketing institutions. Long-established models and methods of selling, researching, product planning, distribution, and promotion are facing the challenge of adaptation. As an integral part of our culture, marketing resonates throughout society, influencing lifestyles, values, attitudes, and self-images.

Purpose of the book The purpose of this book is to involve the reader in analysis and spirited debate concerning macromarketing issues that are not only fundamental to the discipline but also germane to their lives as consumers, concerned citizens, and future practitioners. Analyzing and presenting a persuasive case is much like selling a product and is essential to the practice of marketing. Also, readers should recognize that a dominant share of society's controversial issues involves marketing. Why? Because marketing is the business function that "touches" the public through product usage and communication. A crucial component of marketing management involves analysis, persuasion, and the selling of ideas. This book provides the means for developing these skills through the process of debate. Since these marketing topics are mainstream public issues that often dominate the news media, marketing students in particular need to be versed in the subjects and positioned to defend their views on these omnipresent controversies.

Plan of the book This volume presents 20 issues in marketing supported by 40 selections presented in a pro-con format. A brief summary of each selection is presented along with a concise *introduction* designed to frame the issue. This element usually contains a historical scenario, including significant points that convey the evolution of each issue and illustrate its impact on contemporary marketing. It also directs the student toward the major points and questions to be considered.

Each issue concludes with a *postscript* that lends some final observations and provides references to additional books, articles, URLs, and other sources that are pertinent to the issue. It also notes developments that may have transpired since the featured selections were written. Usually, the postscript leaves the reader with some final thoughts pertaining to future research and conceivable developments that will likely impact marketing's relationship with each of us as consumers, practitioners, and concerned citizens.

In addition, URLs have been provided on the *On the Internet* page that accompanies each part opener. And at the back of the book is a listing of all the *contributors to this volume,* which will give you information on the economists, sociologists, and commentators whose views are debated here.

A word to the instructor   An *Instructor's Manual With Test Questions* (multiple-choice and essay) is available through the publisher for the instructor using *Taking Sides* in the classroom. A general guidebook, *Using Taking Sides in the Classroom,* which discusses methods and techniques for integrating the pro-con approach into any classroom setting, is also available. An online version of *Using Taking Sides in the Classroom* and a correspondence service for *Taking Sides* adopters can be found at http://www.dushkin.com/usingts/.

Taking Sides: Clashing Views on Controversial Issues in Marketing is only one title in the Taking Sides series. If you are interested in seeing the table of contents for any of the other titles, please visit the Taking Sides Web site at http://www.dushkin.com/takingsides/.

Acknowledgments   We would like to acknowledge all of our students who became involved in research and ideas for this project. Special recognition belongs to Laura Dykstra and Kevin Frenette for their research assistance. Jean Avery, Margo DeL'Etoile, Courtney Eshelby, Ken Mills, Linda Lamirande, Mary Robinson, Heather Turner, and Karen Urciuoli also made valuable contributions. Our thanks to Marjorie Houdegbe for her patience and help in researching and organizing the project. Martha Hogan was of great assistance with her insights and editorial expertise.

We appreciate feedback from our colleagues. Bart would especially like to thank Bill Benoit, Colleen Brickley, Frank Kopczynsky, Warren Mason, and Duncan McDougall. Thanks to President Don Wharton of Plymouth State College for granting my sabbatical. Abhi would like to thank the marketing faculty at Boston University, especially Professors Paul Berger, Ronald Curhan, and C. B. Bhattacharya for their advice. He is exceptionally indebted to his wife, Mousumi, and daughter, Sukanya, for their love and support in completing this project.

A very sincere thanks to Ted Knight for overseeing and managing the project. Without his advice, direction, and encouragement, this project would not have been possible.

Barton Macchiette
Plymouth State College

Abhijit Roy
Boston University

Contents In Brief

Contents

D. Kirk Davidson, an assistant professor of marketing, explores the development and ethical dimensions of applying marketing techniques to "sin products," such as tobacco, alcohol, pornography, and gambling. While he does not applaud these marketing efforts, he emphasizes the relevance of freedom of speech and the rights of consumer choice. Michael F. Jacobson, executive director of the Center for Science in the Public Interest, and Laurie Ann Mazur, a writer and consultant, consider the intrusiveness and pervasiveness of "hybrid advertising," such as the video news release (VNR), advertorial, and product placement in sitcoms and movies and conclude that these messages transcend the perceptual boundaries of traditional advertising.

Writer Dale D. Buss depicts the booming growth of multilevel marketing (MLM) in various arenas. He outlines the techniques of one-to-one selling as well as the home party method. Buss also notes how the legitimate companies in the MLM industry take special care to distance themselves from phony operations. Retired psychiatrist Stephen Barrett argues that people who join in the later stages of an MLM operation will likely not do well. He discusses the example of health-related food supplements, where claims are subject to government intervention and public scrutiny as to their effectiveness. Barrett also examines questionable claims and people's motivations and methods of selling.

Regis McKenna, chairperson of the McKenna Group, proclaims that the era of "adaptive" marketing has arrived—now driven by new technologies of communications and information. Keeping in close touch with ever-changing consumer needs is now the only constant for marketing managers, he concludes. Jack Trout, president of the marketing firm Trout & Partners, and Steve Rivkin, a faculty member of the Department of Economics at Amherst College, see an overcommunicated culture of clutter. They argue that simplicity and the "focused benefit" must be encoded into one integrated singular message and emphasize the importance of a consistent "value proposition" packaged into a simple message, which is memorably positioned in the minds of consumers and prospects in a creative way.

Law student Jennifer Bresnahan describes the new era of information technology, which enables marketers to serve every consumer, one at a time, and develop long-term mutually beneficial relationships. James R. Rosenfield, chairperson and CEO of Rosenfield & Associates, maintains that relationships in marketing are not always like those between human beings; customers want more of a one-way street. He shares "nine big mistakes" that impede successful development of marketing relationships.

Paul Holmes, editor of *Reputation Management,* defines cause-related marketing (CRM) as tying a company and its products to a special interest group, social issue, or charitable organization. The result is a deepened trust and relationship with customers, improved corporate image, and increased sales and promotional benefits for the related cause. Professors of economics James T. Bennett and Thomas J. DiLorenzo argue that product endorsements by charitable organizations put the public confidence at risk and can erode the integrity of the cause. They question the practice of the cause becoming leverage for increasing the brand's market share.

Investment writer Erick Schonfeld argues that the move to customization in manufacturing and services is irrefutable. He concludes that by making full use of cutting-edge technology, this service to the customer is becoming more important than the brand. Professor of sociology George Ritzer presents a view of the influence of McDonaldization, or the domination of society by standardized franchise systems, on consumers' lifestyles and values and demands from marketers.

Writer Lucette Lagnado asserts that 19 million elderly citizens of the United States have little or no coverage for life-sustaining drugs, yet they are the most disadvantaged consumers. High-priced prescriptions represent an absolute inequity in the system, she argues. Writer Elyse Tanouye explains that the high prices and profits associated with pharmaceutical drugs are driven by demand, research, and new marketing-driven costs. She contends that a profusion of new drugs has revolutionized the industry but resulted in spiraling costs, which consumers have been forced to absorb.

Mary Modahl, vice president of Forrester Research, establishes that 52 percent of the U.S. population is optimistic about technology and "marching happily toward on-line shopping." She considers this to be the beginning of a dramatic 10-year transition in consumer behavior. *Forbes* editor Mary Beth Grover argues that despite the allure of no sales payroll or the fixed costs of bricks-and-mortar merchants, turning a profit in cyberspace is no easy task. Furthermore, the hurdles can be even higher for traditional retailers going online.

Writer Beth Belton explains how technology is rapidly displacing "selling as it used to be" with an entirely new job definition. This coincides with the 50th anniversary of the classic Arthur Miller play *Death of a Salesman,* as marketers ponder the future of the stereotypical salesman as portrayed by the character of Willy Loman, a symbol of this dying breed. Psychiatrist Edward M. Hallowell argues that the new communications technology, while ostensibly creating an efficient cost-saving mechanism for doing business, has created a deepened and neglected need for what he terms the "human moment," an authentic encounter that can begin only when two people share the same physical space. The destructive power resulting from the absence of the human moment will become more apparent as the stress levels associated with e-commerce rise, he concludes.

Pierre M. Loewe and Mark S. Bonchek, executive director and research director, respectively, of the global strategy innovation firm Strategos, argue that consumers are more empowered in challenging retailers to meet their needs for convenience, service, and price. Marcia Stepanek, a regular contributor to *Business Week,* suggests that the guiding rule of providing whatever the customer wants is now whatever the company can afford to offer based on the value of that customer.

Writer Evan I. Schwartz explains how building brands is accomplished by using the interactive attributes of the Internet. He concludes that emotional branding does not work well on the Internet, so mass media and interactive media should reinforce one another. Writer Rebecca Piirto Heath makes a case for the importance of a known and trusted brand as a primary influence on a purchase decision. Building a strong brand image strikes an emotional bond with the consumer through brand character and memorability, she asserts.

Karl Taro Greenfeld, a business issues writer, asserts that "extreme sports," such as snowboarding and mountain biking, have enjoyed incredible growth in contrast to the demise of baseball, touch football, and aerobics. He offers evidence to illustrate parallel behavior for risk taking and thrill seeking in many aspects of other national behaviors. Myra Stark, director of knowledge and management insight at Saatchi and Saatchi, highlights the appeal of extreme sports to its target market, emphasizing the quest for individualism and self-expression. Competitiveness and the development mindset are also derivatives of these unique recreational challenges, maintains Stark.

Peter Ferrara, general counsel and chief economist for Americans for Tax Reform, defends Channel One as a much-needed 12-minute documentary news program designed to educate students about current events, social studies, economics, and history. Peggy J. Farber contends that the outrage over commercialism in American classrooms is intensifying, as the private sector becomes inventive with sophisticated techniques and innovative ways of marketing to students in schools. She offers large-scale marketing research, exclusive contracts, and computer ads as current examples of marketing that has been spawned from the origins of Channel One.

Edward J. Stanek, president of the North American Association of State and Provincial Lotteries, argues for the benefits derived from state-promoted lotteries and against time-worn criticisms of state-sanctioned lotteries. The National Gambling Impact Study Commission, based on a two-year study of the social and economic impact of gambling in the United States, outlines criticisms of lotteries, such as offering the worst odds, misleading allocation of funds, and deceptive, inappropriate advertising.

Investigative reporter Charles Lewis provides a portrait based on documented research of the sources and financial power behind the marketing of U.S. presidential candidates, focusing on "the most obscenely expensive race in history." He argues that special (and often secret) interest groups heavily invest in politicians who, in turn, become beholden to their political patrons. Professor of labor economics and public policy Russell Roberts deems absurd the idea of purging special interest money from politics. He is concerned that banning soft money may conflict with the First Amendment and suggests alternative means for making politicians accountable.

Introduction

Barton Macchiette

Abhijit Roy

The Nature of Marketing

One standard definition of marketing views it as a total system of business-related activities designed to plan, price, promote, and distribute want-satisfying products and services to current and potential customers.

It is difficult to conceive of a more integrated discipline, especially in the context of subjects related to the Taking Sides series. Actually, marketing is primarily a "borrowed science" and exists only as a composite of physical and behavioral sciences, relying heavily on psychology, sociology, social psychology, cultural anthropology, and economics. Many would argue that marketing is as much an art as it is a science. No one can truly accurately predict how people will react to any marketing campaign. A recent development is the integration of marketing courses into other degree programs. This major trend results from the new focus on concepts such as customer service, cross-functional orientation, satisfaction studies, and customer retention as general management strategies.[1]

In this book, marketing is examined from a broad perspective, including several dimensions of the exchange process. We emphasize that marketing is not limited to traditional products and services. The issues in this book cover many diverse aspects and interpretations of marketing, with a focus on ethical and societal issues as well as on the impact of technology on the marketing process. Conceivably, this book lends support to the notion that marketing is the most pervasive and unavoidable aspect of our culture as well as our personal and professional lives. It is ingrained in the most basic of our instincts—*survival*.

Change As a Constant

When President Bill Clinton first took office in 1993, for all practical purposes e-commerce was a nonentity. Now projections forecast that by the year 2003, half a billion people, or one-twelfth of the world's population will be online[1]. Furthermore, it is also estimated that 80 percent of all business transactions will be carried out online. Marketers are facing an entirely new frontier of challenge and opportunity.

Marketing and the notion of change are truly interwoven. Although the fundamental needs that are served by marketers remain constant, specific wants are constantly spawned from new technologies, changing lifestyles, and the endless emergence of media-dominated social concerns. The past decade has welcomed revolutionary changes in every aspect of marketing and consumer behavior; this revolution is the central theme of this book.

The Challenge of Issue Selection and Criteria for Choice

The task of selecting the topics for this book was imposing in light of the expansive scope and spectrum of marketing. Also, the impact of the Internet is represented in the majority of issues due to its irrefutable influence in every facet of marketing. We have purposely avoided many of the more theoretical debates in academia. Instead, the emphasis is on more practitioner-oriented and broad-based societal issues, which the reader will find personally engaging. We have sought to strike a balance by presenting issues that appeal equally to practitioners, academics, and students of marketing.

Most welcomed are comments and direction from you, the reader, in terms of which issues should be sustained, augmented, or deleted in future editions of *Taking Sides: Clashing Views on Controversial Issues in Marketing*. What other issues deserve to be included?

Organization of the Book

The parts are organized by topics that generally follow most marketing texts.

Part 1, The Role of Marketing: Theory, Practice and Conceptual Conflict, examines definitional perspectives and interpretations of marketing. The first issue, "Does Marketing Have Appropriate Boundaries?" addresses the pervasiveness and ethical relevance of marketing applications. The practice of multilevel marketing is examined in Issue 2. Views on conceptual orientations and relationship marketing are also considered.

Part 2, Strategic Planning and the Marketing Mix, focuses on sweeping changes in strategic applications that are relevant to the marketing mix. How, for example, has the changing environment created a new climate that is ripe for the strategy of cause-related marketing?

Each of the elements of the marketing mix is discussed in this section. For the product domain, the focus is on mass customization. The pricing of essential drugs has been chosen as a major controversy. Most salient to the issue of distribution is the question of reducing or entirely eliminating intermediation: Will intermediaries survive the onslaught of e-commerce? Finally, the promotion issue questions the demise of the traditional salesman.

Part 3, Consumer Behavior in the New Millennium, deals with the emergence of an entirely new frontier for purchasing, searching for information, decision making, and evaluating products and services. Has the basic consumer/marketer relationship been reversed by a new paradigm of marketing? The new marketplace also raises questions concerning the future of brand loyalty development.

What new motivators and buying behaviors are typically reflected in the analysis of "extreme sports"? An equally evocative consumer behavior issue is the question of commercial exposure to students in the classroom.

Part 4, Segmentation, Positioning, and Target Marketing, examines the most basic and crucial tools utilized by marketers in tailoring market offerings to satisfy consumer needs. Changing demographics, lifestyles, and new technologies are forcing marketers to reengineer and adapt. What is the future of marketing with regard to vulnerable populations such as children, the elderly, and minority consumers? Are cohorts more significant than generations in terms of market segmentation? In relation to students and professors, the future market for online education is a relevant and exciting controversy.

Finally, Part 5, Societal and Regulatory Influences, considers the effects of marketing on society. For example, some critics agree that the incidence of violence in society is inextricably bound to media and the marketplace, which they feel has created a "culture of violence."

The marketing of "sin products," such as tobacco, alcohol, and guns, is highly controversial. So, too, are the ethics of marketing lotteries, which become particularly debatable when the government promotes a questionable practice. Finally, campaign financing and political marketing are highly disputed issues among aspiring politicians and the public at large. We hope that readers will be sparked with a passion to debate these highly evocative issues, which closely affect their everyday lives.

Selection Choice

The following criteria served as guidelines in choosing the specific selections for this volume:

Source credibility Our goal was to seek authors and sources that are recognized, legitimate, qualified, and respected in their fields. We have taken care to avoid Web sites of questionable integrity and articles that do not present a strong position. Reliable and credible studies were given priority. Top-quality journals, magazines, newspapers, and books are represented in the selections. They include articles from top business magazines (e.g., *Business Week, Fortune, Forbes,* and *Nations Business*), top academic and management journals (e.g., *Harvard Business Review* and *Management Review*), major newspapers (*Wall Street Journal* and *USA Today*), and best-selling, contemporary books.

We are particularly proud to have selections from an eclectic group of experts in their respective fields. Contributors from academia include Charles D. Schewe (marketing), George Ritzer (sociology), David Grossman (psychology), Russell Roberts (economics), and Edward M. Hallowell (psychiatry), among others. Seasoned writers such as Karl Taro Greenfeld, Rebecca Piirto Heath, and Wendy Melillo are also distinguished contributors.

Marketing relevance Marketing focus and connectedness were the most important requisites in choosing the selections. Essentially, we feel that the selections should be truly germane to the traditional marketing textbook but also relate to contemporary media coverage. An example is the issue on violence in America (Issue 17). While tangentially related to marketing, most of the popular debate on violence focuses on political and regulatory factors. However, we have chosen the alleged role of marketing in promoting America's entire "culture of violence" as the focus of this issue.

Temporal durability   To be included in this book, we felt that an issue must meet the test of time endurance and signal some future trend or significant development. For example, rather than choose tobacco as an issue, we selected alcohol (Issue 18) because it appears to be the next arena of legislative activity, as are video games and media violence. Sometimes seemingly significant products and events soon lose the public's interest and become fads or yesterday's news. Meaningful issues have staying power, and many classic marketing articles are still incredibly relevant to today's subjects of debate. It is a sure bet that the linkage of violence to marketing, the impact of e-commerce on retailing, and the controversies surrounding marketing and politics will be topics of sustained interest and will continue to embrace the challenge of public scrutiny.

Inherent drama   The element of passion is essential to a stimulating controversy and "clashing views." Assuming that our two target audiences are students and professors, we have chosen selections that hopefully strike a responsive chord with both groups. Most of the selections do relate to aspects of marketing that truly touch the lives of these individuals and should engage their interest. Extreme sports, commercial-free classrooms, online education, and the impact of e-commerce should have equal appeal to professors and students, as well as the community at large.

Academic integrity   We have chosen selections that provide insights for analysis and debate on concepts related to the marketing text. Journals, seminars, and conferences are bound with new tools, techniques, and theories that challenge traditional marketing thought. Several of the selections target newly evolving developments, such as information technology, that are dramatically influencing changes in consumer behavior. How must academia change to meet the new challenges for understanding our dynamically changing marketing environment?

Questions to Contemplate

1. How and to what extent will consumers purchase products differently as the Internet becomes more completely embedded in American culture?
2. How will lifestyles, demographics, and changing values (psychographics) influence the future of marketing? Will services continue to emerge as a major factor? Will cause-related marketing continue to grow?

3. How will society respond to the problem of media violence and marketing of inherently damaging products (tobacco, alcohol, gambling, and the video/entertainment industry)?

Summary

Three central themes—conflict between the traditional and the new, causal factors identifying change agents, and future predictions—form the backbone of *Taking Sides.* To support these themes, several new ideas and concepts have been introduced for your thoughts and future research in the postscripts.

A marketing revolution is heavily influencing every aspect of our lives. Fragmented markets, changing lifestyles, communications/information technology, and the global neighborhood are forcing marketers to adapt. What does the future hold? How will we respond to these changes as consumers and marketers?

Note

1. "Everybody's Teaching Marketing Today," *Marketing News* (October 25, 1999).

On the Internet . . .

Affinity Marketing Promotes Your MLM

This is the home page of Affinity Marketing, whose members are part of the ProSTEP organization, a networking company that provides training, support, lead generation, and technological resources.

`http://www.affinitymarketing.com`

RightPoint Software Incorporated

RightPoint Software Incorporated was recently acquired by E.piphany software, the leading provider of customer-focused analytic, campaign management, and real-time personalization applications. E.piphany's customer analytics and personalized marketing solutions create a single view of the customer and provide real-time insight and action across all customer touchpoints.

`http://www.rightpoint.com`

Association for the Advancement of Relationship Marketing

The Association for the Advancement of Relationship Marketing is a nonprofit organization dedicated to meeting the needs of individuals who wish to understand and apply the concepts of relationship marketing.

`http://www.aarm.org`

PART 1

The Role of Marketing: Theory, Practice, and Conceptual Conflict

Can you think of a theory, concept, or practice that has not been influenced by the recently revolutionized marketing environment? For example, communications and information technology is causing marketers to rethink the most basic tenets of its traditional institutions. These developments represent major benchmarks for theory relating to the evolution of marketing. The expanded boundaries for reaching consumers with an explosive array of product choices in new and different ways has created questions concerning levels of pervasiveness and ethical issues.

Are age-old practices such as "cold calls" and "prospecting" for customers becoming obsolete? Now the Internet allows interaction with thousands of multilevel marketers in ways that were previously unimaginable. Long-established theories that product positioning requires a singular, focused, unique selling proposition that is sustained through large promotional budgets committed to brand building and repetition are now in a state of flux. Are today's real-time consumers with insatiable demands for immediate satisfaction threatening these traditional marketing concepts?

New technologies are forcing marketers to reinvent how they form lasting consumer relationships, and concepts such as customer retention, customer-delivered value, and augmented services are emerging as dominant themes. The industrial revolution was to manufacturing what the information revolution is to marketing. Traditional models of marketing are being challenged on every front. Questions of ethics and societal influence are also becoming inordinately significant as "e-life" is shaping the marketing environment for the new millennium.

- Does Marketing Have Appropriate Boundaries?

- Is the Practice of Multilevel Marketing Legitimate?

- Has the "Keep It Simple" Concept Become "All Change, All the Time"?

- Is Relationship Marketing a Tenable Concept?

ISSUE 1

Does Marketing Have Appropriate Boundaries?

YES: D. Kirk Davidson, from *Selling Sin: The Marketing of Socially Unacceptable Products* (Quorum Books, 1996)

NO: Michael F. Jacobson and Laurie Ann Mazur, from *Marketing Madness: A Survival Guide for a Consumer Society* (Westview Press, 1995)

ISSUE SUMMARY

YES: D. Kirk Davidson, an assistant professor of marketing, explores the development and ethical dimensions of applying marketing techniques to "sin products," such as tobacco, alcohol, pornography, and gambling. While he does not applaud these marketing efforts, he emphasizes the relevance of freedom of speech and the rights of consumer choice.

NO: Michael F. Jacobson, executive director of the Center for Science in the Public Interest, and Laurie Ann Mazur, a writer and consultant, consider the intrusiveness and pervasiveness of "hybrid advertising," such as the video news release (VNR), advertorial, and product placement in sitcoms and movies and conclude that these messages transcend the perceptual boundaries of traditional advertising.

The origins of the issue of "where should marketing be applied?" can be traced to the mid-1960s with a position paper by the Ohio State University faculty, which viewed marketing as a "social process" while the American Marketing Association (AMA) prior to 1985 considered it to be a set of "business activities." In the July 1969 issue of the *Journal of Marketing*, Philip Kotler and Sidney J. Levy prescribed broadening the concept of marketing to include non-business organizations like churches, police stations, and public schools, since they all had products and customers and implemented the normal tools of the marketing mix. William Lazer supported some of the same views in the same issue of the journal, calling for a broader view of marketing rather than just looking at it as the technology of the firm. David J. Luck (1970), however, disagreed and felt that the field had a broad enough scope by considering *just* organizational business practices that resulted in market transactions.

As we fast forward to the new millennium, four specific categories of marketing boundaries can be delineated. They include matters of deception and taste, where marketing is applied, acceptable methods of marketing, and the pervasiveness of marketing in society.

Matters of deception and taste are perhaps the most common criticisms. Unsubstantiated claims and false statements challenge the dimensions of marketing, while examples of taste relate more to socially acceptable boundaries. The clothing company Bennetton has been criticized for utilizing an actual photograph of a dying AIDS victim and real mug shots of convicted criminals as a form of "shock advertising." These are contextual issues raising questions of tactics appeal and intent.

The second dimension, applications of marketing, has demonstrated a radical shift in philosophy in the past three decades toward the acceptance and growth of this *broadened concept* of marketing. But are contemporary applications of marketing transcending appropriate boundaries? For example, The Vatican recently opened the first of 400 worldwide theme stores in New York, promoting Pope Paul II china and sheets, replicas of Italian art, and assorted religious artifacts. Frito-Lay was a sponsor for the Pope's last trip to Mexico. The Pope's licensing agent was quoted in *Newsweek* as saying, "There is no better brand name in the world."

D. Kirk Davidson discusses acceptable marketing methods for questionable sin products. He explores the issues unique to marketing applications of sin products, such as gambling, pornography, firearms, and alcohol. All of these industries confront the challenge of a hostile environment—the public and a variety of special interest groups. Davidson examines the importance of establishing the *legitimacy* of marketing's role in these industries. He notes that established traditional tools of marketing, such as targeting new customers and increasing product usage, take on negative dimensions when applied to sin products. Davidson considers the strategies common to marketers in their efforts to legitimize applied marketing in the gray areas of sin products.

The dimensions of pervasiveness and methods of "hybrid" marketing have surfaced with public concerns for privacy and the alleged intrusiveness of direct markets and "Spam," or advertising in the form of unsolicited e-mail. Michael F. Jacobson and Laurie Ann Mazur focus on the negative attributes of hybrid marketing practices such as advertorials, infomercials, product placement, and the video news release (VNR). The VNR, a commercial message that is generated from a company's public relations agency and ostensibly portrayed as actual news, is the quintessential example of "blurred distinctions" in commercial messages. Since it is most often perceived by the audience as actual news, the credibility factor is much higher than that of an advertisement. It is much more cost effective because it is programming rather than commercially bought time. Should consumers be better informed to distinguish VNRs, product placement, and other hybrid marketing techniques? Who should be responsible? Do these methods transcend acceptable boundaries of marketing?

D. Kirk Davidson

 **YES**

Selling Sin

In the long run a company's right to continue in business is granted by society, not by its profitability. If an organization is to maximize its return to its shareholders, it must maximize its contribution to the society in which it operates. This means earning and maintaining the trust of that society—in other words, establishing the firm's legitimacy—and marketers have a critical role to play in this.

The marketing questions we have explored... are extraordinary ones. They are different from the problems discussed in most marketing texts because these deal with the fundamental relationship between business and society. This is an interactive relationship. It is clear that the decisions made by marketers will affect how society accepts the firm and its products. Equally clear is that the extent to which society grants its approval—grants legitimacy—will have a major impact on the firm and especially on its marketing function.

[We have] focused on five specific industries because they are good examples of what happens when an industry begins to lose its legitimacy. In the United States of the mid-1990s, tobacco, alcoholic beverages, firearms, gambling, and pornography all face the challenges of a hostile environment and significant opposition by various groups for a variety of reasons.

In other industries, under other circumstances, similar marketing challenges can arise in regard to specific products even though the company and the industry are given a relatively clean bill of health by society. For example, there is little criticism of the chemical industry in its entirety although specific products, such as certain agricultural chemicals and napalm for military use, have encountered severe opposition. No one finds the athletic shoe industry, qua industry, unacceptable, although there has been sharp criticism of the marketing of very expensive shoes in low-income neighborhoods. There is general acceptance now of biotechnology products used for medical purposes, although genetically engineered bovine growth hormone to stimulate milk production in the dairy industry, and other biotech products used in the food industry, still encounter severe opposition. In other words, problems of legitimacy and social unacceptability can crop up in specific areas of otherwise perfectly respected and accepted product lines, companies, and industries.

Marketers, therefore, across all industries can benefit from studying the lessons, experiences, and challenges described [here]. Of course, there are no universally applicable solutions. More precisely, there are no "solutions" at all. Even among the five industries studied here, there are no tactics or strategies that can be considered applicable across the board. Just as one product's marketing strategy, no matter how successful, cannot be replicated and used with any guarantee of similar success for a different product, or in a different industry, so one company's approach to dealing with problems of social unacceptability cannot be prescribed across product lines or across industries. In marketing, as in all social science fields, there are simply too many variables: too many differences in products, markets, company cultures, and surrounding environments.

The benefits, then, for marketers will come, as with any case analysis work, from the generation of ideas: from seeing what works or doesn't work under a particular set of circumstances, and from using that knowledge to tailor a strategy to the marketer's unique needs and conditions.

What are some of the lessons we as marketers can learn from the material collected [here]?

Expansion of Market

Perhaps the first lesson to be learned is that the most basic objectives of marketing—to expand the business, to attract new customers, to increase usage of the product—must be reconsidered if the product category or the industry faces questions of social acceptability. Critics may tolerate continued consumption or usage of the product by current customers, but the degree of opposition will increase dramatically when manufacturers are perceived as going after new markets, recruiting new customers, or trying to increase usage. To encourage people to gamble more, to drink more alcoholic beverages, or certainly to smoke more would be totally unacceptable and would be like pouring fuel on the opposition's fire. Giving the appearance of encouraging nongamblers to begin buying lottery tickets (as with the slogan "You can't win if you don't play") or encouraging nonsmokers to take up the habit (you can be cool like Joe Camel or rugged and individualistic like the Marlboro Man) is a dangerous message in terms of inflaming the critics. Even the tobacco companies, in their public relations utterances if not in their actions, eschew recruiting new smokers. After forty years of mounting evidence about the health problems associated with smoking, the firms now acknowledge some risks but counter that many products, even Twinkies, present risks, and insist that adults should make their own individual choices.

The firearms industry presents a definite exception to this rule. To the extent that the National Rifle Association (NRA) represents the views and furthers the strategy of the industry's member firms, the message that they project is that more and more people who do not now own guns should acquire them! In spite of a high level of social protest, in spite of very active and very vocal advocacy groups working to limit the spread of guns, especially handguns, the NRA and the industry are not backing down or softening in any way their marketing efforts to increase the size of the market by recruiting new customers.

The marketers of cigarettes and beer, on the other hand, claim that all of their formidable marketing budgets and efforts are aimed only at current customers. They claim not to be trying to attract new customers, only to defend, or better yet to increase, their current market share. In other words, they say they are not trying to increase the size of the pie, only to get a larger slice of the present pie. [W]e have shown that these claims are widely disputed by the industries' opponents.

This battle of words—of claims and counterclaims—can never be won. Inevitably, consumer advertising that a manufacturer insists is meant to defend or increase its brand's market share will be perceived by critics as meant to entice new users. Circumstantial evidence can be gathered—for example, that 75 percent of underage smokers smoke the three most heavily advertised brands —yet the cigarette companies will insist that the intent of their ads is not to attract new, young smokers. By extension, all consumer advertising for socially unacceptable industries or products becomes suspect because it would seem to legitimate the use of that product in our society.

Under these conditions an argument can be advanced that a manufacturer should emphasize a "push" strategy rather than a "pull" strategy. Promotion budget dollars should be shifted away from consumer advertising and consumer-oriented sales promotion tactics, which are the most visible elements of the entire marketing mix and the most subject to public scrutiny, into increased marketing efforts directed at the trade channels that are less obvious and less likely to incite the product's critics. Larger and more active sales organizations making more calls on retailers and increased dealer incentives should result in increased sales and market share without triggering the level of opposition that consumer advertising is certain to initiate.

It would be naive to suppose that in a mature industry such as cigarettes or beer, dominated a few large, powerful competitors, that any one company could unilaterally reduce its consumer advertising dramatically. Even though the benefits of advertising are notoriously difficult to measure, very few marketing executives are daring enough to cut back on advertising their brands and risk losing some market share that would be very expensive to regain. The threat is simply too great. What is suggested here is that in the planning of an overall marketing strategy and in the budget allocation process, the avoidance of social criticism is an additional factor to consider in weighing the relative merits of consumer advertising versus trade promotions.

The Woes of Targeting: Pricing and Distribution Issues

As important as precise, careful targeting is in the marketing of most products, it is almost certain to backfire in the marketing of socially unacceptable goods. As we have seen, targeting is meant to identify segments of the market with some common characteristics so that a specific marketing strategy can be developed that will be especially effective with that defined group. Critics of the product can readily paint this as a picture of exploitation: a large, billion-dollar corporation zeroing in on a small segment of society, employing all of its marketing muscle and persuasive powers to increase the sales of its product. When the product carries some risk or danger, as do all socially unacceptable products, and when the targeted segment is perceived as being vulnerable in any way, this creates an exploitative situation that is intolerable in our society.

Problems can surface as a result of targeting a wide variety of groups: women, racial or ethnic minorities, the elderly, or lower-income groups. But no targeted group arouses more sympathy and protection than children do.... [T]he five product categories studied [here] have been defined by our society as adult products, and so there is a natural inclination for young people, especially teens, to be attracted to them as a way of assuming adulthood. When cigarette manufacturers or brewers or pornography merchants are perceived as targeting children, therefore, a strong backlash of social pressure and criticism is unleashed. Many possible measures have been suggested to constrain the marketing of tobacco products, including higher excise taxes and the disallowance of advertising as a tax-deductible expense, but the tobacco control program brought forward by the Food and Drug Administration (FDA) in 1995 was all about protecting children because the Clinton administration recognized this would have the widest popular appeal. In a similar vein, it is the protection of children from the pornography found in popular music lyrics, in 900 telephone messages, and in cyberspace that engenders the most widespread attention and support.

The lesson or message to marketers, then, is obvious. If your product is socially unacceptable to some degree, choose targets with the greatest of caution. Targeting almost any group other than well-to-do white males will be criticized. And by all means, avoid even the perception of targeting children.

Just as with targeting, pricing decisions must be made with an eye to how they will be perceived by the market, especially by the product's critics. With mainstream products, low prices are not only accepted but welcomed as an introductory tactic or as a way to move potential customers to the trial or adoption stage of the product adoption process. Not so with socially unacceptable products. Special prices on cigarettes or alcoholic beverages to attract new consumers or encourage present customers to consume more would ignite a storm of protest.

The price lining of the major brewers—Anheuser–Busch's Michelob in the superpremium category, Budweiser at the premium level, and Busch at popular prices, for example—must be administered as simply catering to the needs of beer drinkers in different income brackets. So, too, with the premium, value, and generic or private label cigarette brands. Philip Morris' fateful price cut on Marlboro and its other premium brands in 1993 had to be explained as a desperate measure to regain market share from the generics and private labels, which it indeed was. Handgun control advocates are especially critical of cheap Saturday night specials because they are purposely priced low to encourage increased sales.

Casinos have an advantage in that they can disguise their price promotions. Traditionally they have offered their hotel rooms and meals—and sometimes their Hollywood extravaganza shows—at quite reasonable prices, not to mention free drinks for those gambling at the tables or machines. A thin disguise, perhaps, but the low prices are associated with the rooms, food, and drinks rather than directly with the gambling.

Distribution strategies used by producers of socially unacceptable products have received less attention than targeting, pricing, promotion, and product line management decisions. If a product, such as any one of our five, is subject to a significant degree of social criticism, it would seem to make sense to shorten, to whatever extent possible, the channel of distribution. The longer the product is in the stream of commerce and the more hands it passes through, the more public exposure it receives and the more likely it is to be criticized.

From the producer's viewpoint, the ideal form of distribution is direct to the consumer. This entails the least amount of public exposure. For convenience goods such as beer and cigarettes, which in theory and in practice require the longest channels and the widest distribution, this would be impossible. However, it is widely accepted that the major cigarette manufacturers are building enormous databases of their customers, in the hopes of being able to turn this information into a direct marketing program at some point. Pornographic conversations through 900 telephone numbers are a form of direct distribution, as are the various pornography sites on the World Wide Web.

Public policy interests point in the opposite direction. Whether the product is guns, alcoholic beverages, cigarettes, lottery tickets, or slot machine bets, whatever social and regulatory controls are to be exercised—and whatever taxes are to be collected—require that these products be distributed through a totally open and transparent system. There are already prohibitions against distributing guns and alcoholic beverages through the mail. Cigarette companies have been stymied so far in selling by mail by the problem of verifying minimum age requirements. But there are plenty of proposals being floated for at-home betting on horse races, lotteries, or even casinos in cyberspace, and the prospect of 500 channels being available for television viewing raises the prospects of direct access to more X-rated movies or perhaps entire channels devoted to pornography.

Addressing the Issues

There comes a time for every firm facing social pressures, criticism, and disapproval when the issues on which those difficulties are based must be addressed. How will the firm defend itself, its products, and its right to continue in business? Making adjustments in the firm's marketing strategy—promotion mix, product line management, pricing decision, choice of targets, and so on—while necessary and helpful, does not deal with the underlying problem. Can the criticism at least be blunted, if not silenced? Can the critics be isolated and industry supporters be organized and energized? Can some degree of legitimacy be restored?

Accomplishing these tasks goes well beyond the normal duties of the firm's public relations department and beyond the traditional scope of marketing strategy. But we have considered them [here] because they are in fact public relations issues, they must be coordinated carefully with the everyday marketing activities of the firm, and they are absolutely crucial to the success of the firm over the long run.

In reviewing the five industries we have studied [here], several common themes emerge.

Deflect the Criticism

Perhaps the most common ploy in attempting to deal with social criticism is to deflect the criticism away from the firm's core products. The alcoholic beverage and gambling industries have been rather successful in doing this; the National Rifle Association, as a stand-in for the firearms industry, has used this tactic with somewhat less success.

Alcoholic beverages are not the problem, insist the industry representatives, certainly not as they are normally used and as they should be used. The problems are excessive drinking, underage drinking, and drunk driving. The industry strives to focus social attention on these limited issues and works with its critics on developing and financing programs to deal with them. The hope, of course, is that this will leave the industry relatively free to produce and market wine, beer, and spirits with a minimum of controversy.

"Guns don't commit murders; people do" is the message from the NRA. Firearms themselves are simply tools: essential for various sports and personal protection. It is the criminal use or careless use of guns that must be curbed. To this end the NRA and the industry sponsor training classes in the proper use of guns and safe shooting for both children and adults.

The gambling industry has followed the same course. Gambling per se is not the problem; it is excessive gambling that society must prevent, and the industry demonstrates its concerns by providing money and initiative to ameliorate the problem. Changing the word "gambling" to "gaming" also is a tactic to deflect criticism, as is the transformation of a casino into a family entertainment complex. How can anyone criticize games and family fun?

The tobacco industry has stumbled badly in its inability to deflect criticism from its core products and now confronts an intractable problem. Scientific studies have confirmed that any level of smoking is harmful to one's health —and to the health of those around the smoker. For sixty years the tobacco firms have known about these health concerns and have attempted to hide them. Even since the 1950s and 1960s, when the smoking and health problems first came to the public's attention, the firms have reduced the tar and nicotine content in many of their cigarettes but have been unwilling to remove all of it—to develop a "safe" cigarette—because smokers prefer the taste and the "lift" that the tars and nicotine provide. The long-run viability and legitimacy of the industry was sacrificed to meet quarterly and annual sales and profit goals.

Cure Is Worse Than the Disease

An alternative to the deflection strategy is to try to show that whatever social concerns are raised by the industry's products, they are less serious than the critics' proposed solutions. Marketers of pornography answer their critics by waving the First Amendment banner. Censorship, they proclaim, and the loss of freedom of speech are a far more serious threat to our society than porno-graphic magazines and videos that people, after all, can either buy or ignore, as they choose.

The NRA also uses this approach, but its rallying cry is the Second Amend-ment. Whatever social ills gun critics complain about, whatever the level of violence in our society, however many deaths are the result of guns and their proliferation, as serious as these problems may be, they are not as serious as the threat to Americans of whittling away at the freedoms guaranteed by the Bill of Rights. When gun control advocates warn of violence and death resulting from handguns and assault weapons, the NRA and allied organizations warn of midnight searches of homes and property by "jackbooted" federal agents.

This is also the thrust of the 1994–1995 institutional ad campaigns spon-sored by Philip Morris and Reynolds Tobacco. In response to the FDA's proposals for limiting the sale of cigarettes to minors, Reynolds ran full-page newspaper ads showing a smirking, corpulent, generally unattractive man asking whether a parent or some government bureaucrat is better able to guide and care for children. The ads called for a rational debate and urged that the industry and its critics work out public policy issues together. Here again the message is perfectly clear. As Reynolds framed the debate, whatever social problems are associated with tobacco, they are not nearly so dangerous as the proposed so-lution, which would mean more regulation (i.e.., more bureaucracy) and less freedom of individual choice.

The Economics Card

If there is one thing that the five industries represented [here] have in common, it is that each of them, when confronted with criticism based on social concerns or moral values, responds with a justification based on economics. This funda-mental struggle between personal, material well-being and moral principles is as old as Adam and Eve's fateful decision to taste the forbidden apple.

Every proposal for a new gambling enterprise—a riverboat for Indiana, a casino for Baltimore, a racetrack for Tennessee—promises more jobs and more tax revenues for the state. Never does the proposal try to convince us that gam-bling is a virtuous and healthy form of entertainment; the argument is that the economic benefits outweigh the social costs. How does a state government rationalize being in the business of owning and operating a gambling enter-prise (i.e., a lottery)? Only by citing the economic necessities of the state and assuring the electorate that the social consequences will not be so bad.

What is the tobacco industry's response when the federal government pro-poses a stiff hike in the excise tax on cigarettes? The benefits to society would seem unassailable: reduced consumption, especially among teenagers, and the resulting improvements in public health. Inevitably, the response comes in the form of warnings of economic chaos. Hundreds of thousands of jobs would be lost just in the convenience store industry. End U.S. government interven-tion that ensures advertising of American cigarettes in foreign countries? This would have a terrible effect on our balance of payments. Restrict cigarette adver-tising in any of a dozen ways? The entire advertising industry joins the chorus warning of lost jobs and economic disruption.

Even in the business of pornography, adult videos are defended by explaining just how important they are to the profitable operation of most video rental stores.

And so the debate is framed. With the exception of the firearms industry, or more specifically the NRA, the marketers of these socially unacceptable products do not try to convince us that the character of their products has been unfairly impugned. Alcoholic beverage and gambling proponents readily admit that their products are sometimes used to excess and, as noted, join with their critics in looking for solutions. Purveyors of pornography recognize that their product should be purchased only by adults and are willing to join in the effort to keep it away from children. Even cigarette marketers now reluctantly admit that there are health risks associated with their product. For all of these industry representatives, however, the economic justification is sufficient: jobs for workers and managers, taxes for governments, contracts for suppliers, and profits for shareholders.

Cynics may assume that economics will always win out over morality, but such is not the case. Questions of heath and safety, and especially the protection of children, often are enough to tip the balance in favor of social and moral values. Tobacco products are still with us, but because of the now unassailable health concerns, significant restrictions have been imposed on how they are marketed. Economic pressures, along with social preferences, may have rescued the alcoholic beverage industries from Prohibition, but when Mothers Against Drunk Driving framed the issue as the safety of our children, society was willing to get tough on the problem of underage drinking. And the setbacks for gambling in the 1994 elections show that in some states and under some circumstances, the electorate will give social and moral values the priority over economic arguments.

Legitimacy: Lost, Maintained, Regained?

Finally, a review of these five industries and their marketing strategies must offer some insights regarding the question of legitimacy: for individual companies or for entire industries. Legitimacy itself is difficult to define, because it is dependent on the shifting sands of public opinion and social mores; it is all the more difficult to try to measure the legitimacy of a firm or an industry or to determine whether that legitimacy is waxing or waning.

Over the years a number of scholars have developed approaches and models that can help in this effort, even if they do not provide definitive or precise answers. For example, Charles Summer suggested that when firms find themselves in the "conflict stage" of their life cycle—and all of our five industries are in such a conflict situation—the question becomes whether the "zone of opposition" or the "zone of approval" will expand at the expense of the other. In these terms we can conclude that for the tobacco companies, their zone of opposition has without question been growing at the expense of their zone of approval. The gambling firms are experiencing just the opposite.

Ed Epstein and Dow Votaw have suggested three strategies by which firms can deal with challenges to their legitimacy: adapt to society's values, change society's values, or associate with other organizations that enjoy legitimacy. The major brewers have taken some steps along the first of these paths, the tobacco firms and the NRA have chosen the second, and the gambling companies, to the extent they have allied themselves with the hospitality industry, have opted for the third.

Christine Oliver has created a framework... for classifying companies' responses to societal pressures. The tobacco and firearms industries have been pursuing the manipulation and defiance strategies, alcoholic beverages and gambling have chosen avoidance and sometimes compromise, while pornography lies in between, choosing defiance on some occasions and avoidance on others.

Accommodation or Opposition

More is at stake here than simply marketing a product. We are discussing the marketing of the firm, or perhaps the entire industry: how that firm or industry will relate to and respond to the society in which it is operating. But the different levels of marketing are inescapably linked. The decision of Reynolds Tobacco to continue the Joe Camel ad campaign for a year or more, even after strong protests from critics, is a part of the firm's, and the industry's, broader decision to choose a defiant stance against its detractors. The brewers' willingness to promote responsible drinking and similar messages are part of their choice of "compromise" and "pacify" as their corporate and industry marketing strategies.

Ultimately, the marketing of socially unacceptable products comes down to a choice of accommodation or opposition between a firm and the society in which it is embedded. Can the firm find a way to adapt its product and the way it promotes and distributes it, perhaps even shift its choice of markets, to fit more comfortably within society's constraints? Or will it choose opposition and continue to fight a rearguard, minimize-our-losses kind of action?

The tobacco firms have operated very profitably under the latter strategy for several decades, so one cannot dismiss that choice. It is carried out, however, at great cost to the firms and to society, and there is scant hope for anything but a continuously deteriorating situation. For any kind of healthy, long-term relationship—if there is to be any hope for legitimacy—there must be a congruence between the operating decisions of the firm and the expectations of society. Achieving this relationships falls on the shoulders of the firm's manager's and especially its marketers; it will depend on the decisions they make, the tactics they choose, and the strategies they develop.

**Michael F. Jacobson and
Laurie Ann Mazur**

Blurring the Distinctions: Infomercials, Advertorials, and More

Late-breaking news bulletin: To announce the introduction of its new Almond Kiss, Hershey Foods drops a 500-pound replica of the candy from a building in Times Square. Cut to commercial. *Good Morning America* host Joan Lunden sits behind an anchor desk, reporting authoritatively on a breakthrough in "skin science"—the discovery that Vaseline Intensive Care lotion helps dry skin.

Frequently, news items bear an uncanny resemblance to commercials, and commercials masquerade as news. Who can tell the difference? Often we can't, and that's the point. Knowing that consumers view ads with skepticism, marketers sneak through our defenses by blurring the lines between advertising, news, and entertainment.

Newsfakers: The Video News Release

One of the most sinister line-blurring innovations is the video news release (VNR). Descendants of the printed press release, VNRs are supplied to news broadcasters on tape or by satellite. VNR providers include corporations, public relations firms, government, advocacy groups—virtually anyone with a product to plug or a spin to doctor. A VNR may contain background footage on a particular issue or a complete, ready-to-roll canned news story. It usually offers a news "hook," however manufactured or self-serving, and features compelling visuals. "A good VNR should be indistinguishable from a news story," says producer Larry Pintak. "The key is to look like, sound like, and have the elements of a news story."

VNRs blend seamlessly into news programs. In June 1991, for example, 17 million Americans watched a "news" story on the fiftieth anniversary of Cheerios cereal. The feel-good report included a tour of the Cheerios factory and some footage of a giant Cheerio made specially for the occasion. Few viewers suspected—and were not told by newscasters—that the segment was conceived, filmed, and produced by Cheerios manufacturer General Mills, then beamed via satellite to local television stations across the country. Similarly, when *Good Morning America* ran a light-hearted human-interest story about a Maine farmer's cow with spots shaped like Mickey Mouse's head, few guessed that the tape had been supplied by a thoughtful Disney World.

Why, you may ask, do newscasters air these obvious promotional pieces? In a word, desperation. Competition from cable and other factors has forced deep budget and staff cutbacks at many stations. At the same time, programmers have allotted more time for news shows, which are less expensive to produce than entertainment programs. As a result, news departments have lots of airtime to fill, but they must do so cheaply. VNRs, which offer high-quality, prepackaged "news" for free, are an irresistible temptation. According to Nielsen Media Research, 80 percent of the nation's news directors say they use VNR material at last several times every month. A 1993 Nielsen study found that every one of the ninety-two stations surveyed used VNRs, and another study found that less than 50 percent of the VNR segments identified their source. Medialink, a company that distributes VNRs, says that 5,000 VNRs were sent to newscasters in 1991, up from 700 in 1986.

For marketers, VNRs are an inexpensive way to reach a huge audience. It costs between $15,000 and $80,000 to produce and distribute a VNR nationwide; in comparison, a thirty-second commercial can run to $250,000. There is no guarantee that stations will air VNR footage, but many have achieved astonishingly high visibility. McDonald's VNR on the introduction of its McLean Deluxe hamburger was seen by approximately 22 million Americans, and Coors reached 27 million with news of a court victory in a battle over its ads.

Disturbingly, some corporations use VNRs to circumvent restrictions—or bans—on advertising their products. For instance, in 1987 the James B. Beam Distilling Company issued a VNR congratulating itself for using only American grains in the manufacture of Jim Beam bourbon. The video was seen by TV viewers in forty cities, although network and industry guidelines expressly forbid television advertising of distilled spirits.

Drug companies have also used this ruse. Advertising claims about pharmaceutical products are strictly regulated by the Food and Drug Administration (FDA), but for many years the FDA did not screen VNRs sent out by drug companies. Not surprisingly, drug-company VNRs touted new products as miracle cures and neglected to mention side effects or contraindications. In one case, a VNR was used to hype a drug that proved deadly. In 1982, Eli Lilly and Company sent out a video extolling the virtues of Oraflex, its new arthritis drug. Within a few months, Oraflex had been blamed for twenty-six deaths in the United States, and the drug was discontinued. Lilly was later found guilty of suppressing information about severe adverse reactions, including deaths, during Oraflex trials overseas. Newscasters contributed to this tragedy by uncritically airing Lilly's video as though it were an unbiased source of news. In response to criticism, the FDA has begun to review pharmaceutical VNRs before they are sent to stations.

But drug companies plant news stories in other media as well. *Consumer Reports* magazine raised the issue, stating, "So much of what we are told about health and disease now comes in some way from the people in business to sell drugs." *Consumer Reports* interviewed several freelance health writers, who reported that drug companies had offered them money to write stories about their products and pitch them to national magazines without revealing the financial arrangement to the editors of those magazines.

VNR producers say they offer a valuable public service. The videos, they say, provide broadcasters with free footage that might otherwise be costly or impossible to obtain. Moreover, they argue, a VNR is just a high-tech version of the press release, which has long been considered a legitimate news source for reporters. But VNRs and other planted news stories give corporations an unparalleled opportunity to define and interpret current events. Would a news organization run a story about the anniversary of a breakfast cereal—*unless* it were ready-made with a catchy visual? Corporate propaganda also fills airtime that might otherwise be devoted to real news. Faced with a choice between running a prepackaged bit of commercial fluff or sending out a news crew to do some investigative reporting, many news directors choose the former. Furthermore, when corporate videos are the *only* source of information on a given topic—as is often the case in stories on medical or technical subjects—how can we know the information they provide is objective?

Press releases, too, have been subject to abuse; reporters have been known to write entire articles straight from releases. But good reporters always attribute information drawn from press releases; most VNR broadcasts go unacknowledged. Eugene Secunda, a professor of marketing at Baruch College, believes that news directors fear disclosure would hurt their image of objectivity. "If you are a news director," he says, "why would you do anything that might in any way compromise the believability of your program?"

Clearly, the biggest problem with VNRs is that viewers usually don't know they're watching them. For marketers, this is the whole point. A commercial is immediately identifiable as corporate propaganda, but a VNR masks propaganda as fact, borrowing the objective aura of the newsroom. "That's the great thing about VNRs," said Susan Fleming, an account executive at a company that produces VNRs. "Everybody sees them, but nobody realizes it. You have a corporate message to get across, and there's television news anchor saying it to millions of the people. It's one of the most legitimate ways to get your message to the public."

Many marketers conduct slick publicity campaigns to promote "new" or "improved" products, and the media obligingly present them as news. For instance, when Polaroid introduced its new min-instant camera, *USA Today* ran a half-page editorial spread, complete with sample photos and customers' praise. Suzanne Somers showed up in various gossip columns endorsing the sequel to her Thighmaster fitness gadget.

Public relations experts are eager to win over traditional advertisers to such free—and quality—publicity. Writing in the *Advertiser,* Thomas Mosser of Burson-Marsteller Public Relations urged companies to work the news media into their ad campaigns. "The implied editorial endorsement created by national publicity efforts can give a brand promotion added impact," said Mosser. "Just think how much more credible the advertising for McDonald's McLean sandwich was after the *New York Times* ran a Sunday front-page about how good the sandwich tasted."

It's a Program ... It's an Ad ... It's an Infomercial!

When they're not sneaking into the evening news, commercials are posing as regular TV shows. "Infomercials" or "program-length commercials," as these impostors are known, mimic the format of talk shows, newscasts, sitcoms, or investigative news programs. These half-hour-long superblurbs have many of the trappings of regular programs: theme music, production credits, listings in the television-guide sections of newspapers, and a "studio audience" of regular-looking folks who have been paid $50 or $75 apiece to feign enthusiasm. They even have "commercial breaks"—for the same product that has been advertised throughout the "show," of course.

Typical of the genre is "Morgan Brittany on Beauty," an infomercial that appeared to be a late-night talk show hosted by the former *Dallas* star. Brittany first introduced the actor George Hamilton, promising, "Today, for the first time ever, he's going to reveal his very own personal method for looking so good." His secret turned out to be the George Hamilton Skin Care System, which viewers were urged to purchase for $39.95 by calling a toll-free number. Alert viewers may have noticed a few departures from talk-show convention. For example, Hamilton was the only guest, and the conversation did seem peculiarly limited to the subject of skin care. But the talk-show illusion was carefully maintained: Brittany welcomed "my guest today" as though she were hosting an ongoing program that had other days, other guests. And at another point, Brittany said to Hamilton, "When I heard you were going to be on the show ..." as if he were not the show's sole reason for being.

The infomercial concept is not new; for decades marketers have tried to get their commercials to blend in with the shows they interrupt. In the 1970s, "Great Moments in Music" and "100 Paintings" were mail-order ads in the guise of cultural programs. But these early infomercials were forced off the air by limits on commercial length and other regulations. It was not until 1984, when Reagan's FCC lifted restrictions on broadcast ads, that infomercials truly began to flourish. (Appropriately enough, Reagan's deregulation paved the way for his son, Michael, to appear in a 1990 infomercial for the Euro Trym Diet Patch, a bogus weight-loss aid. Euro Trym's manufacturer was nabbed by the FTC and forced to refund money to its many disgruntled customers.)

Deregulation, along with the availability of cheap airtime that accompanied the soaring popularity of cable TV, brought forth a deluge of infomercials. By 1993, some 175 products vied for infomercial spots, and according to *Advertising Age*, 90 percent of all U.S. television stations broadcast infomercials. Cable was the first to exploit the infomercial genre and continues to support it heavily: Lifetime airs about forty-three hours of infomercials per week and the Family Channel averages twenty-eight hours a week. Regular broadcasters are also waking up to the $400 million spent on infomercial airtime per year; noncable stations now make 60 percent of infomercial sales.

Initially confined to off-peak time slots, infomercials can now be seen at all hours of the day and night, with nearly 15 percent shown during prime time, according to a 1993 industry survey. Cable executives are developing many infomercial-based channels as part of their interactive TV ventures. In 1994, CBS announced plans to run on the stations it owns prime-time promotions of late-night infomercials, urging early-to-bed audiences to *videotape* the infomercials for later viewing.

In addition to the usual dice-o-matics and costume jewelry, infomercials increasingly feature mainstream companies such as General Motors' Saturn division, McDonald's, Volvo, and Philips Electronics. In fact, one ABC affiliate in Miami preempted the popular *Wheel of Fortune* to air the Philips CD video player infomercial in prime time. Meanwhile, *Wheel's* hostess, Vanna White, stars in her own infomercial for Perfect Smile tooth whitener.

Although most infomercials feature bouncy, entertaining formats, some companies are going after the skeptical, upscale audience with a softer sell. For instance, McDonald's produces "The Mac Report," which masquerades as a sophisticated business newsmagazine—but only about McDonald's. As infomercials earn broader acceptance, they are also attracting a higher order of celebrity hosts: Ted Danson, Cher, and Jane Fonda have appeared in recent infomercials.

Infomercials are likely to continue thriving with the expected boom in new cable channels. Tele-Communications Inc. (TCI) is creating as many as twenty-five single-subject channels, primarily to showcase the products of sponsors. William Airy, a TCI executive overseeing the marketing of new cable ventures, prophesized, "The future... includes special-interest channels that will provide opportunities for infomercial advertisers that are able to target by lifestyle, target demographically, psychographically." The only channels to survive, according to Craig Evans, author of *Marketing Channels: Infomercials and the Future of Televised Marketing,* "will be the advertiser-supported channels that in some way, shape, or form promote product brands or images."

The success of infomercials leads inescapably to the conclusion that *people must be watching them.* Infomercials sold between $750 million and $900 million worth of products in 1993 alone. "What people seem to want from the infomercial is an experience that is wholly and brainlessly affirmative," said Mark Crispin Miller, professor of media studies at Johns Hopkins University. And as Rick Marin concludes in a *New York Times* article, "In a decade with much talk about dysfunction, the world of the infomercial is mesmerizingly functional, even multifunctional. Everything works, or seems to. And if it doesn't? There's always the money-back guarantee."

So what's wrong with infomercials? First, despite the proliferation of infomercials for better-quality products, many of the goods sold this way are ripoffs: weight-loss plans, get-rich-quick schemes, "cures" for baldness, aging, and impotence. And like the home-shopping channels, infomercials owe their success to impulse buying based on limited, biased information. Moreover, infomercials further convert the news and information medium of television into a sales device and add to the chorus of voices urging us to *consume.*

Proliferating infomercials are also forcing conventional shows off the programming schedule. That arrangement suits both advertisers and broadcasters: Infomercial time is cheaper for advertisers than the equivalent in traditional advertising, and television stations can make more money on one thirty-minute block than on a series of thirty-second ads within a regular broadcast. "It's schlock TV," admitted one broadcasting executive at a major station. "But it's a lot of money. If your competitors do that business and you don't, then you lose." Jayne Adair, program director at Pittsburgh's KDKA-TV, is equally positive. "[Infomercials] are the fastest-growing program segment in terms of production values and the quantity of programs being produced," she said. "They are a legitimate form of programming."

But perhaps the biggest problem with infomercials is the element of deception. Infomercials invariably seek to make viewers forget that they are watching a commercial and believe that the advertised product is really the subject of a talk show or news report. Most infomercials provide only cursory notice of their true commercial nature at the beginning or end and at the "commercial" breaks. In an age of remote-controlled electronic "grazing" among channels, many viewers are likely to miss these disclaimers entirely. According to Rader Hayes, a professor of consumer science at Marquette University, there has been no research to determine whether a "reasonable consumer" could distinguish infomercials from regular programming. Hayes, who has studied infomercials since 1985, says they can escape detection even by a trained eye. "Even after all my years of watching," she says, "I was fooled by one this spring." More troubling still are infomercials aimed at kids, who have even fewer skills to make the call. . . .

In their defense, marketers argue that infomercials offer an opportunity to provide in-depth product information. "What better mass vehicle to inform, educate, convince, motivate and sell is there than thirty minutes of TV time?" asked Gene Silverman, vice president of marketing at Hawthorne Communications, in a letter to *Advertising Age.* That is a defensible proposition as long as viewers *know* they are watching a commercial. Broadcasters could, for example, superimpose an easily recognized icon—say, the word "AD" in a circle—in a corner of the TV screen during infomercials. (A similar icon could be used to identify VNR tapes on newscasts.) This simple remedy has been suggested by media critics and consumer advocates but has been rejected by marketers and broadcasters.

The New Hybrid Breed

Marketers continue to experiment with new hybrid formats that merge news, entertainment, and advertising. Bell Atlantic, for example, has produced a "sitcommercial" ad that poses as a situation comedy. "The Ringers," as the show is called, follows the adventures of a suburban family that gets out of typical sitcom dilemmas with the help of call waiting, speed dialing, and other telephone services. The *Wall Street Journal* observes that the sitcommercial's "jokes aren't any worse than any network sitcom" (a depressing commentary on current network fare). The ads' creators believe that by drawing in viewers with a story line, they'll improve sales. "If people actually enjoy watching it and get interested in the characters, they will respond more positively," says Richard Alston, vice president of marketing at Bell Atlantic. In the same spirit, Sominex sleeping pills were the focus of "The Good Night Show," a skit-filled infomercial from the fictional Cable Snooze Network. To its credit, the Sominex infomercial did contain many on-screen disclaimers.

Ads also impersonate documentary films. For example, SmithKline Beecham USA produced a half-hour "documercial" on the importance of calcium in women's diets. SmithKline Beecham makes TUMS antacid, which has been promoted as a source of calcium. Here, the company is trying to fool not only viewers but television stations as well. "When we go to stations and try to get them to run this, we don't want them to think this is a commercial," said Pat McGrath, president of the ad agency Jordan, McGrath, Case and Taylor, which is credited for developing both the sitcommercial and the documercial.

Ads have even been disguised as TV movies. In 1994, NBC sold Mirage Resorts an hour of prime time to broadcast a mini-movie promoting Mirage's new Las Vegas casino, Treasure Island. "Anyone can do a thirty-second commercial," said Mirage spokesman Alan Feldman. "This is much more fun." And much more effective, if viewers get swept away in the adventure-saga formula. NBC tried to keep viewers blissfully unaware that they were viewing a commercial; NBC spokeswoman Mary Neagoy said they were calling it "an entertainment show, an extravaganza." Neither the TV listings nor the network promotions made reference to the show's sponsor.

Another recent innovation that blurs the line between advertising and entertainment is the use of celebrity endorsers who play their TV-character roles in television commercials. Advertisers have always used celebrities to pitch their products; the new wrinkle is that the celebrities appear not as themselves but as the characters they play on TV. For example, Tim Allen, star of *Home Improvement,* played the quirky do-it-yourselfer in a commercial for Kmart's Builders Square. Craig T. Nelson and Shelley Fabares star in a commercial for Kraft Healthy Favorites that could pass for a scene from their popular serial *Coach.* Jerry Seinfeld jokes his way through a commercial for American Express, Sinbad performs his characteristic antics in a Polaroid commercial, and Bart Simpson and family advertise Butterfingers in their trademark dysfunctional style.

Similarly, talk shows have revived the practice of live endorsements, whereby the show's host personally plugs a sponsor's product. When Jay Leno announced that he would endorse products on the *Tonight Show,* the *Wall Street Journal* reported that advertisers "applauded Mr. Leno's move, since they believe viewers are less likely to zap a commercial if it's performed as part of the show." In one episode, Leno held up a giant Intel Inside logo and welcomed the chip manufacturer as a new sponsor on the air. (Late-night rival David Letterman refuses to endorse sponsors on his show.)

Particularly disturbing is the use of former or current newscasters in ads to create an impression of objectivity. For instance, former *CBS This Morning* host Kathleen Sullivan appeared in an ad for the Collagen Corporation. In what looked like a scientific news show, Sullivan presented collagen injection as a safe, effective treatment of skin problems—despite intense debate within the medical community over its safety. Mary Alice Williams also used her credibility as an Emmy Award–winning newsanchor to flack for NYNEX, a telecommunications company. "My job is to stay on top of what they're doing and keep you posted," she said in a TV ad.

One of marketers' newest gambits appeared in September 1994 in the form of a hybrid TV show called *Main Floor*. The half-hour show includes brief features about fashion and beauty. The catch is that some of the features are paid commercials, while others are not; viewers may not be told which are which until the credits at the end. For a fee of about $25,000 (much cheaper than a typical thirty-second commercial), Lee jeans, Chanel cosmetics, and other sponsors can buy two-to three-minute spots to feature their products in the show.

Walt Disney Co. has sponsored what is perhaps the most egregious example of hidden advertising. The company bought time in local newscasts for its "Movie News" spots. The ads, which include an anchorman who sits behind a desk and clips from *The Lion King* and other ... movies, are designed to look exactly like the entertainment segment of a newscast, but they are pure hype for the movies. Only an easy-to-miss notice at the end of the minute-long spots indicates they are "Paid for by Buena Vista," Disney's distribution company.

Blurring the Lines on Radio

Radio, too, is breaking down the barriers between ads and programming. In Washington, D.C., WPGC-AM runs several talk shows on financial topics that are actually program-length ads for their sponsors' products. Ron Petersen hosts a show about investments, which serves to drum up business for his brokerage firm; Jerome Wenger's talk show is really an ad for his financial newsletter. A single sentence at the beginning of each program informs viewers that the show is "furnished," "sponsored," or "brought to you" by its hosts. However, most listeners miss the implications of the disclaimer. The shows are effective marketing tools precisely because most people do not identify them as ads. According to Arnold Sanow, a small-business marketing consultant who once hosted a weekly busienss show on WPGC, "Having *you* on the radio, nobody realizes that you've paid to be the host of that show. They don't think of that."

Moreover, having one's own radio show provides instant respectability. Carolann Brown, who uses her WPGC program *The Money Manager* to promote her book of the same name, says, "It does give you a lot of credibility.... Somehow [people] think that if you're on TV or on the radio that you're already credible." Such deceptions are particularly disturbing when used to sell financial services, where life savings are invested on the strength of perceived reputation and objectivity.

Imitation Editorial

In 1988, Ann Landers received a letter from a reader wanting more information on a miraculous diet pill that dissolves fat while you sleep, based on what appeared to be a legitimate news story. Landers replied, horrified, "What you read wasn't a news story but an advertisement.... How these charlatans get away with this stuff is beyond me."

Landers and her reader had stumbled upon the print media's version of the infomercial—the "advertorial," or advertising disguised as editorial copy.

Advertorials—and consumer complaints about their deceptive nature—have been around for decades. They evolved from "reading notices" of the late 1800s, in which advertisers paid newspapers—or promised them future business—to publish news stories lauding their product or service. Although a 1912 provision to the Newspaper Publicity Act banned advertising disguised as news copy, advertisers and publishers today continue to push the legal limits.

In 1967 the FTC ruled that advertorials must carry the word "advertisement" at the top of the page. Still, it's easy to get fooled. An advertorial spread in the August 1993 issue of *Mademoiselle* titled "What's Next" plugs a variety of products: clothes, makeup, shampoo. The ad's copy style, layout, and photos all mimic the magazine's regular features. A quiz prepared by Centrum titled "How healthy is your diet?" is placed next to an ad for Centrum vitamins. An advertorial in *Travel and Leisure* for Stouffer's Vinoy Resort includes an engaging essay by George Plimpton about a friend with writer's block who checks into the hotel to finish a novel. Again, the ad's title, byline, and typography closely match the magazine's editorial articles.

Advertorials are proliferating madly. According to *Advertising Age,* the recession of the early 1990s gave advertisers more power, which they are using to demand advertorials as part of their contract deals with publishers. In 1992, advertorials filled 6,998 pages in the magazines tracked by the Publisher's Information Bureau. This number was down slightly from the previous year, but up 51 percent from 1986. Even industry organ *Advertising Age* worries about the ethical implications of advertorials. Reporter Scott Donaton writes that "there's a danger that it becomes more difficult for readers to make the distinction between regular editorial matter and special advertising sections."

But fooling the reader is what advertorials are all about. As Ruth Whitney, editor in chief of *Glamour,* told Donaton, "The only thing that's bad about [advertorials] is the effort to deceive the reader, which was really their purpose in the beginning, to convince the reader that this was editorial material. It's imitation editorial."

Now, marketers are taking the advertorial one step further by producing entire magazines to flaunt their products and advertising. Called magalogs, these custom publications sell at newsstands, contain articles and regular ads—but, unlike real magazines, they are published expressly to promote the sponsor's products. For instance, Mary Kay cosmetics publishes *Beauty* magazine, which could be easily mistaken for any other women's magazine. General Motors puts out *Know How,* which covers car matters for women. (*Know How's* premiere issue was even reviewed in *USA Today.*) Pepsi publishes *Pop Life,* which claims to be a "magazine for today's teens." The publication—full of Pepsi ads —includes interviews with Cindy Crawford and Pepsi's other celebrity spokespeople. Although magalog publishers claim to offer a legitimate information source, the contents are biased by definition; single-sponsor magazines will not include any information that could threaten the profits of their backers.

What People Have Done

VNRs, infomercials, and advertorials all disguise their advertising content in order to fly beneath consumers' commercial-detecting radar. The only way to make these "stealth ads" less deceptive is to require a clear indication of their commercial nature. For example, radio infomercials would be punctuated with clear announcements every several minutes, and TV infomercials would include a constant on-screen notice identifying the broadcast as an advertisement. In 1991, the Center for the Study of Commercialism (CSC), together with other consumer-advocacy groups, petitioned the Federal Communications Commission (FCC) to require better identification of infomercials (the FCC had not acted by October 1994). In 1993 the FCC also invited comments on whether to impose commercial time limits on broadcasters; CSC recommended a daily or weekly maximum of commercial content, which would restrict the amount of commercially blurred material allowed on the public airwaves.

POSTSCRIPT

Does Marketing Have Appropriate Boundaries?

J acobson and Mazur emphasize the horrific consequences of commercialism, which "engulf everything from schools to professional sports to scientific research." Examples of "stealth marketing" (like the stealth bomber—unforeseen attacks camouflaged to an unsuspecting target) practices are more apparent every day. For example, a recent article in *Business Week* (February 28, 2000) critiques the use of promotional deals between hospitals and TV stations, whereby consumers are fed paid "news reports" instead of unbiased medical information. The editorial integrity of the *Los Angeles Times* was recently questioned when the editors aggressively publicized the "Staples Center" while simultaneously sharing ad revenues with the company.

There is little question that commercialism has grown by leaps and bounds in newer arenas, and marketers may be culpable for "crossing the line" in many cases. But shouldn't we also consider *demand side* factors, such as audience taste and our tolerance for such lowest common denominator forms of entertainment and programming? "Shock jock" Howard Stern and talk show host Jerry Springer are on TV because there is a sizable and lucrative audience that continues to tune in. As critics consider the degradation of popular culture, are irresponsible marketers culpable for this decline, or are they merely reacting to the demands of the marketplace?

Suggested Readings

Bart Macchiette and Abhijit Roy, "Social Issues and Sensitive Groups: Are You Marketing Correct?" *Journal of Consumer Marketing* (vol. 11, no. 4, 1994)

Richard Ohmann, ed., *Making and Selling Culture* (Wesleyan University Press, 1996)

Paul Raeburn, "The Corruption of TV Health News," *Business Week* (February 28, 2000)

Leigh Eric Schmidt, *Consumer Rites: The Buying and Selling of American Holidays* (Princeton University Press, 1995)

Barry Schwartz, *The Costs of Living: How Market Freedom Erodes the Best Things in Life* (W. W. Norton, 1994)

R. George Wright, *Selling Words: Free Speech in a Commercial Culture* (New York University Press, 1997)

ISSUE 2

Is the Practice of Multilevel Marketing Legitimate?

YES: Dale D. Buss, from "A Direct Route to Customers," *Nation's Business* (September 1997)

NO: Stephen Barrett, from "The Mirage of Multilevel Marketing," *Quackwatch*, <http://www.quackwatch.com/01QuackeryRelatedTopics/mlm.html> (August 26, 1999)

ISSUE SUMMARY

YES: Writer Dale D. Buss depicts the booming growth of multilevel marketing (MLM) in various arenas. He outlines the techniques of one-to-one selling as well as the home party method. Buss also notes how the legitimate companies in the MLM industry take special care to distance themselves from phony operations.

NO: Retired psychiatrist Stephen Barrett argues that people who join in the later stages of an MLM operation will likely not do well. He discusses the example of health-related food supplements, where claims are subject to government intervention and public scrutiny as to their effectiveness. Barrett also examines questionable claims and people's motivations and methods of selling.

M ultilevel marketing (MLM) is used by a wide range of companies to distribute their goods in the marketplace without significant promotional cost. According to Dale D. Buss, there are over 1,000 companies employing more than 7 million people involved in this industry. A diverse range of products and services are sold extensively using this strategy, such as personal care products, home and family care products, vitamins, long distance telephone plans, books, and educational leisure products and services.

MLM can be practiced in two distinct ways—through one-to-one selling or the home party method. Two-thirds of the companies use individual, one-to-one selling either at home, in the workplace, at public events such as fairs, or over the phone. The rest (primarily women) try to sell in a social gathering by offering products "whose sales are enhanced by the strong marketing context" provided by the occasion. What distinguishes a legal MLM company from a pyramid scheme is that by law it limits the maximum number of overrides on distributors generating new distributors. Conversely, pyramid schemes truly afford continuing payoffs for its top originators as the pyramid grows exponentially. Such schemes allow the top numbers to accumulate great wealth at the expense of later entrants to the system.

MLM firms have largely shed their spurious image, and today there are numerous independent distributors selling products to neighbors, friends, and relatives. Many individuals have achieved great success in recruiting others and building a "downline" from which they receive commissions. Buss notes that the legitimate MLM industry is very careful to maintain its clean image.

Some major MLM companies have gone public in recent years with several stocks listed on both the New York Stock Exchange (NYSE) and NASDAQ. Amway, Avon, Tupperware, and Shaklee are examples of companies that have established legitimacy and distanced themselves from the fear of deceptive practices. However, skepticism still exists, states Stephen Barrett. He warns people not to be surprised if a friend or acquaintance tries to sell them vitamins, herbs, homeopathic remedies, weight loss powders, or other health-related products. Barrett sees the attraction as being in tune with the trend toward out-of-home businesses, whereby for a few hundred dollars, working part-time holds the promise of a successful entrepreneurial venture. He comments that many of the pyramid-type MLM companies still exist and seem more prevalent in health care and cosmetic industries. They often prey upon the faith of unsuspecting distributors that the products will provide the results they promise.

Barrett also portrays the attraction of MLM as a derivation of aging baby boomers, who are vulnerable to sales pitches, often from relatives and friends, that promise a healthier and more youthful lifestyle. Such sales pitches also promise monetary rewards devoid of a truthful depiction of the time and effort the undertaking really requires for success. The distributors most frequently are not trained in health and nutrition but simply pass on to their customers the promotional information provided by the company. They can easily become victims of their own hype when they listen to company-made tapes, telephone conference calls, and propaganda at company rallies.

MLM offers the benefits of short-cutting retail distribution, reducing costs, selling new customers in a personal way, and initiating a cult of followers equally committed to making the venture a success. However, the actual hours of commitment and market development are often underplayed by MLM providers. Once initiated, the new MLM recruits sell to everyone and anyone to whom they have access, which is usually a circle of friends, family, and business colleagues. Frequently, after purchasing the "minimal inventory" or sample kits, they are stuck with excessive product.

While thousands of MLM endorsers have profited from their efforts, just as many have struggled in their support without achieving the riches of their sponsors. Although major MLM participants, such as Amway, claim over 10,000 distributors, many of these are people who like and endorse the product but become distributors only to secure access to discounted prices of the product for themselves and a close circle of friends.

Dale D. Buss

 **YES**

A Direct Route to Customers

If she's done it once, she's done it 458 times—literally. But on a sunny June evening in the flower-splashed back yard of a home in Menomonee Falls, Wis., Mary Adashek is using all her enthusiasm to demonstrate the patented peeler-corer-slicer marketed by the company she represents, Pampered Chef.

Over a card table, Adashek uses the gee-whiz tool to prepare fresh apple rings, to spiral-slice fillings for pie, to ready apples for the dehydrator—even to peel potatoes and create curly fries.

"I wish I'd had this all the years I've been making apple pies," says one convinced customer among the half-dozen women who have accepted homeowner Laurie Barker's invitation to see Pampered Chef products and to socialize.

By the time Adashek is done for the evening and leaves for her home in nearby Cedarburg, she has sold about $400 worth of gizmos, including the apple tool, clay "baking stones," and measuring cups with a plunger so butter won't stick to the inside. Add that amount to the more than $250,000 in Pampered Chef sales she has rung up the past four years.

Adashek's earnings from the evening are about $100, below her average of about $125. But by arranging with hostesses to appear at about 10 such parties a month and by reaping commissions from other "sales consultants" she has helped establish, Adashek netted more than $17,500 last year—"enough to pay the mortgage," she says. And that doesn't count the free trips she gets: all-expense-paid sales-reward junkets that Adashek and her husband, a property manager, have taken to London, San Diego, Disney World, and Alaska. Hawaii beckons next year.

"The more people I share this with, the more benefits there are for myself, yes," says the 33-year-old Adashek, a former cardiovascular technician who likes to be able to stay home during the day with her 4-year-old daughter. Sarah. "But we also offer people a way to make life in the kitchen easier and more enjoyable.... And people love these products!"

Indeed, as Adashek climbs the ladder of success, she actually is doing a lot more than selling kitchen implements and enlarging the family budget: She's building her own micro-enterprise while promoting a business opportunity for other women. She is one of the more than 7 million Americans who work,

From Dale D. Buss, "A Direct Route to Customers," *Nation's Business*, vol. 85, no. 9 (September 1997). Copyright © 1997 by The United States Chamber of Commerce.

mostly part time, as sales representatives for companies—such as Pampered Chef Inc., based in Addison, Ill.—that rely on multilevel marketing.

Such marketing—also known as MLM, direct selling, or network marketing —is being used by a growing number of companies to get their goods into the marketplace without the expenses of advertising or staffing a sales department.

Each MLM sales representative is, in effect, a business owner working as an independent contractor for a company that may have few "real" employees. Reps earn commissions on their own sales. They also share commissions with the "upliners" who recruited them and manage them. And, in turn, they recruit and supervise salespeople, called "downliners," who learn from and share commissions with them. Low overhead, work-time flexibility, and lots of potential are all part of the allure.

Cosmetics to Cookware

MLM is booming, with sales reaching an estimated $18 billion in 1995, the latest year for which figures are available. That's up from about $13 billion in 1991, according to the Direct Selling Association, a trade group in Washington, D.C.

To be sure, MLM has a highly notorious side. Some companies create a cultlike environment, motivating sales reps to lean on friends and family to join them. Dozens of firms have been pursued by law-enforcement authorities amid allegations that the companies are using pyramid schemes—illegal scams in which large numbers of people at the bottom of the pyramid pay money that flows to a few people at the top. The illegal operations typically focus on recruiting downliners and sweeping in their signup fees rather than on selling products.

The legitimate MLM industry takes great pains to distance itself from these seamy pretenders.

More than 1,000 companies now use MLM as their primary distribution method, compared with fewer than 700 five years ago, the association says. Personal-care products such as cosmetics and jewelry accounted for about 39 percent of revenues in the direct-selling industry in 1995; home and family-care products, including cleaning solutions and cookware, made up 34 percent; services such as telephone long-distance plans accounted for 10 percent; vitamins, weightloss products, and other health formulas, 9 percent; and books and educational and leisure products or services, 8 percent.

Home is the primary venue of operation, and personal relationships are the main vehicle. About 59 percent of MLM sales occur in homes, according to the Association; an additional 16 percent are made over the phone; 15 percent in the workplace; 5 percent at public events such as fairs; and 5 percent elsewhere.

Two Approaches

In-person salesmanship is the common denominator, but MLM methodology falls into two basic camps: Two-thirds of the companies use individual, one-to-one selling, the association says, while one-third use the home-party method.

Many MLM companies strive to duplicate the accomplishments of renowned direct marketers such as Tupperware, the consumer-products company, Mary Kay, the cosmetics enterprise, and Amway, the home-care-products giant.

One company that takes the one-on-one sales approach developed so successfully by Amway is Excel Communications Inc. Founded by Kenny Troutt in 1989, the Dallas-based provider of long-distance phone service grew from a $20 million company [in the early 1990s] to $14 billion in revenues [in 1996] with its army of 979,000 independent sales reps. The company buys huge blocks of long distance time from the big providers and resells it to consumers at very competitive prices. In May 1996, Excel went public as one of the New York Stock Exchange's youngest new listings ever.

A decade ago, when Troutt got into the business of reselling long-distance capacity—after holding jobs selling life insurance and working in the construction and oil industries—he chose MLM without hesitation. Most Americans obviously knew how to use their phones, he reasoned, but "nobody really understood their rates, nobody really cared what company they were with."

As long as the price is right, he deduced, many phone customers would rather let a relative or friend pocket sales commissions from their purchase if it's a purchase virtually everyone is going to make anyway.

Troutt also correctly concluded that sales reps prefer not having to manage an inventory.

A Way That Works

Robert Montgomery has built Reliv International Inc. into a huge organization in less than 10 years via one-to-one selling of the firm's line of about 25 nutritional supplements and weightloss products, such as Cellebrate. It is a powder that is mixed with water to make a drink, and Reliv says it has been designed to "burn and block fat, curb appetite, and reduce food intake... without side effects." The company has more than 50,000 distributors worldwide.

Montgomery says he considered offering Reliv's line through pharmacies, health-food stores, even gyms and health clubs, but he chose MLM because of the effectiveness of personal salesmanship.

"We believe that our products could be put in a health-food store or a grocery store and just sit there and really not do anything but gather dust unless people can demonstrate them, and talk to someone about what's in the product, and tell them why they should be taking the product," says Montgomery, who is president, chairman, and CEO of the Chesterfield, Mo.-based company.

Such "value-added" selling allows most MLM companies to price their goods higher than they could at retail, says Greg Martin, CEO of ShapeRite Concepts Ltd., another marketer of nutritional products. ShapeRite, based in Sandy, Utah, has more than 70,000 sales reps.

"You need a fairly adequate or hefty margin to be able to pay your distributors fairly for their efforts," says Martin, who founded the company in 1989 with an imported dietary supplement. Compensation for ShapeRite's reps amounts to 54 percent of sales revenue.

Selling in a Social Gathering

Home-party companies, the other MLM camp, typically offer products whose sales are enhanced by the strong marketing context provided by a social gathering of women.

Rhonda Anderson, a Montana homemaker, already knew from demonstrations she had given that her hobby of producing heirloom-quality albums for family photos was party-friendly and that it struck a strong emotional chord in her mostly female audiences. So when she and a friend, Minneapolis business woman Cheryl Lightle, decided to form a business, Creative Memories Inc., home parties seemed the right way to go.

Creative Memories mushroomed from six consultants and $20,000 in sales in 1988 to more than 15,000 reps and $40 million in sales last year. The company just completed a 30,000-square-foot headquarters building in St. Cloud, Minn.

The reason for this exponential growth is a "passion that is common in the consultants who stay with us," says Susan Iida-Pederson, vice president of promotion and communications. "You're not just selling [customers] a product or teaching them a skill, you're really contributing to a tradition they're starting, and it feels good."

"Unit managers"—those with several downliners—earn about $25,000 to $40,000 a year, Iida-Pederson says; a small number of managers earn $60,000 to $80,000; and the rare superstars break $125,000. Some upliners do so well that they quit pitching at parties and spend all their time managing their corps of reps.

Longaberger Co., a Dresden, Ohio, manufacturer of baskets, ceramics, and other goods for the home, also benefits from the warm feelings that home parties generate. Last year its 38,000 reps across the country generated sales of more than $500 million.

Getting Out of the House

As a regional sales manager for Longaberger, Heidi Proefrock is a certifiable MLM star and another weaver of the social fabric in homey Cedarburg, a Milwaukee suburb of 10,000 people. Proefrock has steadily built her business from $8,000 in annual revenues with just six downliners 11 years ago, when she was a part-time water-aerobics instructor, to $40,000 to $50,000 a year net and nearly 60 downliners in nine states.

The operation has grown so big that she is moving it out of the basket-bedecked restored farm home where she and her husband, Steve, a real-estate agent, live. She is relocating her business to an old schoolhouse nearby that she refurbished as an office.

"When I got started with this, I wasn't thinking of making a business out of it at all," says the 38-year-old mother of four. "Like most people, I was just looking to get out of the house a little bit and make some extra grocery money."

In fact, the hallmark of some of the most successful MLM companies is that the business aspect, at least initially, seems secondary to the participants' convictions about the good that they're doing.

Twenty years ago, for example, Lane Nemeth wanted to open a store to demonstrate educational toys. But because parents were her target, her husband suggested the Tupperware-party method. Someone else suggested that she reward people for recruiting. Now Discovery Toys, based in Martinez., Calif., has more than 30,000 reps, and it reached $85 million in sales last year in the United States alone.

"It was all sort of learn-as-you-go," says Nemeth, a former teacher. "What I did have was this enormous, driving mission to get parents to understand that the right kinds of products, the right kinds of stimulation... produce a significantly different child. I was not going into business for the sake of the business." That kind of passion for a quality product or service—a commitment that is easily embraced by others—is the biggest predictor of success for an MLM company, practitioners say.

Successful and reputable MLM companies share a number of other attributes. Among them:

- They make it easy to get in.
- Low barriers to entry are crucial to getting a strong flow of new reps. MLM companies rarely set education or experience requirements.
- There's no commitment by the contractor to a specific tenure, and part-time work is the norm.

The average initial investment required of MLM consultants is only about $100, according to the Direct Selling Association, and its members pledge to buy back at 90 cents on the dollar any resalable goods held by reps who want to exit the business. If a company requires more than an initial small amount for a kit of product samples and other materials, the association says, it could be trying to boost its revenues by making contractors pay in advance for vast supplies of goods regardless of whether they have customers' orders for the products.

The required initial order for a new rep of Biogime International Inc., a Houston-based company that sells skin-care products via MLM, is just $40.

And instead of asking new reps to place orders for a large inventory of skin creams that would have to be stored in a garage or basement, Biogime set up a toll-free telephone line for reps or their customers to call in their orders. The company then credits the rep with the amount of the sale and ships the goods directly to customers, who are billed directly.

"This way doesn't prevent distributors from having a good ongoing relationship with customers, but it stops them from having to invest in inventory and spend unnecessary time delivering products, which really is downtime," says Julie Martin, CEO and co-owner of Biogime. "You don't want people to regret their investment in your program."

They make it attractive to stay on.

Most sales reps leave just as easily as they arrive. Turnover for some MLM companies is 100 percent a year.

Commissions, of course, greatly affect each company's turnover rate because they're the only form of compensation offered by nearly all MLM companies. While commission formulas range widely in the industry, consumables such as nutritional supplements generally carry lower percentage commissions than big-ticket items such as vacuum cleaners. The commissions that sales reps receive from downliners also vary greatly and can have a big impact on contractors' incomes. To help stem departures and to build their reps into successful sellers, good MLM companies produce a wide stream of information for reps on the company's new products and services, sales techniques, and other topics.

The companies also offer regular and continual training sessions that are held one-on-one or at local, regional, or national gatherings.

Longaberger, for example, starts a new consultant with a kit containing printed, video, and audio information, including sample scripts for recruiting hostesses. The company sends out a monthly newsletter as well as a separate monthly publication that suggests product uses, and it hosts a three-day annual national convention, including a full day of training on sales and recruiting.

The company aggressively discourages hyped claims about products and services.

As independent and largely unsupervised agents with strong incentives to attract downliners, MLM reps can be tempted to make unsubstantiated or even outlandish claims about their products, services, and incomes.

Companies such as ShapeRite and Reliv have to be especially vigilant in educating their distributors to ensure that they do not run afoul of recent federal regulations regarding health claims. These companies' training materials and newsletters make clear what distributors should not say when pitching products.

The enterprise avoids fast-buck opportunists.

Because business opportunities can ebb and flow, some reps become what the industry calls "junkies" or "poster boys" who move from company to company trying to get in, and out, at the right times—often taking hundreds or even thousands of downliners with them.

"They're not for long-term companies." says Biogime's Martin. "They're a flash in the pan. It's a big problem in this industry."

The company jealously protects its niche.

The most successful MLM companies quickly attract imitation products, often in conventional retail settings. Consequently, continued innovation in products and services is essential. It prompted Longaberger, for example, to add the ceramic bowls, wallpaper designs, and other housewares to its original focus on baskets.

And Creative Memories has acted assertively to protect its coattails, urging reps not to subscribe to, distribute, or promote a magazine produced by a firm that could become a competitor.

The firm understands the awkwardness of working for an MLM company.

The biggest obstacle for sales reps—and, therefore, for MLM companies—is the fact that reps need to rely on family members and friends for sales, at least initially. Awkwardness often prevails in these social and personal interactions, and the best MLM companies help reps work through that problem—and refrain from pressuring them into feeling like they must turn everyone they know into a customer or a downliner.

"It requires that you commercialize noncommercial relationships," says Robert L. Fitzpatrick, an industry critic and author of a new book, *False Profits: Seeking Financial and Spiritual Deliverance in Multi-Level Marketing and Pyramid Schemes* (Herald Press, $12.95). "It means that you will approach your son-in-law, your girlfriend, your wife, your brother-in-law, your next-door neighbor, your customers—you will invite people who perhaps you have a very different kind of relationship with based on trust, based on family, blood, love, nationalities, something—and you're going to convert that into a business relationship."

The best way for MLM companies to avoid the appearance of exploitation is to market a highly desirable, thoroughly genuine product or service with the utmost integrity—and to let it do its own "talking."

We really are out there as a mission company which happens to have a wonderful learning opportunity," says Nemeth of Discovery Toys. "You'd never come to a Discovery Toys opportunity event and hear all about the people who got rich. You hear about all the parents who got helped."

Stephen Barrett

The Mirage of Multilevel Marketing

Don't be surprised if a friend or acquaintance tries to sell you vitamins, herbs, homeopathic remedies, weight-loss powders, or other health-related products. Millions of Americans have signed up as distributors for multilevel companies that market such products from person to person. Often they have tried the products, concluded that they work, and become suppliers to support their habit.

Multilevel marketing (also called network marketing) is a form of direct sales in which independent distributors sell products, usually in their customers' home or by telephone. In theory, distributors can make money not only from their own sales but also from those of the people they recruit.

Becoming an MLM distributor is simple and requires no real knowledge of health or nutrition. Many people do so initially in order to buy their own products at a discount. For a small sum of money—usually between $35 and $100—these companies sell a distributor kit that includes product literature, sales aids (such as a videotape or audiotape), price lists, order forms, and a detailed instructional manual. Most MLM companies publish a magazine or newsletter containing company news, philosophical essays, product information, success stories, and photographs of top salespeople. The application form is usually a single page that asks only for identifying information. Millions of Americans have signed up, including many physicians attracted by the idea that selling MLM products can offset losses attributable to managed care.

Questionable Financial Opportunity

Distributors can buy products "wholesale," sell them "retail," and recruit other distributors who can do the same. When enough distributors have been enrolled, the recruiter is eligible to collect a percentage of their sales. Companies suggest that this process provides a great money-making opportunity. However, it is unlikely that people who don't join during the first few months of operation or become one of the early distributors in their community can build enough of a sales pyramid to do well. And many who stock up on products to meet sales goals get stuck with unsold products that cost thousands of dollars. Some companies permit direct ordering of their products, which avoids

From Stephen Barrett, "The Mirage of Multilevel Marketing," *Quackwatch*, <http://www.quackwatch.com/01QuackeryRelatedTopics/mlm.html> (August 26, 1999). Copyright © 1999 by Stephen Barrett. Reprinted by permission.

this problem. In July 1999, the National Association of Attorneys General announced that complaints about multilevel marketing and pyramid schemes were tenth on their list of consumer complaints.

An Amway Corporation report indicates that the vast majority of its distributors make very little money. Amway's 1998 "Business Review" tabulates figures gathered from April 1994 through March 1995, from distributors who attempted to make a retail sale, presented the Sales and Marketing Plan, received bonus money, or attended a company or distributor meeting in the month surveyed. The average "gross income" for these "active distributors" was $88 per month. The report defines "gross income" as the amount received from retail sales minus cost of products, plus any bonus. It does not take any business expenses into account. If this figure includes purchases for personal use, the potential profit would, of course, be less. The report also notes that "approximately 41% of all distributors of record were found to be active."

Dubious Health Claims

More than a hundred multilevel companies are marketing health-related products. Most claim that their products are effective for preventing or treating disease. A few companies merely suggest that people will feel better, look better, or have more energy if they supplement their diet with extra nutrients. When clear-cut therapeutic claims are made in product literature, the company is an easy target for government enforcement action. Some companies run this risk, hoping that the government won't take action until their customer base is well established. Other companies make no claims in their literature but rely on testimonials, encouraging people to try their products and credit them for any improvement that occurs.

Most multilevel companies tell distributors not to make claims for the products except for those found in company literature. (That way the company can deny responsibility for what distributors do.) However, many companies hold sales meetings at which people are encouraged to tell their story to the others in attendance. Some companies sponsor telephone conference calls during which leading distributors describe their financial success, give sales tips, and describe their personal experiences with the products. Testimonials also may be published in company magazines, audiotapes or videotapes. Testimonial claims can trigger enforcement action, but since it is time-consuming to collect evidence of their use, government agencies seldom bother to do so.

Government enforcement action against multilevel companies has not been vigorous. These companies are usually left alone unless their promotions become so conspicuous and their sales volume so great that an agency feels compelled to intervene. Even then, few interventions have substantial impact once a company is well established.

Recent Promotions

During the past 15 years, I have collected information on more than 100 multilevel companies marketing health products. Here are some examples of improper marketing activities:

- Body Wise International, of Carlsbad, California, markets "fitness" products and weight-management products. In 1995 the FTC [Federal Trade Commission] charged the company with making unsubstantiated claims that *Cardio Wise* was "designed to give an extra margin of insurance against heart disease" and that its weight-management products would foster weight loss without dieting. The company signed an FTC consent agreement prohibiting it from making unsubstantiated health-related claims in the future.

- Mary Kay, well known for its cosmetic products, is now marketing a $29.50-per-month daily supplement packet alleged "to help bridge the gap between what a healthy diet provides and what a woman needs for optimum health and beauty." *Tufts University Diet & Nutrition Letter* has observed: (1) the supplements contain huge amounts of thiamin, riboflavin, vitamin B6, and vitamin B12, which almost all Americans get from their food; (2) they lack iron, which might benefit some women of childbearing age; and (3) more rationally formulated multivitamin/mineral preparations are available elsewhere for one tenth the cost.

- In 1993, Melaleuca Inc., of Idaho Falls, Idaho, began offering a "wellness assessment" by a company that provided in-home testing. The procedure included a questionnaire, a blood cholesterol test, a blood-pressure reading, and an estimate of the percentage of body fat. The resultant report evaluated personal risk factors and recommends modifications in diet, exercise habits, and lifestyle. The recommendations include taking a "balanced vitamin/mineral supplement every day" and "working closely with a 'Vitality for Life counselor'" (a Melaleuca distributor) to implement the suggested changes. Prospects were then encouraged to purchase a "Vitality Pack" of "55 different vitamins, minerals, and other nutrients, all in the proper amounts and proper proportions," which wholesales for $263.40 for an annual supply. Although the health-risk appraisal could provide useful information, the Vitality Pack is a waste of money. People who wish to take a multivitamin/multimineral formula can obtain equivalent nutrients at a drugstore for less than $50 per year. The company also marketed a patented "fat conversion activity bar," an expensive candy bar whose ingredients are claimed to make exercise easier by "inhibiting the body's ability to hold on to fat."

- Matol Botanical International, a Canadian firm, markets *Km,* a foul-tasting extract of 14 common herbs. *Km* was originally marketed as *Matol,* which was claimed to be effective for ailments ranging from arthritis to cancer, as well as for rejuvenation. Canada's Health Protection Branch took action that resulted in an order for the company to advertise only the product name, price, and contents. In 1988 the FDA [Food and Drug Administration] attempted to block importation of *Matol* into the United States. However, the company evaded the ban by adding an ingredient and changing the product's name. The product literature acknowledges that *Km* has never been tested for effectiveness against any disease and states that distributors should not diagnose or recommend its products for any specific disease. However, many distributors do so.

- Nature's Sunshine Products, of Spanish Fork, Utah, markets herbs, vitamins, other nutritional supplements, homeopathic remedies, skin and hair-care products, water treatment systems, cooking utensils, and a weight-loss plan. Its more than 400 products include many that are claimed to "nourish" or "support" various body organs. Its salespeople, dubbed "Natural Health Counselors," are taught to use iridology (a bogus diagnostic procedure in which the eyes are examined), applied kinesiology (a bogus muscle-testing procedure), and other dubious methods to convince people that they need the products.

- Nu Skin International, Inc., of Provo, Utah, sells body-care products and dietary supplements. Nu Skin's Interior Design division markets expensive antioxidant, phytochemical, and "active enzyme" products. The enzyme products are said to be important because "the majority of cooked or processed foods we eat lack an ideal level of enzyme activity" needed for digestion. This statement is nonsense because the enzymes needed for digestion are made by the body's digestive organs. In 1993, the company and three of its distributors agreed to pay a total of $1,225,000 to settle FTC charges that they made unsubstantiated claims for *Nutriol Hair Fitness Preparation* and two skin-care products. In 1997, the company agreed to pay $1.5 million to settle charges that it had made unsubstantiated claims for five more of its products. The products, which contained chromium picolinate and L-carnitine, were falsely claimed to reduce fat, increase metabolism, and preserve or build muscle.

- Sunrider Corporation, of Torrance, California, claims that its herbal concoctions can help "regenerate" the body. Although some ingredients can exert pharmacologic effects on the body, there is little evidence they can cure major diseases or that Sunrider distributors are qualified to advise people about how to use them properly. During the mid-1980s the FDA ordered Sunrider to stop making health claims for several of its products. In 1989 the company signed a consent agreement to pay $175,000 to the state of California and to stop representing that its products have any effect on disease or medical conditions. The company toned down its literature but continued to make therapeutic claims in testimonial tapes included in its distributor kits. In 1992 a jury in Phoenix, Arizona, concluded that Sunrider had violated Arizona's racketeering laws and awarded $650,000 to a woman who claimed she had been misled by company representations and had become ill after using some of its products. On January 7, 1997, *The Wall*

Street Journal reported that Sunrider's president Tei-Fu Chen and his wife Oi-Lin Chen were indicted for conspiracy, tax evasion, and smuggling. The article stated that they had (1) underreported their 1987–90 income by more than $125 million, (2) used foreign companies they controlled to overcharge Sunrider for ingredients so the company could understate its profits, (3) wired millions of dollars to pay the inflated charges, but "recycled" the money to purchase U.S. real estate and Chinese antiques, and (4) filed falsely low customs declarations to reduce the import duty on dozens of art works. In September 1997, the Chens and the company pled guilty to tax and customs frauds. Mr. Chen was sentenced to two years in federal prison, to be followed by two years of supervised release including six months of home detention. Mrs. Chen was sentenced to two years probation, including six months of home detention. The financial penalties totaled $99.8 million. The Corporation was fined $500,000 for filing a false tax return for 1989. Mr. Chen agreed to pay the Customs Service $4 million to avoid forfeiting antique items that had been seized. In related actions, the Chens had paid the Internal Revenue Service $93 million in back taxes, interest, and penalties, and paid the Customs Service $2.3 million in additional duties. In 1998, the FDA issued a warning letter citing manufacturing violations and stating that it was illegal for the company to market "spray vitamins" as dietary supplements.

Motivation: Powerful but Misguided

The "success" of network marketing lies in the enthusiasm of its participants. Most people who think they have been helped by an unorthodox method enjoy sharing their success stories with their friends. People who give such testimonials are usually motivated by a sincere wish to help their fellow humans. Since people tend to believe what others tell them about personal experiences, testimonials can be powerful persuaders.

Perhaps the trickiest misconception about quackery is that personal experience is the best way to tell whether something works. When someone feels better after having used a product or procedure, it is natural to give credit to whatever was done. However, this is unwise. Most ailments are self-limiting, and even incurable conditions can have sufficient day-to-day variation to enable bogus methods to gain large followings. In addition, taking action often produces temporary relief of symptoms (a placebo effect). For these reasons, scientific experimentation is almost always necessary to establish whether health methods are really effective. Instead of testing their products, multilevel companies urge customers to try them and credit them if they feel better. Some products are popular because they contain caffeine, ephedrine (a stimulant), valerian (a tranquilizer), or other substances that produce mood-altering effects.

Another factor in gaining devotees is the emotional impact of group activities. Imagine, for example, that you have been feeling lonely, bored, depressed or tired. One day a friend tells you that "improving your nutrition" can help you feel better. After selling you some products, the friend inquires regularly to find out how you are doing. You seem to feel somewhat better. From time to time you are invited to interesting lectures where you meet people like your-self. Then you are asked to become a distributor. This keep you busy, raises your income, and provides an easy way to approach old friends and make new ones—all in an atmosphere of enthusiasm. Some of your customers express gratitude, giving you a feeling of accomplishment. People who increase their income, their social horizons, or their self-esteem can get a psychological boost that not only can improve their mood but also may alleviate emotionally-based symptoms.

Multilevel companies refer to this process as "sharing" and suggest that everyone involved is a "winner." That simply isn't true. The entire process is built on a foundation of deception. The main winners are the company's own-ers and the small percentage of distributors who become sales leaders. The losers are millions of Americans who waste money and absorb the misinformation.

Do you think multilevel participants are qualified to judge whether prospective customers need supplements—or medical care? Even though cu-rative claims are forbidden by the written policies of each company, the sales process encourages customers to experiment with self-treatment. It may also promote distrust of legitimate health professionals and their treatment methods.

Some people would argue that the apparent benefits of "believing" in the products outweigh the risks involved. Do you think that people need false beliefs in order to feel healthy or succeed in life? Would you like to believe that something can help you when in fact it is worthless? Should our society support an industry that is trying to mislead us? Can't Americans do something better with the billion or more dollars being wasted each year on multilevel "health" products?

Physician Involvement

During the past few years, many physicians have begun selling health-related multilevel products to patients in their offices. The companies most involved appear to be Amway, Body Wise, Nu Skin (Interior Design), and Rexall. Doctors are typically recruited with promises that the extra income will replace income lost to managed care. In June 1999, the AMA House of Delegates approved ethical guidelines emphasizing that physicians should not coerce patients to purchase health-related products or recruit them to participate in marketing programs in which the physician personally benefits, financially or otherwise, from the efforts of their patients. The guidelines clearly frown on doctors prof-iting from the sale of health-related nonprescription products such as dietary supplements.

Recommendations

Consumers would be wise to avoid health-related multilevel products alto-gether. Those that have nutritional value (such as vitamins and low-cholesterol foods) are invariably overpriced and may be unnecessary as well. Those promoted as remedies are either unproven, bogus, or intended for conditions that are unsuitable for self-medication.

Government agencies should police the multilevel marketplace aggressively, using undercover investigators and filing criminal charges when wrongdoing is detected. People who feel they have been defrauded by MLM companies should file complaints with their state attorney general and with local FDA and FTC offices. A letter detailing the events may be sufficient to trigger an investigation; and the more complaints received, the more likely that corrective action will be taken.

POSTSCRIPT

Is the Practice of Multilevel Marketing Legitimate?

While many perceptual concerns of MLM exist, and legal public scrutiny is certain to endure, the simple reality is that this marketing practice is here to stay, and it has become embedded in America's controversial marketing culture. Financial success portends the growth of more sophisticated versions of MLM augmented by the growth of the Internet, affinity marketing, and the quest for building relationships. As we face the new millennium, many factors are collectively creating a fertile environment of MLM. Baby boomers' desire to "cocoon" (i.e., work out of the home), computer technology, and the quest for independence are alluring for a large percentage of many demographic segments seeking autonomy and financial success.

The method of multilevel marketing has made millions of dollars for distributors of Amway products, Mary Kay Cosmetics, and thousands of companies embracing the benefits of utilizing friendships, contacts, and person-to-person selling with the motive of having one's own distributorship. Given its uniqueness, how should this form of distribution be evaluated?

Despite the illegality of pyramid schemes, action from the government in enforcing regulations against such companies has not been forthcoming. Unless their promotions become so conspicuous and sales so extreme that an agency feels compelled to intervene, there will likely be less than vigorous law enforcement. The burden of the decision will remain with the consumer.

The direct sales appeal has not been without criticism, because of the negative connotation inherent in "pyramid selling." Enhanced by e-commerce, chat lines, and databases, multilevel marketing is experiencing unprecedented growth with its unique advantages and alleged savings to all parties involved.

Suggested Readings

Norm Brodsky, "Multilevel Mischief," *Inc.* (June 1998)

Cheryl Coward, "How to Spot a Pyramid Scheme," *Black Enterprise* (February 1998)

Richard Eisenberg, "The Mess Called Multilevel Marketing," *Money* (June 1987)

Constance Gustke, "Multi-Level Investing: Some of the Hottest Stocks Around Are Issued by Network Companies. Here's How to Analyze and Invest in Them," *Success* (September 1998)

Rob Laymon, "Multi-Level Marketing Proves a Hit on 'Net," *Philadelphia Business Journal* (August 20, 1999)

Jim Salter, "Multi-Level Marketing Goes Mainstream," *Marketing News* (September 1997)

Kristine Zwica, "ABCD . . . MLM," *Success* (May 1999)

"What's Wrong With Multi-Level Marketing?" `http://www.vandruff.com/mlm.html`

Spree.com. `http://www.spree.com`

ISSUE 3

Has the "Keep It Simple" Concept Become "All Change, All the Time"?

YES: Regis McKenna, from *Real Time: Preparing for the Age of the Never Satisfied Customer* (Harvard Business School Press, 1997)

NO: Jack Trout with Steve Rivkin, from *The Power of Simplicity: A Management Guide to Cutting Through the Nonsense and Doing Things Right* (McGraw-Hill, 1999)

ISSUE SUMMARY

YES: Regis McKenna, chairperson of the McKenna Group, proclaims that the era of "adaptive" marketing has arrived—now driven by new technologies of communications and information. Keeping in close touch with ever-changing consumer needs is now the only constant for marketing managers, he concludes.

NO: Jack Trout, president of the marketing firm Trout & Partners, and Steve Rivkin, a faculty member of the Department of Economics at Amherst College, see an overcommunicated culture of clutter. They argue that simplicity and the "focused benefit" must be encoded into one integrated singular message and emphasize the importance of a consistent "value proposition" packaged into a simple message, which is memorably positioned in the minds of consumers and prospects in a creative way.

Two distinct schools of thought have emerged as contemporary marketing orientations. Recent developments in information technology have tended to galvanize these perspectives. The first can be summarized by the following illustration: How many times have you been to a friend's or relative's house and seen the time on their VCR perpetually blink "12:00"? It is not a very difficult task to set the time correctly, but many lack the motivation to try and figure out how to do it. This is why many companies follow the KISS (Keep it simple, stupid!) policy. The origins of this theme can be traced to the early theory of Rosser Reeves, who introduced the concept of the Unique Selling Proposition (USP). He emphasized identifying and focusing on one differentiating attribute that can be "hammered" into the minds of consumers. Advertising mogul David Ogilvy then refined the concept by stressing the importance of developing a clear product personality, or the complex symbol known as the *brand image*. The need for clarity, simplicity, and consistency are essential in each advertising campaign, which is creating an "investment" in building the brand.

Product positioning emerged as the strategic mantra of the late 1970s and remains the core concept for Jack Trout and Steve Rivkin. Their quest is for a clear value proposition binding the essence of consumer benefit to the market offering. For example, in the automotive industry, Volvo has established the safety position, Mercedes prides itself upon engineering quality, while Porsche touts itself as being the best sports car. It is necessary to provide customers with a salient reason to patronize one company's brand over the competitive offering. A simple positioning platform must carry a clearly construed core message and provide a meaningful idea for differentiation. The rationale for returning to simplicity and clarity is also at the heart of the integrated marketing communication (IMC) concept, which is defined by the American Association of Advertising Agencies (AAAA) as "a concept of marketing communications planning that recognizes the added value of a comprehensive plan that evaluates the strategic roles of a variety of communications disciplines—for example, general advertising, direct response, sales promotion and public relations—and combines these disciplines to provide clarity, consistency and maximum communications' impact through the seamless integration of discrete messages."

In other words, instead of a heavy reliance on any one promotional tool, several tools are blended to deliver a consistent and coherent brand image, which is presented to the customer at every brand contact.

The common thread for all these developments is what might be termed the *complexity avoidance syndrome*. Consumers seek to avoid confusion, hassles, and clutter. Bombarded by thousands of stimuli, they are loathsome of intrusive telemarketers and the onslaught of the thousands of "me, too" products found in the supermarket.

The opposing perspective focuses on the necessity for "real-time marketing" or "adaptive marketing." This assumes that consumers are constantly driven by their wants and needs, possessed by instant gratification, and empowered with product information. Regis McKenna argues that the advancements in communications technology and interactive advantages of the Internet can devastate loyalty to the company, as customers can eliminate geographic constraints and literally "shop the world." He believes that the need for extraordinary flexibility and instant reaction time has become crucial in offering consumers both choice and access.

Experts say that the themes of *speed* and *innovation* should replace the outmoded notion of celebrating consistency. This is a logical extension of *turbomarketing*, whereby companies are trying to establish a competitive advantage by responding faster to the fickle and ever-changing demands of the marketplace. Other sources suggest that adaptations, customization, and rapid response to smaller-niche markets are the themes for marketing in the new millennium.

Regis McKenna

 **YES**

Real Time

The Real Time Message

Society and technology are in a continual dance, each moving and swaying in response to unanticipated moves by the other. Real time technology swiftly embeds itself in everything, everywhere, profoundly affecting the marketplace and every business participating in it. To discover how best to use the new technological tools to cross traditional market or geographic boundaries, adapt their modus operandi, and still keep their customers happy, managers must first get acquainted with the dimensions of the new technological power and its incipient social effects.

The Never Satisfied Customer

Right here. Right now. Tailored for me. Served up the way I like it. If the new consumer's expectations were spelled out on a billboard, that is how they would read. Top managers monotonously repeat, as if intoning mantras, that this is the age of customer service or the age of the consumer. Yet few of these managers realize what they must do for that customer to earn his or her complete approval. Consumer criteria for absolute satisfaction from supplier organizations, whether a company or a branch of government, have become so stringent as to seem unreal by the standards of the past.

Still, some of the most unlikely institutions have gotten parts of the message ahead of the rest: they have understood the need for extraordinary flexibility and have adapted accordingly, offering consumers both choice and access. One of these is a public agency upending government's reputation for sloth and rigidity. The Department of Motor Vehicles (DMV), seeking to maximize public cooperation with the enforcement of driving laws, offers some traffic offenders—as an alternative to steep fines and a hike in their auto insurance rates—a staggering array of choices for remedial instruction, known as traffic school. These are among the options available in several states to a driver who has earned, say, one too many speeding tickets: seven hours of daytime instruction on any day of the week, including Saturday and Sunday, or three and a half hours each on two consecutive weekday evenings. In California, the reforming speeder can attend any of 3,000 classrooms scattered across the state, run by certified, independent instructors (not government employees). The class offerings include those run by comedians who sugarcoat the predictable lessons with unpredictable wit and those held in pizzerias where students also get their dinner. There are the "Escuela Latina De Trafico-Espanol," an "Armenian-Persian-Spanish Classes" outfit, variations on "Finally a Gay Traffic School," budget-conscious operations such as the "Ultimate Discount and Fun Safety Traffic School," and the catchall establishment that advertises itself as "Laffs & Comedy—Low Cost—AM/PM—7 Days."

Traffic offenders of the near future can, of course, be expected to take their punishment over the Internet, from on-line schools. But the DMV had a glimmer of consumer attitudes to come way back in 1986, when it handed over the job of remedial teaching to outside contractors who, being in competition with each other, have every incentive to be accommodating.

The Conditioning of the Consumer

Choice gives the customer power. An empowered customer becomes a loyal customer by virtue of being offered products and services finely calibrated to his or her needs. That amounts to a reversal of the pattern of the past, in which consumers or users of things had to arrange their lives according to the product or service desired. People had to shop during relatively limited store hours, to buy an automobile from one of the Big Three, to make phone calls from fixed locations, to treat the office computer room like a temple, approaching it only through intermediary MIS [mass information systems] priests.

The personal computer [PC] remains the most stunning marker for the transition, putting personal information and network access into the hands of consumers and reinforcing consumers' growing sense of autonomy by giving them access to ever more finely tuned information on which to base buying decisions. Personal computers surpassed television set sales in revenues in 1994, outpaced VCR unit sales in 1996, and are expected to outpace TV unit sales in 1997. At the time of the PC's invention in the 1970s, the idea of buying a low-cost computer for use by one person from a specialty retail store like Circuit City (www.circuitcity.com) seemed about as plausible as purchasing a personal aircraft or personal train from Sears Roebuck (www.sears.com) or JCPenney (www.jcpenney.com).

Yet the conditioning of the new empowered consumer, expecting more or less instant gratification, took place at a steady pace over many decades. Most middle-aged adults probably have some equivalent of my first glimpse of the possibilities of real time. One summer in the early 1950s, I remember racing with my friends down to the new dry cleaner in town, in whose window flashed a big red neon sign announcing, "One Hour Shirt Cleaning." Amazed at the efficiency, we stuck our noses against the glass to watch the astonishing maneuvers of the automatic shirt-pressing machine.

Like every other technology-toned consumer, I have in the intervening years come to take for granted other marvels of compressed time: direct-dial telephone and fax services for communicating almost anywhere in the world; packages delivered overnight, with the bonus of being able to discover, at almost any time of day, the whereabouts of a parcel in transition with an 800 call to a customer service representative or with track-it-yourself software. Other time-compressed, mind-altering technologies include instantaneous, worldwide news from CNN, pagers, cellular phones, mobile and wireless computing, video conferencing, and instant credit card verification with the swipe of a plastic card through a machine.

The expanding expectations of choice characteristic of the new consumer are one effect of growing time pressure. To the time-conscious shopper, the most generous possible menu of purchase options offering several different price-points cuts down on time spent driving around hunting and comparison shopping. Category-killing, price-sensitive retail chains like Wal-Mart (www.wal-mart.com) and "warehouse clubs" like Price-Costco (www.wal-pricecostco.com) and Sam's Club (www.samsclub.com) serve the needs of discount-minded and low-income shoppers who want to pile up the largest number of bargains with the smallest outlay of time and effort. Pier 1 Imports (www.pier1.com) actually urges shoppers to take home a piece of rattan furniture or a dhurrie rug and try it out. It wants to encourage would-be buyers put off by not having the time to make the perfect selection and afraid of making a costly mistake. The no-questions-asked, hassle-free policies for exchanging or returning goods pioneered by stores like Nordstrom in the early 1980s are similarly motivated.

Yet even these leaders in serving the new consumer's needs have little cause to relax into smug self-congratulation. Today's consumers are made more aware by modern communications, they have more choice, they are more diverse and mobile; yet the pace of life has also made them more discontented. As a result, the American consumer's demands on the supplier appear, for all the world, to be increasing exponentially.

The New Consumer Is Never a Satisfied Consumer

A 1995 report in *Fortune* (*http://pathfinder.com/fortune*) set out the results of a customer satisfaction survey by the University of Michigan Business School (www.bus.umich.edu) and the American Society for Quality Control (www.asqc.org). Not even Federal Express—"a service star"—earned a rating above 85 on a scale of 0 to 100. (Although Dole Foods, purveyor of pineapple rings and other packaged consumables, did earn a top score of 90. See www.dole5aday.com.) According to the report:

> "(I Can't Get No) Satisfaction" is the theme song of consumers who clearly believe the nation's companies are doing a lousy job of meeting their needs.... Many of the losers on the list are champs in both size and reputation. Citicorp [www.citicorp.com] has the most advanced ATM system in the world and a global strategy as ambitious as Coca-Cola's [www.cocacola.com]. But consumers find banking there anything but

refreshing.... Nordstrom [www.nordstrom.com], famous for taking shoppers by the hand, is not the crowd pleaser you might think, either: The department store barely broke 80.

Companies with the clearest view of the new consumer's time-conscious mental landscape that are willing to adapt their modus operandi to its features will have the edge over their competition.

New consumers expect from organizations if not obeisance then, at the very least, the respect accorded an equal. Traditional business language reveals a different attitude on the part of managers, who have unthinkingly referred to marketing "targets" slotted into market "segments" of people with wants and needs assumed to be virtually identical. Consumers have been thought of in terms of classification statistics—"30–40 age bracket, $70,000–$100,000 income range, 2.5 children, 2.5 cars"—or categories—such as DINKS (dual income, no kids)—to be manipulated into desiring the goods or services a company has to purvey. The general idea has been that if you could name it, classify it, and put it in a database, you had half the marketing problem solved. These practices are symptomatic of an obsession with measurement in the interests of control (over the partitioned groups).

The other half of the misguided marketing equation has dictated that dealing with individual consumers is a waste of time. And time is money. Therefore, the argument goes, it is necessary to classify consumers into large monolithic groups and address them as if they all think and act alike. While this approach may have been expedient in the age of mass marketing, it is unlikely to survive the reign of the new consumer.

A New Model to Fit the New Consumer

The new marketing model reflects a shift from monologue to dialogue in dealings with customers. The result is a reversal of traditional consumer and producer roles, with the consumer dictating exactly how he or she would like to be served. New consumers expect to be asked about their individual preferences and treated—to the most extreme degree possible—as if these preferences are being respected.

A pioneering example of the consultative approach in action is the way Philips Electronics N.V. (www.philips.com), the Dutch multinational giant, developed an on-line product for children in the early 1990s. Philips dispatched industrial designers, cognitive psychologists, anthropologists, and sociologists in mobile vans to communities in Italy, France, and the Netherlands. The researchers invited adults and children to brainstorm ideas for new electronics products. Instead of conducting a survey of these volunteer product designers, Philips arranged discussions in which specialists and customers imagined new possibilities. After examining all the propositions the dialogues produced, Philips reduced them to a short list, then chose one new interactive product. In the next stage, the researchers revisited the communities and tested the new product idea on the same children whose aid had been enlisted.

The gains to be had from consulting consumers in this fashion are also demonstrated by a progressive Parisian designer of women's clothes, Emanuel

Ungaro, which licenses a line of garments to Gruppo GFT, which in turn distributes them in America. The "relaxed career wear" bearing the Emanuel label has been one of the few upscale collections in the business to thrive in a shrinking market, the result of an apparent decline in women's interest in high-fashion clothing. Analyzing Emanuel's success in a report on the garment industry, the *New York Times* said in 1996:

> In fashion, manufacturers usually rely on intuition and on feedback from retailers. Instead, Emanuel executives went right to customers, in suburbs as well as cities. "We're doing a lot more analysis today than we did in the past because now the customer wants to tell the designer what she wants," said Maura de Vischier, chief executive of Emanuel.

TQM [total quality management] supplies the model. Enlightened companies invite customers to sit on advisory boards, work as partners in the refinement of specifications and testing, share benchmark data, and fine-tune the balance of supply and demand. Customers have an equal say in such areas as design and inventory management. Customers—like vendors—are treated like partners.

Caution: Slow-Moving Vehicles Ahead

In addition to such exemplary exercises in paying attention to market feedback as displayed by Philips and Emanuel, recent history supplies cautionary tales about companies taking the opposite tack. German automaker Porsche (www. porsche.be), for instance, lost 80 percent of its share of the American luxury car market to Japanese rivals in just five years in the late 1980s and early 1990s. Until the company ran into trouble, it refused to lower its prices—even over a period in which the dollar lost more than half its value against the mark.

Both Porsche and Mercedes (www.daimler-benz.com) mistakenly believed that the appeal of brand exclusivity—and in the case of Mercedes, outstanding engineering—gave them license to price as they pleased. In 1990 I attended a J. D. Power conference at which the keynote address was delivered by the director of marketing for Mercedes America. He boasted that while other automakers were lowering prices and so devaluing their brands, Mercedes would soon announce even more expensive models. Only a few months later, Lexus appeared on the scene, forcing Mercedes to modify its pricing and change many of its other entrenched marketing practices. But a great deal of damage had been done. Daimler-Benz lost almost $4 billion in 1995.

In Porsche's case, large portions of its potential market, in which baby boomers were heavily represented, were starting families and rapidly switching from deluxe cars to minivans or buying the smart new Lexus. In addition, the government slapped on new luxury sales and gas taxes, and the economy was in a recession. Finally, with Porsche in the red and its unit sales dropping steeply, the company, like Mercedes, was sufficiently humbled to introduce new cars with more modest tags. The result was a dramatic increase in sales by 1997. Porsche's slow response was almost catastrophic and its market share growth much slower. Brand name was no protection.

Companies poorly oriented to the technology-toned consumer's changing behavioral terrain often describe their preferences in clever-sounding terms derived from interpretations of research rather than interactive information. But the properly oriented company will set itself the goal of understanding the consumer through dialogue. It knows that customers bombarded with sales propositions that do not reflect responsiveness to their needs will increasingly react with Procrustean fury or, worse, fatal indifference.

Real time marketing permits the constant updating of information about consumers' likes and dislikes; communications and computer technologies are now closely meshed for a constant exchange of information between distributors, retailers, and customers. Networks of this sort already exist and register rapidly changing consumer wishes. Computer-based design and manufacturing technologies are allowing companies to go even further, actually responding to those wishes with fiercely compressed product cycles and processes that incorporate more options and variety.

Virtual Customization Through Service

The fact is, now that the technological means for enormous flexibility exist, what customers expect is customization or personalization of some kind. The costs of customizing manufactured goods are falling steadily as technical refinements and managerial innovations allow flexible production plants with short runs to get closer to the low unit costs of long mass production runs. Undifferentiated manufactured goods are a steadily diminishing proportion of the output of advanced economies.

Manufacturers like Levi Strauss (www.levi.com) have been lighting the way to the future: since 1995, Levi's sales clerks have taken the measurements of women shopping for jeans and entered the numbers into computers that calculate fit. The customized jeans are sewn at a Levi's factory from a computer-generated pattern. A shoe-store chain, the Custom Foot, (www.thecustomfoot.com) lets women design their own shoes, using a three-dimensional foot scanner. Variety, when it is broad enough, can amount to virtual customization—whether in the form of products actually sitting on retail shelves or capable of being ordered directly from the factory in a quantity of one.

From the consumer's viewpoint, individual attention also amounts to virtual customization. For instance, though doctors and lawyers usually draw on the same database of knowledge—a combination of their training and experience—to serve patients or clients, they apply that knowledge to specific clients in specific ways, tailored to individual needs. Every ulcer patient may be prescribed the same drug and dietary regimen, but feels as if he or she has received customized attention.

Unfortunately, health care today is being driven by health care maintenance organizations (HMOs), which are degrading patient care to a one-prescription-fits-all commodity business. Consumers are becoming increasingly dissatisfied with the severe constraints on choice of physicians; cumbersome procedures for treatment approval, endless paperwork, and red tape associated with their health insurance. This approach to service will eventually fail because it violates the basic tenets of good service: interaction, a willingness to listen on the part of the service provider, customized responsiveness, and real time.

Real time technology holds the potential for restoring substance and meaning to the care in health care. I have been a diabetic for more than forty years. In that span of time, I have been able to take advantage of specialized new products and medical technologies—everything from a huge and growing range of sugar-free foods to pen-size, thirty-second test glucose monitors to a miniature pump that acts as an electronic pancreas supplying insulin twenty-four hours a day whenever and wherever I need it. I frequently correspond via e-mail with my doctor, Joe Prendergast. A practicing diabetologist for more than twenty-five years, he runs the Endocrine Metabolic Medical Centre (EMMC) in Atherton, California (www.diabeteswell.com).

EMMC is a model of futuristic responsiveness in health care. Its operation is guided by the findings of the Diabetic Control and Complications Trial, released in 1993. This study showed that any improvement in blood glucose control reduced the risk of the various complications associated with the disease. EMMC has been conducting an experiment with Caresoft, a Silicon Valley startup (www.caresite.com), to help a subset of its patients who are having trouble maintaining their blood glucose levels within desired ranges and happen to be connected to the Internet. Caresoft has developed "condition management" software that enables clinic staff to assist such patients, directly and proactively, over the Internet in a secure environment. "Data are the key to control," says Dr. Prendergast. Hence diabetics upload data from their digital glucose monitoring devices and transmit these to the care givers, and in return they get recommendations and reminders from the system, and instant feedback on actions to take from the care giver.

While the number of patients in this pilot project is small, preliminary results show a marked improvement in their ability to control their ailment. "Patient empowerment," Dr. Prendergast believes, is "probably the most philosophically exciting idea to emerge in medicine in recent years." He is trying to extend many of his findings about the effectiveness of patient power to a wider public through an organization he founded, the Pacific Medical Research Foundation. Empowerment is inextricably linked to customization.

Technology-toned consumers do not merely want a customized end product. They also require some sign that a company acknowledges their individuality in almost all of its dealings with them. Personalized greetings at a hotel—"Welcome back, Mr. McKenna, thanks for staying with us. Your favorite room is available for you"—are not the half of it. I didn't realize what heights my own expectations had reached until a remark I made to a shirt salesman earned a look of horror from my wife. "We sell lots of these," he said, pressing one selection on me. "Now why would I want to wear a shirt that everyone else is wearing?" I snapped at him reflexively.

A similarly harsh and thoroughly contemporary attitude is expressed in the *New York Times* report on the garment industry, mentioned above:

> Walk through the Macy's in Herald Square and experience the world of a lab mouse. Go to the contemporary department, home to shiny sheath dresses and polyester hip huggers, and realize that a coat to wear over them means a trip to another floor. Like that suit and want a nice scarf to wear with it? Trek downstairs to accessories. Over at coats, an indifferent sales clerk, punching sales tags into the computer with all the enthusiasm of a child being immunized, should not be asked to recommend a nice pair of matching boots. They will be nowhere nearby.

New customers want to feel that they have the ear of employees with the authority to make swift decisions and, increasingly, that they can reach someone who can take action. The most progressive companies allow customers access to huge corporate product-related and service databases. Today an 800 number is even printed on a package of M&M's (1-800-627-7852) and a bar of Hershey's chocolate (1-800-468-1714). Some companies have already taken the step of printing the address of their Web site on their products (Pepsi is an example: www.pepsi.com), thereby providing the consumer with a gateway to galaxies of information. Information provided at a hypothetical M&M's site, for instance, could range from a graphical demonstration or video of how the candy is manufactured to research information about the profiles of people who prefer eating green M&M's to red ones. Some day a customer with a malfunctioning electric toaster will be able to download diagrams demonstrating troubleshooting procedures—unless she decides to return or exchange the appliance and is instructed as to how to go about this painlessly over the Internet or by fax.

Making Choice Transparent

Above all, what the new consumers want is control, which chiefly means choice, even if they are not sufficiently conscious of that desire for control (or choice) to be capable of expressing it in a focus group. They want not only the widest array of choices but a choice among choice-making routes.

One route, for instance, would spare people the burden of choosing at all. Someone wanting this option might share the opinion of Natan Sharansky, a member of the Israeli Knesset, who after nine years in Soviet prisons and labor camps complained of feeling lost in the West. Forced to make "thousands of mundane choices [about] all these kinds of orange juice and cereals," he said, "[y]ou lose your life in all these things. Your life becomes very shallow." Precisely that sentiment is echoed at the start of the 1996 film *Trainspotting*, adapted from the novel of the same name, about young, heroin-addicted Scottish dropouts. A voiceover conveys the disgust the main character, Mark Renton, feels over the commercial rituals of modern society:

> Choose life. Choose a job.... Choose a ... big television, choose washing machines, cars, compact disc players and electrical tin openers.... Choose fixed-interest mortgage repayments. Choose a starter home.... Choose leisurewear and matching luggage. Choose a three-piece suit ... in a range of ... fabrics.... Choose your future. Choose life.

For Renton, the burden of choice is overwhelming, but there are constructive new alternatives to his drug-induced oblivion. In 1996, Rates Technology of Long Island patented a telecommunications device that can automatically select the cheapest carrier—among all carriers nationwide, a total of 867 at the time—for every long-distance call placed. As soon as a phone number is punched in, the computerized processor scans all the rates of all the carriers before it makes its selection.

Choice ultimately becomes transparent to the user, by virtue of either an easy-to-use interface or simple familiarity. Transparency means never having to say, "Damnit!" When information is available at the touch of a fingertip, you have transparency. Software developed by the Colorado start-up Netdelivery enables publishers of catalogs, newspapers, newsletters, and any sort of material that requires constant updating to be placed on a subscriber's computer automatically without the user phoning, searching, clicking, or downloading. Transparency! Using such software delivers your daily financial newsletter or Lands' End catalog to the desktop—always current, prices, pictures, and all (www.netdelivery.com). The most successful transparent human interface is the simple, twelve-button alphanumeric telephone keypad, which offers an almost infinite choice of communication links—not just to other owners of telephones but to information services and directories—with the user exerting little thought or effort.

For the majority who actually enjoy being offered a choice, the options provided by real time technology will be unprecedented. The person buying a car, probably long before he or she visits a showroom to kick actual tires and take a test drive, will have done these things "virtually," in some sense, through on-line services. The potential buyer will have browsed through comparative data and the Web site of, say, *Consumer Reports* (www.consumer.org); J. D. Power & Associates (www.JDPower.com), the organization that monitors automobile trends and performance; or the Consumer Information Center at www.pueblo.gsa.gov. Nationally distributed car magazines have Web sites, as do brokers stocked with vast reservoirs of data about the relative costs and benefits of purchasing and leasing. There are Internet bulletin boards linking de facto communities of owners of different makes and models of cars, through which additional help and advice can be sought.

A friend of mine recently purchased a new minivan after using the Internet to gather data and a fax machine to send out requests for bids to dealers. She said it was the "best and most efficient experience I have ever had of buying a car." The automobile business is being reshaped from the bottom up by the discovery of exactly this sort of potential. "The consumer-driven marketplace is changing the heart and soul of this industry," Dave Power, J. D. Power & Associates founder, told me. "The franchise retail system is a hundred years old! Things have to change. The whole system is broken."

Today's leaders—embryonic real time organizations—are already putting in place the managerial and technical infrastructure to give consumers more information and assistance, making choice as easy as possible. They understand the edge this gives them with customers pressured on all fronts: putting in longer work days to stay ahead of the competition or to assuage fears of downsizing; straining to find time to spend with children and equally harassed mates; longing for increasingly scarce leisure time or the time to simply get chores done.

All Information Superhighways Lead to Service

Companies have long competed largely through building brand names—sowing desirable associations in the minds of potential customers with advertising slogans, discounts, and promotions. Customers have been treated like clay to be molded into loyal brand buyers. Today's enlightened company understands that lasting brand loyalty is won only one way: by dynamically *serving* customers. Here *dynamic* means constant interaction and dialogue based on real time information systems.

Real time service is the key to winning the hearts and minds of new consumers, with their seemingly reset circadian clocks. It means being in touch all the time, creating an experience, adding information that addresses individual needs and circumstances, responding without delay, and gaining valuable feedback for new and improved offerings.

Internet enthusiasts eagerly await access to devices that will allow them to be on-line without interruption—or, in the telling phrase they use, "turned on" twenty-four hours a day. Rising businesses aiming to excel in the real time arena have as their goal ubiquitous, nonstop, and transparent service.

The new consumers hate to be kept waiting and are being conditioned, in all spheres of life, to become ever more impatient. "The advances of technology contradict theories of human satisfaction expounded by... psychoanalysis," Nobel Prize–winning novelist Nadine Gordimer observes. "Apart from its purely sexual application, Sigmund Freud's deferred pleasure as a refinement of emotional experience does not compare with the immediate joy of hearing a lover's voice, or getting a friend's reply to a letter at once by e-mail."

As I have noted elsewhere, what customers want most from a product is often qualitative and intangible: it is the benefit and service that is integral to the product. Service is not an event; it is the process of creating a customer environment of information, assurance, and comfort. Technology has made it possible to establish such an environment with unprecedented finesse. Many companies are using call centers, kiosks, 800 numbers, expert software, and on-line services to meld marketing and technology, creating a feedback loop that binds their best interests to those of their customers. This circuit has immensely enhanced sensitivity to customers' requirements and to many of their preoccupations with information and service, most of which have a time-related component.

From its earliest days, the world's leading microprocessor company, Intel, discussed plans for future models of microchips with designer-engineers at customer companies, such as computer makers. As Dave House, a former senior vice president at Intel, explained to me, by blending marketing and engineering, the company has been able to achieve a faster return on investment in new products. Working closely with key customers on specifications—balancing prototype products' technical capabilities against customers' receptivity to new features and requirements—Intel has developed a remarkable relationship with those customers, who are then primed to use the products they helped design. As with Philips and the children who participated in its brainstorming meetings, or the customers of the fashion design firm Emanuel, the consultees not only help to make salable products but become potential buyers of them.

This sort of intimate dialogue between a company and its customers creates a brand loyalty immeasurably deeper than catchy jingles riding on advertising blitzes ever could. It creates a quasi-symbiotic tie. The new interactive technologies collapse the space between consumer and producer. The extraordinary attentiveness to customers' desires by companies using these tools leads their customers to expect a similar response from other companies.

The galloping expectations of the technology-toned consumer can be expected to gain velocity as an electronic infrastructure allowing intensifying interactivity between producers and customers spreads wider. This is the infrastructure composed of the communication revolution's profusion of linked media. Collectively, these media represent a critical watershed. For businesses and branches of government serving the public, the important media of the past were channels for broadcast. The vital new media, by contrast, are channels of access.

Access media hold the key to satisfying the consumer's runaway demands for real time results. This is because access media help organizations serve customers better by making it possible for customers to serve *themselves*. Without any sense of effort, customers are satisfied by means of sophisticated, hidden, or "transparent" technologies about whose workings they need know nothing.

The Real Time Message

New consumers are never satisfied consumers. Managers hoping to serve them must work to eliminate time and space constraints on service. They must push the technological bandwidth with interactive dialogue systems—equipped with advanced software interfaces—in the interest of forging more intimate ties with these consumers. Managers must exploit every available means to obtain their end: building self-satisfaction capabilities into services and products and providing customers with access anytime, anywhere.

The Power of Simplicity

Simplicity

Why People Fear It So Much

> Simple Simon met a pieman going to the fair.
> Said Simple Simon to the pieman,
> Let me see your ware.
> Says the pieman to Simple Simon,
> Show me first your penny.
> Says Simple Simon to the pieman,
> Indeed, I have not any.
>
> — Mother Goose

Through the years, being called "simple" was never a plus. And being called "simpleminded" or a "simpleton" was downright negative. It meant you were stupid, gullible, or feebleminded. It's no wonder that people fear being simple.

We call it the curse of "Simple Simon."

When psychologists are asked about this fear, they get a little more complex. (Not surprising.) Psychologist John Collard of the Institute of Human Relations at Yale University described seven kinds of common fears. (All of us have some of them.)

1. Fear of failure
2. Fear of sex
3. Fear of self-defense
4. Fear of trusting others
5. Fear of thinking
6. Fear of speaking
7. Fear of being alone

It would appear that not being simple—or not seeking simple solutions—stems from number 5, "fear of thinking."

The problem is that instead of thinking things through for ourselves, we rely on the thinking of others. (This is why the worldwide management consulting business is expected to grow to about $114 billion by the year 2000.)

Says Dr. Collard: "Not only is it hard work to think, but many people fear the activity itself. They are docile and obedient and easily follow suggestions put forward by others, because it saves them the labor of thinking for themselves. They become dependent on others for headwork, and fly to a protector when in difficulty."

This fear of thinking is having a profound impact in the business of news. Some even wonder whether it has much of a future.

Columnist Richard Reeves suggests that "the end of news" may be near. The avalanche of news about the rapid changes of modern life is turning people off. Audiences "do not want complicated and emotionally complex stories that remind them of their own frustrations and powerlessness."

Reeves is probably right about the growing avoidance of complexity. People don't want to think.

That's why simplicity has such power. By oversimplifying a complex issue, you are making it easy for people to make a decision without too much thought. Consider the complex trial of O. J. Simpson and how Johnnie Cochran put the essence of his argument into one memorable line: "If the glove doesn't fit, you must acquit."

"Make your scandals complex and you can beat the rap everytime," says speechwriter Peggy Noonan referring to Whitewater, which, unlike Watergate, lacked the easily grasped story line that people want.

But psychologist Dr. Carol Moog comes at the problem from another vantage point. She states that in our culture there's a "paranoia of omission." There's a sense that you have to cover all your options because you could be attacked at any moment. You can't miss anything or it could be fatal to your career.

In other words, if you have only one idea and that idea fails, you have no safety net. And because we are so success-driven, it magnifies the number one fear, "fear of failure."

You feel naked with a simple idea. A variety of ideas enables a person to hedge his or her bets.

Our general education and most management training teach us to deal with every variable, seek out every option, and analyze every angle. This leads to maddening complexity. And the most clever among us produce the most complex proposals and recommendations.

Unfortunately, when you start spinning out all kinds of different solutions, you're on the road to chaos. You end up with contradictory ideas and people running in different directions. Simplicity requires that you narrow the options and return to a single path.

Dr. Moog also had some interesting observations about buzzwords. To her, a management buzzword is like a movie star with whom we fall in love.

The buzzword comes with a beautiful book jacket and a dynamic speaker that has what we all love, charisma. Whether or not I understand this starlet isn't important, because I'm in love. And besides, people are afraid to question somebody who's a big shot or to challenge what they think is a big idea. (That's "fear of speaking.")

The best way to deal with these natural fears is to focus on the problem. It's analogous to how a ballet dancer avoids getting dizzy when doing a pirouette. The trick is to focus on one object in the audience every time your head comes around.

Needless to say, you have to recognize the right problem on which to focus.

If you're Volvo, the problem on which to focus is how to maintain your leadership in the concept of "safety" as others tries to jump on your idea.

That's pretty obvious.

But there are times when the problem isn't so obvious. Such was the case in recent years for Procter & Gamble, the world's preeminent marketer. You might assume that its problem was to find ways to sell more stuff.

The new management recognized the real problem. Does the world need 31 varieties of Head & Shoulders shampoo? Or 52 versions of Crest? As P&G's president, Durk Jager, said in *Business Week* magazine, "It's mind-boggling how difficult we've made it for consumers over the years."

As the article put it, he and CEO John Pepper realized that after decades of spinning out new-and-improved this, lemon-freshened that, and extra-jumbo-size the other thing, P&G decided it sells too many different kinds of stuff.

This solution to that problem was simple, though implementing it was a complex process. The company standardized product formulas and reduced complex deals and coupons. Gone are 27 types of promotions, including bonus packs and outlandish tactics such as goldfish giveaways to buyers of Spic & Span. (Many froze to death during midwinter shipping.) P&G also got rid of marginal brands, cut product lines, and trimmed new product launches.

So with less to sell, sales went down, right? Wrong. In hair care alone, by slashing the number of items in half, the company increased its share by 5 points.

Our friends at P&G certainly weren't afraid of simplicity. Over the past five years they've used it to increase their business by a third.

That's the power of simplicity.

Common Sense

It Can Make Things Simple

> *You must draw on language, logic and simple common sense to determine essential issues and establish a concrete course of action.*

> — Abraham Lincoln

The real antidote for fear of simplicity is common sense. Unfortunately, people often leave their common sense out in the parking lot when they come to work.

As Henry Mintzberg, professor of management at McGill University, said, "Management is a curious phenomenon. It is generously paid, enormously influential and significantly devoid of common sense."

Common sense is wisdom that is shared by all. It's something that registers as an obvious truth to a community.

Simple ideas tend to be obvious ideas because they have a ring of truth about them. But people distrust their instincts. They feel there must be a hidden, more complex answer. Wrong. What's obvious to you is obvious to many. That's why an obvious answer usually works so well in the marketplace.

One of the secrets of the buzzword gurus is to start with a simple, obvious idea and make it complex. A *Time* magazine commentary on a Stephen Covey book captured this phenomenon:

> His genius is for complicating the obvious, and as a result his books are graphically chaotic. Charts and diagrams bulge from the page. Sidebars and boxes chop the chapters into bitesize morsels. The prose buzzes with the cant phrases—empower, modeling, bonding, agent of change—without which his books would deflate like a blown tire. He uses more exclamation points than Gidget.

If you look up the dictionary definition of "common sense," you discover that it is native good judgment that is free from emotional bias or intellectual subtlety. It's also not dependent on special technical knowledge.

In other words, you are seeing things as they really are. You are following the dictates of cold logic, eliminating both sentiment and self-interest from your decision. Nothing could be simpler.

... [T]he new management at Procter & Gamble clearly saw the world of the supermarket as it really was: confusing. And that clarity of vision led management to the simple, commonsense strategy of simplifying things.

Consider this scenario. If you were to ask 10 people at random how well a Cadillac would sell if it looked like a Chevrolet, just about all they would say is, "Not very well."

These people are using nothing but common sense in their judgment. They have no data or research to support their conclusion. They also have no technical knowledge or intellectual subtlety. To them a Cadillac is a big expensive car and a Chevrolet is a smaller inexpensive car. They are seeing things as they really are.

But at General Motors, rather than seeing the world as it is, those in charge would rather see it as they want it to be. Common sense is ignored and the Cimarron is born. Not surprisingly, it didn't sell very well. (And we're being kind.)

Was this a lesson learned? It does not appear to be so. GM is now back with the Catera, another Cadillac that looks like a Chevrolet. Like its predecessor, it probably won't sell very well because it makes no sense. You know it and I know it. GM doesn't want to know it.

Leonardo da Vinci saw the human mind as a laboratory for gathering material from the eyes, ears, and other organs of perception—material that was then channeled through the organ of common sense. In other words, common sense is a sort of supersense that rides herd over our other senses. It's supersense that many in business refuse to trust.

Maybe we should correct that. You don't have to just be in business to ignore simple common sense. Consider the complex world of economists, a group that works hard at outwitting simple common sense.

There is nothing economists enjoy more than telling the uninitiated that plain evidence of the senses is wrong. They tend to ignore the human condition and declare that people are "maximizers of utility." In econo-talk we become "calculators of self-interest." To economists, if we all have enough information we will make rational decisions.

Anyone who's hung around the marketing world for a while realizes that people are quite irrational at times. Right now, we're overrun by four-wheel-drive vehicles designed to travel off the road. Does anybody ever leave the road? Less than 10 percent. Do people need these vehicles? Not really. Why do they buy them? Because everyone else is buying them. How's that for "rational"?

The world cannot be put into mathematical formulas. It's too irrational. It's the way it is.

Now some words about intellectual subtlety.

A company often goes wrong when it is conned with subtle research and arguments about where the world is headed. (Nobody really knows, but many make believe they know.) These views are carefully crafted and usually mixed in with some false assumptions disguised as facts.

For example, many years ago Xerox was led to believe that in the office of the future everything—phones, computers, and copiers—would be an integrated system. (Bad prediction.) To play in this world, you needed to offer everything. Thus Xerox needed to buy or build computers and other noncopier equipment to offer in this on-rushing automated world.

Xerox was told it could do this because people saw the company as a skilled, high-technology company. (This was a false assumption. People saw it as a copier company.)

Twenty years and several billion dollars later, Xerox realized that the office of the future is still out in the future. And any Xerox machine that can't make a copy is in trouble. It was a painful lesson in technical knowledge and intellectual subtlety overwhelming good judgment.

Finally, some thoughts about a business school education, which seems to submerge common sense.

By the time students finish their first year, they already have an excellent command of the words and phrases that identify them as MBA wanna-bes. They have become comfortably familiar with jargon like "risk/reward ratio", "discounted cash flow", "pushing numbers", "expected value", and so forth.

After a while, all this uncommon language overwhelms critical thought and common sense. You get the appearance of deliberation where none may exist.

Ross Perot, in a visit to the Harvard Business School, observed, "The trouble with you people is that what you call environmental scanning, I call looking out the window."

To think in simple, commonsense terms you must begin to follow these guidelines:

1. **Get your ego out of the situation.** Good judgment is based on reality. The more you screen things through your ego, the farther you get from reality.
2. **You've got to avoid wishful thinking.** We all want things to go a certain way. But how things go are often out of our control. Good common sense tends to be in tune with the way things are going.
3. **You've got to be better at listening.** Common sense by definition is based on what others think. It's thinking that is common to many. People who don't have their ears to the ground lose access to important common sense.
4. **You've got to be a little cynical.** Things are sometimes the opposite of the way they really are. That's often the case because someone is pursuing their own agenda. Good common sense is based on the experiences of many, not the wishful thinking of some. . . .

Marketing

It's Turning Simple Ideas Into Strategy

Marketing, in the fullest sense, is the name of the game. So it better be handled by the boss and his line. Not staff hecklers.

— Robert Townsend
Up the Organization

If a CEO conducts the symphony, it's marketing that oversees the arrangement of the music.

Academics have written tomes about the complexity of marketing and all its functions. Ad agencies and consultants have constructed convoluted systems for building brands. One of our favorite pieces of complexity comes from a U.K. consulting firm that claims a brand has nine positioning elements in a customer's mind: functional needs, objective effects, functional roles, attributes, core evaluators, psychological drives, psychological roles, subjective character, and psychological needs. Then the consultants turn all this into a "bridge matrix" [see Figure 1].

(Help, I'm trapped on a bridge to nowhere.)

Another piece of complexity is [what] some agency is pushing [see Figure 2].

(Help, I'm trapped in a marketing labyrinth.)

We'll give you the essence of marketing in two sentences: First, it's marketing's responsibility to see that everyone is playing the same tune in unison.

Figure 1

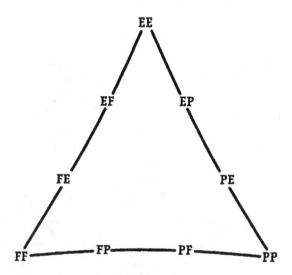

Second, it's marketing's assignment to turn that tune or differentiating idea into what we call a coherent marketing direction.

The notion of a differentiating idea requires some thought. What kind of idea? Where do you find one? These are the initial questions that must be answered.

In order to help you answer these questions, we propose using the following specific definition. A differentiating idea is a *competitive mental angle.*

This kind of idea must have a *competitive* angle in order to have a chance for success. This does not necessarily mean a better product or service, but rather there must be an element of differentness. It could be smaller, bigger, lighter, heavier, cheaper, or more expensive. It could be a different distribution system.

Furthermore, the idea must be competitive in the total marketing arena, not just competitive in relation to one or two other products or services. For example, Volkswagen's decision in the late fifties to introduce the "first" small car was an excellent competitive idea. At the time General Motors was manufacturing nothing but big, heavily chromed patrol boats. The Beetle was a runaway success.

The VW Beetle was not the first small car on the market, of course. But it was the first car to occupy the "small" position in the mind. It made a virtue out of its size, while the others apologized for their small size by talking about "roominess."

Figure 2

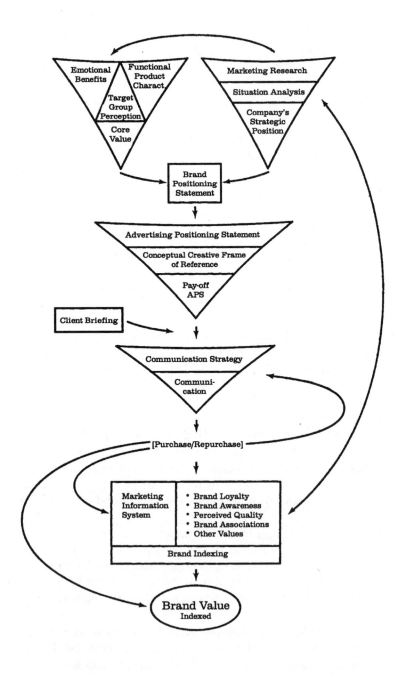

"Think small," said the Volkswagen ads.

An example of a new bad idea is Volvo's sporty coupe and convertible. We see no competitive angle against BMW, Mercedes, and Audi (just to name a few).

Second, a differentiating idea must have a competitive *mental* angle. In other words, the battle takes place in the mind of the prospect.

Competitors that do not exist in the mind can be ignored. There were plenty of pizza places with home delivery operations when John Schnatter launched Papa John's. But nobody owned the "better ingredients" position in the mind.

On the other hand, there are competitors who enjoy strong perceptions that do not agree with reality. It's the perception that must be considered in the selection of an idea, not the reality.

A competitive mental *angle* is the point in the mind that allows your marketing program to work effectively. That's the point you must leverage to achieve results.

But an idea is not enough. To complete the process, you need to turn the idea into a strategy. (If the idea is a nail, the strategy is the hammer.) You need both to establish a position in the mind.

What's a strategy? A strategy is not a goal. Like life itself, a strategy ought to focus on the journey, not the goal. Top-down thinkers are goal-oriented. They first determine what it is they want to achieve, and then they try to devise ways and means to achieve their goals....

But most goals are simply not achievable. Goal setting tends to be an exercise in frustration. Marketing, like politics, is the art of the possible.

When Roger Smith took over General Motors in 1981, he predicted that GM would eventually own 70 percent of the traditional Big Three domestic car market, up from about 66 percent in 1979. To prepare for this awesome responsibility, GM began a $50 billion modernization program. Boy, was Roger wrong.

Currently, General Motors' share of the Big Three domestic market is 30 percent and falling. His goal was simply not achievable because it was not based on a sound idea.

In our definition, a strategy is not a goal. It's a *coherent marketing direction*. A strategy is *coherent* in the sense that it is focused on the idea that has been selected. Volkswagen had a big tactical success with the small car, but it failed to elevate this idea to a coherent strategy. It forgot about "small" and instead elected to bring into the U.S. market a family of big, fast, and expensive Volkswagens. But other car manufacturers had already preempted these automotive ideas. This opened the way for the Japanese to take over the small car idea.

Second, a strategy encompasses coherent *marketing* activities. Product, pricing distribution, advertising—all the activities that make up the marketing mix must be coherently focused on the idea. (Think of a differentiating idea as a particular wavelength of light and the strategy as a laser tuned to that wavelength. You need both to penetrate the mind of the prospect.)

Finally, a strategy is a coherent marketing *direction*. Once the strategy is established, the direction shouldn't be changed.

The purpose of the strategy is to mobilize your resources to preempt the differentiating idea. By committing all your resources to one strategic direction you maximize the exploitation of the idea without the limitation that the existence of a goal implies.

What are you looking for? You are looking for an angle—a fact, an idea, a concept, an opinion on the part of the prospect that conflicts with the positions held by your competitors.

Take laundry detergents, for example. What does detergent advertising suggest that customers are looking for? Cleanliness. That's why Tide gets clothes "white." Cheer gets clothes "whiter than white." And Bold goes all the way to "bright."

Did you ever watch a person take clothes out of a dryer? If you read the ads, you might think he or she puts on sunglasses so the glare won't ruin the eyes.

In fact, most people hardly look at the clothes at all. But they almost always smell them to see if they smell "fresh." This observation led Unilever to introduce Surf, a detergent whose sole distinguishing characteristic is that it contains twice as much perfume as the competition. *Result:* Surf came in and grabbed a respectable piece of the $3.5 billion U.S. detergent market.

Did you ever watch a commuter buy a cup of coffee to carry on a train or bus? The commuter will often carefully rip a drinking hole in the lid so the coffee won't spill while he or she is drinking it during the trip.

Someone at the Handi-Kup Division of Dixie Products noticed. Handi-Kup introduced a plastic lid with the drinking hole built in.

Some angles are hard to spot because customers express them in the negative. The Adolph Coors Company invented light beer. (Even today there are fewer calories in regular Coors than in Michelob Light.) Yet Coors ignored its own invention until Miller introduced Lite beer.

It was hard to ignore. Before Lite saw the light of day, any Denver bartender could have told you how their customers ordered a Coors. "Give me a Colorado Kool-Aid."

Coors could have preempted the light category with a major advertising program. It didn't. Miller did. So Miller Lite became the first successful light beer.

Most angles are hard to spot because they almost never look like big winners in advance. (If they did, others would already be using them.) Marketing bombshells burst very quickly.

"Great ideas," said Albert Camus, "come into the world as gently as doves. Perhaps then, if we listen attentively, we shall hear amid the uproar of empires and nations a faint flutter of wings, the gentle stirring of life and hope." ...

When you saw your first bottle of Lite beer, did you say, "This brand is going to become one of the biggest-selling beers in America"? Or did you say, "Here's another Gablinger's"? (The first low calorie beer.)

When you saw the first Toys "R" Us store, did you say, "This is going to be a $10 billion business selling one-fourth of all the toys in America"? Or did you say to yourself, "Why did they make the letter R backward?"

Did you buy a McDonald's franchise in 1955 when it would have cost you all of $950? Or did you wait in line saying to yourself, "How can they make money selling hamburgers for 15 cents?"

Did you buy Xerox stock in 1958? Andy Warhol soup cans in 1968? A condo in Manhattan in 1979?

Did you save your baseball cards? Your Superman comic books?

Opportunities are hard to spot because they don't look like opportunities. They look like angles—a lighter beer, a more expensive car, a cheaper hamburger, a store that sells only toys. Marketing's responsibility is to take that angle or idea and build it into a strategy so as to unleash its power.

Market leader Pizza Hut could have neutralized one or two Papa John's "better ingredients" delivery units. With the strategy of expanding into a nationwide chain of better ingredient delivery units, Papa John's effectively drove a powerful wedge into the competition. It is first into the mind with this idea.

The idea dictates the strategy. Then the strategy drives the idea. To say that one is more important than the other is to miss the essence of the process. It's the relationship between the two that is the crucial aspect of marketing success.

What's more important in aircraft design: the engine or the wing? Neither. It's the relationship between the two that determines whether your design will get off the runway.

The idea differentiates your business from your competitor's. Strategy gives wing to the idea that can make your business soar.

POSTSCRIPT

Has the "Keep It Simple" Concept Become "All Change, All the Time"?

In 1996 Proctor & Gamble (P&G) went through a drastic simplification program, recognizing that 31 varieties of Head and Shoulders shampoo and 52 varieties of Crest toothpaste were overwhelming to the average consumer. Wal-Mart has consistently used an "every day low prices" (EDLP) pricing policy to their advantage. In advertising, some of the more enduring slogans are simple and short: "Just Do It" (Nike), "Diamonds Are Forever" (DeBeers), and "Compassionate Conservative" (George W. Bush). As far as consumer behavior is concerned, a 1999 *Time* magazine cover story examined how most of us are opting for simpler celebrations in life.

We live in an era of "sound bites," and research has shown that simpler and shorter slogans are easier to process cognitively. The argument can be traced back to Claude C. Hopkins (considered the father of advertising), who, in his book *Scientific Advertising* (Chicago, 1923), advised keeping the message as simple as possible. Both David Ogilvy and Hopkins believed in caution with the use of humor in advertising, since it may overwhelm the central message differentiating the product. Conversely, Wendy's "Where's the Beef?" campaign was a humorous means of driving home the simple product advantage of the "beef-to-bun ratio."

Basically, positioning theory and, more recently, integrated marketing communications propose that the proliferation of media and exposure of consumers to exponential increases in marketing stimuli (noise) have created an overcommunicated society and a confused, oversaturated consumer. In an effort to break through this promotional jungle, the need for a single, cohesive, seamless marketing communication is the fundamental common denominator and mandate of both of these viewpoints.

McKenna focuses on the notion of *constant change* and argues that speed and innovation matter more than consistency. Furthermore, customers adapt faster than firms, so companies must "turn not on a dime but a pixel" just to keep pace. The well-received contributions of Don Peppers and Martha Rogers in terms of one-to-one marketing and mass customization lend substantial credence to McKenna's real-time concept.

Does real-time marketing necessarily imply "chaos and complications"? Does the growth of "keep-in-touch" tools like the Internet, e-mail, customer call centers, and the simultaneous decline of broadcast budgets imply the importance of real-time service? The "simple" camp might argue the importance of keeping these tools as user-friendly and uncomplicated as possible so that average customers are not confused. The users might demand something that is consistent in format and easy to read. In 1999 many major retailers (e.g., Toys 'R' Us) did not do well with e-commerce, since most of their customers were unable to easily navigate through their Web sites.

Suggested Readings

Gerrard Macintosh and James W. Gentry, "Decision Making in Personal Selling: Testing the KISS Principle," *Psychology and Marketing* (August 1999)

"Make It Simple," *Business Week* (September 9, 1996)

Regis McKenna, "Real Time Marketing," *Harvard Business Review* (July–August 1995)

Rachel McLaughlin, "Marketing in Real Time," *Target Marketing* (March 1999)

Christopher Meyer, *Fast Cycle Time* (Free Press, 1993)

Richard O. Oliver, Ronald T. Rust, and Sanjeev Varki, "Real-Time Marketing," *Marketing Management* (Fall 1998)

Don Peppers and Martha Rogers, *Enterprise One to One: Tools for Competing in an Interactive Age* (Doubleday/Currency, 1997)

Rosser Reeves, *Reality in Advertising* (Alfred A. Knopf, 1960)

Al Reis and Jack Trout, *Positioning: The Battle for Your Mind* (Warner Books, 1982)

Sarah Schaefer, "Have It Your Way," *Inc.* (November 18, 1997)

"Simple Marketing Hits the Mark," *Discount Store News* (October 1999)

"The Simple New Year's Eve: Why We're Saying No to the Hype and Opting for a Quiet, Meaningful Evening," *Time* (November 29, 1999)

George Stalk, Jr., and Thomas M. Hout, *Competing Against Time* (Free Press, 1990)

Michael Treacy and Fred Wiersema, *The Discipline of Market Leaders: Choose Your Customers, Narrow Your Focus, Dominate Your Market* (Addison-Wesley, 1997)

ISSUE 4

Is Relationship Marketing a Tenable Concept?

YES: Jennifer Bresnahan, from "Improving the Odds," *CIO Enterprise Magazine* (November 15, 1998)

NO: James R. Rosenfield, from "Whatever Happened to Relationship Marketing? Nine Big Mistakes," *Direct Marketing* (May 1999)

ISSUE SUMMARY

YES: Law student Jennifer Bresnahan describes the new era of information technology, which enables marketers to serve every consumer, one at a time, and develop long-term mutually beneficial relationships.

NO: James R. Rosenfield, chairperson and CEO of Rosenfield & Associates, maintains that relationships in marketing are not always like those between human beings; customers want more of a one-way street. He shares "nine big mistakes" that impede successful development of marketing relationships.

Roger Dow, vice president of Marriott Hotels, has stated, "It takes five times the effort to attract a new customer as it does to keep an old one." In the context of our current information-rich empowered consumer, this claim is now likely to be terribly understated. The loss in profits from defecting customers is a revolutionary concern for marketers, and it has served as a wake-up call for relationship marketing. No longer does the average consumer habitually buy from the same car dealer. Recent reports reveal that almost 50 percent of all auto purchasers have searched the Internet for the greatest deal.

Most sources associate Leonard Berry with the first published works on relationship marketing, and in the last two decades the field has received significant attention by academicians as well as marketing practitioners. Although varied definitions of relationship marketing have been provided, it basically consists of attracting, developing, and retaining customers. The guiding principle of relationship marketing is to increase the value of a company's customer base by indentifying, tracking, and interacting with individuals and then reconfiguring products/services to meet specific needs. Thus, it is rooted in the idea of establishing a "learning relationship" with each customer—starting with those that are most valuable. An important question is, How feasible is this today? Is it really possible to build strong customer relationships when consumers are now "armed to the teeth" with competitive information and can gain alternative access to major providers at the click of a mouse?

While there is an apparent need and urgency for relationship marketing, its actual implementation and successful program maintenance is another question. Can every company adequately identify its end-user customers and gather the relevant information essential for the marketing plan? It is essential to differentiate customers based on their value to the company and their unique needs. The ability and willingness for customers to interact is an important consideration. Can the company actually customize its products and services based upon the available information? Finally, are customers sure to respond—will they care enough to adopt the modified offering? Certainly the development of a customer relationship program is a complex and highly integrated task. Yet the "lifetime value" of consumers over the short-term profits of building new ones serves as an important goal. The crucial tools to create these relationship opportunities are interaction and information technologies. It is fair to presume that the trend toward consumer use of these technologies will continue to experience exponential growth.

As Jennifer Bresnahan contends, marketing was the last great holdout of the technology revolution, but it has embraced this major vehicle for accomplishing new goals. She offers several examples of successful relationship marketing programs—within companies such as Charles Schwab, British Airways, Dell computers, and Eddie Bauer—and illustrates the necessity of implementing database techniques.

Unfortunately, companies can fall into the trap of collecting data only because the technology is available and then fail to analyze and apply the information in a meaningful way. *Frequency buying programs* are often misused as a tool for relationship building. The strength of the database is only as good as the marketing strategists capable of developing it into a viable and innovative marketing plan.

Another question relates to the *profitability* of maintaining customer relationships. Consumers by nature keep consistently increasing demands on their provider to at least match, if not exceed, the competition's prices, services, or added incentives to switch brands. Companies risk being forced into reacting to every new gimmick that hits the market, losing control of their own unique identity.

Despite the benefits, relationship marketing demands diligent management and perpetual caution. In the following selections, Bresnahan expresses optimism about the future of relationship marketing. In contrast, James R. Rosenfield identifies the potential hazards of pursuing this strategy, which, he argues, have resulted in the premature death of relationship marketing.

Jennifer Bresnahan  **YES**

Improving the Odds

Get with the program. E-commerce, ERP [enterprise resource planning] and other temporary fashions that have recently hogged our attention are yesterday's news. The next big thing has arrived. Call it "Customer Relationship Management," "One-to-One Marketing," "Enterprise Marketing Automation" or any of the other catch phrases that have cropped up, but the coming competitive frontier is about finding, knowing and delighting customers. In the past, businesses competed by making stellar products and later by meeting the needs of the average customer. Today the goal is to know and serve every consumer, one at a time, and to build long-term, mutually beneficial relationships.

Information technology (IT) is the key to achieving customer intimacy. But the people who need to wield the key are, ironically, in the one department that hasn't yet been flattened and reshaped by the IT thumbprint: marketing. Until recently, marketing was the last great holdout of the technology revolution because technology didn't seem to address marketing's imprecise, creative mandate. In addition, marketers and IT people tended to regard each other with distrust, misunderstanding and misgivings about one another's priorities. "If you had one of these continuums on a circle, marketing and IS would probably be 180 degrees opposite each other," says John Boushy, senior vice president of IT and marketing services at the Memphis, Tenn.-based casino and entertainment company Harrah's Entertainment Inc.

But that's all changing now as marketing takes a dominant role in shaping organizations' interactions with consumers. Marketing thus becomes the company's darling and the information systems (IS) department's new best friend. Together, marketing and IS are finding innovative ways to understand and reach customers. In the process, they are discarding their ancient enmity and fundamentally reinventing the relationships between businesses and their customers. "Marketing is about designing things that meet the needs and wants of customers, and today the use of information is how you meet some of those needs," says Boushy. "So IT very much becomes the means to the marketing ends. It's like you must join these entities with Velcro."

All Grown Up: Database Marketing

The root of all IT-enabled marketing is the common database. Marketing outfits have been using databases for years to get a picture of their customers, either working with IS to leverage a companywide, huge data warehouse or creating their own simple, stovepipe database. Using data mining tools, companies can figure out which of their customers are most likely to buy a given product, respond to a certain communication medium or defect to the competition. Companies can even gauge which of their competitors' customers are ripe for the taking. This is all basic stuff. But now that IT and marketing are making a concerted effort to know and please customers, databases are becoming more strategic and even a little sexy.

Marketers have many new windows available to them for viewing the customer, and warehouses are jampacked with the additional information this provides. Besides the ubiquitous telemarketing center and direct mail campaign, companies can communicate new products, services or promotions to consumers via e-mail, Web-based product registration or customer service and community forums on the Internet. Hitachi Semiconductor (America) Inc. notes the interests and needs of its corporate customers electronically through cookies [a message given to a Web browser by a Web server, containing user information] that track their comings and goings on the site. British Airways uses basic observation as a path to customer intimacy. According to Bob Dorf, president of the Stamford, Conn.-based marketing consultancy Marketing 1 to 1/Peppers and Rogers Group, British Airways flight attendants notice what their most valuable passengers choose and then enter that into a laptop computer onboard so that the next time the passenger in seat 3B flies with the airline, she automatically receives an extra pillow or a Diet Coke with no ice, as she prefers.

Marketers are also becoming more sophisticated in their use of data warehouses, applying their results of data mining in the pursuit of customer intimacy. For example, Mary H. Kelley, vice president of database and relationship marketing at Charles Schwab & Co. Inc. in San Francisco, told the audience at the July 1998 DCI Marketing Automation conference in New York City that Charles Schwab is striving to use its data warehouse to discover how much money a customer isn't investing with Charles Schwab. "If a customer invests $10,000, we want to know if he has a million dollars elsewhere that he isn't investing with us and why not," Kelley says. Spiegel Inc.'s Redmond, Wash.-based Eddie Bauer Inc. subsidiary uses catalog sales information in its data warehouse to determine the best sites for new stores and to eliminate duplicate retail mailings to customers who shop at both retail and catalog channels, says CIO [chief information officer] Jon K. Nordeen. The $14 billion Dallas-based consumer products company Kimberly Clark Corp. uses its data warehouse in the business-to-business sector to market to its customers' customers. The company identifies individuals its distributors market to, such as the building manager of a particular company, and targets that person with mailings about the benefits of Kleenex, Scott towels and other Kimberly Clark products, says Tom Ahonen, director of business systems.

One to One

The next evolutionary step in database marketing is targeting one customer at a time. BMG Direct, the New York City-based direct marketing division of BMG Entertainment, uses its data warehouse to coordinate the 50 variations of a single promotion that are mailed out to its 8 million club members in any given period. BMG's customers are classified into 14 different musical genre preferences and further divided by length of membership. Based on those factors, each member receives different promotional offers, lists of music titles on sale and monthly featured music selections. The longer customers have been in the club, the bigger the discounts they receive. "Our entire business is dependent on our ability to segment our customers so that members receive catalogs and offers with the right kind of music, a featured selection we think they would like and at a discount level in line with their membership in the club," says Elizabeth Rose, vice president of strategic planning and electronic commerce. "There's virtually nothing we can do as marketers that doesn't have systems implications. For me, there are certain people whose phone calls I will pick up every time, and they include the top three systems guys I work with."

Harrah's is also mastering the art of one-to-one marketing. In 1997 it launched its Total Gold national guest-recognition program, which rewards loyal customers with points and complimentary offerings. When a customer swipes her Total Gold identification card at a slot machine or presents it when checking into a Harrah's hotel, the account number is transmitted to Harrah's data warehouse in Memphis, Tenn. The data warehouse sends back her detailed history to the casino property and alerts the property employees via an electronic pager or a PC screen that this customer needs to be welcomed. "When an Atlantic City customer who's never been to Las Vegas goes there and inserts a Total Gold card into a slot machine, within seven seconds we know who that customer is and make sure that information is accessible in Las Vegas," says Boushy. The program engenders such loyalty that in its first four months, from September through December 1997, there was a 60 percent increase in customers that chose Harrah's when traveling to a new casino over the same time period before the Total Gold card program was started and has continued through August 1998. The Vegas property almost doubled its cross-market visitation (Atlantic City customers going to Las Vegas and vice-versa) revenue, and cross-market play overall increased by more than $16 million, says Boushy.

Cleveland-based KeyCorp uses its data warehouse to cross-sell new products to existing customers, says former Vice President of Direct Marketing Jonathan T. Hill. For example, if the warehouse "notices" that a customer is buying a lot of home improvement products, it may suggest to a customer service representative that he offer the customer a low-interest-rate home equity loan. This capability in itself isn't particularly new. But Key has taken it a step further and now generates customer leads without any human intervention. At the end of a customer call to the bank's voice response unit, the system automatically informs the customer that she's been approved for a home equity loan and asks if she'd like to receive an application. "I was afraid they'd hear [the voice response unit] and hang up, but that's not what's been happening at all," says Allen J. Gula, chairman and CEO of Key Services, the IS arm of KeyCorp. "We've had better success than we ever thought we would."

Enter the Internet

More than anything, the Internet has precipitated the trend toward one-to-one marketing. It is certainly the most economical way to communicate with customers, says Tom Haas, vice president of consulting at Hunter Business Direct Inc., because it only costs about 5 cents to e-mail a customer, compared with as much as $5 for direct mail, $8 to $24 for telephone sales and $40 to $400 for a field call from a sales rep. And it's definitely faster. Planning and executing a traditional marketing campaign used to take three months; today it can be done over the Internet in four hours, says Hal Steger, vice president of marketing at enterprise marketing-automation vendor Rubric Inc. in San Mateo, Calif.

The $15.2 billion computer giant Dell Computer Corp. of Round Rock, Texas, uses the Internet to provide key customers with personalized Premier Web pages. Sitting inside Dell's firewall, the pages contain product, technical and industry information of interest to the particular customer. By taking advantage of this innovation, the customer doesn't have to waste time trying to find what it needs among Dell's reams of information, and Dell gets a more loyal customer, says Joe Marengi, senior vice president and general manager of the relationship group at Dell. Customers can communicate with their Dell account team and buy additional products online. Dell even coordinates discounted employee purchase programs through the customized page. Executives on the customer side can use the site to look at their company's entire order history.

Hitachi has gone a step further, actually allowing customers to download sample products for use in product simulations. In the past, Hitachi's customers had to buy a semiconductor device and range through mountains of paper documentation to see how it worked in the electronic equipment they were building. But now they will have the ability to download technical "CAE/CAD [computer-aided engineering/computer-aided design] symbols" from Hitachi's extranet that summarize how the product works, and they can use that information for testing in computer simulations. "In the past you would have to buy it, have some administrative people put in those footprints manually and then import it into your CAD system," says Jim Rey, director of marketing communication. "Now it's a matter of going to your Web site and downloading it." The result may be fewer actual purchases upfront, but in the long run Rey expects this capability to win Hitachi more customers. Eventually, Hitachi will expand this extranet offering to the public Internet, he says.

The BMG Music Service Web site is linked to its data warehouse. As soon as a customer logs onto the site, the page automatically reconfigures to reflect the customer's musical preferences and account history. BMG music customers receive different prices and music selections and can use the Web site to refuse a featured selection, which otherwise is automatically sent. Customers can also search 12,000 titles of music (20 times as many as listed in BMG's paper catalogs), listen to sound samples, view account history, submit customer service transactions, change listening preferences and, for classical club members, submit questions to BMG's music editors. In addition to the customer loyalty it fosters, BMG's Web site enables the company to learn from and react to customer preferences in a timely manner, says Rose. Prior to the site, by the time marketing received a comment or knew how well a particular musical selection or promotion did, it was already working on several mailings down the line. But now they can analyze response rates and individual preferences for each marketing campaign and make adjustments more quickly to upcoming mailings.

Internal Affairs

To rise to the challenge of leading the rest of the company into the new customer-centered paradigm, marketing must get itself in shape. Many software vendors have created programs that automate such basic internal marketing tasks as lead generation and campaign management. . . . And marketing is increasingly turning to IS to integrate its various data sources to yield a complete picture of the customers. The Internet is also helping marketers coordinate as teams. For example, Charles Schwab's Schweb intranet allows 300 Schwab marketers around the country to access the company's aggregate customer information from the data warehouse and perform simple point-and-click customer queries. They can find out who their best customers are and offer discounts, for example, or generate lead lists for a particular campaign. In the past, when marketers wanted to draw up a list of suitable customer leads, they had to put in a request to the data analysis department. Now they can simply use their browser, says Kelley.

Unlike some of its younger competitors, Hewlett-Packard Co. (HP) of Palo Alto, Calif., enters this era of customer intimacy with baggage from the old way of thinking. Until a few years ago, HP's more than 70 business units didn't work together, nor did they care much about understanding the customer. Each operated nearly autonomously with its own marketing budgets and IS projects. Many were targeting the same customers without even knowing it, says J. Andrew Danver, senior consultant in relationship marketing at HP. Changing this mind-set to work together for a 360-degree view of the customer was no easy task. HP's marketing managers worked with IS to create an intranet site to pass the word that customer intimacy was the way to go and the only way to get there was to become more tightly integrated. The intranet, called 1:1/Relationship Marketing, contained best practice commentary, advice from consultants, a bimonthly newsletter, slide presentations, outside research and discussion groups about how and why to adopt a customer-centered mentality. Slowly but surely, the intranet is helping to change attitudes, says Danver. "It takes a long time to turn a Queen Mary around," he says.

Everyone's a Marketer

Perhaps the most important way that IT supports marketing's mission is by helping it transform the entire company into a customer-centered environment. On the front end, marketing must be able to share knowledge with sales and customer support so everybody has a complete picture of the customer. On the back end, the shop floor must be able to respond to customer demands and deliver what marketing promises, be it mass customization or the ability to track packages. Technology makes this level of integration possible.

Hitachi is among those at the forefront of this integrated company-as-marketing-unit mentality. With 33,000 different semiconductor and integrated circuit products, remembering which customer to tell about which semiconductor update is a tall order. Engineers continually come up with new products or upgrade existing ones. But now customers receive information about new products as a matter of course without any human involvement. Customers fill out a profile on the Web highlighting which products they're interested in and the information is automatically linked to Hitachi's engineering or sales departments. As the product design engineers make changes to existing products or create new semiconductor solutions, they use a standard template to enter their work into a document-management system. The system automatically routes the engineer's changes to the appropriate people in the company for approval and then e-mails it to customers who have requested related documentation online, says Rey.

Dell is probably one of the most highly integrated companies today. Starting with sales reps helping customers configure a system from scratch, every process under Dell's roof is integrated, says CIO Jerry Gregoire. First, the order-management system prevents sales reps from offering a product that can't be built. Once the customer places the order, the system immediately sends it to the shop floor to be constructed and simultaneously to Dell's procurement department and Web site. That way Dell's suppliers know a particular part was used, and the customer can track the order's delivery status. Dell's tight integration wins and retains highly lucrative customers, according to Marketing 1 to 1's Dorf. For instance, if a global company such as KPMG Peat Marwick LLP hires five actuaries in Cleveland, two consultants in Bahrain, Saudia Arabia, and one executive in Paris, each of them will receive new, uniquely configured computers that will be shipped the very next day, provided the order gets to Dell by 4 p.m. The fact that the computers arrive already loaded with the programs that each employee needs saves KPMG from having to employ an additional dozen IS employees, and the employees can be up and running faster. These extra benefits make Dell almost irreplaceable to its customers, says Dorf—the ultimate goal of customer relationship management. Or enterprise marketing automation. Or one-to-one marketing.

Whatever you call it, customer intimacy is the name of the game. And marketing is an organization's coach and clutch player all at once. Companies that figure out how to leverage IT to build loyal, lasting relationships with consumers will be tomorrow's winners.

James R. Rosenfield  **NO**

Whatever Happened to Relationship Marketing? Nine Big Mistakes

Looking at my mailbox, thinking about the companies I do business with, making my consulting rounds, a thought occurs to me:

Whatever happened to relationship marketing?

Boomtown America... is all about getting rich quick. Customer churn seems to be regarded as a quite acceptable cost of doing business. Customer service is at an all-time low—just think about your own life as a customer. Consumers are battered, bothered, and bewildered.

None of this was supposed to happen. People like me used to predict that by the end of the century relationship marketing, abetted by information technology, would rule the world. Instead, mass marketing seems to prevail, to the point that direct mail itself has turned into a mass marketing medium.

When you look at relationship marketing efforts, the bad and the ugly seem to be driving out the good, in a sort of crazed variation of Gresham's Law. Amazon.com begins to mess up a good thing by "selling" favorable reviews, a practice it quickly backed down on, but not without some brand equity damage. The airlines beat up their best customers—on a recent three-hour Delta flight that left at 8:00 p.m., THERE WAS NO FOOD! A whole panoply of things keeps going wrong. Here are nine of them:

Mistake #1: Assuming Customers Want a Relationship

Relationships in private life are always two-way streets. But customers want more of a one-way street, with the company doing the work of nurturing and maintaining things. They don't want a relationship with us unless we make it worth their while, and unless the basis of the relationship is on the customer's terms. This becomes especially important as loyalty and frequency programs multiply, competing for the same finite pocketbooks and attention spans.

We want relationships, because we know relationships make us money. But what does the customer want?

The customer wants *solutions*. Providing solutions, rather than merely products, creates the basis for a true customer relationship.

As it stands right now, there are too many products, too few solutions. The average suburban supermarket had 8,000 products in 1978, according to the Food Marketing Institute, and over 30,000 10 years later! No one needs 30,000 products, and in fact the sheer number of choices in itself becomes a problem.

The manufacturers are taking notice. A few years back, Procter & Gamble [P&G] stunned the world by de-extending some of its product lines, a radical departure from the epidemic line extension and product proliferation of the last generation. P&G is beginning to understand that customers want solutions, and that simplification is part of the solution process.

Suggestion: Provide solutions, rather than products, and your customers will be willing to have a relationship with you.

Mistake #2: Assuming Customers Are Willing to Work

About 20 percent of American consumers seem to be addicted to the gamelike minutiae of loyalty and frequency programs. These are the same people who transfer credit card balances and switch long-distance carriers. They know how to work the system.

But the other 80 percent of consumers... are already working hard enough, and have no desire to put in extra work for you.

What does this mean? It means that the overly complex, difficult-to-figure-out awards schemes that now abound are beginning to turn people off. Customers are dropping out of the game, because the rules are too complicated (or have been changed in midstream—see Mistake #7).

The consumer is sending this message loud and clear: "I've lived without your rewards up until now, and I'm not willing to put in the work to master your complications."

Another example: Have you taken a good look lately at your frequent flyer statements? Most of them were designed by the Marquis de Sade. Awards are often printed in light grey mousetype, guaranteed to be unreadable, especially by the middle-aged frequent flyers who comprise the airlines' single most profitable customer segment.

Suggestion: Relationship marketing programs need to be engineered so that simplicity is built into them, and so that simplicity remains. The customer wants solutions, and simplicity is a solution.

Mistake #3: Assuming Customers Will Be Fair

You can get things right 900 times, but if you make a mistake on the 901st transaction, you'll get a quick lesson in the highly contingent nature of customer relationships. Customers will not be fair. They'll key in on the last event, which will subsume all the good things that came before. It's human nature: That terrible meal you had last night at a once favorite restaurant obviates the 20 excellent meals you had there previously.

Even worse, dissatisfied customers talk. Dissatisfied customers tell as many as 15 other people about their experience, naturally exaggerating the story with each re-telling.

However, customers' lack of fairness gives you a sterling opportunity for relationship building. The most loyal customer is a customer who complains in the first place (light users don't bother to complain, they merely go away), and who then gets the problem fixed expeditiously. This not only re-cements the bond, it makes it stronger than ever before.

Who's good at this these days? Not many companies, since customer abuse seems to be the... standard. But you might audit MBNA, the credit card issuer, for whom customer service is the core competency.

Suggestion: You don't have to be perfect, but your customer service does. Otherwise, you will pay the price... at some point.... Relationship marketing is impossible without excellent customer service, and customer service must be regarded as one of the most essential marketing functions of the millennial period....

Mistake #4: Assuming Customer Satisfaction Is Enough

Most customers polled in surveys claim to be satisfied. Worldwide, in fact, about 82 percent of all customers everywhere say they're satisfied. Yet everyone suffers from customer defections. What's going on here?

What's going on is that satisfaction is not enough. All satisfaction means is "You're doing OK." And in fact the... American consumer actually has diminished expectations, because quality and service really have declined in so many categories. Businesses need to strive for customers who claim to be "very satisfied." When companies ratchet themselves up from "satisfied" to "very satisfied," customer attrition decreases significantly.

More important than offering frequent flyer miles or rebates is making sure that customers are "very satisfied." In fact, another hidden danger of relationship marketing is to substitute rewards for satisfaction. A dissatisfied participant of a frequency/loyalty program will find some other program to join.

Suggestion: Don't be seduced by customer surveys showing "satisfaction." It's the "very satisfied" customer who creates your most significant long-term profits.

Mistake #5: Tier Inflation

In order to reach its potential, relationship marketing has to be predicated on a good marketing database.

The database allows companies to identify the small percentage of customers who account for the majority of profits (the famous Pareto Principle), and then to launch relationship building programs at these customers.

But like all technologies, the database is filled with temptations. One temptation: segmentation without intelligence.

Case in point: American Airlines is certainly a pioneer in database-driven relationship marketing, via its famous AAdvantage Program. In the early 1990s, the airline spotted a segment of its Gold AAdvantage customers who were superfrequent flyers. Voila! These customers became Platinum AAdvantage customers, with all the rights and privileges appertaining thereto.

The problem was that there were no rights and privileges! The only important tangible benefit, in fact, was the ability to get first-class upgrades 72 hours in advance of the flight, rather than the mere 24 hours allowed to Gold customers. But even this benefit was subverted, because at the same time that the marketers launched the Platinum program American's accountants evidently tightened up the availability of first-class upgrades. In other words, things got worse, rather than better, when customers got their Platinum cards. Their expectations had been raised, and then disappointed. Result: less brand loyalty, rather than more, among American's most profitable customers.

American has long since fixed this problem, but now has a new problem: Me!

I'm now Executive Platinum, one step up from mere Platinum, and I'm nearing 4 million miles. I want a segment all to myself.

Will this be cost-effective? Probably not. The big question: At what point does tier inflation stop paying off. Stay tuned for this one.

Suggestion: Be careful about tier inflation, and avoid the fatal mistake of good marketing followed by poor product.

Mistake #6: Accidental Disenfranchisement

This can be another unfortunate consequence of "infinite tiering upwards." What happens to the Gold people when you add a Platinum tier? Loyalty/ frequency programs revolve not only around rewards, but also special courtesies, prestige, and status: not having to stand in line, a private toll-free number, etc. A Gold person who has been perfectly content to wait in line might resent the fact that a Platinum customer has no queue.

Every aspect of relationship marketing has to be looked at in terms of strategic downsides, as well as upsides. Failure to do this has been endemic in relationship marketing programs to date. Remember the Chinese military theorist who pointed out that strategy necessitates sacrifice? Think through what you're potentially sacrificing before committing yourself to the possible dangers of accidental disenfranchisement.

Suggestion: When the database tells you what you *could* do, make sure your marketing intelligence tells you what you *should* do.

Mistake #7: Changing the Rules

Relationship marketing programs based on frequency rewards have run into problems due to their very popularity. Airlines, for example, were carrying billions of dollars of free trip liability on their books. In an effort to please the accountants and eliminate the liabilities, the airlines changed the rules in the mid-1990s, typically by introducing expiration dates and upping the ante for trips and upgrades.

The result? Customer mistrust, customer disillusionment, and an erosion in the relationships the airlines have tried so hard to build. No one likes unexpected, unilateral rule changes. It's vital to build in rational expiration dates at the inception of a program, so that disappointment doesn't ensue later.

Suggestion: Get the rules right at the beginning. Remember what Thomas Aquinas said: A small mistake at the start can be a big mistake at the end.

One More Suggestion: When you have bad news for a customer, be direct, be honest, be reassuring. And see if there's something you can give customers (better service, for example) at the same time that you're taking something away.

Mistake #8: Incrementality vs. Cannibalization

From a profitability standpoint, this is the crux of the relationship marketing issue. Are you simply cannibalizing yourself by rewarding customers for doing what they would do anyway, or are you truly achieving incremental results?

A bank in New Zealand earlier this year offered an incentive to customers who used their credit card three times in a month. Problem was, customers were already using the card an average of three and a half times per month. The bank was actually rewarding customers for using the card less!

Suggestion: Think and evaluate before launching a program. Make sure that your efforts are incremental otherwise you're merely getting bogged down in a zero-sum game.

Mistake #9: Confusing Necessity With Loyalty

I have close to 4 million miles on American Airlines, but American doesn't know whether that's because I'm loyal or because I have no choice: I live in San Diego, but I base my working life in the U.S. out of New York. American runs the only nonstop between San Diego and New York.

If you need to travel through the booming cities of the Southeast—Charlotte, for example—it's hard not to travel on USAirways. But I've yet to meet a frequent business traveler who actually prefers USAirways (although I think they're getting better). Anyone traveling back and forth between Charlotte and New York will rack up the miles, but out of necessity, not because of loyalty.

This has some serious implications. Loyalty builds barriers against competition. Necessity, on the other hand, can make competition welcome indeed. Loyalty leads to long-term profits. Necessity can simply lead to customer defections, once they have a competitive choice.

Suggestion: Survey your frequent users to ascertain who is loyal and who uses you out of necessity. Launch cultivation programs at the "necessity" people, in order to convert them to "loyalists."

When all is said and done, the truth is that "relationship marketing" is a misleading term. In fact, if I ran the buzzword factory, I'd try to come up with better stuff.

Why is it misleading? Because the underlying metaphor of the term isn't really appropriate to the situations that marketers address. After all, when do you use the term "relationship?"

You use it when you're talking about your spouses, your children, your bosses, or your employers and clients—all of the people who require energy to deal with.

Relationships, by their nature, are energy-intensive on both ends. And as pointed out earlier, the stressed-out, overloaded and overworked... consumer typically doesn't have any leftover energy these days. And certainly doesn't want to work at maintaining a relationship with your company.

POSTSCRIPT

Is Relationship Marketing a Tenable Concept?

In their seminal 1998 *Harvard Business Review* article, Susan Fournier et al. cite an Oxford University study on rules of friendship: "Provide emotional support, respect privacy, preserve confidence and be tolerant of other friendships." If companies violate these rules, how can they show consumers that they are valued partners—gaining their trust—for a chance to build intimacy?

Seth Godin and Don Peppers have introduced an interesting concept in their book *Permission Marketing: Turning Strangers into Friends, and Friends into Customers* (Free Press, 1999). They argue that businesses can no longer rely completely on traditional forms of "interruption advertising" in magazines, mailings, and TV commercials. Once they get the consumer's attention, they must reward that attention and be receptive to interaction with the firm. This appears to be the real imperative for developing successful relationship marketing.

The key is to establish an easy way to make purchases automatic and to position the provider as a source for solving problems and providing solutions to the consumer. It is important to understand how to send a message and establish a communication system whereby the customer is willing to accept the message and is open to communication. Does every message encourage and reward a consumer response? What kinds of firms or market situations are most appropriate for relationship marketing to be successful? Firms have to consider the economics of using such a strategy. The lifetime value of a customer is of paramount importance. A recent study showed that the lifetime revenue stream from a loyal pizza customer can be $8,000; from a Cadillac car customer it can reach $332,000; and, in the case of a corporate purchaser of commercial aircraft, lifetime revenue can amount to billions of dollars.

Understanding the motivations of customers is crucial to the success of this strategy. Are customers primarily concerned with their own personal economic benefits or do they also have an emotional bond with the company? Certainly, with the incredible growth of potential promotional sources because of advancement of technology and communication tools, the few relationships we make in life are meaningful and welcomed. Focusing on relationship marketing may not be a new concept but it may be more important than ever before.

Finally, the importance of the appropriate use of technology to manage customer relationships should never be overlooked. Application of "Customer Relationship Management" (CRM) software has grown by leaps and bounds in the last couple of years, but does the emphasis on technology enhance or undermine such relationships?

Suggested Readings

Gary Abramson, "Seen the Light: Companies Learn the Hard Way That Over-Emphasis on Technology Can Undermine Customer Strategies," *CIO Enterprise Magazine* (June 15, 1999)

M. J. Baker, "Relationship Marketing in Three Dimensions," *Journal of Interactive Marketing* (Autumn 1998)

Jay Curry and Adam Curry, *The Customer Marketing Method: How to Implement and Profit from Customer Relationship Management* (Free Press, 2000)

Merly Davids, "How to Avoid the Ten Biggest Mistakes in CRM," *The Journal of Business Strategy* (November–December 1999)

Susan Fournier, Susan Dobscha, and David Glen Mick, "Preventing the Premature Death of Relationship Marketing," *Harvard Business Review* (January–February 1998)

Thomas W. Gruen, "Relationship Marketing: The Route to Marketing Efficiency and Effectiveness," *Business Horizons* (November–December 1997)

Laura Mazur, "Dotcoms Place CRM Staff Skills in High Demand," *Marketing* (March 9, 2000)

Frederick Newell, *The New Rules of Marketing: How to Use One-to-One Relationship Marketing to Be the Leader in Your Industry* (McGraw-Hill, 1997)

Don Peppers, Martha Rogers, and Bob Dorf, "Is Your Company Ready for One-to-One Marketing?" *Harvard Business Review* (January–February 1999)

Don Peppers and Martha Rogers, *The One-to-One Manager: Real-World Lessons in Customer Relationship Management* (Currency/Doubleday, 1999)

John V. Petrof, "Relationship Marketing: The Wheel Reinvented," *Business Horizons* (November–December 1997)

CRM-Forum. `http://www.crm-forum.com`

RealMarket Research. `http://www.realmarket.com`

Relationship Marketing Systems. `http://www.smart-marketing.com`

CRM Guru.com. `http://www.crmguru.com`

Andersen Consulting. `http://ac.com/services/crm/crm_thought.html`

On the Internet ...

Cable in the Classroom

This Web site provides background and other information on Cable in the Classroom, a public service effort supported by national cable networks and local cable companies. These networks and cable companies act as partners in learning with teachers and parents by providing free cable connections and over 540 hours per month of commercial-free educational programming to schools across the United States.

> http://www.ciconline.com/about.htm

McDonald's U.S.A.

This is the home page of McDonald's, the largest and best-known global food-service retailer.

> http://www.mcdonalds.com

Prescription Drug Prices Articles

This Web site offers a collection of articles from the *New York Times,* the *Wall Street Journal,* and other notable publications.

http://www.house.gov/waxman/drugs/News_Articles/
00009/body_00009.html

CommerceNet

CommerceNet's membership includes over 600 companies and organizations worldwide, including leading banks, telecommunications companies, value-added networks, Internet service providers, online services, software and services companies, and major end-users.

> http://www.commerce.net

PART 2

Strategic Planning and the Marketing Mix

*H*ow can the marketer break through the thousands of products, messages, and choices to which consumers are exposed every day? Today, with over 8 million Web sites and 800 million online Web pages, "striking a responsive chord" with the right message, to the right consumer, with the best-tailored market offering is the goal of strategic planning and the blueprint for the marketing mix.

Cause-related marketing is a strategy that links the brand/ company to a special interest group or social cause. Increasingly visible, this trend is in response to public demand for a greater commitment to social responsibility from the private sector, but it has also become a powerful tool for product differentiation and the development of brand equity. As the cause becomes a part of the product, it is an attribute that builds an emotional bond with the consumer by creating a "sentiment connection" with the brand.

In relation to the marketing mix, the product issue in this section deals with mass customization and its future. The pricing issue relates to the problems faced by senior citizens in paying for prescription drugs that are priced far beyond what they can afford on their limited incomes. The distribution issue addresses the tremendous impact of e-commerce on traditional middlemen. And the promotion issue deals with trends in personal selling and the demise of the "human moment" in the selling process.

- Does Cause-Related Marketing Benefit All Stakeholders?

- Is Mass Customization the Wave of the Future?

- Are Outrageous Prices Inhibiting Consumer Access to Life-Sustaining Drugs?

- Will E-Commerce Eliminate Traditional Intermediaries?

- Is Communications Technology "Death of the Salesman"?

ISSUE 5

Does Cause-Related Marketing Benefit All Stakeholders?

YES: Paul Holmes, from "Just Cause," *Reputation Management* (January/February 1997)

NO: James T. Bennett and Thomas J. DiLorenzo, from "Health Charities: Reputation for Sale?" *Consumers' Research* (July 1997)

ISSUE SUMMARY

YES: Paul Holmes, editor of *Reputation Management,* defines cause-related marketing (CRM) as tying a company and its products to a special interest group, social issue, or charitable organization. The result is a deepened trust and relationship with customers, improved corporate image, and increased sales and promotional benefits for the related cause.

NO: Professors of economics James T. Bennett and Thomas J. DiLorenzo argue that product endorsements by charitable organizations put the public confidence at risk and can erode the integrity of the cause. They question the practice of the cause becoming leverage for increasing the brand's market share.

Cause-related marketing (CRM) is defined as the public association of a for-profit company with a nonprofit organization, intended to form a mutually beneficial partnership between the company and its supporting cause. It is distinguished from *corporate philanthropy* in that the donations involved in CRM are not outright gifts to a nonprofit association and are thus not tax-deductible. The term was introduced in 1983 when American Express began a crusade to help restore the Statue of Liberty. In recent years, CRM has grown exponentially as corporate responsibility has taken on a renewed significance. With campaign spending close to a billion dollars, cause-related marketing has sparked a high degree of controversy centered upon corporate motives, program credibility, and the ultimate benefits to the parties involved.

Cause-related marketing programs are a logical outgrowth of the historical "charitable donations" in which companies rather arbitrarily contributed back to the community as a basic practice of public relations. As marketers recognized this as a potential long-term social investment, the function emerged into "corporate philanthropy" with the goal of reaping a more positive brand identity. "Strategic giving" and "focused philanthropy" began as marketers analyzed the no-nonsense approach to *getting* something back in the process of *giving* something back. Soon marketers realized that carefully planned cause-related marketing programs could act as a "tiebreaker" for many purchase decisions, especially "product parity" situations where consumers face a plethora of look-alike brands. Establishing partnerships with a charitable cause can clearly differentiate the brand as it becomes an integral part of the market offering. It also may serve as a shield against public criticism in times of crisis. Evidence suggests that cause-related marketing groups are translating into an emotionally powerful appeal to an increasingly large proportion of potential buyers. In 1997, 70 percent of Americans claimed that when price and quality are equal, they would switch to brands or retailers having a good cause. This was a 20 percent increase over 1993.

The affinity credit card industry is a prime example of success in aligning one's market offering with a cause-related component. This tactic provides a "shared-incentive" for affinity cardholders who use their card knowing that part of their fees go directly to their group's cause. Sometimes, however, these benefits are marred. When a company's decisions are based strictly on market potential, with little consideration accorded to the value for the cause, the essential elements of compassion and credibility in corporate philanthropy are lost. If consumers perceive insincere motives, the most well-intentioned campaign can backfire.

Product endorsements by large health charities such as the American Heart Association, the American Lung Association, and the American Cancer Society are illustrating a trend toward commercial affiliations, signaling other such organizations to follow their lead. For many of these certificate mark endorsements that appear on packaging, the sponsoring company has merely paid a fee to the charitable organization. Most frequently, the criteria for certification from the health groups are the same standards set by the Food and Drug Administration or the U.S. Department of Agriculture's regulatory requirements. While such arrangements are only a fraction of all cause-related programs, they risk the public's confidence in the charitable organization. Critics point out that many such campaigns are inherently deceptive by associating the sponsor with the implied standards of the organization's endorsement.

As consumers increasingly demand more from marketers in terms of social responsibility, it is extremely probable that the trend toward CRM will continue its accelerated growth. Research reveals that 92 percent of Americans consider it important for companies to "seek out ways to be good corporate citizens." Greater acceptance and research in cause-related marketing will likely result in the development and refinement of more sophisticated procedures and fewer ill-fated programs. This emphasis on planning and common sense will truly add to the benefit of all stakeholders involved.

Paul Holmes

 **YES**

Just Cause

American corporations spent an estimated $600 million on cause-related marketing activity in 1996. While that represent a significant increase, it is still only a fraction of what is spent on sports sponsorship, despite mounting evidence that association with a good cause can build trust and loyalty between a company and its customers in ways few other promotional activities can match.

When Jay Vestal gets a call from one of those long-distance company sales reps—the ones who call only in the middle of an important business meeting or at the precise second you're getting dinner out of the oven—he doesn't wait for them to tell him how great their rates are or how many cents he can save on a call to Rome. Instead he asks them what causes their companies support. It seems to be an effective technique for stopping a sales pitch dead in its tracks, especially when Vestal goes on to tell them about his current long-distance company, San Francisco's Working Assets, which donates one percent of each long-distance bill to not-for-profit organizations such as Amnesty International, Greenpeace and Planned Parenthood.

Vestal may not exactly be a typical consumer—as a senior vice president at Bozell/Bonneville, a subsidiary of the Bozell Advertising empire that specializes in cause-related advertising, corporate reputation issues are always top of his mind—but he is increasingly not an aberration. More and more consumers are making purchasing decisions based not only on product attributes but also on other ways in which the company behind the product touches their lives. Empowered by growing quality and price parity between products, they are feeling free to indulge their consciences every time they open their pocketbooks.

"There's evidence to suggest that when price and quality are equal, consumers will make their purchasing decisions based on what they know about the company that makes the product, and particularly whether that company is a good corporate citizen," says Carol Cone, president of Boston public relations firm Cone Communications, which specializes in developing and implementing cause-related programs. "Cause-related marketing is a way for companies to demonstrate that they are committed to addressing the issues that impact their customers' lives."

From Paul Holmes, "Just Cause," *Reputation Management* (January/February 1997). Copyright © 1997 by *Reputation Management*. Reprinted by permission of EMMI, Inc.

Cone, working with research giant Roper Starch Worldwide, has studied the attitudes of both consumers and corporate executives toward cause-related marketing (CRM) and predicts that the growth of the past few years—American corporations will spend nearly $600 million on cause-related marketing events in 1996 according to IEG Sponsorship Report, up from $314 million in 1993—will continue as more and more companies recognize that CRM can deliver not only customers but also more importantly loyal customers.

Roper senior vp Bradford Fay agrees. "Consumers in the 1990s take for granted that they can buy high-quality products and services at low prices," he says. "Therefore marketers need to stand out from the crowd. Offering a connection to a good cause is an excellent—and increasingly effective—way to do that."

Cone defines cause-related marketing as "a marketing discipline that ties a company and its products and services to an issue." She adds, "The goal of cause-related marketing is to deepen the trust and the relationship with customers, improve corporate image and ultimately sales while providing benefits to the cause."

Most observers credit American Express marketing maven Jerry Welch for the resurgence of cause-related marketing. His pioneering American Express campaign raised $1.7 million to restore the Statue of Liberty in 1984, but says Cone, "it lasted just a few months and offered limited opportunity to build the brand and create enduring relationships with customers." The credit card company learned a valuable lesson, however. Its current Charge Against Hunger campaign is now in its sixth year and has contributed more than $15 million for domestic hunger relief while generating a 10% increase in credit card usage last year.

Reebok—a Cone client—took the whole trend to a higher level in 1988 when it extended a corporate commitment to human rights to include sponsorship of the Human Rights Now! Tour, which featured artists including Bruce Springsteen and Sting performing to raise funds for Amnesty International, and also introduced its human rights award. Far more than just a short-term promotion, Reebok's CRM effort seemed to permeate the whole company, the whole year round. It blended old-fashioned corporate philanthropy with an insistence that the philanthropy be leveraged as a marketing and corporate image-building tool: the performers wore Reeboks on stage and the company linked the human rights theme to its "Reeboks Let U.B.U." advertising.

Over the past decade, the list of companies creating their own CRM programs has read like a who's who of American business. Pepsico's Pizza Hut subsidiary has devoted itself to children's reading, while the Coors Brewing Co. enjoyed a lengthy association with adult literacy. Liz Claiborne has campaigned against violence against women, and Avon has become active in the fight against breast cancer. Wendy's is a major supporter of adoption, and Polaroid is trying to enhance children's self-esteem.

And [recently], even American Express's arch-rival Visa got in on the act, running ads that touted its donations to a children's reading charity.

In a benchmark study of consumer attitudes toward cause-related marketing conducted in 1993, Cone and Roper found that 71% of consumers believed

CRM to be a good way to help solve social problems, and 64% believed it should be a standard part of a company's activities. Two-thirds (66%) said they would be likely to switch brands to one associated with a good cause when price and quality are equal, and 62% said they would be likely to switch retailers to one associated with a good cause in similar circumstances.

A tracking study conducted in 1996 indicated that consumers are becoming even more accepting of CRM. In the 1996 study, 76% said they would be likely to switch brands based on a company's association with a cause, and the same number said they would be likely to switch retailers for the same reason. Among influentials and those with a household income above $50,000, the percentages are even higher. Moreover, cynicism about CRM had declined, with only 21% saying they questioned the motives of companies that give to good causes, compared to close to 60% in the 1993 study.

According to another Roper survey sponsored by The Pearlman Group, a Los Angeles-based advertising and public relations firm with a strong tradition in the cause marketing arena, 92% of Americans say it is important for companies to seek out ways to be good corporate citizens, and 68% say it is very important.

"As government funding to solve public ills dries up, the public has come to expect corporate America to step in," says agency president Dan Pearlman. "It's redefining corporate responsibility to mean social responsibility. Companies need to realize that if they don't fill the void, their competitors probably will. Nonprofits themselves recognize this and more than ever are actively seeking corporate partners."

Pearlman has worked on a number of major cause-related marketing programs, including two for General Motors. For Geo trucks and cars, he created a program called We're Planting Ourselves in Your Community, which linked the Geo—the most fuel-efficient car on the market, and therefore environmentally friendly—with tree planting, working with the nonprofit American Forests and creating a Geo Award for Environmental Excellence. For Chevrolet trucks, he devised a program that was an extension of the company's Like a Rock advertising theme, linking the product with outdoor restoration and conservation and partnering with the National Fish & Wildlife Foundation.

"One-third of the public frequently bases its purchase decisions on causes a company supports, and another 37% occasionally do," says Pearlman. "Yet our survey shows that one in three Americans does not think most large companies are fulfilling their social responsibility at the local level. Either companies are not communicating their involvement very well, or they have not yet realized the tremendous opportunity to support and differentiate their brands, enhance their image and help society all at the same time."

Pearlman says his research shows that the obverse is also true. Close to 20% of respondents say they frequently refuse to buy the best quality product because they do not like the company that makes it, while 37% say they occasionally do.

Some observers question those numbers, pointing out that people may not behave the way they tell pollsters they behave, and that they may just be telling researchers what they think they want to hear. Pearlman concedes that there may well be some exaggeration, but he says, "The numbers themselves are not the most important thing. It doesn't matter whether it's 70% or 30% or 10%, there are clearly a growing number of consumers out there who are willing to reward a company that commits itself to the issues they care deeply about. Our research and observations indicate that effective cause marketing translates into added value, enhanced customer loyalty and brand equity."

His point is reinforced by recent studies indicating that increasing loyalty and reducing brand defections can have a greater impact on profits than almost any other factor traditionally thought to be a source of competitive advantage. According to Pearlman, there is evidence to suggest that reducing defections by just 5% can generate a jump of 85% in profits.

The public's interest in and support of cause-related marketing is being mirrored by increasing acceptance in the corporate world. The second Cone/ Roper survey questioned executives from 70 major companies actively involved in CRM and found that most believed its primary benefit to be the building of deeper relationships with customers and the creation of long-term customer loyalty.

More than 90% of respondents gave this as the most important objective of their own CRM efforts, while almost the same number gave enhancing corporate image and reputation as a reason. Other popular reasons for CRM included creating and maintaining a compelling corporate purpose and differentiating a product and services. On the other hand, only 50% said that increasing sales was a major reason to engage in CRM.

For this reason, some executives are inclined to view cause marketing with some skepticism. Says Joe McCann, senior vice president of public affairs at PepsiCo, "Like any other kind of marketing, cause-related marketing has to achieve its goals. If the goal is to move product, which is implied in the name, then you had better move product, and frankly a lot of cause-related marketing efforts just don't do that. If that's the case, I don't necessarily think they should be discontinued, but they more properly belong under corporate philanthropy, the kind of things, very legitimate things, a company does just to be a good citizen."

But Carol Cone sees the fact that CRM is no longer simply about boosting sales as an indication that it has come of age.

"In the decade since its inception, cause-related marketing has moved from being seen as a short-term sales promotion tool to being a strategic positioning and marketing practice," says Carol Cone.

"Practiced strategically, CRM is an enormously powerful tool for companies to build brand awareness and help create lifetime customer relationships. CRM programs extend and leverage marketing and communications budgets and complement traditional advertising by using the content and richness of CRM to align the company with its customers' values."

McCann raises a valid question, however. Does cause-related marketing translate into bottom-line results? Does it deserve a place in the marketing strategy, or should it more rightly be regarded as part of a company's corporate philanthropy activity?

The answer is that most cause-related marketing programs are not sufficiently well focused to be successful on marketing terms, but when they are they can be extremely powerful, particularly in terms of creating a deeper bond between the company and its customers and in turning ordinary customers into what marketing experts are coming to call "apostles"—people who will go out and tell their friends about a brand they really like.

"For the marketer, cause marketing is an ideal tool for brand-image support and management," Pearlman says. "Targeting today's socially conscious consumers, it offers an ideal way to differentiate a parity product from its competition, giving the brand an edge with customers and prospects who support the cause. It creates a greater emotional affinity with the brand."

In other words, while the Lady Liberty campaign and other early cause-related marketing campaigns were promotional in nature, today's CRM is much more about brand building.

"Cause-related marketing and cause-related promotion are no longer synonymous," says Carol Cone. "Cause-related promotion is a tactic to spike sales quickly and give corporate image a short-lived boost. It is best when implemented within the context of a comprehensive strategic CRM program that also includes advertising, publicity and special events. When a cause-related promotion stands on its own, it is increasingly subject to public cynicism. Consumers will nail you hardest if you are insincere. They can see through an image that is not real."

The most important element of a successful cause-related marketing program, according to the executives interviewed for Cone/Roper II, is integrity, cited by 96% of respondents. Its not an attribute every company in the cause-related arena has. "In the environmental area, you saw a lot of companies jumping on the bandwagon," says Dan Pearlman. "For the most part, consumers saw right through it. Cause-related marketing has to be credible, and that credibility needs to emanate from your product and from how an organization treats all its various stakeholder groups."

Liz Claiborne is a company that has demonstrated a genuine commitment to a single issue, an issue that many competitive companies might have shied away from. The company's focus for the last five years has been domestic violence, and it has worked closely with New York's Patrice Tanaka & Co. to educate men and women about the issue, commissioning a number of well-known women artists to create a poster campaign, and more recently working with college football players to produce a series of public service announcements that were broadcast at football games and on network affiliates.

"There are two kinds of cause-related marketing programs that really work," says Madeline de Vries, president of a New York PR firm that bears her name. "There are some companies that seem totally impassioned about something. Hugo Boss, for example, is very impassioned about art as a stimulus for creativity, and does a lot of work with the Guggenheim. The company brings artists in to talk to its people about creativity. It's an integral part of the company's way of doing things. Then there are other companies that find an issue that's strategically appropriate. Janzen, the swimwear manufacturer, was involved in clean water in the northeast, for example. It was a great issue for that company.

"The most important thing is that the commitment be genuine. Consumers expect it, and there's nothing quite as transparent as bad marketing."

The executives questioned in the Cone/Roper survey also say that it is important for companies to devote enough resources, both human and financial, to a program, and to secure long-term senior management commitment.

"Cause marketing is not making a donation and simply running advertising that tells the world what you did," says Jay Vestal. "Cause marketing is developing programs whereby you use the emotional power of the issue to bring your consumers into a partnership with you, you and the consumer together are going out to try and solve the issue. You're trying to build the type of friendship that can't be accomplished with a single sales promotion. You're going to have to do it over the years. If it's not important enough to have that type of relationship with your customers over the years, you probably ought to do something else."

It's less important that the issue be unique to the company, according to Cone's respondents. Indeed, with more and more companies getting involved in CRM and a finite number of issues to choose from, it is inevitable that some issues will attract multiple sponsors—as the explosion in the number of breast cancer programs in the past 12 months demonstrates.

Avon, however, has succeeded in cutting through the breast cancer clutter with a program designed to take ownership of one aspect of that issue: access to early-detection services for low-income, minority and older women.

"We spent six months prior to the launch looking for the best issue for us to be involved with," says Joanne Mazurki, Avon director of global public affairs. "We wanted something that would resonate with our sales force, because we wanted something that would maximize the potential involvement of 450,000 representatives across the country. We also wanted an issue that would resonate with our consumers, the vast majority of whom were women, and when we asked them what they were interested in, breast cancer was the overwhelming response."

The company has underwritten a national teleconference on breast cancer, working in partnership with the Centers for Disease Control and Prevention and linking about 25,000 physicians, nurses, educators, religious groups and clinical workers with a panel of medical experts to develop cancer-screening and outreach programs. The company funded half the show's $600,000 production costs and its reps served as facilitators.

As the program has grown, Avon reps have raised $25 million selling pink ribbon pins and pens, says Patrice Tanaka, whose New York firm has worked on aspects of the campaign. "It's a great grassroots campaign," she says. "It really gets both the reps and the customers involved, working together to solve a problem."

Says Mazurki, "We knew we couldn't own the issue, but we could own the early-detection part of the issue."

"More important than owning the issue is coming up with a program that really breaks through in a cluttered environment," says Pearlman.

Creativity was the most important element of the Coors literacy campaign, called Literacy. Pass It On, which came to end recently after five years and an expenditure of $40 million. Coors partnered with several nonprofits, including the National Volunteer Literacy Campaign and SER-Jobs for Progress, which addresses the literacy needs of the Hispanic community. It staged "graduation days" for adults who had learned to read through its programs and most memorably created, with the help of Denver public relations agency Schenkein/Sherman, Wordless U.S.A., a three-dimensional interactive town where no comprehensible written language existed, to give literate people an opportunity to experience what it means to be illiterate.

"Visitors to Wordless were guided through six 14-foot high buildings with audiotapes that told stories about typical non-readers and their thoughts as they attempted to complete everyday tasks that require the ability to read, from purchasing a birthday card to ordering lunch," says a Schenkein/Sherman executive. "Within each room, actors portrayed shopkeepers, waiters and others, reacting to the participants in various different ways."

For a component of the program designed to reach out to women, meanwhile, Patrice Tanaka & Co. came up with another provocative communications vehicle: a romance novel written by best-selling author Judith McNaught. The agency found not only that the romance genre was among the fastest-growing but also that the demographics of romance readers closely mirrored the demographics of women most likely to support charitable causes. McNaught for her part was so moved by the cause that she volunteered to rewrite a recently completed manuscript, transforming the heroine into an illiterate orphan who evolves into an elementary school teacher and literacy volunteer.

Literacy is an important issue to many companies—an educated, literate workforce is vital to the future of corporate America—but others prefer to find causes that are more directly associated with either their products or with the lives of their customers.

"The first thing to remember is, it's not about finding a nonprofit to work with, it's about finding an issue," says Carol Cone. "The issue has to be at the intersection where the company and a societal trend come together." Cone has trademarked what she calls the Cause Relationship Maximization Process and uses it to bring companies and issues together. She assesses the kind of commitment the company wants to make, its willingness to take a risk—Reebok is risk oriented, she says, Avon risk averse—and its current activities at the brand and corporate level and through its Foundation.

At the next stage, she analyzes the issues available to the company, and in particular those issues that resonate with the company's customers. She has helped put Heinz together with family issues, for a multi-year multimedia program called Family Works, and Avon together with breast cancer. Other clients have included American Express, Reebok, Coors, Burger King, and Polaroid, which recently launched a campaign called See What Develops that focuses on the issue of kids and self-esteem.

Polaroid was motivated, in part, by a survey that showed how dramatically children's self-esteem drops during their formative years. When they entered school, 95% of all young children said they liked themselves. By their senior year in high school, that was true for just 5%. When the company then heard that experts in the field, like children's author Diane Loomans, thought that photography could help kids with self-esteem issues, the company saw an opportunity.

"Working with parents nationwide, we've repeatedly seen that an instant photograph enhances the impact of an encouraging word or an affectionate hug," says Lisa Santerian, the company's senior marketing manager. "Whether they're hung on the refrigerator or proudly passed around the classroom, photographs help kids to feel good about themselves."

The company is distributing a brochure that lets parents know how they can improve their kids' self-esteem. It suggests a variety of ideas, from volunteering at an organization that is meaningful to the child to "role reversal day" —with parents and children switching roles.

Similarly, Home Depot has chosen to focus primarily on the issue of affordable housing, which is a brilliant strategic fit with its main business.

"We are in the home improvement business, so we have unique resources that we can bring to this issue," says Suzanne Apple, the company's director of public affairs. "Not only that, but one of the basic principles on which this company is founded is that everyone deserves a quality place to live." The company gets involved with the issue in a number of ways, from offering advice and expertise to building houses as part of the Habitat for Humanity project. The company helped the charity build 100 homes in Atlanta prior to [the] Olympics. The last of the 100 was built by a Home Depot team led by president Arthur Blank and consisting entirely of officers of the company. That's what is meant by the commitment of senior management.

"It started off as part of our good citizenship and corporate responsibility activities," says Apple, "but it has become a vital part of our marketing activity. We could not talk about ourselves without talking about the beliefs we have and the activities we are engaged in that spring from those beliefs."

Some companies, like Avon, even involve their customers in the creation of a program, seeking their input before deciding what causes to support. California-based Sassaby Cosmetics, which markets a line of inexpensive beauty products targeted to teens and called Jane, reached out electronically to its target audience. Sassaby sponsored "Jane's Brain," a computer bulletin board where teenage girls could chat with peers. The company used the board to ask the girls to identify important issues they would like to see addressed, then donated a percentage of profits to the causes they selected.

Pearlman's research also indicates that not all causes are created equal. While 80% of respondents said their opinion of a company would be much more favorable if it sponsored after school programs to keep children out of gangs, and 73% said opinions would be much more favorable if it sponsored a local program to plant trees [to] beautify the community, adopt-a-highway and nutrition education programs were considerably less likely to impress.

"The two biggest issues are crime and kids," says Pearlman. "Those are the issues that score highest among consumers. There's also a strong preference for programs that have a local as well as a national component, that touch people where they live. And there's a bias towards action. Consumers prefer companies to do something rather than just talk about it. Advertising to raise awareness of an issue is not, by itself, enough. Best of all is a program that includes a volunteerism element, some way to work side-by-side with your customers."

The Spirit of Community program launched [recently] by Prudential Insurance Company is a perfect example of a national campaign that reaches people at a grassroots level, uniting the company's employees, agents and customers behind a cause. Inspired by the story of a New Jersey boy who collected old, discarded bicycles, rebuilt them, and gave them to underprivileged children in his community, the company conceived a program to find and honor youth volunteers across the country, and encourage others to follow their lead.

The program, which has been implemented in part by New York consulting firm Geduldig & Ferguson, is designed to stimulate youth volunteerism; demonstrate the company's support for its employees; build closer bonds between the Prudential, its people and the communities they serve; and enhance the company's reputation as a responsible corporate citizen. It includes an awards program for "exceptional self-initiated youth volunteerism," administered in partnership with the National Association of Secondary School Principals.

In its first year, the program uncovered more than 6,000 nominees, with judging panels in each state—a total of 350 prominent state educators and non-profit-organizations—selecting two honorees. The company crafted 52 custom releases—one for each state, plus the District of Columbia and Puerto Rico—and announcements were made jointly by the company and state officials.

The Cone survey, meanwhile, puts improving local schools at the top of a list of issues that concern consumers, with sponsorship of youth programs, cleaning up the environment, and providing college scholarship funds also strong issues that appear to be gaining in support. Cone also suggests some issues that are not currently owned. "I think menopause is a very powerful issue," she says. "But all these companies are run by men, and they don't know how to approach it. I think Alzheimer's is another issue. And assisted living. Anything that deals with the aging population. And women and computers, or girls and computers."

With so many good issues as yet unclaimed, and so many corporations waking up to cause-related marketing for the first time, it seems likely that the amount being spent in this arena will continue to grow. Ninety percent of executives interviewed in the Cone/Roper survey say their commitment to cause-related marketing will continue, with more than half projecting that the dollar expenditure will increase. As it does, the creativity needed to select the right cause and initiate a program that is truly valuable to both parties will be greater than ever.

NO

**James T. Bennett and
Thomas J. DiLorenzo**

Health Charities: Reputation for Sale?

In the fall of 1994, the "Arthritis Foundation" line of pain relievers was launched onto store shelves across the country. By all appearances, the then 46-year-old health charity had come out with a series of medicines that consumers could especially rely on; after all, why else would the charity make such an offering related so closely to its mission? This impression was reinforced by national advertising and direct-marketing campaigns, featuring actress/singer Julie Andrews.

But the pain relievers were not the nonprofit's products. Not readily evident from the packaging or marketing materials, the line of acetaminophen, coated aspirin, and ibuprofen was produced, marketed, and owned by Johnson & Johnson's McNeil Consumer Products Company—maker of the familiar Tylenol brand of pain relievers. The Arthritis Foundation had simply licensed its name to be used by McNeil on the packaging and in various advertising pitches. In exchange, McNeil offered purchasers a year's membership to the Arthritis Foundation and informed them that a portion of the receipts would go to support the charity; the Arthritis Foundation, under a royalty arrangement, would receive at least $1 million a year, plus huge exposure to millions of pain-reliever buyers. For this, McNeil would be able to use the Foundation's good name to leverage increasing market share in the pain reliever market.

The "Arthritis Foundation" line was no different in formulation from competing brands. All that was "new" was the marketing arrangement and the cooperative exposure each organization brought to the other. The mutually beneficial partnership was widely considered to be the first in which a charity's name was featured as a product's brand name. Nevertheless, it blurred the line between nonprofit and for-profit enterprise to such an extent that law enforcement officials cried foul. The relationship was so vague that 19 state Attorneys General charged McNeil with deceptive advertising, alleging that consumers were misled to believe the drugs were new medications created by the Foundation, among other charges. It simply wasn't clear, the Attorneys General argued, as to who was behind the product, what was inside the package, or where the money was going. Although McNeil denied the charges, it settled with the states without admitting wrongdoing and quietly discontinued the line [in] September [1996], citing disappointing sales.

From James T. Bennett and Thomas J. DiLorenzo, "Health Charities: Reputation for Sale?" *Consumers' Research* (July 1997). Copyright © 1997 by *Consumers' Research*. Reprinted by permission.

This foray into so-called cause-oriented marketing, in which corporations link specific products and product lines with major charitable organizations, was not unique to the Arthritis Foundation. Product tie-ins have become a hot trend among business firms, which, in seeking an economic edge in an increasingly competitive marketplace, are attempting to capitalize on various charities' reputations. The charitable organizations, particularly the major health charities, have been willingly signing on to these arrangements, even actively seeking them out, in their quest for new sources of funding and/or wider public exposure. Essentially, they are becoming partners—and beneficiaries—of corporate marketing strategies.

At risk in these endeavors is the public's confidence in the charitable organizations. The marketing arrangements, as typically set up, are inescapably misleading to the buying public. As will be evident in the discussion below, the essential problem is the implied endorsement from association with a charity, even when it is at pains to hold these relationships at arm's length. Moreover, such commercial relationships increase the likelihood that a charity's independence from outside influences will be compromised; and even if it is not, there will develop the perception among many donors that it has been—just as threatening to reputation and public support of the nonprofit's mission.

Of course, not all commercial ties are ill considered; many are beneficial to all parties involved, without threatening charities' integrity—e.g. corporate sponsorship of concerts, "walkathons," or other such events to raise funds for charitable causes. The problems result from the specific practice of product endorsements or other specific product tie-ins that link the charity directly to the profitability of its commercial partner.

Following, we review some of the recent corporate-charity tie-ins by some of the best known and largest health charities—the American Heart Association, the American Cancer Society, and the American Lung Association. The increasing commercialism of these popular groups is important because they are bellwethers for many other organizations, which may well be encouraged to follow their lead.

Product 'endorsements'   American Heart Association (AHA), through its Food Certification Program, conducts one of the most visible and wide-ranging product-endorsement campaigns. Walk through most any supermarket in America, especially down the cereal aisle, and you'll see on selected brands the AHA's heart-check certification mark. This program, as determined by guidelines established in late 1992, is "designed to help consumers easily select foods in the grocery store that can be part of a balanced, heart-healthy diet," as the AHA explains.

As of March this year, some 45 companies pay the association to carry the heart-check mark on more than 450 products. These include portions of the Campbell Soup line, various Del Monte fruits and raisin offerings, nearly 50 brands of Kellogg cereals and breakfast products (such as PopTarts, Cocoa Krispies, Special K, and Common Sense Oat Bran), brands from General Mills (Cheerios, Wheaties, Yoplait yogurts), Con Agra, Milk-Made ("Cool Cow," 99% Fat Free Milk Product), Neighbors Quality House Coffee (such as Banana Nut

Cappuccino Products), and products from Pillsbury and Quaker Oats, according to the AHA. This is hardly a large number in light of the thousands of various foods offered to Americans, many of which are whole, unprocessed meats, vegetables, and grains that as most any nutritionist would explain is generally preferable to processed foods.

The certification-mark endorsements on packaging for the products is generic and offers consumers little information: "This product meets American Heart Association guidelines for healthy people over age 2 when used as part of a balanced diet." Depending on the product, additional AHA-approved statements may be carried, such as: "Diets low in saturated fat and cholesterol and high in grains, fruit and vegetables that contain fiber, may reduce the risk of heart disease, a condition associated with many factors," which appears on Quaker Oatmeal.

And what are the criteria for the certification of these various products? Actually, not much is involved. According to the AHA's "Corporate Relations Policy" the product must first meet Food and Drug Administration (FDA) and U.S. Department of Agriculture (USDA) regulatory requirements for making a coronary heart disease health claim. In other words, the heart-check symbol serves as sort of an extension of federal public health information and guidelines, a signal that a product meets government standards, but not much more.

Remarkably, given the sheer abundance of products that would seem to fit this criterion, the AHA's approach falls well short of any systematic, consumer-friendly survey of the marketplace. Its second major criterion limits the extent of the program significantly: the product cannot be manufactured by a tobacco company or subsidiary since AHA Corporate Relations Policy "prohibits formal corporate relationships" with any company with 5% or greater ownership by a tobacco company. This thus excludes brand-name giants such as Kraft, Nabisco, Post, and Jell-O from the program. Whatever one may think about smoking products, the fact that Post's Raisin Bran cannot carry the heart-check symbol, but Kellogg's Raisin Bran and even Kellogg's Froot Loops can, suggests the inherent hollowness of the program's information.

The AHA's "certification" may guide consumers to some products that arguably can be part of a good diet, but it would be incorrect to say the program offers any accurate distinctions among individual brands, despite the clear implication that this is what the symbol conveys—an implication no doubt on the minds of corporate executives fighting for market share in the competitive cereals market. As the 1996 General Mills Annual Report notes: "Consumers today have higher standards than ever, demanding food products that offer better taste... better value—and stronger nutritional credentials." The AHA's endorsement program, despite the limited informational content, offers excellent "credentials" to the brands allowed to participate, given that the charity is "this country's most trusted source for cardiovascular health information," as it asserts. Judging by the number of companies signed up for certification so far, such a good reputation clearly has value to marketers.

Interestingly, the AHA had long opposed such product endorsements; from its inception in 1924 its charter expressly "prohibited the endorsement of any product." This changed, however, in June of 1988 when the AHA's House of Delegates voted overwhelmingly to permit such endorsements. The purpose was to institute the charity's ill-fated "HeartGuide Seal" program. The storm generated by this program revolved around the large fees charged participants —depending on a company's size, the fee ranged from $45,000 to $640,000 per brand, per year, for a minimum of three years—as well as controversy about the informational quality of the label. Among other critics were officials with the FDA and USDA. Under pressure from the federal government (and the threat of a lawsuit), the AHA abandoned the program in 1990.

When the AHA resurrected a version of the HeartGuide program in the form of its current heart-check initiative, it initially indicated that there would be "no charge" to participating manufacturers, save for a nominal administrative fee. This ranges from $350 to $850 per product per year. But the AHA still gains extensive (and otherwise expensive) exposure from the program; all participating companies are required to plug the AHA certification at least once a year.

However, the financial arrangements seem to have been modifiable. On February 21, 1996, the AHA and the Florida Department of Citrus—a state agency promoting citrus sales—announced a cooperative effort to promote the sale of grapefruit and grapefruit juice which would "receive the AHA's heart-check food certification mark." For this endorsement, the AHA will "receive a $100,000 donation." But this sum is merely the tip of the iceberg, for the contract between Florida and the AHA specifies that, over the period December 1, 1996 to June 1, 1999, the AHA will be paid a total of $450,000. Of interest is the title of the AHA executive officer who signed the contract: "Vice President —Marketing and Creative Services."

Educational partnerships   Not all the AHA's product tie-ins are related to its certification program. The charity, like the American Cancer Society (ACS) and American Lung Association (ALA), also associates its name with specific products in so-called educational partnerships. These often exclusive relationships are commonly presented as arm's length arrangements by which the charity makes no endorsement of the product. Rather, the association is presented as taking mutual advantage of a "shared mission."

The result, for example, is the recent full-page advertisement in newspapers such as *The Wall Street Journal* by Bristol-Myers Squibb for its cholesterol drug, Pravachol. In the ad, the drug maker surrounds its pitch for Pravachol with eyes-catching messages about cholesterol and heart disease from the AHA. "Ask your doctor if Pravachol is right for you," the ad notes. "Or call 1-800-PREVENT for more information on first heart attack prevention including a free brochure from the American Heart Association. It's all provided by Bristol-Myers Squibb."

The major health charities have long received grants from corporations, especially pharmaceutical companies, to help nonprofit missions. The rise of cause-oriented marketing and ensuing product tie-ins, however, has been shifting the association from one of relatively straight-forward philanthropy to one of *quid pro quo* marketing.

As the ACS notes in its 1995 Annual Report: "We are also forging a new breed of partnership with corporations...." The essentials of this type of partnership bear directly on the corporate bottom line. In a recent issue of *Focus: The Fundraising Magazine of the American Cancer Society,* an article entitled "Developing Corporate Relationships in Fundraising" advises that "Advertising, marketing, and public relations departments have their own budget and their own motivations for making a gift: increased profit through increased visibility, enhanced company image, and stronger customer perception that the company and/or its products can be trusted." Or, as one pitch to corporate partners by the ALA puts it: "You can leverage the credibility, visibility and good will of the American Lung Association by working with us to create an educational partnership that gives you a marketing advantage...."

In exchange for the marketing advantage products gain when associating with charities' good reputation, the charities can receive sizable sums of money and significant exposure. In a move mirroring that of the AHA, the ACS signed, in the spring of 1996, a $1 million-a-year deal with Florida in which the Society licensed its logo for use to promote Florida citrus fruits. In August 1996, the SmithKline Beecham to allow the company exclusive use of the ACS name on its Nicoderm brand smoking-cessation patches. The ALA signed a similar, $2.5-million-a-year deal with McNeil Consumer Products' Nicotrol-brand nicotine patches this past April.

In defending its actions, the ACS says in a position statement that it "does not formally endorse products," adding that it "does not offer an opinion as to the superiority of one product versus another." This may seem odd when one views a pack of Nicoderm exclusively emblazoned with the ACS logo, but the ACS finesses the association:

"We have formed educational awareness-building partnerships with companies whose products match our established mission and which offer us the opportunity to reach people with ACS messages through media [i.e., product advertising] previously unavailable to us. These partnerships also generate significant new income with which we can advance our over-all cancer control mission."

And what is the buying public supposed to make of these arrangements? The ACS recognizes the marketing value of its name: "Research shows us that the public trusts and respects the American Cancer Society beyond virtually any other American institution. We know that the power of that public recognition adds valuable credibility to the companies and products with which we partner. It is for this reason that we will choose to partner only with those products and companies which can further the mission of the ACS."

To be sure, the ACS "publicly partners with good companies and organizations," as it explains. But, as indicated by the statement above, the charity will associate only with groups that will help finance its programs. By keeping the relationship at arm's length, that is, by making no formal appraisal of the product's particular merits against other products, the group seems to believe it can escape accountability. Yet at the same time it acknowledges that the public may be deceived.

As one ACS vice president was quoted in a recent report for the on-line policy magazine *Slate*: "Is there an implied endorsement? The answer to that has to be 'yes.' There is no way around it." An executive for the ALA made a similar acknowledgement: "If you're standing there looking at the shelf, you might say, 'Hmm, maybe I'll buy the product with the logo as opposed to the one that doesn't have any.' That's a reality."

The slippery slope   The risk to charities' reputations from these activities should be readily evident. They allow misperceptions about their associations to persist so long as they license their names to individual products. Should one product prove controversial, the associated charity may have some explaining to do. Likewise, the quality of the information put out directly by the charity may become suspect. For example, the use of cholesterol-lowering drugs has been controversial. So association with one particular therapy would seem to create potential conflicts should more effective or appropriate therapies become clear. (See "Diet and Heart Disease: Not What You Think," *CR*, July 1996.) Will the charity trumpet this new information to the public?

Additionally, product tie-ins may tempt charities to become involved on behalf of business interests in other ways. A slippery slope exists where charities' actions, while perhaps fitting their own mission, also directly benefit particular businesses. Consider, for example, how the ALA's lobbying activities benefited one of its corporate partners, American Sensors, maker of carbon monoxide and natural gas detectors.

In July 1994, American Sensors "formed an educational alliance" with the ALA. The company has the exclusive use of the ALA logo and its message about carbon monoxide poisoning in its packaging and advertising; its promotional materials state that: "American Sensors is working closely with the American Lung Association (ALA)... to raise public awareness of the health and safety risks from indoor air pollution."

This educational campaign goes far beyond telling consumers about the dangers of carbon monoxide; it includes lobbying elected officials to adopt regulations mandating the installation of detection devices in homes and businesses. Such laws obviously benefit firms that produce the detectors, such as American Sensors. If the manufacturers lobbied for such legislation, the financial self-interests would be apparent; but, under the guise of being concerned solely with public health, the ALA can lobby far more effectively.

In any case, relative to many health concerns, carbon monoxide poisoning is a comparatively minor problem: the National Safety Council estimates that 600 people died in the United States in 1994 as a result of non-fire-related carbon monoxide poisoning. Nearly five times as many people die at home from other forms of suffocation each year. And the CO death rate had been dropping steadily—long before detectors hit the market. Does the ALA note this in its lobbying efforts? Does it put this risk in perspective for the public?

Such positions, while beneficial to gas-detector companies, can backfire. An ordinance requiring a carbon monoxide detector in every home was enacted in Chicago in October 1994. Two months later, thousands of detectors sounded warnings over a two-day period, and concerned homeowners flooded the fire department with calls. The alarms were caused by a harmless buildup of pollution, but the net effect was to *increase* risk to the public health as dozens of emergency units responded to false alarms rather than to real emergencies.

The ALA is not one to shy from lobbying for the benefit of one particular company. In another case, the national office of ALA placed newspaper advertisements urging that a private firm—Envirotest, Inc. of Tucson, Arizona—be awarded a contract to conduct the controversial "enhanced auto emissions test" that the Environmental Protection Agency mandated for Pennsylvania. According to the *Harrisburg Patriot*, "not only did [the ALA] recently fund an ad campaign supporting the embattled [emissions test] program's expansion, the American Lung Association has accepted $200,000 in contributions over the past three years from Envirotest, Inc., the firm that won the lucrative contract to implement the plan."

In response to charges of influence peddling, ALA lobbyist Paul Billings responded that: "In the 90s, you have to make money where you can." *The Pittsburgh Post-Gazette* reported that hundreds of Pennsylvania donors were "outraged that the lung association was paying for ads for a private enterprise" instead of helping the victims of lung disease, the central theme of its fund-raising appeals. Outraged, as well, was the head of the local Western Pennsylvania ALA chapter: "The perception that... the ALA of Western Pennsylvania is involved in those ads is damaging to us," he told the paper. Donors were calling him to say they wouldn't contribute to the program anymore.

The nonprofit motive   Such behavior damages the credibility of not only the ALA, but other charities as well. Although in the short run revenue is enhanced by grants and contracts to undertake such activities, in the long run, the public's confidence and willingness to contribute are undoubtedly compromised.

Nonprofit organizations are not subject to the pressures of marketplace competition, as are for-profit business firms, nor are they subject to electoral competition, as are governments. Economic and political competition provide incentives for both businesses and governments to serve the interests of their customers and constituents (however imperfectly), but the "customers" of nonprofit organizations (i.e., donors) do not benefit from these competitive pressures. There is no bottom line, in an accounting sense, in the nonprofit sector; there are no shareholders or customers to satisfy; and there are no public elections for top officials.

With nonprofit organizations, potential donors must rely almost exclusively on trust—on the belief that their donations will be spent wisely to carry out the organization's charitable purpose. Thus, a charity's "brand name" is by far its most valuable asset; indeed, without it no charity could long survive.

Commercial endorsements by health charities may jeopardize their reputations which have been built up though good works over many decades. The long-term financial viability of these organizations and the public's trust in and willingness to support nonprofits may be eroded by their increasing ties to profit-seeking firms. As stated by former Food and Drug Administration commissioner Donald Kennedy: "Voluntary agencies that support research ought to be very wary of putting their reputation of scientific objectivity in jeopardy. I think [product] endorsements do constitute that kind of jeopardy."

Professor Arthur L. Caplan, director of the Center for Bioethics at the University of Pennsylvania Medical Center, believes the practice of nonprofits' charging for "seals of approval" is "ethically dubious." And Michael Jacobson, founder of the Center for the Study of Commercialism in Washington, D.C., believes that "in the long run, the nonprofit sector is being jeopardized" as "the health groups are getting a little greedy.... As soon as a nonprofit organization takes money from a company, they have sold off a bit of their independence."

Charities inevitably "sell off" some of their independence and cash in part of their good will when they endorse products and participate in marketing ventures with for-profits. Although such partnerships may seem beneficial in the short run for both the nonprofit and the commercial firm (a "win, win" arrangement), in the long run the commercialization of nonprofits will likely diminish the reputations of charities with both donors and the public at large, especially if the endorsements are dubious. As Patty Oertel, executive director at the Center for Nonprofit Management, observed "There are risks associated with... giving up some control of the [charity's] name and what the general public will perceive of them granting use of the name.

In competitive markets, the profit motive generates incalculable human benefits by motivating businesses to outdo each other in providing the public with higher quality goods and services at competitive prices. But the major health charities, renting their reputations out as they do, erode public trust in their own distinctly separate mission in society by essentially shilling for various corporate interests. These relationships do not always advance the cause of improving public health and, at times, may even hinder it.

POSTSCRIPT

Does Cause-Related Marketing Benefit All Stakeholders?

T wo parallel trends have emerged in reference to CRM programs. While becoming inordinately more dominant on the consumer-marketing scene, they are inviting unprecedented scrutiny from critics challenging their credibility and effectiveness. Even consumers who patronize these programs often believe that the marketers are motivated by profit and market share rather than by pure altruism. Critics will continue to question the distinguishing attributes that legitimize the "heart smart" logo as a cause-related symbol on the cereal Cocoa-Frosted Flakes.

Cause-related marketing's role is escalating in a consistently growing array of product/service categories. Consider the campaign for Flutie Flakes, which promotes the cause of autism through celebrity NFL football star Doug Flutie. The actual product—cereal—is barely referenced in the advertising, and it serves only as a backdrop, or conduit, for the *real* product, which is the related cause. This is a concept that raises cause-related marketing to a new plateau—*cause-based marketing*. This occurs when the cause becomes the *core* product and is the central theme of the promotional campaign. This opens an entirely new arena of competition, as the actual product becomes "commoditized" and of secondary importance. Segmentation research must focus on articulating levels of attitudes toward cause-relatedness and identify the causes that are most salient to specific target audiences.

Suggested Readings

Sue Adkins, "The Wider Benefits of Backing a Good Cause," *Marketing* (September 2, 1999)

Karen File and Russ Prince, "Cause-Related Marketing and Corporate Philanthrophy in the Privately Held Enterprise," *Journal of Business Ethics* (October 1998)

Rachel Fox, "Employees and Consumers Like Cause Marketing," *Incentive* (September 1999)

Harvey Meyer, "When the Cause Is Just," *Journal of Business Strategy* (November–December 1999)

CONE, Inc. http://www.conenet.com

AVON: The Crusade. http://www.avoncrusade.com

ISSUE 6

Is Mass Customization the Wave of the Future?

YES: Erick Schonfeld, from "The Customized, Digitized, Have-It-Your-Way Economy," *Fortune* (September 28, 1998)

NO: George Ritzer, from *The McDonaldization of Society: An Investigation into the Changing Character of Contemporary Social Life,* rev. ed. (Pine Forge Press, 1996)

ISSUE SUMMARY

YES: Investment writer Erick Schonfeld argues that the move to customization in manufacturing and services is irrefutable. He concludes that by making full use of cutting-edge technology, this service to the customer is becoming more important than the brand.

NO: Professor of sociology George Ritzer presents a view of the influence of McDonaldization, or the domination of society by standardized franchise systems, on consumers' lifestyles and values and demands from marketers.

J ust as the industrial age allowed consumers to obtain more standardized products due to cost efficiencies, the information age allowed them the option of customized products, involving consumers in the process through their personal choice of product attributes. Now the information revolution is transforming standardized formats for mass markets by customizing unique products for markets of one. It represents a strategy change from pushing completed products to involving consumers in customized design. The key change requires the involvement of consumers as an integral part of the marketing process. Due to enhanced technology, database prices have fallen and the software and algorithms now allow comparisons and can scan data faster. But one-to-one marketing needs more than a database system; interaction with the customer is crucial to the customized strategy. It is not "better-targeted" harassment but a response to what the customer has expressed as needs in terms of price, form, service, and delivery.

This is a major departure from the price-driven, market-oriented "rat race" of the industrial age when customers perceived products as being the same and price became the tiebreaker. Instead, co-opting the consumer builds relationships through the partnering that takes place in the marketing process. Customers become more loyal and committed due to their actual involvement. Products are less likely to be returned, and inventory costs can be slashed.

Mass customization is actually less expensive on a unit basis than mass production. It is a digital configuration of a product from many different components and models. But unlike traditional manufacturing, the product is only made when you have a customer. Millions of standardized consumer products are being customized due to the benefits of more sophisticated microprocessors —organizing and managing customer information into an automated production process. Erick Schonfeld provides several examples, such as Motorola's ability to mass customize over 29,000 variations of its pager.

Mass customization has primarily been most approachable in business-to-business marketing with success stories like Hewlett-Packard—producing in modules and assembling the final product at the last step of the supply chain based on specific consumer requests. John Deere Harvester has revamped its manufacturing process to accommodate customized orders. Now it only needs to keep 20 crop planters in finished goods inventory. Their customers can now choose from a large number of options best suited to their needs.

But do we really live in a customized world? Another growing pillar of American culture looms in stark contrast to this trend. Proposed by George Ritzer, the concept is *McDonaldization*, which is a process whereby the principles of fast-food restaurants dominate more and more sectors of American society as well as the rest of the world. The basic premise is that "McDonaldized" institutions have successfully programmed consumers to accept and internalize standardized products, services, and franchised types of consumer experience as the marketplace norm. Ace Hardware, Ammco, Holiday Inns, H&R Block, and even *USA Today* are cases in point. Why is *USA Today* left outside almost every hotel room in America each morning? Because people know the format and can readily find their hometown news and weather, as well as national events.

But deeper societal criticisms are associated with Ritzer's concept. Is marketing culpable for roles in trashing the environment by converting the unique character of American cities into endless indistinguishable landscapes of looka-like franchises? Another criticism of McDonaldization is that the standardized formula for "pushbutton" service is dehumanizing to both employees and consumers, eliciting a robotic attitude that stifles creative thinking and the entrepreneurial spirit. Basic to the issue is whether or not consumers have the time and willingness to become that involved in the "learning relationship" sought by mass customization. Mass customization is a powerful means of *corporate differentiation* because "the product becomes the service." It adds a progressive image to the firm and is invigorating for employees. Still, it is not without problems, and the long-run success of mass customization remains to be seen. Consumer apathy versus their quest for individualized products is the ultimate question.

Erick Schonfeld

 **YES**

The Customized, Digitized, Have-It-Your-Way Economy

Mass customization will change the way products are made—forever.

A silent revolution is stirring in the way things are made and services are delivered. Companies with millions of customers are starting to build products designed just for you. You can, of course, buy a Dell computer assembled to your exact specifications. And you can buy a pair of Levi's cut to fit your body. But you can also buy pills with the exact blend of vitamins, minerals, and herbs that you like, glasses molded to fit your face precisely, CDs with music tracks that you choose, cosmetics mixed to match your skin tone, textbooks whose chapters are picked out by your professor, a loan structured to meet your financial profile, or a night at a hotel where every employee knows your favorite wine. And if your child does not like any of Mattel's 125 different Barbie dolls, she will soon be able to design her own.

Welcome to the world of mass customization, where mass-market goods and services are uniquely tailored to the needs of the individuals who buy them. Companies as diverse as BMW, Dell Computer, Levi Strauss, Mattel, McGraw-Hill, Wells Fargo, and a slew of leading Web businesses are adopting mass customization to maintain or obtain a competitive edge. Many are just beginning to dabble, but the direction in which they are headed is clear. Mass customization is more than just a manufacturing process, logistics system, or marketing strategy. It could well be the organizing principle of business in the next century, just as mass production was the organizing principle in this one.

The two philosophies couldn't clash more. Mass producers dictate a one-to-many relationship, while mass customizers require continual dialogue with customers. Mass production is cost-efficient. But mass customization is a flexible manufacturing technique that can slash inventory. And mass customization has two huge advantages over mass production: It is at the service of the customer, and it makes full use of cutting-edge technology.

A whole list of technological advances that make customization possible is finally in place. Computer-controlled factory equipment and industrial robots make it easier to quickly readjust assembly lines. The proliferation of bar-code scanners makes it possible to track virtually every part and product. Databases now store trillions of bytes of information, including individual customers' predilections for everything from cottage cheese to suede boots. Digital printers make it a cinch to change product packaging on the fly. Logistics and supply-chain management software tightly coordinates manufacturing and distribution.

And then there's the Internet, which ties these disparate pieces together. Says Joseph Pine, author of the pioneering book *Mass Customization:* "Anything you can digitize, you can customize." The Net makes it easy for companies to move data from an online order form to the factory floor. The Net makes it easy for manufacturing types to communicate with marketers. Most of all, the Net makes it easy for a company to conduct an ongoing, one-to-one dialogue with each of its customers, to learn about and respond to their exact preferences. Conversely, the Net is also often the best way for a customer to learn which company has the most to offer him—if he's not happy with one company's wares, nearly perfect information about a competitor's is just a mouse click away. Combine that with mass customization, and the nature of a company's relationship with its customers is forever changed. Much of the leverage that once belonged to companies now belongs to customers.

If a company can't customize, it's got a problem. The Industrial Age model of making things cheaper by making them the same will not hold. Competitors can copy product innovations faster than ever. Meanwhile, consumers demand more choices. Marketing guru Regis McKenna declares, "Choice has become a higher value than brand in America." The largest market shares for soda, beer, and software do not belong to Coca-Cola, Anheuser-Busch, or Microsoft. They belong to a category called Other. Now companies are trying to produce a unique Other for each of us. It is the logical culmination of markets' being chopped into finer and finer segments. After all, the ultimate niche is a market of one.

The best—and most famous—example of mass customization is Dell Computer, which has a direct relationship with customers and builds only PCs that have actually been ordered. Everyone from Compaq to IBM is struggling to copy Dell's model. And for good reason. Dell passed IBM last quarter to claim the No. 2 spot in PC market share (behind Compaq). While other computer manufacturers struggle for profits, Dell keeps reporting record numbers; in its most recent quarter the company's sales were up 54%, while earnings soared 62%. No wonder Michael Dell has become the poster boy of the new economy. As Pine says, "The closest person we have to Henry Ford is Michael Dell."

Dell's triumph is not so much technological as it is organizational. Dell keeps margins up by keeping inventory down. The company builds computers from modular components that are always readily available. But Dell doesn't want to store tons of parts: Computer components decline in value at a rate of about 1% a week, faster than just about any product other than sushi or losing lottery tickets. So the key to the system is ensuring that the right parts and products are delivered to the right place at the right time.

To do this, Dell employs sophisticated logistics software, some developed internally, some made by i2 Technologies. The software takes info gathered from customers and steers it to the parts of the organization that need it. When an order comes in, the data collected are quickly parsed out—to suppliers that need to rush over a shipment of hard drives, say, or to the factory floor, where assemblers put parts together in the customer's desired configuration. "Our goal," says vice chairman Kevin Rollins, "is to know exactly what the customer wants when they want it, so we will have no waste."

The company has been propelled by this thinking ever since Michael Dell started selling PCs from his college dorm room in 1983. The Web makes the process virtually seamless, by allowing the company to easily collect customized, digitized data that are ready for delivery to the people who need them. The result is an entire organization driven by orders placed by individual customers, an organization that does more Web-based commerce than almost anyone else. Dell's future doesn't depend on faster chips or modems—it depends on greater mastery of mass customization, of streamlining the flow of quality information.

It's not much of a surprise that a leading tech company like Dell is using software and the Net in such innovative ways. What's startling is the extent to which companies in other industries are embracing mass customization. Take Mattel. Starting by October [1998], girls will be able to log on to barbie.com and design their own friend of Barbie's. They will be able to choose the doll's skin tone, eye color, hairdo, hair color, clothes, accessories, and name (6,000 permutations will be available initially). The girls will even fill out a questionnaire that asks about the doll's likes and dislikes. When the Barbie pal arrives in the mail, the girls will find their doll's name on the package, along with a computer-generated paragraph about her personality.

Offering such a product without the Net would be next to impossible. Mattel does make specific versions of Barbie for customers such as Toys "R" Us, and the company customizes cheerleader Barbies for universities. But this will be the first time Mattel produces Barbie dolls in lots of one. Like Dell, Mattel must use high-end manufacturing and logistics software to ensure that the order data on its Website are distributed to the parts of the company that need them. The only real concern is whether Mattel's systems can handle the expected demand in a timely fashion. Right now, marketing VP Anne Parducci is shooting for delivery of the dolls within six weeks—a bit much considering that that is how long it takes to get a custom-ordered BMW.

Nevertheless, Parducci is pumped. "Personalization is a dream we have had for several years," she says. Parducci thinks the custom Barbies could become one of [the] hottest toys. Then, says Parducci, "we are going to build a database of children's names, to develop a one-to-one relationship with these girls." That may sound creepy, but part of mass customization is treating your customers, even preteens, as adults. By allowing the girls to define beauty in their own terms, Mattel is in theory helping them feel good about themselves even as it collects personal data. That's quite a step for a company that has stamped out its own stereotypes of beauty for decades, but Parducci's market testing shows that girls' enthusiasm for being a fashion designer or creating a personality is "through the roof."

Levi Strauss also likes giving customers the chance to play fashion designer. For the past four years it has made measure-to-fit women's jeans under the Personal Pair banner. In October [1998], Levi's will relaunch an expanded version called Original Spin, which will offer more options and will feature men's jeans as well.

With the help of a sales associate, customers will create the jeans they want by picking from six colors, three basic models, five different leg openings, and two types of fly. Then their waist, butt, and inseam will be measured. They will try on a plain pair of test-drive jeans to make sure they like the fit before the order is punched into a Web-based terminal linked to the stitching machines in the factory. Customers can even give the jeans a name—say, Rebel, for a pair of black ones. Two to three weeks later the jeans arrive in the mail; a bar-code tag sealed to the pocket lining stores the measurements for simple reordering.

Today a fully stocked Levi's store carries approximately 130 ready-to-wear pairs of jeans for any given waist and inseam. With Personal Pair, that number jumped to 430 choices. And with Original Spin, it will leap again, to about 750. Sanjay Choudhuri, Levi's director of mass customization, isn't in a hurry to add more choices. "It is critical to carefully pick the choices that you offer," says Choudhuri. "An unlimited amount will create inefficiencies at the plant." Dell Computer's Rollins agrees: "We want to offer fewer components all the time." To these two, mass customization isn't about infinite choices but about offering a healthy number of standard parts that can be mixed and matched in thousands of ways. That gives customers the illusion of boundless choice while keeping the complexity of the manufacturing process manageable.

Levi's charges a slight premium for custom jeans, but what Choudhuri really likes about the process is that Levi's can become your "jeans adviser." Selling off-the-shelf jeans ends a relationship; the customer walks out of the store as anonymous as anyone else on the street. Customizing jeans starts a relationship; the customer likes the fit, is ready for reorders, and forks over his name and address in case Levi's wants to send him promotional offers. And customers who design their own jeans make the perfect focus group; Levi's can apply what it learns from them to the jeans it mass-produces for the rest of us.

If Levi's experiment pays off, other apparel makers will follow its lead. In the not-so-distant future people may simply walk into body-scanning booths where they will be bathed with patterns of white light that will determine their exact three-dimensional structure. A not-for-profit company called [TC]2, funded by a consortium of companies including Levi's, is developing just such a technology. [Recently] some MIT business students proposed a similar idea for a custom-made bra company dubbed Perfect Underwear.

Morpheus Technologies, a wacky startup in Portland, Me., hopes to set up studios equipped with body scanners. Founder Parker Poole III wants to "digitize people and connect their measurement data to their credit cards." Someone with the foresight to be scanned by Morpheus could then call up Eddie Bauer, say, give his credit card number, and order a robe that matches his dimensions. His digital self could also be sent to Brooks Brothers for a suit. Gone will be the days of attentive men kneeling on the floor with pins in their mouths. Progress does have its price.

Thirty years ago auto manufacturers were, effectively, mass customizers. People would spend hours in the office of a car dealer, picking through pages of options. But that ended when car companies tried to improve manufacturing efficiency by offering little more than a few standard options packages. BMW wants to turn back the clock. About 60% of the cars it sells in Europe are built to order, vs. just 15% in the U.S. Europeans seem willing to wait three to four months for a vehicle, while most Americans won't wait longer than four weeks.

Now the company wants to make better use of its customer database to get more Americans to custom-order. BMW dealers save about $450 in inventory costs on every such order. Reinhard Fischer, head of logistics for BMW of North America, says, "The big battle is to take cost out of the distribution chain. The best way to do that is to build in just the things a consumer wants."

Since most BMWs in the U.S. are leased, the company knows when customers will need a new car. Some dealers now call customers a few months before their leases are up to see whether they'd like to custom-order their next car. Soon, however, customers will be able to configure their own car online and send that info to a dealer. Fischer can even see a day when the Website will offer data about vehicles sailing on ships from Germany, so that people can see whether a car matching their preferences is already on the way. That does, of course, raise the question, Why not send the requests directly to BMW, circumventing dealers altogether? Says Fischer: "We don't want to eliminate their role, but maybe they should have a 7% margin, not 16%." Ouch.

Such dilemmas are inevitable, given that mass customization streamlines the order process. What's more, mass customization is about creating products —be they PCs, jeans, cars, eyeglasses, loans, or even industrial soap—that match your needs better than anything a traditional middleman can possibly order for you.

LensCrafters, for instance, has made quick, in-store production of customized lenses common. But Tokyo-based Paris Miki takes the process a step further. Using special software, it designs lenses and a frame that conform both to the shape of a customer's face and to whether he wants, say, casual frames, a sports pair, sunglasses, or more formal specs. The customer can check out on a monitor various choices superimposed over a scanned image of his face. Once he chooses the pair he likes, the lenses are ground and the rimless frames attached.

While we tend to think of automation as a process that eliminates the need for human interaction, mass customization makes the relationship with customers more important than ever. ChemStation in Dayton has about 1,700 industrial-soap formulas—for car washes, factories, landfills, railroads, airlines, and mines. The company analyzes items that are to be cleaned (recent ones in its labs include flutes and goose down) or visits its customers' premises to analyze their dirt. After the analysis, the company brews up a special batch of cleanser. The soap is then placed on the customer's property in reusable containers ChemStation monitors and keeps full. For most customers, teaching another company their cleansing needs is not worth the effort. About 95% of ChemStation's clients never leave.

Hotels that want you to keep coming back are using software to personalize your experience. All Ritz-Carlton hotels, for instance, are linked to a database filled with the quirks and preferences of half-a-million guests. Any bellhop or desk clerk can find out whether you are allergic to feathers, what your favorite newspaper is, or how many extra towels you like.

Wells Fargo, the largest provider of Internet banking, already allows customers to apply for a home-equity loan over the Net and get a three-second decision on a loan structured specifically for them. A lot of behind-the-scenes technology makes this possible, including real-time links to credit bureaus, databases with checking-account histories and property values, and software that can do cash-flow analysis. With a few pieces of customized information from the loan seeker, the software whips into action to make a quick decision.

The bank also uses similar software in its small-business lending unit. According to vice chairman Terri Dial, Wells Fargo used to turn away lots of qualified small businesses—the loans were too small for Wells to justify the time spent on credit analysis. But now the company can collect a few key details from applicants, customize a loan, and approve or deny credit in four hours—down from the four days the process used to take. In some categories that Wells once virtually ignored, loan approvals are up as much as 50%. Says Dial: "You either invest in the technology or get out of that line of business."

She'd better keep investing. Combine the software that enables customization with the ubiquity of the Web, and you get a situation that threatens Wells' very existence. If consumers grow accustomed to designing their own products, will they trust brand-name manufacturers and service providers or will they turn to a new kind of middleman? Frank Shlier, a director of research at the Gartner Group in Stamford, Conn., sees disintermediaries emerging all over the Net to help people sift through the thousands of choices presented to them. In financial services, he suggests, there is "a new role for a trusted adviser, maybe someone who doesn't own any banks."

Shlier's middleman sounds a lot like Intuit, which lets visitors to its quicken.com Website apply for and purchase mortgages from a variety of lenders, fill out their taxes, or set up a portfolio to track their stocks, bonds, and mutual funds. Tapan Bhat, the exec who oversees quicken.com, says, "The Web is probably the medium most attuned to customization, yet so many sites are centered on the company instead of on the individual." What would lure someone to Levi's if she could instead visit a clothing Website that stored her digital dimensions and ordered custom-fit jeans from the manufacturer with the best price and fit? Elaborates Pehong Chen, CEO of Internet software outfit BroadVision: "The Nirvana is that you are so close to your customers, you can satisfy all their needs. Even if you don't make the item yourself, you own the relationship."

Amazon.com has three million relationships. It sells books online and now is moving into music (with videos probably next). Every time someone buys a book on its Website, Amazon.com learns her tastes and suggests other titles she might enjoy. The more Amazon.com learns, the better it serves its customers; the better it serves its customers, the more loyal they become. About 60% are repeat buyers.

The Web is a supermall of mass customizers. You can drop music tracks on your own CDs (cductive.com); choose from over a billion options of printed art, mats, and frames (artuframe.com); get stock picks geared to your goals (personalwealth.com); or make your own vitamins (acumins.com). And you can get all kinds of tailored data; NewsEdge, for example, will send a customized newspaper to your PC.

These companies want to keep customers happy by giving them a product that cannot be compared to a competitor's. Acumin, for instance, blends vitamins, herbs, and minerals per customers' instructions, compressing up to 95 ingredients into three to five pills. If a customer wants to start taking a new supplement, all Acumin needs to do is add it to the blend.

Acumin's products address what Pine calls customer sacrifice—the compromise we all make when we can't get exactly the product we want. CEO Brad Oberwager started the company two years ago, when his sister, who was undergoing a special cancer radiation treatment, couldn't find a multivitamin without iodine. (Her doctor had told her to avoid iodine.) "If someone would create a vitamin just for me, I would buy it," she told her brother. So he did.

The Web will make that kind of response the norm. Sure, there are any number of ways for consumers to provide a company with information about their preferences—they can call, they can write, or, heck, they can even walk into the brick-and-mortar store. But the Web changes everything—the information arrives in a digitized form ready for broadcast. Says i2 CEO Sanjiv Sidhu, "The Internet is bringing society into a culture of speed that has not really existed before." As new middlemen customize orders for the masses, differentiating one company from its competitors will become tougher than ever. Responding to price cuts or quality improvements will continue to be important, but the key differentiator may be how quickly a company can serve a customer. Says Artuframe.com CEO Bill Lederer: "Mass customization is novel today. It will be common tomorrow." If he is right, the Web will wind up creating a strange competitive landscape, where companies temporarily connect to satisfy one customer's desires, then disband, then reconnect with other enterprises to satisfy a different order from a different customer.

That's the vision anyway. For now, companies are struggling to take the first steps toward mass customization. The ones that are already there have been working on the process for years. Matthew Sigman is an executive at R.R. Donnelley & Sons, whose digital publishing business prints textbooks customized by individual college professors. "The challenge," Sigman warns, "is that if you are making units of one, your margin for error is zero." Custom-fit jeans do come with a money-back guarantee. Levi's can't afford for you not to like them.

NO

George Ritzer

An Introduction to McDonaldization

Ray Kroc, the genius behind the franchising of McDonald's restaurants, was a man with big ideas and grand ambitions. But even Kroc could not have anticipated the astounding impact of his creation. McDonald's is one of the most influential developments in twentieth-century America. Its reverberations extend far beyond the confines of the United States and the fast-food business. It has influenced a wide range of undertakings, indeed the way of life, of a significant portion of the world. And that impact is likely to expand at an accelerating rate.

However, this is *not*... about McDonald's, or even the fast-food business, although both will be discussed frequently throughout these pages. Rather, McDonald's serves here as the major example, the "paradigm," of a wide-ranging process I call *McDonaldization*, that is,

> the process by which the principles of the fast-food restaurant are coming to dominate more and more sectors of American society as well as of the rest of the world.

As you will see, McDonaldization affects not only the restaurant business, but also education, work, health care, travel, leisure, dieting, politics, the family, and virtually every other aspect of society. McDonaldization has shown every sign of being an inexorable process by sweeping through seemingly impervious institutions and parts of the world.

McDonald's success is apparent: in 1993 its total sales reached $23.6 billion with profits of almost $1.1 billion. The average U.S. outlet has total sales of approximately $1.6 million in a year. Many entrepreneurs envy such sales and profits and seek to emulate McDonald's success. McDonald's, which first began franchising in 1955, opened its 12,000th outlet on March 22, 1991. By the end of 1993, McDonald's had almost 14,000 restaurants worldwide.

The impact of McDonaldization, which McDonald's has played a central role in spawning, has been manifested in many ways:

- The McDonald's model has been adopted not only by other budget-minded hamburger franchises such as Burger King and Wendy's, but also by a wide array of other low-priced fast-food businesses. Subway, begun in 1965 and now with nearly 10,000 outlets, is considered the fastest-growing of these businesses, which include Pizza Hut, Sbarro's, Taco Bell, Popeye's, and Charley Chan's. Sales in so-called "quick service" restaurants in the United States rose to $81 billion by the end of 1993, almost a third of total sales for the entire food-service industry. In 1994, for the first time, sales in fast-food restaurants exceeded those in traditional full-service restaurants, and the gap between them is projected to grow.

- The McDonald's model has also been extended to "casual dining," that is, more "upscale," higher-priced restaurants with fuller menus. For example, Outback Steakhouse and Sizzler sell steaks, Fuddrucker's offers "gourmet" burgers, Chi-Chi's and Chili's sell Mexican food, The Olive Garden proffers Italian food, and Red Lobster purveys... you guessed it.

- McDonald's is making increasing inroads around the world. In 1991, for the first time, McDonald's opened more restaurants abroad than in the United States. As we move toward the next century, McDonald's expects to build twice as many restaurants each year overseas than it does in the United States. By the end of 1993, over one-third of McDonald's restaurants were overseas; at the beginning of 1995, about half of McDonald's profits came from its overseas operations. McDonald's has even recently opened a restaurant in Mecca, Saudi Arabia.

- Other nations have developed their own variants of this American institution. The large number of fast-food croissanteries in Paris, a city whose love for fine cuisine might lead you to think it would prove immune to fast food, exemplifies this trend. India has a chain of fast-food restaurants, Nirula's, which sells mutton burgers (about 80% of Indians are Hindus, who eat no beef) as well as local Indian cuisine. Perhaps the most unlikely spot for an indigenous fast food restaurant, war-ravaged Beirut of 1984, witnessed the opening of Juicy Burger, with a rainbow instead of golden arches and J. B. the Clown for Ronald McDonald. Its owners hoped that it would become the "McDonald's of the Arab world."

- Other countries with their own McDonaldized institutions have begun to export them to the United States. For example, the Body Shop is an ecologically sensitive British cosmetics chain with 893 shops in early 1993, 120 of which were in the United States, with 40 more scheduled to open that year. Furthermore, American firms are now opening copies of this British chain, such as The Limited, Inc.'s, Bath and Body Works.

- As indicated by the example of the Body Shop, other types of business are increasingly adapting the principles of the fast-food business to their needs. Said the vice chairman of Toys R Us, "We want to be thought of as a sort of McDonald's of toys." The founder of Kidsports Fun and Fitness Club echoed this desire: "I want to be the McDonald's of the kids' fun and fitness business." Other chains with similar ambitions include Jiffy-Lube, AAMCO Transmissions, Midas Muffler & Brake Shops, Hair Plus, H & R Block, Pearle Vision Centers, Kampgrounds of America (KOA), Kinder Care (dubbed "Kentucky Fried

Children"), Jenny Craig, Home Depot, Barnes & Noble, Petstuff, and Wal-Mart (the nation's largest retailer with about 2,500 stores and almost $55 billion in sales).

- Almost 10% of America's stores are franchises, which currently account for 40% of the nation's retail sales. It is estimated that by the turn of the century, about 25% of the stores in the United States will be chains, by then accounting for a whopping two-thirds of retail business. About 80% of McDonald's restaurants are franchises.

McDonald's As "Americana"

McDonald's and its many clones have become ubiquitous and immediately recognizable symbols throughout the United States as well as much of the rest of the world. For example, when plans were afoot to raze Ray Kroc's first McDonald's restaurant, hundreds of letters poured into McDonald's headquarters, including the following:

> Please don't tear it down! . . . Your company's name is a household word, not only in the United States of America, but all over the world. To destroy this major artifact of contemporary culture would, indeed, destroy part of the faith the people of the world have in your company.

In the end, the restaurant was not only saved, but turned into a museum! A McDonald's executive explained the move: "McDonald's . . . is really a part of Americana." Similarly, when Pizza Hut opened in Moscow in 1990, a Russian student said. "It's a piece of America." Reflecting on the growth of fast-food restaurants in Brazil, the president of Pepsico (of which Pizza Hut is part) of Brazil said that his nation "is experiencing a passion for things American."

McDonald's truly has come to occupy a central place in popular culture. It can be a big event when a new McDonald's opens in a small town. Said one Maryland high-school student at such an event, "Nothing this exciting ever happens in Dale City." Newspapers avidly cover developments in the fast-food business. Fast-food restaurants also play symbolic roles on television programs and in the movies. A skit on the television show *Saturday Night Live* satirized specialty chains by detailing the hardships of a franchise that sells nothing but Scotch tape. In the movie *Coming to America*, Eddie Murphy plays an African prince whose introduction to America includes a job at "McDowell's," a thinly disguised McDonald's. Michael Douglas, in *Falling Down*, vents his rage against the modern world in a fast-food restaurant dominated by mindless rules designed to frustrate customers. *Moscow on the Hudson* has Robin Williams, newly arrived from Russia, obtain a job at McDonald's. H. G. Wells, a central character in the movie *Time After Time*, finds himself transported to the modern world of a McDonald's, where he tries to order the tea he was accustomed to drinking in Victorian England. In *Sleeper*, Woody Allen awakens in the future only to encounter a McDonald's. Finally, *Tin Men*, ends with the heroes driving off into a future represented by a huge golden arch looming in the distance.

Many people identify strongly with McDonald's; in fact to some it has become a sacred institution. At the opening of the McDonald's in Moscow, one journalist described the franchise as the "ultimate icon of Americana," while a worker spoke of it "as if it were the Cathedral in Chartres . . . a place to experience 'celestial joy.' " Kowinski argues that shopping malls, which almost always encompass fast-food restaurants, are the modern "cathedrals of consumption" to which people go to practice their "consumer religion." Similarly, a visit to another central element of McDonaldized society, Walt Disney World, has been described as "the middle-class hajj, the compulsory visit to the sunbaked holy city."

McDonald's has achieved its exalted position because virtually all Americans, and many others, have passed through its golden arches on innumerable occasions. Furthermore, most of us have been bombarded by commercials extolling McDonald's virtues, commercials that are tailored to different audiences. Some play to young children watching Saturday-morning cartoons. Others solicit young adults watching prime-time programs. Still others coax grandparents to take their grandchildren to McDonald's. In addition, these commercials change as the chain introduces new foods (such as breakfast burritos), creates new contests, and ties its products to things such as new motion pictures. These ever-present commercials, combined with the fact that people cannot drive very far without having a McDonald's pop into view, have served to embed McDonald's deep in popular consciousness. A poll of school-age children showed that 96% of them could identify Ronald McDonald, second only to Santa Claus in name recognition.

Over the years, McDonald's has appealed to people in many ways. The restaurants themselves are depicted as spick-and-span, the food is said to be fresh and nutritious, the employees are shown to be young and eager, the managers appear gentle and caring, and the dining experience itself seems fun-filled. People are even led to believe that they contribute, at least indirectly, to charities such as the Ronald McDonald Houses for sick children.

The Long Arm of McDonaldization

McDonald's has strived to continually extend its reach within American society and beyond. As the company's chairman said, "Our goal: to totally dominate the quick service restaurant industry worldwide. . . . I want McDonald's to be more than a leader. I want McDonald's to dominate."

McDonald's began as a phenomenon of suburbs and medium sized towns, but in recent years it has moved into big cities and smaller towns, in the United States and beyond, that supposedly could not support such a restaurant. You can now find fast-food outlets in New York's Times Square as well as on the Champs Elysees in Paris. Soon after it opened in 1992, the McDonald's in Moscow sold almost 30,000 hamburgers a day and employed a staff of 1,200 young people working two to a cash register. McDonald's plans to open many more restaurants in the former Soviet Union and in the vast new territory in Eastern Europe that has now been laid bare to the invasion of fast-food restaurants. In early 1992, Beijing witnessed the opening of the world's largest McDonald's with 700 seats, 29 cash registers, and nearly 1,000 employees. On its first day of business, it set a new one-day record for McDonald's by serving about 40,000 customers.

Small satellite, express, or remote outlets, opened in areas that cannot support full-scale fast-food restaurants, are expanding rapidly. They have begun to appear in small store fronts in large cities and in nontraditional settings such as department stores, service stations, and even schools. These satellites typically offer only limited menus and may rely on larger outlets for food storage and preparation. McDonald's is considering opening express outlets in museums, office buildings, and corporate cafeterias.

No longer content to dominate the strips that surround many college campuses, fast-food restaurants have moved onto many of those campuses. The first fast-food restaurant opened at the University of Cincinnati in 1973. Today, college cafeterias often look like shopping-mall food courts. In conjunction with a variety of "branded partners" (for example, Pizza Hut and Subway), Marriott now supplies food to almost 500 colleges and universities. The apparent approval of college administrations puts fast-food restaurants in a position to further influence the younger generation.

More recently, another expansion has occurred: People no longer need to leave the highway to obtain fast food quickly and easily. Fast food is now available at convenient rest stops along the highway. After "refueling," we can proceed with our trip, which is likely to end in another community that has about the same density and mix of fast-food restaurants as the locale we left behind. Fast food is also increasingly available in service stations, hotels, railway stations, airports, and even on the trays for in-flight meals. The following advertisement appeared in the *Washington Post* and the *New York Times* a few years ago: "Where else at 35,000 feet can you get a McDonald's meal like this for your kids? Only on United's Orlando flights." Now, McDonald's so-called "Friendly Skies Meals" are generally available to children on Delta flights. Similarly, in December 1994, Delta began to offer Blimpie sandwiches on its North American flights, and continental now offers Subway sandwiches. How much longer before McDonaldized meals will be available on all flights everywhere by every carrier? In fact, on an increasing number of flights, prepackaged "snacks" have already replaced hot main courses.

In other sectors of society, the influence of fast-good restaurants has been subtler, but no less profound. Though McDonald's and other fast-food restaurants have begun to appear in high schools and trade schools, few lower-grade schools as yet have in-house fast food restaurants. However, many have had to alter school cafeteria menus and procedures to make fast food readily available. Apples, yogurt, and milk may go straight into the trash can, but hamburgers, fries, and shakes are devoured. Furthermore, fast-food chains are now trying to market their products in school cafeterias. The attempt to hook school-age children on fast food reached something of a peak in Illinois where McDonald's operated a program called, "A for Cheeseburger." Students who received A's on their report cards received a free cheeseburger, thereby linking success in school with rewards from McDonald's.

The military has also been pressed to offer fast food on both bases and ships. Despite the criticisms by physicians and nutritionists, fast-food outlets increasingly turn up *inside* hospitals. Though no homes yet have a McDonald's of their own, meals at home often resemble those available in fast-food restaurants. Frozen, microwavable, and prepared foods, which bear a striking resemblance to meals available at fast-food restaurants, often find their way to the dinner table. Then there is also home delivery of fast foods, especially pizza, as revolutionized by Domino's.

McDonald's is such a powerful model that many businesses have nicknames beginning with *Mc.* Examples include "McDentists" and "McDoctors," for drive-in clinics designed to deal quickly and efficiently with minor dental and medical problems; "McChild" Care Centers, for child care centers such as Kinder-Care; "McStables," for the nationwide racehorse-training operation of Wayne Lucas; and "McPaper," for the newspaper *USA TODAY.*

However, it is worth noting that McDonald's is not always crazy about this proliferation. Take the case of *We Be Sushi,* a San Francisco chain with three outlets. A note appears on the back of the menu explaining why the chain was not named "McSushi":

> The original name was *McSushi.* Our sign was up and we were ready to go. But before we could open our doors we received a very formal letter from the lawyers of, you guessed it, McDonald's. It seems that McDonald's has cornered the market on every McFood name possible from McBagle (sic) to McTaco. They explained that the use of the name McSushi would dilute the image of McDonald's.

As powerful as it is, McDonald's has not been alone in pressing the fast-food model on American society and the rest of the world. Other fast-food giants, such as Burger King and Kentucky Fried Chicken, have played a key role, as have innumerable other businesses built on the principles of the fast-food restaurant.

Even the derivatives of McDonald's and the fast-food industry in turn exert their own influence. For example, the success of *USA TODAY* has led many newspapers across the nation to adopt, for example, shorter stories and color weather maps. As one *USA TODAY* editor put it, "The same newspaper editors who call us McPaper have been stealing our McNuggets." The influence of *USA TODAY* is blatantly manifested in *The Boca Raton News,* a Knight-Ridder newspaper. This newspaper is described as "a sort of smorgasbord of snippets, a newspaper that slices and dices the news into even smaller portions than does *USA TODAY,* spicing it with color graphics and fun facts and cute features like 'Today's Hero' and 'Critter Watch'. As in *USA TODAY,* stories in *The Boca Raton News* usually do not jump from one page to another; they start and finish on the same page. To meet this need, long, complex stories often have to be reduced to a few paragraphs. Much of a story's context, and much of what the principals have to say, is severely cut back or omitted entirely. With its emphasis on light news and color graphics, the main function of the newspaper seems to be entertainment. Even the *New York Times* has undergone changes (for example, the use of color) as a result of the success of *USA TODAY.*

The expansion deep into the newspaper business suggests that McDonaldization may be inexorable and may therefore come to insinuate itself into every aspect of society and people's private lives. In the movie *Sleeper,* Woody Allen not only created a futuristic world in which McDonald's was an important and highly visible element, but he also envisioned a society in which even sex underwent the process of McDonaldization. The denizens of his future world were able to enter a machine called an "orgasmatron," which allowed them to experience an orgasm without going through the muss and fuss of sexual intercourse.

Sex actually has, like virtually every other sector of society, undergone a process of McDonaldization. "Dial-a-porn" allows people to have intimate, sexually explicit, even obscene conversations with people they have never met and probably never will meet. There is great specialization here: Dialing numbers such as 555-FOXX will lead to a very different phone message than dialing 555-SEXY. Those who answer the phones mindlessly and repetitively follow "scripts" that have them say such things as, "Sorry, tiger, but your Dream Girl has to go . . . Call right back and ask for me." Escort services advertise a wide range of available sex partners. People can see highly specialized pornographic movies (heterosexual, homosexual, sex with children, and sex with animals) at urban multiplexes and can rent them from local video stores for viewing in the comfort of their living rooms. Various technologies (vibrators, for example) enhance the ability of people to have sex on their own without the bother of having to deal with a human partner. In New York City, an official called a three-story pornographic center "the McDonald's of sex" because of its "cookie-cutter cleanliness and compliance with the law." These examples suggest that no aspect of people's lives is immune to McDonaldization.

The Dimensions of McDonaldization

Why has the McDonald's model proven so irresistible? Four alluring dimensions lie at the heart of the success of this model and, more generally, of McDonaldization. In short, McDonald's has succeeded because it offers consumers, workers, and managers efficiency, calculability, predictability, and control.

First, McDonald's offers *efficiency,* or the optimum method for getting from one point to another. For consumers, this means that McDonald's offers the best available way to get from being hungry to being full. (Similarly, Woody Allen's orgasmatron offered an efficient method for getting people from quiescence to sexual gratification.) Other institutions, fashioned on the McDonald's model, offer similar efficiency in losing weight, lubricating cars, getting new glasses or contacts, or completing income-tax forms. In a society where both parents are likely to work, or where there may be only a single parent, efficiently satisfying the hunger and many other needs of people is very attractive. In a society where people rush, usually by car, from one spot to another, the efficiency of a fast-food meal, perhaps even without leaving their cars by wending their way along the drive-through lane, often proves impossible to resist. The fast-food model offers people, or at least appears to offer them, an efficient method for satisfying many needs.

Like their customers, workers in McDonaldized systems function efficiently. They are trained to work this way by managers, who watch over them closely to make sure they do. Organizational rules and regulations also help ensure highly efficient work.

Second, McDonald's offers *calculability,* or an emphasis on the quantitative aspects of products sold (portion size, cost) and service offered (the time it takes to get the product). Quantity has become equivalent to quality; a lot of something, or the quick delivery of it, means it must be good. As two observers of contemporary American culture put it, "As a culture, we tend to believe deeply that in general 'bigger is better.' " Thus, people order the *Quarter Pounder,* the *Big* Mac, the *large* fries. More recently, there is the lure of the "double this" (for instance, Burger King's "Double Whopper With Cheese") and the "triple that." People can quantify these things and feel that they are getting a lot of food for what appears to be a nominal sum of money. This calculation does not take into account an important point: the extraordinary profitability of fast-food outlets and other chains, which indicates that the owners, not the consumers, get the best deal.

People also tend to calculate how much time it will take to drive to McDonald's, be served the food, eat it, and return home; then, they compare that interval to the time required to prepare food at home. They often conclude, rightly or wrongly, that a trip to the fast-food restaurant will take less time than eating at home. This sort of calculation particularly supports home-delivery franchises such as Domino's, as well as other chains that emphasize time saving. A notable example of time saving in another sort of chain is Lens Crafters, which promises people, "Glasses fast, glasses in one hour."

Some McDonaldized institutions combine the emphases on time and money. Domino's promises pizza delivery in half an hour, or the pizza is free. Pizza Hut will serve a personal pan pizza in five minutes, or it, too, will be free.

Workers at McDonaldized systems also tend to emphasize the quantitative rather than the qualitative aspects of their work. Since the quality of the work is allowed to vary little, workers focus on such things as how quickly tasks can be accomplished. In a situation analogous to that of the customer, workers are expected to do a lot of work, very quickly, for low pay.

Third, McDonald's offers *predictability,* the assurance that their products and services will be the same over time and in all locales. The Egg McMuffin in New York will be, for all intents and purposes, identical to those in Chicago and Los Angeles. Also, those eaten next week or next year will be identical to those eaten today. There is great comfort in knowing that McDonald's offers no surprises. People know that the next Egg McMuffin they eat will taste about the same as the others they have eaten; it will not be awful, but it will not be exceptionally delicious, either. The success of the McDonald's model suggests that many people have come to prefer a world in which there are few surprises.

The workers in McDonaldized systems also behave in predictable ways. They follow corporate rules as well as the dictates of their managers. In many cases, not only what they do, but also what they say, is highly predictable. McDonaldized organizations often have scripts that employees are supposed to memorize and follow whenever the occasion arises. This scripted behavior helps create highly predictable interactions between workers and customers. While customers do not follow scripts, they tend to develop simple recipes for dealing with the employees of McDonaldized systems. As Robin Leidner argues,

> McDonald's pioneered the routinization of interactive service work and remains an exemplar of extreme standardization. Innovation is not discouraged... at least among managers and franchisees. Ironically, though, 'the object is to look for new, innovative ways to create an experience that is exactly the same no matter what McDonald's you walk into, no matter where it is in the world.'

Fourth, *control*, especially through the *substitution of nonhuman for human technology*, is exerted over the people who enter the world of McDonald's. A *human technology* (a screwdriver, for example) is controlled by people; a *nonhuman technology* (the assembly line, for instance) controls people. The people who eat in fast-food restaurants are controlled, albeit (usually) subtly. Lines, limited menus, few options, and uncomfortable seats all lead diners to do what management wishes them to do—eat quickly and leave. Further, the drive-through (in some cases walk-through) window leads diners to leave before they eat. In the Domino's model, customers never come in the first place.

The people who work in McDonaldized organizations are also controlled to a high degree, usually more blatantly and directly than customers. They are trained to do a limited number of things in precisely the way they are told to do them. The technologies used and the way the organization is set up reinforce this control. Managers and inspectors make sure that workers toe the line.

McDonald's also controls employees by threatening to use, and ultimately using, nonhuman technology to replace human workers. No matter how well they are programmed and controlled, workers can foul up the system's operator. A slow worker can make the preparation and delivery of a Big Mac inefficient. A worker who refuses to follow the rules might leave the pickles or special sauce off a hamburger, thereby making for unpredictability. And a distracted worker can put too few fries in the box, making an order of large fries seem skimpy. For these and other reasons, McDonald's has felt compelled to steadily replace human beings with nonhuman technologies, such as the soft-drink dispenser that shuts itself off when the glass is full, the french-fry machine that rings and lifts itself out of the oil when the fries are crisp, the preprogrammed cash register that eliminates the need for the cashier to calculate prices and amounts, and, perhaps at some future time, the robot capable of making hamburgers. This technology increases the corporation's control over workers. Thus, McDonald's can assure customers that their employees and service will be consistent....

A Critique of McDonaldization:
The Irrationality of Rationality

Though McDonaldization offers powerful advantages, it has a downside. Efficiency, predictability, calculability, and control through nonhuman technology can be thought of as the basic components of a *rational* system. However, rational systems inevitably spawn irrationalities. The downside of McDonaldization will be dealt with most systematically under the heading of the *irrationality of rationality;* in fact, paradoxically, the irrationality of rationality can be thought of as the fifth dimension of McDonaldization. The basic idea here is that rational systems inevitably spawn irrational consequences. Another way of saying this is that rational systems serve to deny human reason; rational systems are often unreasonable.

For example, McDonaldization has produced a wide array of adverse effects on the environment. Take just one example: the need to grow uniform potatoes to create those predictable french fries that people have come to expect from fast-food restaurants. It turns out that the need to grow such potatoes has adversely affected the ecology of the Pacific Northwest. The huge farms that now produce such potatoes rely on the extensive use of chemicals. The need to produce a perfect fry means that much of the potato is wasted, with the remnants either fed to cattle or used for fertilizer. However, the underground water supply is now showing high levels of nitrates that may be traceable to the fertilizer and animal wastes. There are, of course, many other ecological problems associated with the McDonaldization of society—the forests felled to produce paper, the damage caused by polystyrene and other materials, the enormous amount of food needed to produce feed cattle, and so on.

Another unreasonable effect of the fast-food restaurant is that it is often a dehumanizing setting in which to eat or work. Customers lining up for a burger or waiting in the drive-through line and workers preparing the food often feel as though they are part of an assembly line. Hardly amenable to eating, assembly lines have been shown to be inhuman settings in which to work.

Of course, the criticisms of the irrationality of the fast-food restaurant will be extended to all facets of the McDonaldizing world. For example, at the opening of Euro Disney, a French politician said that it will "bombard France with uprooted creations that are to culture what fast food is to gastronomy." This clearly indicates an abhorrence of McDonaldization, whatever guise it may take.

... [T]here *are* great gains to be made from McDonaldization. However, [there are] great costs and enormous risks of McDonaldization. McDonald's and the other purveyors of the fast-food model spend billions of dollars each year outlining the benefits of their system. However, the critics of the system have few outlets for their ideas. There are, for example, no commercials between Saturday-morning cartoons warning children of the dangers associated with fast-food restaurants.

A legitimate question may be raised about this critique of McDonaldization: Is it animated by a romanticization of the past and an impossible desire to return to a world that no longer exists? Some critics do base their critiques on the idea that there was a time when life was slower and less efficient, and offered more surprises; when people were freer; and when one was more likely to deal with a human being than a robot or a computer. Although they have a point, these critics have undoubtedly exaggerated the positive aspects of a world without McDonald's, and they have certainly tended to forget the liability associated with such a world. As an example of the latter, take the following case of a visit to a pizzeria in Havana, Cuba:

> The pizza's not much to rave about—they scrimp on tomato sauce, and the dough is mushy.
>
> It was about 7:30 P.M., and as usual the place was standing-room-only, with people two deep jostling for a stool to come open and a waiting line spilling out onto the sidewalk.
>
> The menu is similarly Spartan. . . . To drink, there is tap water. That's it —no toppings, no soda, no beer, no coffee, no salt, no pepper. And no special orders.
>
> A very few people are eating. Most are waiting. . . . Fingers are drumming, flies are buzzing, the clock is ticking. The waiter wears a watch around his belt loop, but he hardly needs it; time is evidently not his chief concern. After a while, tempers begin to fray.
>
> But right now, it's 8:45 P.M. at the pizzeria, I've been waiting an hour and a quarter for two small pies.

Few would prefer such irrational systems to the rationalized elements of society. More important, critics who revere the past do not seem to realize that we are not returning to such a world. In fact, fast-food restaurants have begun to appear in Havana. The increase in the number of people, the acceleration of technological change, the increasing pace of life—all this and more make it impossible to go back to the nonrationalized world, if it ever existed, of home-cooked meals, traditional restaurant dinners, high-quality foods, meals loaded with surprises, and restaurants populated only by chefs free to fully express their creativity.

While one basis for a critique of McDonaldization is the past, another is the future. The future in this sense is defined as human potential, unfettered by the constraints of McDonaldized systems. This critique holds that people have the potential to be far more thoughtful, skillful, creative, and well-rounded than they are now. If the world were less McDonaldized, people would be better able to live up to their human potential. This critique is based not on what people were like in the past, but on what they could be like in the future, if only the constraints of McDonaldized systems were eliminated, or at least eased substantially. The criticisms put forth [here] reflect the latter, future-oriented perspective rather than a romanticized past and a desire to return to it.

POSTSCRIPT

Is Mass Customization the Wave of the Future?

Two conflicting theories of motivation and views of consumer behavior are embedded in the selections by Schonfeld and Ritzer. Schonfeld sees the consumer as an innovator, seeking new market opportunities and willing to invest the time to enter into learning relationships with mass customizers. Ritzer, conversely, portrays the consumer as a Pavlovian buyer, a creature of habit, conditioned and content with the homogenized marketplace of standardized products and services.

It is likely that *levels of involvement* play a significant role in determining consumer attitudes toward mass customization. The concept of *value-ladenedness* is also relevant. How strong is the consumer's affinity with the product? Also, attitudes toward technology and the extent of "consumer sophistication" are rooted in the success of a customization strategy. Are teenage girls with high-tech skills more likely to order Levi's customized jeans than their grandmothers?

With regard to privacy issues, companies like IBM, Disney, and Microsoft refuse to advertise on Internet sites that do not have privacy policies, and reports show that 92 percent of consumers are uncomfortable about Internet sites sharing information. Regulations repressing e-commerce or sharing information can strike to the heart of mass customized strategy. The information age makes customers as the industrial age made products, so consumer information is the most valuable asset. Mass customization companies are keenly aware of the importance their customers place on this issue, and most include a clearly stated "privacy pledge."

Perhaps the idea of customization will trickle down into franchises with user-friendly variations of everything from McDonalds Big Macs to H&R Block tax returns. But research shows that too many choices can turn consumers off. Either way, McDonaldization will likely continue to be a force to be reckoned with.

Suggested Readings

Mark Alfino, John S. Caputo, and Robin Wynward, *McDonaldization Revisted* (Greenwood, 1998)

Steve Alexander, "Mass Customization," *Computerworld* (September 6, 1999)

W. Michael Cox and Richard Alm, "America's Move to Mass Customization," *Consumers' Research Magazine* (June 1999)

Alice Greene, "Two Faces of Mass Customization," *Manufacturing Systems* (March 1999)

John D. Oleson, *Pathways to Agility: Mass Customization in Action* (John Wiley, 1998)

B. Joseph Pine II and Stan Davis, *Mass Customization: The New Frontier in Business Competition* (Harvard Business School Press, 1999)

B. Joseph Pine II, Bart Victor, and Andrew C. Boynton, "Making Mass Customization Work," *Harvard Business Review* (September–October 1993)

George Ritzer, *The McDonaldization Thesis: Explorations and Extensions* (Sage Publications, 1998)

Barry Smart, *Resisting McDonaldization* (Sage Publications, 1999)

John Vidal and Ralph Nader, *McLibel: Burger Culture on Trial* (New Press, 1998)

Mass Customization. `http://www.kellyallan.com/html/mass_customization.html`

Leading Lights: B. Joseph Pine II. `http://www.webcom.com/quantera/llpine.html`

Levi.com. `http://www.levi.com`

Mattel.com. `http://www.mattel.com`

ISSUE 7

Are Outrageous Prices Inhibiting Consumer Access to Life-Sustaining Drugs?

YES: Lucette Lagnado, from "Choosing Between Drugs, Necessities," *The Wall Street Journal Interactive Edition,* <http://www.msnbc.com/news/215703.asp> (January 20, 2000)

NO: Elyse Tanouye, from "U.S. Develops Expensive Habit With Drug Sector Growth Spurt," *The Wall Street Journal Interactive Edition,* <http://www.msnbc.com/news/215163.asp> (January 19, 2000)

ISSUE SUMMARY

YES: Writer Lucette Lagnado asserts that 19 million elderly citizens of the United States have little or no coverage for life-sustaining drugs, yet they are the most disadvantaged consumers. High-priced prescriptions represent an absolute inequity in the system, she argues.

NO: Writer Elyse Tanouye explains that the high prices and profits associated with pharmaceutical drugs are driven by demand, research, and new marketing-driven costs. She contends that a profusion of new drugs has revolutionized the industry but resulted in spiraling costs, which consumers have been forced to absorb.

The sale of prescription drugs is vital to the health care industry, at nearly $1.2 trillion and forecasted to rise even more as baby boomers leave the workforce and require more care in future years. The cost of prescription drugs is now rising at a 20 percent annual increase (up from 12 to 16 percent in 1992). The hardship these rising costs create for the elderly and low-income families is emotionally documented in the cases presented by Lucette Lagnado. She states that one in five elderly take at least five prescription drugs a day, spending as much as 30 percent of their average annual income of $16,000. Nineteen million American senior citizens—or one out of three—have no health insurance coverage, and Medicare does not currently pay for prescription drugs (43 million younger Americans have no coverage). These consumers make the tragic choice between life-sustaining drugs and food for their table. Also, many insurance companies are increasing costs of copayments in response to rising costs.

There are convergent developments responsible for the rapid escalation of the cost of prescription drugs: increasing research and development and an aging population that requires more prescriptions. Drug companies spend 16 to 20 percent of revenues on research and development while the average is 4 to 6 percent for other companies like Boeing Co. and IBM Corporation. Research and development jumped to $21 billion in 1998 alone. Clinical tests are extremely expensive and labor intensive.

But most relevant to this issue is the major influence of direct-to-consumer (DTC) marketing. There is a relatively recent phenomenon in which Americans demand the latest brand name medications, when older and even cheaper medications might be adequate. It seems that DTC marketing was an effort to counteract the effects of generic drugs that provide a lower cost to consumers—but fewer revenues to manufacturers. When drug manufacturers introduce newly patented drugs, they are marketed as differentiated brands at a much higher cost.

Although the trend really began in the mid-1980s, since 1997 the FDA began allowing drug makers to tout the benefits of specific prescription drugs to patients. Advertising spending has skyrocketed to more that $1.3 billion in 1998, up from 1.1 billion in 1994. Industry sources estimate that consumer ad spending has increased 50 percent in the year 2000. Has all of this promotion led to a higher impact on consumers' perception of prescription drugs?

Prescription drugs are one of the fastest growing components of U.S. health care costs. This is fielded by the endless stream of drugs marketed to consumers as a "pull-strategy." Most holding insurance, and spurred by the print and TV ad campaigns, consumers demand that doctors prescribe remedies for everything from depression to toe funguses. The industry spends a fortune on "push" marketing as well. Salespeople, promotions, and print ads to doctors and medical technicians persuade them to prescribe their drugs.

Some of the heaviest advertising has been for *life-enhancing*, rather than *life-sustaining* drugs for problems like baldness, seasonal allergies, and erectile dysfunction. Consumers are now more favorably disposed toward seeking prescribed drugs that enhance their quality of life. As Elyse Tanouye suggests, Americans are demanding the latest brand name drugs in a ferocious attempt to preserve their health and their youth.

Pharmaceutical companies maintain that prescription drugs are extremely cost effective in cutting absenteeism and avoiding expensive medical treatments. While this may be true, there is an increasing demand for the constant flow of new and expensive drugs, whose promotional costs are felt by the entire marketplace. Products like Claritin—with an advertising budget of close to $2 million—generated a payoff of $2.1 billion in 1998. Now consumer groups are bonding together in an effort to buy drugs in bulk, as hospitals do, and gain the savings of group purchasing.

Lucette Lagnado  **YES**

Choosing Between Drugs, Necessities

An aging black-and-white photograph sits on a coffee table in Jewel Brown's immaculate home on a quiet street in Durham, N.C. It shows her as she was half a century ago, a dazzlingly pretty young woman with dark, wavy hair and a hopeful smile.

Today, Mrs. Brown is elderly, ailing and all but broke. She suffers from chronic emphysema, high blood pressure and arthritis. She nearly died from pneumonia [recently] and in October was hospitalized for major complications. Now age 70, she qualifies for Medicare, the federal government's massive program that is supposed to insulate the elderly from the devastating costs of health care.

Yet Medicare has always had a glaring hole in the safety net: With few exceptions, it doesn't cover the costs of prescription drugs—the single largest health-care expense for the elderly.

As a result, some months Mrs. Brown spends up to $400 for medications, more than 30% of her income. Prilosec calms her stomach but sets her back $102.59 for a 30-day supply. Then there are Norvasc for her blood pressure ($43), two inhalers to help her breathe easier ($88 total), two pain medications ($70), nitroglycerin patches for angina ($27.89) and Theophylline to clear her lungs (a bargain at $16.37). Recently, her doctor prescribed Miacalcin, a nasal spray that helps strengthen her bones but depletes her purse by $55.43 a month.

"I need help, I need help real badly," Mrs. Brown says in a raspy voice. She worked for years as a short-order cook and as a caretaker for Alzheimer's patients but gets no pension, living on $780 a month in Social Security and $500 a month in rent from a boarder. She ran up more than $12,000 in credit-card charges between 1994 and 1996 to buy the medications she otherwise couldn't afford. Her daughter, Rebecca, who lives with her, took a second mortgage on their home to pay off her mother's high-interest debt, but Mrs. Brown has had to charge another $2,500 in drugs. She recently resorted to applying for food stamps, but was given only $10 a month in benefits.

Pricey prescription drugs are driving a new surge in health-care costs, but most Americans don't feel it: Their employer insurance plans typically cover most of the expense. But for Mrs. Brown and millions of people in the ranks of "the uncovered," the impact is far more severe.

About 19 million elderly people in the U.S. have little or no drug coverage at all, according to the Congressional Budget Office [CBO]. Nor do an estimated 43 million younger Americans—the unemployed, the working poor, immigrants, illegal aliens, single mothers in part-time jobs—who lack health insurance of any kind.

"There is an absolute inequity in our system," says Aaron Miller, a neurologist who treats multiple-sclerosis patients at Maimonides Medical Center in Brooklyn, N.Y. "The sickest patients are also the most disadvantaged when it comes to drugs." Many of his patients can't afford the $10,000 a year that the newest MS drugs cost, so he tries to get them into clinical trials—even though they have only a 50% chance of getting the real thing rather than a placebo.

The drug crunch is worst for America's elderly. People age 65 or older make up 12% of the U.S. population but consume almost 35% of all prescription drugs. Excluding insurance premiums, drugs account for 34% of older people's total health-care bill, more than doctor visits (31%) and hospital admissions (14%), according to David Gross, a senior policy adviser at the American Association of Retired Persons [AARP].

What's more, about 65% of people 65 and older have two or more chronic diseases, as do 80% of people over 85, the AARP says. As a result, one in five elderly people takes at least five prescription drugs a day. About 2.2 million seniors shell out more than $100 a month for medication, and many pay even more.

Yet Medicare pays for none of it. Medicare, the Great Society program enacted under President Johnson in 1965, now covers health care for nearly 40 million people, including millions with disabilities, at a cost of $200 billion a year. Expanding it to pay for drugs would cost an extra $20 billion annually, according to the CBO. But in an era when balancing the federal budget has been a top priority, Congress has consistently resisted such action—in no small part because of intense opposition from the drug industry, which fears that Medicare coverage might open the way for government price controls.

Five of the 10 top-selling prescription drugs in the U.S. are products heavily used by elderly patients. The aged account for 33% of the sales of No. 1-ranked Prilosec, the anti-ulcer remedy, and generate almost 50% of the sales of the No. 9 entry, Norvasc for high blood pressure, according to Scott-Levin, a research firm in Newtown, Pa.

Roughly half of Medicare-covered patients get some drug assistance, because they are also covered under employer-sponsored insurance plans for retirees, are members of HMOs or are poor enough to qualify for state Medicaid programs, which do pay for prescriptions. But the other half go it alone, and the sicker they are, the less likely they are to get any kind of prescription benefits from insurers. "They don't sell insurance plans to houses already on fire," says Michael Knipmeyer, a lawyer at a legal clinic for seniors run by the George Washington University Law School in Washington, D.C.

Left to their own devices, millions of these elderly resort to resourceful but dubious solutions. They rack up big credit-card debts, plead with their doctors for free samples and forgo basic necessities and little luxuries. Some cross the border into Mexico or Canada, where some drugs are much cheaper because of government price controls. Others go without their prescriptions altogether or skip doses to stretch out their supply, often resulting in medical complications that can send them to the hospital.

Cora Albright, an 84-year-old widow who lives 10 minutes away from Jewel Brown, sometimes skips her medications to make them stretch, a classic habit of the "near poor" elderly. Mrs. Albright, who worked for more than 30 years in a hospital laundry, subsists on a pension of about $90 a month and $700 a month in Social Security. But she spends $200 a month—more than 25% of her income—to stock her medications, including Prilosec, the Astra anti-ulcer drug that costs her more than $100 out-of-pocket, Megace to increase her appetite and Remeron, an antidepressant.

"Then there is the oil bill, the telephone bill, the water bill, the light bill. I have to pay them, and it is a struggle," says Mrs. Albright, who spends much of the day in a wheelchair in her dark living room, her swollen legs swathed in bandages. "It takes about everything I get to make ends meet."

"People are making big-time decisions on what medicines they'll take versus what utility bills they will pay," says Gina Upchurch, director of Senior PharmAssist, an organization she founded in Durham that helps seniors who make too much to qualify for Medicaid but are too poor to afford their medicines. Yet hers is a small program, and there is a long waiting list of people hoping to get in, including Mrs. Brown and Mrs. Albright.

"The system makes no bloody sense," says Frank Larkin, president of Good Samaritan Hospital in Brockton, Mass. "Does it make sense that we give people costly surgeries but we can't give them prescriptions?"

The uncovered elderly, moreover, can end up paying higher prices than the rates paid by HMOs and drug-benefit programs. The drug industry has always denied that such "cost-shifting" occurs. But experience reveals otherwise. At Upchurch Drugs, an independent pharmacy in Durham, owner David Upchurch notes that HMOs get a month's supply of Norvasc, for hypertension, for $33.80—25% less than what Jewel Brown pays.

"Prices are going up for those people who pay cash," Mr. Upchurch says. "We don't have any choice. If you are forced to raise prices, it will happen only where you can—and that tends to be the elderly."

Medicaid's Role

In the absence of a federal drug-benefit program, the poorest of the elderly get some help from Medicaid programs for the indigent. In the past four years, Medicaid's costs have grown by 6% a year, while the cost of drug benefits rose at more than twice that rate, according to data collected by the federal Health Care Financing Administration. "It's one of the fastest-growing parts of the Medicaid budget, and a part that is exceptionally hard to control," says James Verdier, a Medicaid expert at Mathematica Policy Research Inc., a Washington, D.C., social-service research firm.

But even Medicaid is a patchwork. In North Carolina, people's earnings must be 26% below the poverty level to qualify for Medicaid (the federal poverty level is pegged at $8,052 a year for an individual and $10,860 a year for a couple). In Illinois, an older person's earnings must be 46% of the poverty level. In Massachusetts, patients can earn 33% more than the federal poverty level and still get state benefits; that, however, doesn't apply to the elderly, who have to be at the poverty level to qualify, according to Health-Care for All, a Boston advocacy group.

So in some states, thousands of older and disabled people are too poor to afford their prescriptions, yet not impoverished enough to receive coverage. Experts use a buzz-phrase for these patients: the near poor.

Not Poor Enough

Roland and Bessie Pennington, who have been married for 57 years and live in a modest housing project in the shadow of the Capitol in Washington, would seem to be a slam-dunk for Medicaid. Mr. Pennington is 84 and has been retired from his boiler-repairman job for 26 years. He takes 10 prescription drugs to quell high blood pressure, gout, arthritis pain and angina, meticulously tracking every expense and saving every receipt. Last February, for example, he spent $235.09 on drugs, 32% of his monthly Social Security payment of $739. Mrs. Pennington's $350-a-month Social Security check is used by the couple to buy groceries and pay $255 in monthly rent, which was recently reduced to $83.

Yet Mr. Pennington has applied for—and been rejected by—Medicaid four times. Under local Medicaid rules, the couple's combined income is $154 a month over the limit.

So Mr. Pennington improvises. Early each month, he buys only half the prescribed quantity of his most expensive drugs, such as Nitrodur for angina ($51.29 for a full month's supply); then he buys the rest two weeks later—his fear is that he will run low on cash, and so this is his way of budgeting. And rather than use the drugstore a block away from his home, he drives his temperamental 1987 Chevrolet six miles to his old neighborhood and the Safeway he has patronized for 20 years. When he is short of money, the Safeway pharmacist advances him some pills, knowing Mr. Pennington will promptly return to pay up when his Social Security check arrives. The pharmacy near his current home refused to do that.

Sue Andersen, a lawyer at the George Washington University legal clinic, has been trying to help the Penningtons qualify for Medicaid. "The very poor get a free ride, but it is the lower-middle classes who are stuck with bills of $2,000 or more a year," she says.

A $300 a Month Drug Bill

Even aging patients who are financially better-off can feel the pressure. Nathaniel Ashkenaz, 79, a retired appliance repairman, and his wife Thelma, 75, live in El Paso, Texas, on a comfortable pension of $22,800 a year. Yet he worries constantly about how to pay $300 a month in drugs to treat his ulcer and Thelma's diabetes. He crosses the border into Juarez, Mexico, each month to buy 100 Zantac tablets for his ulcer for $24, one-fourth the price he would pay in Texas. But his wife's medications must be purchased stateside: $117 for Rezulin, $126 for cholesterol-lowering Zocor, $33 for Norvasc.

To offset some of the cost, Mrs. Ashkenaz tried to purchase through the AARP a "Medigap" insurance policy, which typically covers half of drug costs. But she was turned down because she was on too many medicines, her husband says. "They said 'Sorry, we can't accept you.'" Then in September, his wife underwent an emergency quintuple-bypass operation, and since has required a slew of additional medications, including Coumadin, at $47, and Amaril for diabetes, at $23.29.

"We are retired and we are getting by, but we aren't rich," Mr. Ashkenaz says. "We can't afford luxuries. We would like to take a trip or go on a cruise, but it isn't feasible."

Waiting for Free Prescriptions

The high cost of drugs also shakes the lives of the young and uninsured. In Brockton, a depressed mill town in eastern Massachusetts, local churches and synagogues have banded together to raise money to dispense free drugs to the poor. On a recent evening, the small waiting room of the Brockton Neighborhood Health Center is crowded with two dozen people hoping to snare free prescriptions—mothers struggling to rein in their children, young men, elderly couples—most of them immigrants from Haiti, Cape Verde, Puerto Rico, Swaziland and the Caribbean.

Maria Chadderton, 41, sits nervously fingering the six prescriptions she has never filled. They are dated from June, and include drugs she needs to manage her diabetes and high blood pressure. "I couldn't fill them. I scarcely have money to get to work," she says. Her take-home pay for working up to 12 hours a day as a home health-care aide has been at most $800 a month, she says. Filling the prescriptions, which include pricey drugs such as Vasotec for blood pressure and Glucophage for diabetes, would set her back a couple of hundred dollars, leaving her unable to pay the rent and buy groceries, she says.

As someone who cares for the ill, Ms. Chadderton has no illusions about the risks she is taking by forgoing the drugs. "I can go into a coma," she says.

"We see this all the time," says Sue Joss, the Brockton clinic's director. "It becomes a choice between filling a prescription and eating." Even so, she says, clinic doctors are under strict orders to give out free medication only to those who expressly state they can't afford it. "If we met all the demand, we would go bankrupt," she says.

The Costs of No Medication

Yet even higher costs loom when people don't get adequate access to prescription drugs, says Stephen Soumerai, who has studied the issue and is chairman of Harvard University's Drug Policy Research Institute. Elderly people who don't get sufficient medication often get too sick to stay independent and end up in the hospital or a nursing home, where care is far more expensive, he says. About

75% of doctor visits result in prescriptions, yet Medicare pays for the visit but won't pay for the resulting therapies, he complains.

"Drugs are the glue that holds the medical system together," Dr. Soumerai says. "We can't afford not to cover people with chronic illnesses, or whose independence rests on access to medications."

Four hours away from Brockton, in the quaint Norman Rockwell country of western Massachusetts, day laborer Ralph Carsno is learning the hard way what it means to be both unhealthy and uninsured. A 38-year-old diabetic, he returned to North Adams, his hometown, a year ago after losing his job in Florida. In July he underwent emergency surgery to clear blocked heart arteries. The surgery was free under a Massachusetts program for the uninsured, but he balked when the pharmacy wanted to charge him more than $200 out of pocket for two pricey medications—Lipitor and Zestril—to manage his cholesterol and hypertension problems.

Half a Prescription

"It was a pretty good chunk of money to spend the day I got out of the hospital, and it really would have put a dent in my budget," Mr. Carsno recalls. He purchased only half the prescription, hoping to scrape together enough money to fill the rest later on. So far, though, he has been recuperating and hasn't earned enough to follow through.

A local aid group, Ecu-Health Care, which comprises local doctors, hospital executives and volunteers, has been trying to help Mr. Carsno. Officials successfully prevailed upon the two companies that make Lipitor and Zestril —the Parke Davis division of Warner-Lambert Co. and Zeneca Group PLC—to hand out free supplies to tide Mr. Carsno over for several months until he can find a job with full drug benefits.

The industry pledged to redouble its efforts to help the indigent even as it fought the Clinton health-reform plan in the early 1990s, but progress has been uneven. The industry says it helped nearly a million people last year with drug giveaways, but the application and approval process differs from company to company.

But Ecu-Health Care officials see the Carsno victory as merely a temporary and unsatisfactory solution. "It's hit and miss—we don't know what we are going to do for folks from month to month," says Charles Joffe-Halpern, Ecu's director. He offers people hope only "on a temporary basis," he says.

Elyse Tanouye

U.S. Develops Expensive Habit With Drug Sector Growth Spurt

America has a new drug problem. A revolution in pharmaceutical research, a billion-dollar marketing blitz and Americans' voracious appetite for Viagra, Claritin and a host of other pricey pills are driving drug spending to record-high levels. And nobody, it seems, knows what to do about it.

Retail pharmacies will rack up an estimated $102.5 billion in sales of prescription drugs by year end, up 85% in just half a decade. Drug sales in the U.S. are rising 16.6% this year, more than four times the increase in healthcare spending overall. And at a time when prices of other manufactured goods have declined by 1%, some generic drug makers have raised the prices of many medications by 10% or more in the past year.

For pharmaceutical companies and their shareholders, the news could hardly be better: Profits for U.S. drug makers are expected to grow 16% to 18% a year for the next four years, far outpacing the 4%-to-7% growth forecast for the nation's top 500 companies.

But the surge is ominous for plenty of others: companies looking to get a handle on employee prescription costs; government-funded health plans weighing the benefits of new therapies against other medical expenditures; uninsured patients who must choose between ever-more-expensive prescriptions and forgoing treatment altogether.

At auto maker Chrysler, spending for employees' prescription drugs has risen 86% in five years to more than $220 million. At Blue Cross Blue Shield of Michigan, drug outlays now represent 28% of total expenditures—more than the amount spent by the health plan on doctor visits. California's Medicaid program for the poor is expected to run 10% over its $1.4 billion pharmaceutical budget for the year because of a spike in drug spending.

The reasons behind the run-up are many and complex. Great advances in research have allowed drug makers to crank out a profusion of new—and expensive—chemicals aimed at treating diseases that were once invincible: AIDS, arthritis, breast cancer, schizophrenia, Alzheimer's, as well as less grave conditions like baldness, wrinkles, toenail fungus and impotence. But with the new

Figure 1

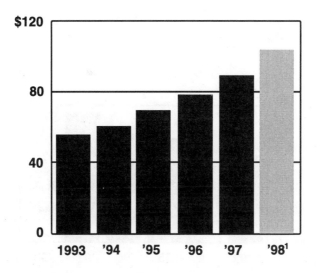

Drug Sales: U.S. Retail in Billions

[1]Forecast

Source: National Association of Chain Drug Stores (outpatient drugs only)

drugs have come soaring development costs, especially for clinical trials, the most expensive part of drug development. At the same time, the growth in generic drugs has failed to bring about a much-anticipated drop in pharmaceutical spending overall.

"Given the rate of innovation in the industry, this situation is going to continue," says Raymond Gilmartin, chairman and chief executive of Merck & Co., maker of the AIDS therapy Crixivan, the cholesterol-lowering Zocor and osteoporosis treatment Fosamax.

Medicating an Aging Population

The pharmaceutical frenzy is expected to get worse in coming years, as drug giants crank out more new medications to salve an aging population. The ranks of people over age 65 will double to about 70 million by the year 2030, growing to 20% of the U.S. population from 13% now. On average, people over 65 fill between nine and a dozen prescriptions a year, compared with two or three for people between the ages of 25 and 44.

"We have a very short window to fix this," says Woodrow Myers, director of health-care management at Ford Motor Co., where drug costs consumed 19% of the $1.5 billion the auto maker spent last year on employee medical costs,

Figure 2

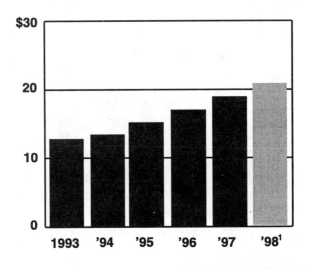

**Research & Development: Drug Companies' Research
and Development Investment, in Billions**

[1]Forecast

Source: Pharmaceutical Research and Manufacturers of America

up from 14% in 1994. "It will get to a point in a couple of years where there will be so many great new products that more and more people can't afford."

While prices of some drugs are rising sharply, higher prices are contributing only 3.2 percentage points of the 16.6% increase in drug spending this year, according to IMS Health Inc., Plymouth Meeting, Pa. A far more important factor: Americans are increasingly demanding the latest brand-name drugs in a ferocious attempt to preserve their health—and their youth.

Marketing Muscle

That owes largely to the marketing might and research prowess of drug makers. They have spent billions building their prescription portfolios, which they once promoted only to doctors, into some of the hottest and most heavily advertised consumer products of the 1990s.

A decade ago, advertising prescription drugs directly to consumers was deemed unseemly. Print advertising began to take off a few years ago after some campaigns, such as Schering-Plough Corp.'s for the antihistamine Claritin, fueled big sales increases. A change in regulatory restrictions on television ads last year unleashed a flood of new commercials.

This year, drug marketers will spend $1.3 billion on consumer ads, seven times what they spent five years ago, according to IMS. In the process, Americans, once merely passive recipients of prescriptions, have turned into savvy and demanding consumers who insist on getting the latest and greatest drugs, even when older and cheaper medications might suffice. And why not? About 192 million Americans, or about three-quarters of the U.S. population, have some sort of prescription-drug insurance that requires them to put up only a small "co-payment" of several dollars to $25 for each prescription.

Pharmaceuticals once were a relatively cheap part of health costs, commonly no more than $2 a pill a few years ago. The new-generation drugs cost $4, $11, even $15 per pill, and they tend to be used far more widely than their predecessors, over longer periods and for a broader range of long-lasting diseases.

The way pharmaceutical companies, as well as many caregivers and patients, see it, investing in drugs now helps avoid far more expensive medical procedures down the road. "Pharmaceuticals are the most cost-effective, value-added, least-invasive part of the health-care system," says Alan F. Holmer, president of the industry's trade group, Pharmaceutical Research and Manufacturers of America, or PhRMA.

The logic is akin to the commercial for one brand of automobile oil filters: "Pay a little more now—or pay a lot later." In recent years, employers and insurers have bought heavily into the pay-me-now premise. But as their drug budgets swell, they will look harder at whether this premise is actually true.

Drug Rations

"All of the new designer technologies . . . have the capacity to increase the quality of life. All are going to be very expensive, and it's going to literally break our bank around the year 2005," says Alan L. Hillman, director of the center for health policy at the University of Pennsylvania. Society will then have to decide how to ration the new technologies, he says.

But how does society calculate the value of drugs that let a 70-year-old woman stave off osteoporosis and spend five more years gardening, when she otherwise might have withered away in a wheelchair? New AIDS drugs have sent mortality rates plunging and pared hospital and other costs, but in the short-term the total costs of treating HIV-infected patients haven't fallen much, according to one study by Merck, maker of Crixivan. The dollars have simply been redirected from hospitals to drug makers.

The federal government has largely left it to private enterprise to hammer out these issues. America is virtually alone among major industrial countries in forgoing controls and letting the market set drug prices. The United Kingdom imposes profit controls, France has a complex system of price controls, and Japan orders broad price cuts every year.

No. 1 in New Remedies

As a result, U.S. firms lead the world in drug development. U.S. companies produced almost half of the new drugs introduced around the world between 1975 and 1994, far more than the next-largest contributor, the U.K. with 14% of the output, according to figures cited by PhRMA. And the pace is accelerating: The drug industry put out 120 new medications from 1995 to 1997, and 30 or so are expected to have made their debut by the end of this year. Merck has introduced eight new drugs and vaccines since 1996, among them Crixivan and the baldness drug Propecia; Warner-Lambert Co. eight, including the cholesterol-lowering Lipitor and diabetes drug Rezulin; and Pfizer five, including the impotence pill Viagra and antibiotic Trovan.

America, says Pharmacia & Upjohn Inc. Chief Executive Fred Hassan, "is the locomotive of growth not only for our company but the entire industry. It is the best market for new products and innovation." Which is why Pharmacia, maker of incontence treatment Detrol and baldness treatment Rogaine, recently relocated its headquarters from London to New Jersey.

But that also means that "the U.S. consumer is subsidizing that investment for the rest of the world. And it isn't fair," says Stephen J. Mock, a spokesman at Warner-Lambert.

Pushing a new drug through years of human trials can run up bills of $150 million or more, and only a tiny fraction ever make it to market. In the U.S., drug prices are typically one-third higher than in Canada and 60% higher than in Britain, according to government studies.

Beating the Generics

"It is the national strategy to rely on a competitive health-care system, and that relies on higher prices in the early phases" of a drug's life, says Patricia Danzon, a professor and drug-pricing expert at the University of Pennsylvania's Wharton School. Prices usually don't come down until later years, after a drug loses patent protection and generic copies start selling at a fraction of the price.

By the time the generics get to market, however, brand-name drug makers have often cranked out a new generation of higher-priced replacements. Case in point: Merck and Monsanto Co. are competing to develop a new class of arthritis painkillers called "Cox-2" inhibitors that promise relief without the severe indigestion that current medications can cause. Such side effects afflict only about 2% to 4% of patients treated for a year with pills currently on the market, several of which are generics. But many people are expected to switch anyway.

Indeed, fully half of the arthritis patients in Michigan's Blue Cross Blue Shield plan are expected to switch when the new medicines hit the market ..., says Marianne Udow, a Blue Cross senior vice president. At an anticipated $2 to $5 a pop, the pills will cost up to 17 times as much as current generic arthritis medications.

Left on their own, drug manufacturers charge rates that often have little to do with actual costs of development. Drugs that can prevent hospital visits carry a big ticket because of the purported savings they offer; others are pricey because they treat such common conditions as baldness or impotence.

Pricing Propecia

Take Merck's baldness treatment, Propecia, which is made from the same chemical, but in a different dosage form, as the company's prostate-shrinking product Proscar. A one-milligram daily dose of the baldness treatment costs $1.25, while a five-milligram daily dose of the prostate medicine costs only 35 cents per milligram, or $1.73 per pill.

"The total amount of active ingredient in a product is only one of many factors in the pricing," says David Anstice, the Merck executive who runs the company's Americas pharmaceutical unit. Other considerations, he says, include competition, the drug's effectiveness, the cost of additional clinical trials, and what the company thinks the patient will perceive as the product's value.

The most important factor, however, is profit. Profit margins in the drug trade are the envy of the corporate world. Prescription pharmaceuticals boast gross profit margins of 90%, and the cost of the raw materials runs only a few cents in pills that often sell for up to $15 apiece. (At the corporate level, of course, profit margins are much lower: Gross margins, which include manufacturing costs, but not selling, research and other expenses, are around 70% industrywide. Net profit margins, after all corporate costs, are about 18% for the industry.) Viagra is pegged by one manufacturing expert at a gross profit margin of 98%, although Pfizer won't comment on that estimate.

The drug giants plow a hefty portion of their returns back into the business. Their research spending runs about 20% of total revenue, compared with 6% at International Business Machines Corp. and about 4% at Boeing Co. The drug industry will spend about $17 billion on research in the U.S. this year, more than the National Institutes of Health's budget of $13.6 billion for fiscal 1998.

Beefing up the Sales Ranks

The business invests billions more—about $11 billion this year, according to IMS Health—to market the newest drugs to doctors and consumers. In the past two years, pharmaceutical companies have hired 40% more sales representatives, called detail people, to pitch prescriptions to doctors, pharmacies and other providers, in large part because of the huge number of new products that the firms have launched.

The recent use of direct-to-consumer advertising has also brought a remarkable change in social perceptions about prescription drugs. "Patients today don't fear them as much as they used to," says Mr. Myers of Ford, almost lamenting the trend. In fact, "patients are specifically looking for a pharmaceutical product as an easy way to deal with whatever malady they have," he says.

Alarmed at the cost, employers and health plans are trying to curb the growth in drug spending by reminding consumers and doctors about cheaper generics. They are also raising co-payments for some drugs and refusing to cover others, such as Viagra and Propecia. More than half of the employers surveyed late last year by William M. Mercer Inc. said they hoped to adopt programs that will better manage their drug costs. In Michigan, a task force of employers, labor unions, health plans, doctors and pharmacies was formed [recently] specifically to look at ways to control pharmaceutical costs.

Figure 3

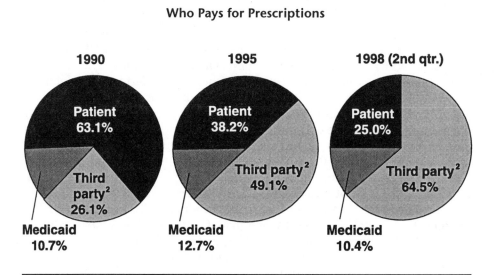

Who Pays for Prescriptions

1990

Patient 63.1%

Third party[2] 26.1%

Medicaid 10.7%

1995

Patient 38.2%

Third party[2] 49.1%

Medicaid 12.7%

1998 (2nd qtr.)

Patient 25.0%

Third party[2] 64.5%

Medicaid 10.4%

[2] Includes health plans and prescription services
Source: IMS Health

Health plans are taking aim first at expensive "lifestyle" drugs that make things more pleasant but don't necessarily tackle life-threatening diseases, such as Viagra, Claritin and rival allergy medicines. Not to mention Lamisil, which was heavily advertised to consumers as "the ultimate pedicure"—truth in advertising, given its cost of about $500 for a 12-week treatment for toenail fungus. A recent "Let Your Feet Get Naked" Lamisil campaign lamented, "People with nail fungus are, well, embarrassed by how their nails look."

'Good Use of Health-Care Dollars?'

"In some cases with respect to the new pharmaceuticals, we are paying lots of money for products that marginally increase the quality of someone's life. Is that a good use of health-care dollars?" asks Bruce Bullen, the Massachusetts Medicaid commissioner and chairman of the National Association of State Medicaid Directors. Five years ago, his state's Medicaid program spent three times as much on hospital stays as it did on drugs. But drug costs are rising so rapidly they will exceed hospital costs within five years, he says.

As a rebuttal, the pharmaceutical industry often cites a 1991 study showing that when New Hampshire restricted the number of prescriptions reimbursed by Medicaid, drug use in the program declined by 35%, but admissions to nursing homes rose by 80%; admissions later returned to normal levels when the restrictions were lifted.

For the time being, the pharmaceutical industry seems more inclined to keep pumping out new drugs and impressive profits than to fret about runaway spending. But that complacency poses risks. Drug companies were vilified for high prices and handsome profits five years ago as the nation debated Clinton health reform, and were impelled to hold back price increases until the furor died down. The business could get whipsawed again if spiraling drug costs once more raise the ire of the public and politicians.

"The pharmaceutical industry is being very shortsighted by not working directly on this problem," says Ford's Mr. Myers. "I hope they don't assume that the pot is limitless, that costs can go up forever."

POSTSCRIPT

Are Outrageous Prices Inhibiting Consumer Access to Life-Sustaining Drugs?

Prescription drug prices in the United States are the highest in the world. Drug companies claim to charge higher prices to pay for product development, yet marketing and administrative costs are shown to be higher than research costs. It seems unconscionable that pharmaceutical companies boast gross profit margins of 90 percent and net profits of 18 percent when so many people are forced to go without necessary drugs due to their prices. Targeting the lucrative profit margins of the pharmaceutical drug trade has not yet been considered as a solution to the runaway costs of prescription drugs, but the notion of price controls may not be ruled out as an alternative.

Several diverse programs are being considered, and there is current speculation over the possibility of the New England states buying prescription drugs in bulk in Canada. Shortly after a shocking *60 Minutes* broadcast, President Bill Clinton launched a task force to examine alternatives and is fighting to have prescription drugs covered by Medicare. This has prompted a $30 million ad campaign by the pharmaceutical industry against such a proposal. The proposed plan would cover one-half of the costs of prescription drugs to $1,000 annually, but the proposal comes with a hefty cost to taxpayers of $168 billion over 10 years. This has indeed become a hot political issue.

Employers are looking for fresh solutions in reining in the escalating costs of new prescription drugs. Some companies, in conjunction with their health plans, have introduced copayment structures designed to encourage employees to use less expensive drug therapies. Others are taking a careful look at their Pharmacy Benefit Management systems (PBMs) in lowering these costs. By forming strategic partnerships with PBMs, companies enjoy economies of scale, which allow them to purchase large amounts of prescription medicines at deep discounts.

Hospitals, too, face a serious struggle with the rising costs of medications as they are increasingly forced to cut costs while trying to provide high-quality care. Since hospitals have no control over the rise in pharmaceutical costs, they are forced to make budget cuts in personnel, which increases their vulnerability to error. Is the high cost of pharmaceuticals indirectly related to the horrifying statistics of 98,000 deaths related to mistakes attributed to U.S. hospitals?

Tanouye poses the question, How does society calculate the value of drugs that let a 70-year-old woman spend five more years gardening when otherwise she might be in a wheelchair? Many agree that marketers have created the demand for quality of life and expensive drugs that work and keep people out of hospitals. But at what cost to society?

Suggested Readings

Alexandra Alger, "Drug Problem," *Forbes* (April 5, 1999)

Catherine Arnst, "Is Good Marketing Bad Medicine?" *Business Week* (April 13, 1998)

Roberto Ceniceros, "Employees Scrutinize Prescription Drug Costs," *Business Insurance* (August 2, 1999)

Matthew Cooper, "The High Cost of Prescriptions May Be the Hot Issue in This Election: What You Should Know About the Problem, and Why the Polls Are Worrying," *Time* (November 22, 1999)

Miles Z. Epstein and David G. Epstein, "Prescription for Success," *HR Magazine* (June 1999)

Scott Hensley, "Another War on Drugs," *Modern Healthcare* (November 15, 1999)

Glen Hess, "Seeking Patent Extension for Branded Drugs," *Chemical Market Reporter* (February 14, 2000)

Matthew F. Hollon, "Direct-to-Consumer Marketing of Prescription Drugs —Creating Consumer Demand," *JAMA* (January 27, 1999)

Rhoda H. Karpatkin, "Are Prescription Drugs Too Expensive?" *Consumer Reports* (October 1999)

J. D. Kleinke, *Bleeding Edge: The Business of Health Care in the New Century* (Aspen, 1998)

Michael Prince, "Health Care Costs on the Rise Again," *Business Insurance* (December 21, 1998)

Adam Zagorin, "Who's Really Raising Drug Prices?" *Time* (March 8, 1999)

Knowledge@Wharton. `http://knowledge.wharton.upenn.edu/articles.cfm?caid=6&articleid=27`

Congress Hears an Outcry Over Prescription Drugs. `http://www.house.gov/bernie/publications/articles/1999-11-07-pharm-stl.html`

ISSUE 8

Will E-Commerce Eliminate Traditional Intermediaries?

YES: Mary Modahl, from *Now or Never: How Companies Must Change Today to Win the Battle for Internet Consumers* (HarperBusiness, 2000)

NO: Mary Beth Grover, from "Lost in Cyberspace," *Forbes* (March 8, 1999)

ISSUE SUMMARY

YES: Mary Modahl, vice president of Forrester Research, establishes that 52 percent of the U.S. population is optimistic about technology and "marching happily toward on-line shopping." She considers this to be the beginning of a dramatic 10-year transition in consumer behavior.

NO: *Forbes* editor Mary Beth Grover argues that despite the allure of no sales payroll or the fixed costs of bricks-and-mortar merchants, turning a profit in cyberspace is no easy task. Furthermore, the hurdles can be even higher for traditional retailers going online.

Even until a few years ago, most goods were sold through marketing channels, which were sets of linearly organized intermediaries, involved in moving products from the manufacturer to the retailer. Intermediaries smoothed the flow of goods and services, which was necessary in order to bridge the discrepancy between the assortment of goods and services generated by the producer and the assortment demanded by the consumer. Manufacturers typically produce a large quantity of goods, whereas consumers usually desire only a limited quantity, but from a wide variety of goods.

Clearly, the influence of e-commerce on traditional intermediaries strikes to the heart of physical distribution. Internet commerce is not a product but a powerful agent transforming the very means by which exchange takes place and titles to goods are moved. *Business Week* estimates that doing business on the Internet could increase the U.S. gross domestic product (GDP) by $10 to $20 billion annually by 2002. Electronic sales to consumers is expected to grow sixfold to almost $200 billion in the next few years. Reduced costs from implementing e-commerce are 5 to 10 percent as a share of sales.

E-commerce has clearly brought about "disintermediation," enabling the customer to transact directly with the firm without involving intermediaries. Mary Modahl highlights the advantages and impact of e-commerce on the transformation of marketing. Identifying customer attitudes and segmenting those favorably disposed toward the new technology is crucial. She believes the Internet is reengineering distribution systems in many diverse industries. Some predict that over 90 percent of consumer products will soon be delivered to the home.

Yet, according to many, the idea of eliminating the middleman is an illusion. Disintermediation is in fact creating an opposite effect, called *hypermediation*—the growth of online intermediaries facilitating transactions. Even insignificant transactions routinely involve several intermediaries, not just the traditional wholesalers and retailers, but content providers, affiliate sites, search engines, portals, Internet service providers, software makers, and several other parties.

Marketing channels created by e-commerce come in many shapes and sizes. Many are familiar with business-to-consumer (B2C) as well as business-to-business (B2B) systems. The network company Cisco reportedly overtook Microsoft recently as being the most valued company, accentuating the growth in the later sector. In some cases, the transactions can take place through intermediaries to both consumers and businesses. CarsDirect.com, an Internet site where many car manufacturers sell their products to end consumers, is a good example of a business-to-intermediary-to-consumer (B2I2C) channel, while VerticalNet exemplifies a business-to-intermediary-to-business (B2I2B) model, since this company has created targeted business-to-business "vertical trade communities" on the Internet. In essence, this enables a central "e-hub" for all B2B stakeholders to aggregate and match their offerings.

In some cases the consumer is the initiator of the channel. Consider the case of Priceline.com for instance. This is a classic exemple of a consumer-to-intermediary-to-business (C2I2B) channel, since the individual originates the transaction. NexTag.com is another example in this category. Consumers can even interact amongst themselves through an intermediary, i.e., consumer-to-intermediary-to-consumer (C2I2C), as exemplified in how eBay or epinions.com operates.

Mary Beth Grover is skeptical about the movement of commerce to the electronic media. She points to the probability that e-commerce will "cannibalize" retail sales. Hidden costs, the complexities of advertising an Internet site, technology expenditures, and the cost of customer support are looming as problems for dot.com ventures. Online shopping provides consumers with a broader array of information, choice, and convenience, but shopping sites cannot truly replace some of the "real-world thrills" of shopping.

Mary Modahl

 **YES**

Now or Never

W e have entered a time when doing business over the Internet is no longer a novelty but a necessity. Electronic sales to consumers will pass $20 billion in 1999, and Forrester [Research] and others project a more than sixfold increase in the next few years (see Figure 1).

In addition, Internet commerce affects business far beyond the scope of actual sales, as start-ups challenge long-standing business practices in many consumer industries. Traditional company managers note alarming trends, such as:

- **New pricing models that undermine existing revenues.** In many cases, Internet companies bet that they can lower prices and make up revenues on volume. In financial services, for example, Internet companies charge individual investors low flat-rate fees instead of variable commissions on trading.
- **Higher customer-service expectations.** Internet businesses are open twenty-four hours a day, seven days a week, and they allow consumers to help themselves to information about products before buying. Some of the busiest hours for these new companies occur during workweek breaks, when consumers at the office take ten minutes to buy a gift or plan a weekend away.
- **New ways to distribute products.** Internet companies build their businesses around home delivery—even in markets where home delivery has never existed before. This has caught traditional companies, which focus on consumers' in-store experience, off guard. For example, traditional booksellers believed that people wanted to touch a book before buying it. And grocers thought that consumers would never trust a service to choose their family's food. In both cases, past experience led to the wrong conclusion.
- **Unexpected market opportunities.** Because the Internet connects people across very wide distances at extremely low cost, start-ups can dream up services that literally were never possible before. Take, as an example, consumer-to-consumer auctions, which bring together millions of people to offer or bid on hundreds of thousands of items daily.

- **High rates of entry—even in very staid markets.** Conservative industries such as newspaper classified advertising, which had not seen a significant entrant in decades, find themselves challenged by newcomers.

Figure 1

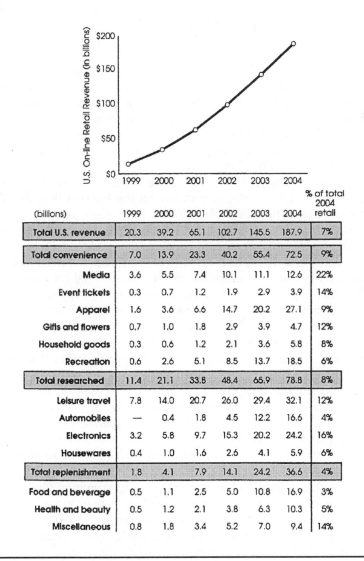

U.S. On-line Retail Projections by Category

(billions)	1999	2000	2001	2002	2003	2004	% of total 2004 retail
Total U.S. revenue	20.3	39.2	65.1	102.7	145.5	187.9	7%
Total convenience	7.0	13.9	23.3	40.2	55.4	72.5	9%
Media	3.6	5.5	7.4	10.1	11.1	12.6	22%
Event tickets	0.3	0.7	1.2	1.9	2.9	3.9	14%
Apparel	1.6	3.6	6.6	14.7	20.2	27.1	9%
Gifts and flowers	0.7	1.0	1.8	2.9	3.9	4.7	12%
Household goods	0.3	0.6	1.2	2.1	3.6	5.8	8%
Recreation	0.6	2.6	5.1	8.5	13.7	18.5	6%
Total researched	11.4	21.1	33.8	48.4	65.9	78.8	8%
Leisure travel	7.8	14.0	20.7	26.0	29.4	32.1	12%
Automobiles	—	0.4	1.8	4.5	12.2	16.6	4%
Electronics	3.2	5.8	9.7	15.3	20.2	24.2	16%
Housewares	0.4	1.0	1.6	2.6	4.1	5.9	6%
Total replenishment	1.8	4.1	7.9	14.1	24.2	36.6	4%
Food and beverage	0.5	1.1	2.5	5.0	10.8	16.9	3%
Health and beauty	0.5	1.2	2.1	3.8	6.3	10.3	5%
Miscellaneous	0.8	1.8	3.4	5.2	7.0	9.4	14%

Not all figures add up due to rounding
Source: Forrester Research, Inc.

These trends suggest that even giant consumer companies can no longer ignore the possible impact of the Internet. Traditional companies must take part in the new market and defend themselves against the incursion of the start-ups.

The stage is set for the battle for Internet consumers—a conflict that will span more than ten years as companies adjust their strategies to take advantage of the Internet's ability to let consumers buy anytime, anywhere. On one side of this battle stand the established corporations—companies and brands that people have known since childhood. On the other stand the "dotcoms," start-ups that believe they can offer consumers a better deal and become a household name in the process.

The battlefield is uneven. Start-ups, with their Internet birthright, have the advantage. Being small, newer companies can move quickly, and their entire business revolves around a single focus. In addition, start-ups have had easy access to venture funding and more risk-tolerant investors than traditional companies. But most important, the dotcoms have nothing to lose if the old ways of doing business fade away.

Traditional companies have developed a core of well-understood business practices. Although this core is valuable, it also creates a gravity field, trapping the company by continually pulling it back toward the way it has always done business. This gravity can make it amazingly difficult for traditional companies to understand fully what changes are possible in their industries. Even when they do understand, it is tough for them to act. So many old, comfortable habits must be broken in order to compete on the Internet that, in truth, few traditional companies have been able to do it well.

The fact that smaller, venture-backed companies have done better on the Internet so far has led many people to conclude that traditional companies have no chance of winning the battle for Internet consumers. But this black-or-white conclusion fails to take account of the fact that traditional companies are only now beginning to fight back. With a few exceptions, start-ups have not yet faced any significant competition for their share of the Internet market.

Moreover, the early success of the start-ups has actually created the single biggest problem they face. As the start-ups grew and investor excitement about their prospects mounted, these barely formed entities found that they could offer public stock without being profitable. As a result, most of the rewards for growing an Internet business from scratch have already been reaped—in advance. Regardless of where the market heads next, the far-too-fast run-up in the value of tiny Internet companies in early 1999 spawned a cancer among the dotcoms. Getting rich quick is now a built-in expectation of start-up employees —a situation that makes it very difficult for a dotcom leader to grow a lasting enterprise.

Traditional companies also bring significant strengths to the battle for Internet consumers. First and foremost, consumers trust the companies they have done business with for decades. This familiarity will turn out to be an important advantage as Internet commerce spreads from the bolder consumers who first got on the Internet in the mid-1990s to the more reluctant mainstream. The more wary consumers are, the more that knowing the brands helps them get on-line and shop. In addition, traditional companies can span on-line and off-line venues. It is tough for any start-up to match the physical presence and consumer awareness of an established company that owns a chain of stores, or runs billboard, TV, and radio advertising.

In the end, the winners—and the losers—in the battle of the Internet will include both traditional companies and start-ups. Among the winners will be traditional companies that can learn to compete on Internet terms and start-ups that manage their way sanely through the turbulence of high growth and inflated expectations. Traditional companies that fail to understand the new environment will be left behind, and start-ups that keep losing money won't survive.

An Overview...

The Internet changes many of the rules of doing business.... But the most important rules, such as "know your customer," "add real value," and "differentiate from competitors," haven't really changed at all. The same frameworks that managers have used to understand business all along still apply.

Both traditional companies and Internet start-ups must accomplish three objectives in order to ultimately succeed....

1. **Understand Internet consumers.** The early adopters of the Internet are far different from the mainstream consumers who follow. As the Internet spreads to a broader cross section of households, the tastes and requirements of the average Internet consumer will change. Only companies that understand the different types of Internet consumers will be able to target the right people with the right products, services, and messages.
2. **Exploit Internet business models.** The Internet makes markets more competitive because buyers and sellers can find each other more easily. Companies must understand how revenues, costs, and value creation are affected by this heightened competitiveness.
3. **Defy the gravity of the old ways of doing business.** As Internet businesses expand, age-old management challenges such as continuous technology change, sales-channel conflict, funding, organization, and leadership take on new forms. At the outset of the battle of the Internet, traditional companies have far more gravity to contend with than start-ups do. Yet every organization, especially those that formed around the World Wide Web, must expect continued rapid technology change, and with it, new ways of doing business. The Web as we know it is not the final word from the computer industry.

Understanding Internet Consumers

[I attempt to] unravel... the mystery of why consumers buy on the Internet. I am going to share with you a very important discovery that we have made at Forrester Research: When it comes to determining whether consumers will or won't go on the Internet, how much they'll spend, and what they'll buy, demographic factors such as age, race, and gender don't matter anywhere near as much as the consumers' *attitudes toward technology.*

Forrester's researchers first began to realize the importance of technology attitudes in mid-1997. At the time, we were writing a report on the personal computer market. PCs cost an average of almost $2,000 apiece back then, and partly for that reason, only about 40 percent of American households had them. Yet some homes had more than one. In fact, some were onto their third and even fourth PC. We wanted to know if all the growth in the industry would come from this same 40 percent of households or if the rest of the population would eventually start buying computers, too. And if so, at what price?

As we analyzed mountains of data about PC purchasing patterns, we noticed that college students and senior citizens had very distinctive PC buying and usage patterns. College students saw their PCs as a necessity for school as well as a source of entertainment. They bought the latest, most powerful PC they could afford, and they often added on graphics accelerators and joysticks to play games. Senior citizens, who were far less likely to buy computers overall, bought standard models and viewed them as fancy typewriters.

But when we looked at the remaining category—the twenty-five to fifty-five-year-olds that make up the majority of the population—we found that age and life interests could not explain PC buying behavior on a consistent basis. If you took three demographically identical families, you would find one family that liked its first PC so much it bought a second one, another that owned a PC but never used it, and another with no plans to buy a PC at any price.

We began to think that maybe something else—something beyond age, income, or number of children—was driving consumer behavior. Maybe people's actions were determined by their *attitude toward technology itself.* Perhaps some consumers were inherently *optimists* about technology, believing that it could help them in their lives, while others were *pessimists* who were afraid of using computers, hostile toward them, or simply indifferent.

Over the next eighteen months, Forrester, with the help of our partners at NPD Group, mounted a massive research effort to test this hypothesis and, if it proved to be correct, to identify which consumer activities were most affected by attitudes toward technology. When all was said and done, the research project involved questionnaires, focus groups, and interviews with more than 250,000 North American consumers—the largest study of consumer technology adoption ever conducted in North America.

When the results were in, we found that attitude toward technology indeed affects consumer PC buying more than any other factor. In fact, it turns out that consumers' attitudes influence their adoption of all kinds of digital technology—including Internet connections, cellular telephones, and digital TV. Not only that, these latent beliefs also affect how quickly consumers will shop on-line, how much money they will spend, and how fast they will progress from merely looking at products on-line to actually buying them.

Forrester used the information we gathered to create a new tool for understanding consumers. We call our tool Technographics because it is a system of classifying consumers, just like demographics or psychographics. Yet unlike these other schema, Technographics is custom-made for the Internet economy.

Rather than separating consumers by age or lifestyle, this new system segments people according to their behavior as *digital* consumers.

Technographics segments consumers according to their attitude toward technology, their motivation to use technology, and their ability to afford technology (see Figure 2 and [the box entitled "Definitions of Technographics Segments"])....

Figure 2

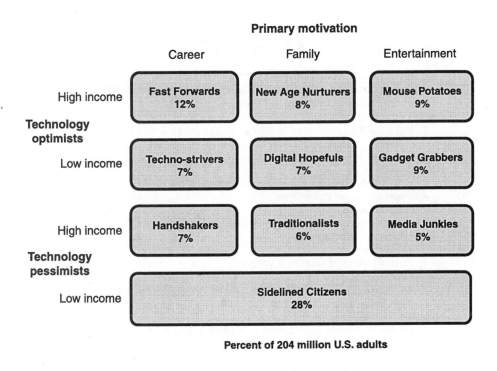

Consumer Technographics Segments in the U.S.

Primary motivation

	Career	Family	Entertainment
High income **Technology optimists**	Fast Forwards 12%	New Age Nurturers 8%	Mouse Potatoes 9%
Low income	Techno-strivers 7%	Digital Hopefuls 7%	Gadget Grabbers 9%
High income **Technology pessimists**	Handshakers 7%	Traditionalists 6%	Media Junkies 5%
Low income	Sidelined Citizens 28%		

Percent of 204 million U.S. adults

Source: Forrester Research, Inc.

Exploiting Internet Business Models

.... [T]he Internet is changing supply and demand, moving consumer industries toward a new competitive environment that Forrester calls *Dynamic Trade*. The changes caused by Dynamic Trade are at once so simple and so profound that their full impact can be difficult to grasp.

Consider, for example, the way minivans are sold today. Somewhere in Texas, at the intersection of two crosstown highways, stands a four-acre square of asphalt where a dealer displays the models currently on sale from Chevrolet.

In the far corner are parked five minivans, all green. In walks a couple with their hearts set on a white minivan.

Now this dealer has a salesman, an ambitious young fellow whose sole job is to convince this couple that what they really want is a green minivan, because the dealer isn't getting a white one in until next month. Luckily, the young salesman is so talented that by the end of the month he has not only convinced *this* couple to buy a green minivan but has sold the remaining four.

DEFINITIONS OF TECHNOGRAPHICS SEGMENTS

Digital Hopefuls *n. pl.*
   1. family-oriented technology lovers with low incomes;
   2. promising future market for low-cost PCs
Fast Forwards *n. pl.*
   1. high-income, career-oriented technology adopters;
   2. driven careerists, time-strapped, often in dual-income households;
   3. leading users of business and productivity software
Gadget Grabbers *n. pl.*
   1. lower-income consumers focused on tech-based entertainment;
   2. Nintendo/Sega games;
   3. buyers of low-cost, high-tech toys
Handshakers *n. pl.*
   1. successful professionals with low technology tolerance;
   2. dealmakers and executives
Media Junkies *n. pl.*
   1. high-income, entertainment-oriented individuals—not PC savvy;
   2. visual consumers;
   3. TV lovers;
   4. early adopters of satellite TV
Mouse Potatoes *n. pl.*
   1. high-income, entertainment-focused technology consumers;
   2. those dedicated to interactive entertainment, especially on a PC
New Age Nurturers *n. pl.*
   1. affluent believers in technology for family and education;
   2. least-served group of future technology consumers
Sidelined Citizens *n. pl.*
   1. low-income technophobes;
   2. the least receptive audience for any technology;
   3. technology laggards
Techno-strivers *n. pl.*
   1. up-and-coming believers in technology for career advancement;
   2. students or young professionals;
   3. of low-income segments, this group has the highest percentage of computer ownership
Traditionalists, *n. pl.*
   1. high-income, family-minded individuals suspicious of technology;
   2. Midwestern and small-town dwellers with little technology beyond VCRs

Source: Forrester Research, Inc.

The dealer is thrilled. He didn't expect to sell the green minivans anytime soon, since consumers vastly prefer white in this Texas town. He gladly pays the salesman fifteen hundred dollars in commission. Back in Detroit, the data comes in: Green minivans are hot in Texas. Make some more.

The lack of information in the selling system results in a loss of value for both the consumers and the manufacturer in this scenario. What would happen if the consumers used the Internet to find their car? For starters, the couple would never even go out to the crosstown dealer because they would know in advance that he doesn't have what they want. Instead, they would locate a dealer who could supply a white minivan. Next, because the information about sales is captured electronically, the manufacturers would not make more *green* minivans; it would make more *white* ones. The salesman and the dealer would lose out. Fewer minivan buyers would require such a hard sell in a market with better information flow....

Defying the Gravity of the Old Ways of Doing Business

[I identify] the impediments to Internet success that traditional companies face. First among these impediments is the challenge that traditional companies, and in fact many start-ups too, face in managing technology change. The Internet has increased the level of dependence of consumer businesses upon technology, and consequently, companies need a new level of competence at technology management....

Many companies avoid selling on the Internet mainly because they fear that doing so would cause a backlash among their retail partners. Being new, start-ups have not had to grapple with the paralyzing reality of angry retailers, dealers, franchisees, and brokers....

The View Through the Crystal Ball

"Yes, yes, yes," you think. "Now tell me what will happen. Who will win and who will lose?"

Personally, I expect that in every consumer industry, at least one or two of the traditional leaders will fail to make the transition to the Internet. Likewise, winners will emerge in every sector from among the start-up companies. Forrester regularly handicaps individual players in most e-commerce segments, and I welcome you to compare notes on the current standings at www.forrester.com.

Yet I think it only fair to say that the winners and the losers in the battle for Internet consumers have yet to be determined. Many of the early hotshot companies will fall prey to unrealistic expectations on the part of their investors, employees, and consumers. Some of the least involved traditional companies will at some point pivot toward the Internet with astonishing impact.

One thing is clear: The time for waiting and watching is past. The Internet is quickly moving from being merely a curiosity to being really useful. Before long, many consumers will see the Internet as a necessity. Any company that wants to be a player on the Internet will have to have its position staked out before that happens.

Mary Beth Grover

Lost in Cyberspace

Electronic commerce is a merchant's dream: no costly stores, no payroll for salespeople, slim inventory costs. In four years almost 90,000 on-line merchants have opened shop. Build a Web site and they will come.

Traditional retailers embrace the dream, too—about 40% are on the World Wide Web and most others plan to join them, according to an Ernst & Young survey. On-line sales totaled $8 billion [in 1998] and could grow tenfold in four years.

Promising, but now comes the hard part: turning a profit. Behind high-tech screens are some distinctly low-tech costs. On-line sellers that had dreamed of avoiding bricks and mortar are now building distribution centers and ware-houses. The Web's ability to compare prices at the click of a button sparks jarring discounts and costly coupon wars. And for all those eyeballs on-line, marketing consumes a frightful chunk of revenues.

The hurdles can be even higher for traditional retailers going digital. Their on-line sales may simply cannibalize sales they would have racked up off-line—that is, in the real world. Their backshop infrastructures were built to dispatch truckloads of goods to hundreds of stores—not ship small orders to millions of individual customers. (Catalog companies are better equipped but have their own worries.)

Manufacturers hoping to sell directly to consumers risk the wrath of the dealers and wholesalers that provide most of their revenues. In short, the Web is both the problem and the opportunity.

No wonder some merchants venture into cyberspace with no small amount of dread. Borders, the second-largest chain of bookstores, opened its Web site last May [1998] but wasn't exactly ecstatic about it. The 1,145-store chain's chief executive, Philip Pfeffer, sounds like one reluctant cybernaut: "Books, music and video have all been substantially discounted. Consumers get good value, but in the long run margins are inadequate to support the business regardless of how much volume is done."

Pfeffer worries that Web profits may never come. Borders expects the Web effort to run a loss of $10 million this year and $20 million the next. The chain's stock tumbled 38% when those prospects and other snags were disclosed in early January [1999]. It hasn't recovered. Seems investors, unfazed by red ink for on-line upstarts with "dot-com" in their names, are unforgiving when the same applies to old-line firms going on the Web.

Yet Pfeffer, like many marketers—like your company, most likely—has little choice but to go on-line. His rivals at Barnes & Noble had preceded him onto the Web, and both chains had good reason to fear the soaring sales of Amazon.com.

Amazon opened up shop in 1995 and offered discounts of 30% on best-sellers. Barnes & Noble turned up the heat on-line in May 1997 by offering 40% off. Wal-Mart, one of the largest booksellers, has a Web outpost slashing 45% off list prices—and upstart Buy.com promises 50% discounts.

So Pfeffer opened a vein and bled, offering on-line discounts even as he jacked up spending for the privilege of doing it. To gear up for shipping tiny orders to thousands of customers, Borders had to build a separate $15 million distribution center in LaVergne, Tenn. All told, the distribution costs of an on-line storefront can be surprisingly high—about 15% of sales for Web sellers like Borders.

At the front end, Borders had to get cybershoppers into its on-line store. On the Web, that can mean paying hefty fees to other sites for referring their visitors to yours. It is a kind of rent: Popular "portals" like Yahoo lure the critical mass of eyeballs, so e-commerce companies pay for prominent placement on Yahoo and for customer "click-throughs." Such rent and other marketing costs can run to 65% of sales, says the Boston Consulting Group.

Borders spent $5 million marketing its new Web site in 1998 and could lay out $20 million this year. Pfeffer won't confirm the numbers but laments: "I can remember hearing this is a great model. With bricks and mortar comes rent. But the fact is, real estate costs on-line are significant. It makes it really difficult to get profits."

For existing retailers, the scary prospect is that the less-profitable setting of the Web—rather than create extra sales from new customers—will simply siphon off the higher-margin sales from their stores. That could happen at Borders. Buying two or more books can be instantly cheaper on its Web site than in its stores largely because customers can avoid state sales taxes. (Retailers must collect the tax only in the states where they have a physical presence. Borders' separate on-line unit has only two such outposts: the warehouse in Tennessee, and headquarters in Ann Arbor, Mich.)

So Pfeffer looks for other upsides. Even if his Web site never turns a profit, he hopes it can increase sales *in stores*. Shoppers frustrated by sold-out stock and hard-to-get titles can now place special orders via Web-linked PCs in Borders outlets. This approach could bring in several million dollars in revenue in each quarter, less than 1% of total sales.

Of course, the Web is supposed to be a sales outlet unto itself, and virtually no on-liner has more experience at it than Amazon. And rarely have so many companies been thrown into so much panic by a company that loses so much money. In the past three years Amazon lost a cumulative $162 million on sales of $774 million. Indeed, the deficit has grown nearly as rapidly as revenue. As a percentage of sales, Amazon's net loss has actually gotten worse, widening from 16.4% in the last quarter of 1997 to 18.4% in the last quarter of 1998. Amazon expects more losses for the foreseeable future.

Even for a pure on-liner like Amazon, distribution costs are a huge drain. When Jeffrey Bezos founded Amazon in 1994, he planned to rely heavily on Ingram Books, the largest book wholesaler in the U.S. The concept: Ingram would keep his inventory—and the costs that go with keeping inventory.

Bezos bragged of offering 1.1 million titles while stocking just 500 best-sellers, in a single 45,000-square-foot warehouse. He set up shop in Seattle in part because of its proximity to some Ingram operations. But he stopped short of letting Ingram handle shipping to individual customers, insisting on deploying his own force to ensure quality of service.

Three years later Amazon relied on Ingram for 60% of its books. That portion has since declined, and today two-thirds of Amazon's 2,100 employees work on customer "fulfillment," placing orders, packing shipments and answering customer e-mails and processing credit card charges. That consumes close to 10% of revenue, and it could go higher.

Now Ingram is being bought for $600 million by Amazon's rival, Barnes & Noble. Ingram hopes to keep supplying Amazon, but Amazon is increasingly sidestepping Ingram to buy directly from publishers.

To house all its new inventory, Amazon is opening its third warehouse—a colossal seven-acre facility in Fernley, Nev.—with plans for a fourth and possibly a fifth one. Staffing costs will grow accordingly.

Worth it? Even Sam Walton of Wal-Mart shaved his cost of goods sold only 2% below his competitors by buying direct. Amazon says its gross margins on books have risen four percentage points in 18 months. But music CDs now provide 13% of sales, a big reason the on-liner's overall gross margin fell by 1.6 points, to 21.1%.

Perhaps Amazon will find profits in becoming an on-line landlord. In December Bezos launched a "shop the Web" program, charging "e-tailers" rent to be featured on Amazon. Cyberspace is getting to be as expensive as a storefront on Rodeo Drive. Barnes & Noble's on-line unit is paying America Online an eye-popping $40 million to lock in space as AOL's exclusive bookseller for four years. A bargain?

"I've always felt these portal deals were way too expensive and lock you in for way too long," says Darryl Peck, head of Cyberian Outpost, a Web seller of computers. "No one knows if they're going to work or not."

Music sellers N2K and CDNow agreed to merge in part because their already-ailing finances were hurt by contracts to spend, between them, $108 million for similar marketing agreements. That is almost half their hoped-for full-year revenue—a costly promotion, to be sure. "We don't want to go out and talk about how it's not working," says N2K Chief Executive Jon Diamond. He has renegotiated some deals, which could reduce the cost by $10 million.

Such savings can get eaten up quickly by other needs. Ad budgets are a big jolt. Last summer software seller Beyond.com began a six-month TV blitz for $10 million—exceeding its entire third-quarter sales. Buy.com, an on-line discount store, paid $1.6 million for a single 30-second spot on the Super Bowl.

Special promotions are *de rigueur*. At the Buy.com site, you can get an Agfa digital camera for $723.95—and a $250 Clik disk drive free of charge. Computer

Literacy, an on-line seller of computer books, offers some software developers $19.95 off any purchase north of that amount.

Technology spending can be a drain, too. 1-800-Flowers poured $13 million into its new Web site and will spend $15 million in the next two years to upgrade it. "We've been profitable thus far. Now we're plunging into the dark," says Chief Executive James McCann. "Still, we do believe it's the future. We're betting all our chips on it."

The Web was supposed to all but wipe out the cost of customer support, letting mouse-clicks replace phone orders. Don't count on it. During the Christmas rush, Shopping.com's support lines were swamped with callers who needed a human touch. Some of them were left on hold for an hour. The Web discounter, which sells watches, Cuisinarts and other goods, doubled its support staff to 50 people, easily adding another $1.5 million a year in costs. Yet revenue for the nine months ended Oct. 31 totaled just $4 million.

Compaq Computer Corp. is willing to forgive Shopping.com its cost problems, for now. It has agreed to buy the upstart for $200 million.

Will these Web selling costs go away? Probably not. Web sellers have noticed that on-line buyers are indecisive, filling up their digital shopping baskets as they proceed through a site, but then erasing two-thirds of their purchases before reaching the checkout. They lose their nerve or can't find their way out.

"The bottom line is that e-commerce companies have to spend more on phone centers than bargained for," says Ajit Pendse, founder of Beaverton, Ore.-based Efusion. His firm offers a fix. He pushes "pop-up" buttons on Web pages that could route frustrated customers who are ready to bail out to a service rep, turning the PC into a speakerphone.

There must be some way to make money. Ebay, the auctioneer, is one of the few Websters to turn a profit, in part because it refuses to fuss with "fulfillment"; customers who use the site must do the work to get the booty shipped from buyer to seller. Beyond.com hopes to cut delivery costs by zapping more copies of software over phone lines into customers' PCs.

Scott Blum, the founder of Buy.com, plans to sell some products below cost—in the expectation of building a large enough audience that he can make money on advertising. He hopes so many customers stampede his way that *other* Web sites will pay him big bucks for customer referrals.

Good luck to him. Someone will get it right, but along the way hype and hope will collide with harsh realities. "This is just a catalog retail business with lower barriers to entry. Margins, if they ever materialize, will always be crummy," grouses Michael Murphy, a veteran tech investor in Half Moon Bay, Calif. He may be right.

POSTSCRIPT

Will E-Commerce Eliminate Traditional Intermediaries?

E. Raymond Corey wrote in his classic text *Industrial Marketing: Cases and Concepts,* 4th ed. (Prentice Hall, 1991) that a distribution system is a key external resource. "Normally, it takes years to build, and it is not easily changed. It represents a commitment to a set of policies and practices that constitute the basic fabric on which is woven an extensive set of long-term relationships."

How much of this is true today with the proliferation of e-markets? With the advent of Internet markets and e-hubs, the lines between what is internal and what is external is increasingly blurring. Proctor & Gamble, Coca-Cola Co., Unilever, and other packaged goods companies have begun buying everything from corn syrup to plastic online. Today's competitive battles are being waged by one "value chain against another," not firm versus firm.

Are the Internet initiatives truly distinguishable from traditional businesses? Some say that most innovative Internet players are integrating their virtual and physical operations in a myriad of ways. Office Depot's Web site, for example, by giving information about store locations and inventory online, has actually increased the traffic at its physical outlets. KB Toys, on the other hand, has relied on a joint venture strategy by partnering with Brainplay.com, an e-tailer of children's products in creating KBkids.com. In that way, the companies were able to capitalize on the advantages of both integration and separation.

Suggested Readings

Russ Arensman, "Distribution's 'Net Threat," *Electronic Business* (February 2000)

"Do-It-Yourself.com," *Time* (March 27, 2000)

Jacqueline Emigh, "E-Commerce Strategies," *Computerworld* (August 16, 1999)

Stanie Holt, "Trading Partners to Get New Options for Communication," *InfoWorld* (June 21, 1999)

Steven Kaplan and Mohanbir Sawhney, "E-Hubs: The New B2B Marketplaces," *Harvard Business Review* (May–June 2000)

"Survey: E-Commerce: We're Off to the Online Mall," *The Economist* (February 26, 2000)

ISSUE 9

Is Communications Technology "Death of the Salesman"?

YES: Beth Belton, from "Technology Is Changing Face of U.S. Sales Force," *USA Today* (February 9, 1999)

NO: Edward M. Hallowell, from "The Human Moment at Work," *Harvard Business Review* (January–February 1999)

ISSUE SUMMARY

YES: Writer Beth Belton explains how technology is rapidly displacing "selling as it used to be" with an entirely new job definition. This coincides with the 50th anniversary of the classic Arthur Miller play *Death of a Salesman*, as marketers ponder the future of the stereotypical salesman as portrayed by the character of Willy Loman, a symbol of this dying breed.

NO: Psychiatrist Edward M. Hallowell argues that the new communications technology, while ostensibly creating an efficient cost-saving mechanism for doing business, has created a deepened and neglected need for what he terms the "human moment," an authentic encounter that can begin only when two people share the same physical space. The destructive power resulting from the absence of the human moment will become more apparent as the stress levels associated with e-commerce rise, he concludes.

Is technology destroying the lifestyle and face-to-face communication that has traditionally defined the job of the salesman? Has the selling process changed so that the salesman's job description has been radically redefined? Has the role of the salesman become less significant, as it has become much less an allocation of the promotional mix?

The recent 50th anniversary of the Arthur Miller play *Death of a Salesman* has ignited a retrospective view of the pathetic character of Willy Loman as the symbol of cultural antagonism toward the sales profession. The traditional image of the salesman encouraging customers to build loyalty through charisma and personality is dying, many say. An annual amount of $12 billion reportedly has been spent on sales-automated software, displacing thousands of field salespeople. Consumers are adamant in demanding delivered value. They want an immediate interactive medium, customized products, and real-time service for their hard-earned dollars. The Internet is now a revolutionary cost-effective tool for providing detailed product information and facilitating the sale. But ironically this may be increasing consumers' sense of isolation rather than drawing them closer to their providers.

The trend is pervasive, from the golf course buyer to the spreadsheet buyer. Thousands of companies are following the lead of Rite Aid drugstores, no longer dealing with salespeople, reducing costs, and speeding up the purchasing process through accessing information and initiating transactions via the Internet. Xerox and thousands of other firms are reorganizing their sales forces to act as "industrial software organizations." The shift is from a one-way, persuasively domineering sales pitch to intelligently analyzing the sales situation and assisting buyers as problem solvers. Computer technology has allowed the customer to plan and design products, compare alternatives, and circumvent the personal assistance of sales technicians.

Consequently, salespeople have far fewer face-to-face conversations and more systems selling approaches that incorporate "encounter teams" with engineers, lawyers, and accountants fine-tuning their offering to the client's specific needs. Of course, electronic technology offers great advantages to sales technicians as well. Communications and actual markets are no longer limited to geographic boundaries. Productivity has been tremendously increased as networks put sales technicians, distributors, competitors, and customers within reach with the click of a mouse.

The key catalyst for impact on the modern salesman is the interactivity so easily accessed on the Internet. Millions of Web sites, neatly categorized, allow consumers to seek out the "real deal" by surfing the competitive offerings with explicit detail in terms of criteria for sale, obviating the need for salesman contact. But, as Beth Belton suggests, this "death of the salesman" represents an end of an era, quintessentially American, that is being snuffed out—the maverick salesman. The canned pitch and step-by-step blueprint for selling from the proven sales manual are now being eliminated along with the unique bantering and freedom of exchange that defined the sales persona. Is this part of the hidden cost to marketing and society?

Most people can recall being caught in the tangled web of the computerized telephone response whereby you long for the sound of a human voice. Edward M. Hallowell describes this frustration, noting that virtually everyone he sees is experiencing some deficiency of human contact resulting in a sense of isolation, anxiety, and confusion at work. Hallowell argues that this has direct implications for *internal marketing*. Lack of the personal contact can inhibit a healthy and progressive spirit within the marketing department. Sales meetings are becoming fewer and farther between. He concludes that while past personal meetings were time-consuming and expensive, they fostered trust, engendered a surge of team spirit, and resulted in a positive corporate culture and strong working relationships. Will relationship marketing suffer as a result of less personal contact?

Beth Belton

 **YES**

Technology Is Changing Face of U.S. Sales Force

Iowa native Morrie Norman Jr. has selling in his blood. He's been a salesman all his life, just like his father and grandfather before him. Two of his brothers are in sales, and his sister used to be. He has won many top awards for selling Dale Carnegie courses, which teach people how to sell. But, uncharacteristically, he hesitates when asked whether he wants his children to go into sales.

"Selling used to be selling," Norman says. "But in the last five years, I'd say there have been dramatic changes. I mean very dramatic."

As the new millennium approaches, globalization, an explosion of communications technology—including telemarketing and Internet commerce—and the ability to sell almost anything as a commodity are starting to demolish a way of life that has defined the infrastructure of corporate America for most of [the twentieth] century.

[It] is the 50th anniversary of the Broadway opening of Arthur Miller's timeless play *Death of a Salesman*. But while the play is being revived, the salesman of American lore is, in many ways, a dying breed.

It is still possible for bright upstarts without college degrees or the right connections to earn fantastic wages using a bit of moxie and the gift of gab and refusing to take no for an answer. But technology and competition are rapidly encroaching. The old school model of the fast-talking, backslapping salesman is becoming as outdated as Willy Loman, the tormented and pathetic protagonist in Miller's drama.

Just [recently], Rite-Aid Drug Stores, third-largest U.S. pharmacy chain, announced it no longer would deal with salespeople in an attempt to reduce costs and speed up its buying process. Late [January 1999], copier giant Xerox announced a sweeping reorganization of its sales division, renaming the direct sales force the "industry solutions operation."

Even the legendary Dale Carnegie course, *de rigeur* training for four decades of salespeople, has been revamped and relaunched for the first time to reflect changes in how the selling process works.

"A few decades ago, salespeople were taught that they should talk fast and dominate the conversation for fear that the prospect might ask a question they couldn't answer," says famed sales coach Zig Ziglar, author of two hit books on how to sell. "We now understand we must probe not as a prosecuting attorney, but as a concerned individual who wants to become an assisting buyer."

Whether hard sell or soft, the role of sales hasn't disappeared. Far from it. There are 15.5 million salespeople out there, according to government data. That's about 12% of the workforce—a percentage that has held steady for at least 15 years. It is the role of the salesperson that is undergoing a radical shift.

Roger Hirl, president and CEO of Dallas-based Occidental Chemical, has given speeches about how different it is now than when he started out in the '60s: "I covered a 10-state territory that ran from Louisiana all the way to Idaho and Montana. I had no pager, no laptop, no cellular phone, fax or e-mail. I used pay phones that took coins. I kept track of appointments with a pocket secretary and a ballpoint pen, and customers with an index card file."

Today, a salesperson who sells just products or services is being displaced by a new breed of *uber*sales types. They have titles like "global sales and marketing consultant," and many follow tried-and-true, company-approved scripts instead of ad-libbing. This salesperson of the 21st century is expected to develop ways for clients to create profit and gain market share, dubbed "value-added sales," because yesterday's clueless customer has turned into today's formidable buyer.

Now, even before the first sales call, customers, via e-mail, can get price quotes. The Internet arms them to the teeth with product information. A global economy has created a 24-hour business cycle, connecting buyers and sellers around the clock. Automation is eliminating the need for traveling salespeople.

Says David Cole, a University of Michigan professor who studies sales in the transportation industry: "There's been a revolution that has almost escaped unnoticed we've been moving so fast."

Salesman of the 21st Century

On a given day, the fairways of the nation's classiest golf courses still are filled with sales executives on the hunt for a big deal.

But increasingly, that personal relationship is considered less and less, says Norbert Ore, head of purchasing at paper-products maker Chesapeake Corp. in Richmond, Va.

"We've gone from the age of the golf course buyer to the spreadsheet buyer," Ore says. "Before, buying was done on a relationship-built basis among companies that probably had done business for years and years together. Now, business is done on an evaluation of quality, price and delivery."

At the heart of the change is a transformation of the salesperson, from job description to gender (nearly half of today's sales force is female, up from less than 35% female 25 years ago).

"The day of the lone wolf is gone," says Marvin Jolson, retired vice president of sales at Encyclopedia Britannica, who still teaches personal selling at the University of Maryland. "You're talking about salesmen who don't have a one-on-one conversation with someone. They're facing a team of buyers that includes engineers, two lawyers and an accountant."

And before that presentation, they're better prepared than ever.

Salespeople are more educated than in the past and receive more training than many executives. The typical salesperson gets 38 hours of training a year —10 hours more than senior executives, according to a December [1998] survey of 3,703 U.S. companies by *Training* magazine.

"The good ol' boy has been left by the wayside," says Patrick Egan, vice president of purchasing at drugmaker Pfizer. "He doesn't know enough technically, and he also doesn't know enough about how his company works." "It used to be we got five different proposals (to pitch a product) and they were all the same and we would pick one," Egan adds. "Now proposals are customized."

Mass customization is the paradigm of the 21st century just as mass production was the paradigm of the 20th century, experts say.

"At one time all you had to worry about was getting a bunch of deals closed," says Lynn Brubaker, vice president of sales and service in the aerospace division of Morristown, N.J.-based AlliedSignal. "Now you have to worry about the (customer's) overall business. You have to be a market leader; you need to be able to identify trends."

Today's sales reps are plugged in—to headquarters and their customers. They're walking electronic wonders, virtual offices of laptop computers, cell phones and pagers. But just as technology has made their job easier, it also has created obstacles. Salespeople must contend with phone mail, e-mail and stressed-out prospective buyers who no longer have the time or the boss's blessing to conduct business over an afternoon of golf or a three-martini lunch.

"It's a 24-hour sales cycle," says Marshall Smith, an account manager at Silicon Valley-based Cisco Systems, which sells computer networking equipment. Smith says he takes his laptop home with him every night and checks his e-mail right before he goes to bed.

The Middleman's Demise

Changing tactics and technology don't tell the whole story, experts say. Most of the biggest changes are affecting the biggest companies. Smaller businesses must still use tried-and-true selling strategies to survive.

Small-business owners know better than anyone that "selling hasn't changed," argues Oliver Crom, president and CEO of Garden City, N.Y.-based Dale Carnegie Inc. "Selling has always been trying to find out what the customer needs, then determining and demonstrating that what you have to sell fits that need."

"What has changed," Crom says, "is the customer. Today the customer is much more knowledgeable. Through the Internet and other sources, the customer has a tremendous amount of information available."

The result, in many instances, is that the traditional role of the salesperson is being eliminated or changed so dramatically as to be unrecognizable. The December [1998] issue of *Sales and Marketing Management* magazine terms it the "invisible sales force," because companies increasingly are transferring duties that used to be handled by salespeople to telephone representatives, direct mail and the Internet.

Here's how some of the new or transformed ways of selling are working:

Computer technology Consumers can now buy a new car on the Internet without ever having to face down a car salesman. Stocks of retailers that sell their goods on line have skyrocketed in recent months due to the forecast that more and more consumers will shop on line. Businesses, too, are ordering raw materials and other supply staples over the Internet.

Consultation selling Historically, most selling was transaction-based, the one-time sale of a good or product without regard to a buyer's future needs or overall corporate vision. Volume was power and it didn't matter who you sold to as long as you kept selling.

But transaction-based selling has gone from 90% or more of all sales down to 65% and the percentage is expected to continue declining sharply, says Bob Davenport, vice president of the sales force effectiveness practice at the Philadelphia-based Hay Group consulting firm.

"Today, we do much more of a consultative sale and we're looking really to figure out what are (the customer's) critical business processes and how can we add value," says Xerox's Joe Valenti, newly named chief of staff for North American solutions. "It's much more than just selling a box."

At the same time, competition and cost-cutting mania have made companies more interested in keeping their biggest customers satisfied. Procter & Gamble, for example, has its Wal-Mart salespeople living in the retailer's headquarters in Bentonville, Ark., devoted to the singular task of keeping Wal-Mart happy.

Indirect selling In the mid-'80s, mainframe computer giant IBM had a sales force 400,000 strong. Today, it's been reduced to 275,000. And it's not just smaller: 15% of the sales force never leaves the office because they're involved in so-called indirect selling, calling smaller customers on the phone to pitch products and take orders. Indirect selling is one of the biggest growth areas in sales as companies grapple with the ever-rising expense of sending people out into the field. A decade ago, none of IBM's sales force did indirect selling.

Corporate selling There's been an explosion of so-called "executive selling," according to sales industry trade magazines. This means a chairman or chief executive will make a personal visit to prospective CEOs to discuss doing business —alongside the traditional salesman. Chairman Manny Fernandez of the Gartner Group, a Stamford, Conn.-based information technology consulting firm, spends more than half his time traveling on sales pitches.

The Fate of the Maverick

In the midst of these changes, something quintessentially American, something unique, may be getting snuffed out.

More and more salespeople now are required to use a blueprint—a step-by-step manual that a sales rep must carry at all times. It's generally a compilation of what has been proven to work for the company's top salespeople. Banter with the customer is discouraged.

Oracle, the giant software supplier based in Redwood Shores, Calif., began using a blueprint in mid-'97 and sales have since rocketed. It's a seven-page, six-phase outline of the sales process that includes up to 21 steps under each phase on how to sell Oracle products.

That's the kind of selling that demoralizes the mavericks. In most companies, salespeople traditionally were kept separate from other areas of a company's operation, partly because they typically were cut from a different cloth than the accountants, technicians and factory line workers.

Behind a desk, they were useless. But out on the road, they were king, doing what they wanted when they wanted and how they wanted—as long as they produced revenue.

But in today's world, they need new skills.

"There is a... fundamental change in the type of person who will be successful," says Davenport, vice president of the consulting firm. "When an organization runs into trouble and the job changes but you've got the same old person, it's like the analogy: you can teach a turkey to climb a tree, but if you need tree-climbers, you hire a squirrel."

NO

Edward M. Hallowell

The Human Moment at Work

T he chief financial officer [CFO] of an international consulting firm holds a cell phone to his ear while waiting for the shuttle from New York to Boston. He listens to the messages that have piled up since he phoned in three hours earlier. After he flips the phone closed, he sits down to wait for his plane and starts to brood. A valued employee has asked for a transfer to another division. Questions begin to ricochet through his mind. What if the employee complains that the CFO is a lousy boss? What if the employee plans to take his team with him in the move? What if, what if...? The CFO becomes lost in a frightening tangle of improbable outcomes, a thicket that will ensnarl his mind the entire flight back to Boston. The minute he gets home he will dash off an e-mail to the employee and eagerly await a reply—which, when it comes the next day, will likely upset him further by its ambiguity. More brooding will ensue, making it difficult for him to focus on his work.

At an electronics company, a talented brand manager is increasingly alien-ated. The problem started when his division head didn't return a phone call for several days. She said she never got the message. Then the brand manager noticed that he hadn't been invited to an important meeting with a new adver-tising agency. What's wrong my performance? he wonders. The man wants to raise the question with the division manager, but the opportunity never seems to arise. All their communication is by memo, e-mail, or voice mail, which they exchange often. But they almost never meet. For one thing, their offices are 50 miles apart, and for another, both of them are frequently on the road. During the rare moments when they do see each other in person—on the run in a corridor or in the parking lot at corporate headquarters—it is usually inap-propriate or impossible to discuss complex matters. And so the issues between them smolder.

In both scenarios, the executives' anxiety has a simple antidote: a face-to-face conversation. Both men are driving themselves crazy for no reason. But to learn that, they need to reconnect with their unwitting partners in (emo-tional) crime—and they need to do it in person. They need to experience what I call *the human moment:* an authentic psychological encounter that can happen only when two people share the same physical space. I have given the human moment a name because I believe that it has started to disappear from modern life—and I sense that we all may be about to discover the destructive power of its absence.

The human moment has two prerequisites: people's physical presence and their emotional and intellectual attention. That's it. Physical presence alone isn't enough; you can ride shoulder-to-shoulder with someone for six hours in an airplane and not have a human moment the entire ride. And attention alone isn't enough either. You can pay attention to someone over the telephone, for instance, but somehow phone conversations lack the power of true human moments.

Human moments require energy. Often, that's what makes them easy to avoid. The human moment may be seen as yet another tax on our overextended lives. But a human moment doesn't have to be emotionally draining or personally revealing. In fact, the human moment can be brisk, businesslike, and brief. A five-minute conversation can be a perfectly meaningful human moment. To make the human moment work, you have to set aside what you're doing, put down the memo you were reading, disengage from your laptop, abandon your daydream, and focus on the person you're with. Usually when you do that, the other person will feel the energy and respond in kind. Together, you quickly create a force field of exceptional power.

The positive effects of a human moment can last long after the people involved have said goodbye and walked away. People begin to think in new and creative ways, mental activity is stimulated. But like exercise, which also has enduring effects, the benefits of a human moment do not last indefinitely. A ten-mile run on Monday is wonderful—but only if you also swim on Wednesday and play tennis on Saturday. In other words, you must engage in human moments on a regular basis for them to have a meaningful impact on your life. For most people, that's not a tall order.

I am concerned, however, that human moments are disappearing and that this trend will be accompanied by worrisome and widespread consequences. I say this not as an executive but as a psychiatrist who has been treating patients with anxiety disorders for 20 years. Because of where I practice and the nature of my expertise, many of my patients are senior business executives who—to the outside world—are pictures of success. But I can tell you without a doubt that virtually everyone I see is experiencing some deficiency of human contact. Indeed, I am increasingly sought out because people feel lonely, isolated, or confused at work. The treatment I provide invariably involves replenishing the human moments in their lives.

The Disappearing Human Moment

Human beings are remarkably resilient. They can deal with almost anything as long as they do not become too isolated. But my patients, as well as my acquaintances in the business world, tell me that as the tide of electronic hyperconnection rises, the landscape of work is in some ways changing for the worse. As Ray, a senior systems manager in a large investment company, told me: "I don't talk to people as much as I used to. And sometimes the results are very damaging."

Ray wasn't complaining—overall, he likes his job quite a bit—but he was concerned. "I've found you can stumble into giant misunderstandings with e-mail. People's feelings can get hurt and wrong information can get picked up."

As an example, he told the following story. "A guy sent me an e-mail that said, 'We were not able to access the following application, and we need to know why,' and he cc'd his supervisor, solely to show the supervisor that he was doing something about the problem. What bugged me was that line, 'and we need to know why.' If he had spoken to me face-to-face we could have solved the problem, but no, I get this e-mail with its peremptory tone, and he's cc'd it My immediate response was, back at you. So I write an officious sounding e-mail, with a cc to a bunch of other people, including his supervisor, explaining that I had submitted a change management ticket, and if he had gone to the meeting where that was discussed he would have known about it and wouldn't have even tried to access that application. I became that guy's adversary instead of solving the problem. But I felt goaded into it."

Ray's story illustrates how letting the human moment fall to the wayside leads to dysfunction in organizations. When human moments are few and far between, oversensitivity, self-doubt, and even boorishness and abrasive curtness can be observed in the best of people. Productive employees will begin to feel lousy and that, in turn, will lead them to underperform or to think of looking elsewhere for work. The irony is that this kind of alienation in the workplace derives not from lack of communication but from a surplus of the wrong kind. The remedy is not to get rid of electronics but to restore the human moment where it is needed.

The absence of the human moment—on an organizational scale—can wreak havoc. Coworkers slowly but surely lose their sense of cohesiveness. It starts with one person, but distrust, disrespect, and dissatisfaction on the job are like contagions. Soon enough there are five or ten people like Ray and his e-mail partner, and then more. Eventually, such people make up the majority. An organization's culture turns unfriendly and unforgiving. Good people leave. Those who remain are unhappy. Mental health concerns aside, such conditions are not good for business. Indeed, they can be downright corrosive.

To be sure, people have felt lonely or isolated at work in the past. Henry Ford's early factories were no love-ins. Nevertheless, from the 1950s onward, executives and middle managers came to expect that they would talk with one another in the office—for business or personal reasons—and would even play together at the end of the day. And when it came time to connect with distant clients or suppliers or colleagues, people got on planes. Meetings happened in person. Yes, they were time consuming and costly. But they fostered trust. Not incidentally, people had more fun.

But in the last ten years or so, technological changes have made a lot of face-to-face interaction unnecessary. I'm talking about voice mail and e-mail mainly—modes of communication that are one-way and electronic. Face-to-face interaction has also fallen victim to "virtuality" —many people work at home or are otherwise off-site. I will certainly not try to make a case that these changes are bad. And indeed, no one planned on reducing face-to-face meetings; this is simply happening naturally, with the inevitability of water flowing downhill. We have the technology, so we are using it.

For the most part, it makes our lives much better. I enjoy the efficiency and freedom that voice mail and e-mail give me. I communicate with people when I want to, from any location. While I'm traveling, I keep up with my messages from patients and the office through voice mail, and I log on from hotel rooms to collect my e-mail every day. Like most people, I don't know how I ever managed without these tools.

But problems that develop when the human moment is lost cannot be ignored. People need human contact in order to survive.

They need it to maintain their mental acuity and their emotional well-being. I make this assertion having listened to and counseled thousands of patients whose jobs have been sapped of human moments. And I make it based on strong evidence from the field of brain science....

Toxic Worry

What happens to the psychology of the mind when the human moment vanishes—or at least fades—from our lives? In the worst case, paranoia fills the vacuum. In my practice, that has been rare. More often, the human moment is replaced by worry. That's because electronic communications remove many of the cues that typically mitigate worry. Those cues—body language, tone of voice, and facial expression—are especially important among sophisticated people who are prone to using subtle language, irony, and wit.

Not all worry is bad, of course. Some of my patients tell me that in business, worry can be a great tool. It is an inner voice telling you that trouble— a new competitor or a new technology that will shake up your industry—is on the way. "Good worry" leads to constructive planning and corrective action; it is essential to success in any endeavor.

"Toxic worry" is another matter entirely. It is anxiety that has no basis in reality. It immobilizes the sufferer and leads to indecision or destructive action. It's like being in the dark, and we all feel paranoid in the dark. Try an experiment. Go into a room at night and turn off the lights. Your whole body will respond. Even if you know the room well, you will probably feel the hairs on the back of your neck rise up a little as you wonder who might be lurking in the corner. The human moment is like light in an otherwise dark room: it illuminates dark corners and dispels suspicions and fears. Without it, toxic worry grows.

Toxic worry is among the most debilitating consequences of vanishing human moments, but much more common are the little misunderstandings. An e-mail message is misconstrued. A voice-mail message gets forwarded to the wrong people. Someone takes offense because he is not included on a certain circulation list. Was it an accident? Such problems can be tolerated by most individuals from time to time—as I've said, people are resilient. But as the number of human moments decreases, the number of little misunderstandings is likely to increase. They compound one another until there is nothing little about them anymore. People begin to wonder if they can trust their organizations and, just as often, they begin to question their own motives, performance, and self-worth.

Consider Harry, a senior partner at a Boston law firm. Harry was representing a bank in a complicated real estate deal with the developer of a commercial property. Many of the details of the agreement were being worked out via e-mail between Harry and the developer's counsel. At a key juncture, when a technical point about interest rates came up, the developer's counsel e-mailed Harry, "Of course your client won't grasp this, because he won't understand what we're talking about."

When Harry's client read this message, which was mixed in with other documents, he became furious and nearly canceled the deal. Trying to patch things up, Harry met with the developer's lawyer, who was stunned to hear how his message had been misconstrued. "I was trying to be ironic!" the lawyer gasped in horror. "Your client is an expert in the field—saying he didn't know what we were talking about was just my way of being funny. I can't believe what a misunderstanding this is!"

When he came to me, Harry was second-guessing himself, asking me if he had some unconscious wish to fail because he had allowed the message to be seen by his client. But the real problem was in the mode of communication, not in Harry's unconscious.

Harry's deal was saved, but sometimes the misunderstandings wrought by the absence of the human moment do permanent damage. I recently treated a man—let's call him Charles—who came to see me because he was waking up in the middle of the night. He was worried about the company he had just sold for $20 million.

"What's wrong?" I asked him.

"I had intended to stay on with the company for at least a couple of years, but I'm worried it's going to be impossible. I can't deal with the COO [Chief Operating Officer]. He's in Texas, where the headquarters are, and I'm in Massachusetts, and he keeps sending me e-mails with lists of things he wants me to do. This may sound petty, but the way he phrases them just makes me crazy. When I sold the company I knew my role would change, but this is totally degrading."

"Can you give me an example?" I asked.

"Sure. I turned on my computer Monday and got an e-mail that simply said, 'Last communication unacceptable. Redo.' I replied, asking for specifics. He e-mailed me back, 'I don't have time to explain. Can't you figure it out?' Suddenly I'm feeling like a third-grader. But I tried to rise above it. The next day he e-mailed me, 'Your people up there have to do longer weekend hours.' Then I started to lose sleep."

"Is this their way of getting rid of you?" I asked.

"It looks like it, but the fact is that they need me. They know that. But I can't deal with this."

"Can you talk to the COO?" I asked.

"He's evasive. When we meet, he's polite but vague. He does all his damage through e-mail."

Although Charles was determined to make the transition and stay with the new company, his resolve broke down as he felt increasingly at odds with headquarters, particularly the COO. And he started to brood about the direction and purpose of the company, issues he had felt confident about when he made the deal. "I've become a worrier instead of a problem solver," Charles told me. "I never used to be this way."

When Charles submitted his letter of resignation, he was deluged with evidence that the company did indeed want him to stay. He received dozens of e-mail messages and phone calls from people pleading with him to reconsider. But by then the damage had been done. Charles's heart was not in it. He was getting interested in new ideas for other businesses, and venture capitalists had approached him the minute he leaked word of his dissatisfaction. The company's attempts to keep him proved to be too little, too late.

When we discussed his resignation, Charles told me how easy it would have been for the new company to have kept him, if only he had been treated with even minimal respect by the COO. "My problems really came down to those e-mail interactions," he said.

It sounded as if the COO couldn't handle his competitive feelings, but instead of dealing with Charles face-to-face, he took him on in e-mail. He used that approach as a weapon for his negative and angry emotions. In person, he would have had to submit to social convention. His dark feelings would have been forced into the light.

The human moment, then, is a regulator when you take it away, people's primitive instincts can get the better of them. Just as in the anonymity of an automobile, where stable people can behave like crazed maniacs, so too on a keyboard courteous people can become rude and abrupt.

Less dramatic but more common are the instances when people come to see me because they feel worn out by all the nonhuman interactions that fill their days. "I feel like I'm going brain-dead," said Lynn, an executive at a health care company. She consulted me because she actually thought she was losing her memory. In meetings, words were not coming to her as quickly, and decisions that she once made in a snap were now taking her hours or days. Lynn had long prided herself on her sharp mind. Now she felt as if her head were swallowed by fog. But she was still wise enough to realize that her problems might be connected to the changing texture of her work. "I do 30% to 40% of my work by leaving voice-mail messages, playing phone tag, or sending e-mail," she said. "It used to be just 10%. I see and talk to people less and less and less."

A few simple tests conducted in my office revealed that Lynn's brain itself was in fine shape. However, she was right. Her work habits were diminishing her brain's performance. Your psyche, just like your muscles, actually needs rest and variation to perform at its peak. Lynn acted as if she had run a marathon through the desert. No wonder her body ached and her mind was numb. Staying on-screen, on-line, or on the telephone for extended periods—just like any other long and monotonous activity—wears you out. The brain becomes starved for fuel: rest and human contact. That is why punishments like exile and solitary confinement are so painful. All the coffee in the world can't make up for the brain-dead state that many people in jobs like Lynn's feel at about 3 o'clock in the afternoon.

The antidote to Lynn's condition was straightforward. She needed some diversity in her work life. I suggested that she refresh her mind with a bit of exercise or, even better, that she regularly seek out conversations with real, live human beings. She did so and today reports that both her work and her brain's performance are much improved. But I am concerned about all the executives out there who have not sought help as Lynn did. Although most executives attend enough meetings and social functions to prevent them from becoming zombies, the anonymity and monotony of technology can—and will—decrease their brain stamina. And for that, both individuals and organizations will pay a price.

High Tech, High Touch

A patient of mine who was a CEO once told me, "High tech requires high touch." When I asked him what he meant, he explained to me that his company had run into a problem. Every time it made another part of its operations virtual—moving salespeople entirely into the field, for instance—the company's culture suffered. So he had developed a policy that required all "virtual" employees to come into the office at least once a month for unstructured face time.

"It's like what happened when banks introduced ATMs," the CEO said. "Once people didn't know Alice behind the counter anymore or any of the lending agents behind those glass walls, the whole loan process got tougher for both the banks and the customers. There was no familiarity, no trust."

"I love ATMs," I replied

"So do I. So does everyone," said the CEO. "But the banks have been scrambling for years now to get their customers into a relationship again. You see, for business to do well, you can't have high tech without high touch. They have to work together."

The CEO was right. But combining high tech and high touch is easier said than done, according to my patients. Technology always seems to take precedence. Recently, however, I encountered two examples of human and "virtual" moments working in tandem and reinforcing each other to great effect.

Jack is a major real-estate developer based in Boston. In the last decade, his offices and interests have become worldwide. He runs his operation from a suite of offices located on the ground floor of a Back Bay brownstone that he calls the "bat cave." A former football player at Yale, Jack considers teamwork the key to his company's success. When I asked him how he dealt with the recent growth of his company, its increasing diversification, the expanding numbers of people working for him, his reply was "Thursday pizza."

"About ten years ago, I realized I wasn't seeing people as often as before," Jack explained. "I was running around and so was everybody else. We never got a chance to sit down and talk." Jack worried about the impact of this disconnectedness on his business, in which sharing information is critical, so he started a Thursday ritual: a free pizza lunch in the office. "I know this is not an advanced management technique, but it does the job," Jack said. "On Thursdays, we sit around the big table in my office and we talk. There is no agenda. The group averages about 15 people and changes members every week, but there is a core of 5 or 6 who provide continuity. They meet even when I'm not there. We all look forward to it not as a business meeting but as an opportunity for informal talk. People catch up with each other, they brainstorm, they bring up stuff that doesn't get discussed elsewhere, and it works." According to Jack, the pizza lunches are largely responsible for his organization's high morale and competitive strength.

Jack's pizza lunch is a simple way of maintaining the human moment at work. Sometimes, however, reinstating the human moment can be more complex. Consider the case of David, who runs a consulting firm that advises independent furniture stores. About a decade ago, he found that many of his clients were becoming increasingly isolated after an industry consolidation left only one or two independents in each city. Sales representatives from the major manufacturers wouldn't service them in person anymore. They were asked to order over the phone or through the Internet. "You used to learn what was going on in the marketplace from the sales reps who stopped by your store. And a lot of those relationships were very close," David explained "With the sales reps gone, the independents felt completely cut off."

In response to this problem, David decided to start what he called "performance groups"—groups of independent retailers from different parts of the country who would get together three times a year to talk business and offer one another support. When he presented this idea to his colleagues at the consulting firm, they hesitated. They worried that the project might fail, given the notoriously guarded, private nature of independent furniture retailers.

But the need for the human moment proved strong. Today, six groups of independent furniture dealers exist, with ten people in each. They meet in two-day sessions with retailers in noncompeting cities. "We've had people in our groups who say that their fathers would roll over in their graves if they knew they were sharing the financials of their company with other retailers," David told me. "But sharing those financials creates trust and a bond. These people share their best ideas, they benchmark performance, and they give one another the support they need."

The sessions can be very emotional, according to David. "We've had guys break down in tears when people in the group have looked at them and said, 'Fire your son.' But the groups put them in touch with people who know the business and can help work things out." They have provided a human moment.

It's important to note that the groups' face-to-face meetings are augmented by electronic communication. The performance groups use e-mail and other electronic means to support and expand what they do in the meetings. But David believes the in-person meetings are indispensable. "I think a sense of caring develops when you're dealing with somebody face-to-face. Over the Internet you tend to be very precise with questions and answers, and you can't register people's emotions. People don't open up over the Internet like they do in person. When you're chatting with somebody, you can see by his facial expression that you've hit on a very sensitive subject. It may be a signal to avoid that subject or it may be a signal to go further. You can't tell that over the computer." But David feels strongly that the Internet is valuable. In fact, he is currently creating a chat room for each performance group. Using a code to enter, members will be able to "talk" between meetings, thereby sustaining, and even building on, the important relationships forged face-to-face.

The performance groups in the retail furniture business seem to me a brilliant example of using the human moment judiciously—even strategically. Obviously, we don't want to turn back the clock and dispense with the tremendous efficiencies afforded us by electronic communications, but we do need to learn how to deal with the hidden problems they can create.

Indeed, the strategic use of the human moment can help reduce the confusion and ambiguity of electronic communications, develop confidence and trust as only in-person meetings can, and reduce the toxic worry, mental fatigue, and disconnection associated with the excessive use of electronics.

Technology has created a magnificent new world, bursting with opportunity. It has opened up a global, knowledge-based economy and unchained people from their desks. We are all in its debt—and we're never going back. But we cannot move forward successfully without preserving the human moment. The price we pay for not doing that is too high, for individuals and organizations alike. The human moment provides the zest and color in the painting of our daily lives, it restores us, strengthens us, and makes us whole. Luckily, as long as we arrange our lives properly, the human moment should be easy enough to preserve. All we have to do is take heed—and make it happen.

POSTSCRIPT

Is Communications Technology "Death of the Salesman"?

Many lament the loss of the "human moment" in marketing. Consider how Web sites like Ameritrade, Travelocity, and Auto Search are displacing thousands of salespeople who were the agent middlemen and backbone of the American marketing system for nearly a century. Empowered consumers now have more pieces of information at their fingertips than even hundreds of experts could ever remember. The recent trend is for Web sites to include and offer attributes, prices, and service information of competitors in an easily digestible format, further removing the need for sales technicians.

John L. Lock, in his book *The De-voicing of Society: Why We Don't Talk to Each Other Anymore* (Simon & Schuster, 1998), summarizes the issue. He states that the widespread use of communication technology systems risks increasing people's sense of isolation instead of drawing them together. He concludes that such communication cannot compensate for the intimacy generated by nonverbal cues in face-to-face communications. The actual presence of another human builds trusting relationships, so crucial to contemporary marketers.

The desire for privacy and security has further isolated people. There have been significant declines in church attendance, union membership, and in participation with traditional groups like the League of Women Voters. It is likely that justifying the cost of business trips with alternatives like video conferencing will further limit the interaction between salespeople and their customers. Thus, the death of the salesman has deeper societal implications. Beyond its significance to marketers, the loss of the human moment has a pervasive, systemic impact on society beyond the marketplace.

Suggested Readings

William C. Copacino, "The 'Human' Moment," *Logistics Management and Distribution Report* (June 1999)

Kim DeMotte, "What Is Sales Automation?" *Industrial Distribution* (November 1996)

Matt Hamblen, "Sales Automation Projects Still Struggle," *Computerworld* (November 2, 1998)

Margaret Kaeter, "Yes, Sales Automation Can Be Motivating," *Potentials* (February 1998)

Nucila Marrow, "Is This the Death of the Salesman?" *Financial Times* (March 24, 1999)

Peter A. Perera, "Sales Automation: Re-engineering Gone Awry," *Computerworld* (October 21, 1996)

Daniel Sweeney and Arnold G. Reinhold, "The Coming Crash of E-Commerce," *America's Network* (December 1, 1999)

Sales Force Automation Solutions. `http://www.salesautomation group.com`

Customer Relationship Management Association. `http://www.saaintl.org`

LEADtrack Software. `http://www.leadtrack.com`

Turnkey Sales Automation and Customer Interaction Solutions. `http://www.tsas.com`

Solutions for Sales Automation, Customer Relationship Management (CRM), and ECommerce. `http://www.salesforce.com`

On the Internet ...

MarketForce Customer Relationship Management

This is the home page of MarketForce, whose mission is to help companies increase the effectiveness and efficiencies of their sales, marketing, and customer service operations through the application of specialized software systems and professional support services.

`http://www.marketforce.com`

PriceSCAN

PriceSCAN's searchable Web site helps consumers to find the best prices on thousands of computer hardware and software products. The company's database consists of publicly available product and pricing information gathered from magazine ads, vendor catalogs, Web sites, and other sources.

`http://www.pricescan.com`

Priceline.com

Priceline.com enables consumers to use the Internet to save money on a wide range of products and services while enabling sellers to generate incremental revenue. Search this Web site to find deals on long-distance telephone service, cars, hotel rooms, groceries, and more

`http://www.priceline.com`

Excite Sports: Extreme Sports

This Web site offers a variety of resources related to extreme sports.

`http://www.excite.com/sports/extreme_sports/`

PART 3

Consumer Behavior in the New Millennium

*T*hink *of the changes that you have made in what, where, how, when, and why you have purchased products and services in the past five years. These are the primary questions examined under the subject of con-sumer behavior. A subset of human behavior, it analyzes the mental and physical activities and the multiplicity of influences involved in the exchange process. Recently, the shift in marketplace power has created previously unimaginable opportunities for interaction and new models by which consumers can search for information. They can join others in leveraging their economic power for securing the most competitive price. But marketers have also garnered formidable power by interpret-ing reams of personal data, which are now available for customizing consumer promotions.*

How the new technologies will affect the meaning and levels of brand loyalty are crucial issues for marketers. What new motivations will drive customer loyalty to a brand, and how will this influence the process of developing brand loyalties for marketers? What will be the effects of the major changes recently made by younger consumers in their brand preferences and attitudes toward extreme sports?

As marketers seek new ways to reach target audiences, issues of privacy and intrusiveness often arise, as in the case of younger stu-dents' being involved in classroom commercial ventures. This brings up questions concerning the appropriateness of relationships between public schools and marketers in the private sector. This constant interplay be-tween consumers, the changing marketing environment, and marketers is the theme connecting the issues in this section.

- The New Marketing Paradigm Shift: Are Consumers Dominating the Balance of Power in the Marketplace?

- Is the Traditional Development of Brand Loyalty Dying?

- Is "Extreme Sports" Marketing Risk and Thrill Seeking to Society?

- Should Classrooms Be Commercial-Free Zones?

ISSUE 10

The New Marketing Paradigm Shift: Are Consumers Dominating the Balance of Power in the Marketplace?

YES: Pierre M. Loewe and Mark S. Bonchek, from "The Retail Revolution," *Management Review* (April 1999)

NO: Marcia Stepanek, from "Weblining," *Business Week Online,* <http://www.businessweek.com/2000/00_14/ebiztoc.htm> (April 3, 2000)

ISSUE SUMMARY

YES: Pierre M. Loewe and Mark S. Bonchek, executive director and research director, respectively, of the global strategy innovation firm Strategos, argue that consumers are more empowered in challenging retailers to meet their needs for convenience, service, and price.

NO: Marcia Stepanek, a regular contributor to *Business Week,* suggests that the guiding rule of providing whatever the customer wants is now whatever the company can afford to offer based on the value of that customer.

In far less than a decade, communications technology has undeniably empowered consumers in every aspect of marketing, with particular emphasis on the purchase decision process. Concurrently, marketers have also achieved market power through access to comprehensive consumer information, enhanced interactivity, and the means of responding more efficiently to the real-time changing demands of the individual consumer.

The new marketing paradigm reflects a major "role reversal" in many purchase situations, as exemplified by "dot.com" companies such as Priceline.com and eBay. Now the "self-invented consumer" controls the product offering and can dictate the attributes of the desired purchase. Conversely, a series of potential Internet providers now compete and "shop" for consumers. They are responding to the customized specifications of market offerings from end consumers. In other words, the consumer becomes proactive by initiating the market offering. This is considered by the marketer seeking the right deal.

The marketer now shops for a customer relationship. "Co-opting" the competence of consumers means marketing is no longer a one-way process. It speaks to the increasingly significant role they play in interacting with providers to more clearly define customer-delivered value. The new breed of consumer has now found empowerment in every aspect of the marketing mix.

Consider the first of the "Four Ps" of the marketing mix—*products*. Envision the quantum leaps in product choices now available to Web-surfing consumers, particularly those shoppers taking advantage of opportunities for mass customization. Not only has the range and spectrum of customized product/service choices exploded, but shopping mobility has brought the world's marketplace into the consumer's living room. The search for product information has become revolutionized with an inordinate amount of data now available for the comparative technoshopper.

The second "P"—*pricing*—is also a new source of consumer empowerment, whereby thousands of Internet-competing providers are forced to be price competitive due to the shared proliferation of comparative product information.

The third "P"—*place*—has been revolutionized by shorter channels of distribution. Home delivery is the lifeblood of distribution convenience—empowering consumers to have products delivered from all corners of the world. The emerging science of automated inventory technologies will soon facilitate the replacement of goods on a routine basis, eliminating the need for reordering.

The fourth "P"—*promotion*—rewards consumers for patronizing many Web sites with premiums and rewards. This may be undergoing a major transition, however. The inundation of one-way "interruptive" advertising is yielding to *consumer compliant-permission* advertising. These are consumer-controlled situations whereby customers agree to be reached through visiting a Web site. They are exposed only to the ads they want to read.

Yet imagine the incredible empowerment of the new "sophisticated" marketer. The age-old marketing formula of "prospecting" for potential markets is over. Oceans of customer information afford marketers the opportunity to *webline*, or utilize, varied product offerings to highly selective target markets' purchasing histories, and even create "Wish Lists," leading to revolutionary opportunities to pinpoint customer wants and promote access to niche markets. However, privacy issues may tend to invite regulations that could limit this free exchange of consumer information. Currently, 92 percent of Internet users have expressed discomfort about Web sites sharing personal information with other sites. The information is the seminal force in giving marketers a competitive advantage, and they are becoming more empowered.

Marketers also benefit from the prodigious cost savings associated with customized products and delivery systems. Direct-to-consumer shipping and interactivity with end consumers has created a nurturing environment. This eliminates many hassles and conflicts in using traditional channels of distribution. However, others contend that the notion of buyer-driven commerce has become just a marketing gimmick rather than the "centerpiece of a revolution." It remains an unproven territory as competition evolves at every turn.

Pierre M. Loewe and
Mark S. Bonchek

 **YES**

The Retail Revolution

An era of unprecedented consumer power is dawning. It will separate the winners from the losers in all types of retail fields.

Retailers everywhere are talking about using "data mining" to learn more about consumers' habits, tastes and buying behavior than ever before. Every credit card transaction, Internet sale and "frequent buyer" purchase leaves behind a trail of information that retailers are exploiting to their advantage. If knowledge is power, then retailers would seem to have the upper hand.

Don't be fooled. We are entering an era of unprecedented consumer power. Armed with their own databases and tracking technologies, consumers are no longer at the mercy of retailers who set the rules and prices.

"What I want, where I want it, when I want it, and how I want it" is the credo of the emerging consumer. If knowledge is power, then consumer knowledge about retailers' products, inventories and profit margins is about to overturn the world of retailing as we know it. Retailers who continue to use old business models and treat customers in old ways will eventually fail. But those who develop new business models around an informed and empowered consumer will thrive. Many of these business models will involve the Internet, but not all. For those interested in capitalizing on consumer power, the lessons and successes of pioneering companies point the way.

The New Consumer

Who is this new consumer, and what does he or she want? It's simple: anything, anytime, anyplace—on his or her terms. Consider:

- When you bought stocks in the past, you could choose among several full-service brokers as long as you initiated your transaction between 9 a.m. and 5 p.m. and were willing to pay a hefty fee. Today, the array of choices is mind-boggling, with discount brokers like Quick & Reilly, online brokers like E*TRADE and combination brokers like Charles Schwab & Co. You can do it in person, by phone, by fax or online—and in the middle of the night if you like. You can choose a full-cost option with advice, a reduced-cost option that involves only a transaction or a bare-bones option where you do all the work.

- Not so long ago, there were two ways to get dinner: You could go out to a restaurant or cook at home. Now, you not only have more food choices in your supermarket and in the mix of restaurants in your neighborhood, but you also can order your food online, have your groceries delivered in person or by overnight delivery, pick up a prepared meal at the supermarket or a restaurant chain, or order a restaurant-quality meal from Waiters-on-Wheels.

No single trend accounts for the rise of the powerful consumer. A convergence of economic, technological, social and cultural forces has given consumers more information, higher expectations, more choices and better products at lower prices. Still, the individual changes are familiar: Globalization of trade increased the number and quality of competitors in many industries. Deregulation of markets as diverse as trucking, telephony, airlines and financial services unleashed new competitors and lower prices. The quality movement raised the standard for product performance and consumer expectations.

Additionally, technology now allows retailers to manage larger inventories at lower cost and ship any size package anywhere overnight. And the Internet enables consumers to research products, compare prices, check availability and buy or sell merchandise, all without leaving their homes. Forrester Research estimates that 9 million households spent $8 billion on online purchases in 1998. By 2003, more than 50 million households are expected to spend in excess of $100 billion.

Above all, lifestyle changes have made consumers more demanding than ever before. Working couples with little time but plenty of disposable income have created a new dynamic between shoppers and sellers. "Shopping used to be a leisurely activity," says Professor Eugene Fram of the Rochester Institute of Technology in New York. "But we've gone 180 degrees. People are now living time-compressed lifestyles. 'Shop 'til you drop' has gone to 'Drop shopping.'" Consumers have little patience for retailers that do not understand them or will not adapt their business practices to today's lifestyles.

Farsighted retailers recognize that the new consumer has markedly different needs. They are migrating to new business models that will allow them to profit from the creation of value for consumers. Their experiences provide a lesson for other retailers making the same transition.

But innovation requires more than imitation. Retailers must re-examine their relationships with customers, suppliers, distributors and competitors, and then design new business models around the following five core principles.

Empower Your Customer

Traditional retail business models rely on weak, uninformed consumers who don't know the actual cost, performance or repair record of a product. By contrast, business models based on consumer power help customers learn about products, know their options and make intelligent decisions.

Consider the market for long-distance telephone service. Matt Pokress, co-founder and chief technology officer at MediaCom Co., observes that "with hundreds of telephone carriers it is practically impossible to figure out which carrier is best for different types of calls." Most telephone carriers use large advertising budgets to make consumers believe their service is the cheapest.

MediaCom, based in Bedford, Massachusetts, has taken a different approach with a business model based on empowering the customer. Its product, PhoneMiser, connects to a personal computer and automatically searches a database of 200 long-distance phone companies to find the cheapest carrier for each number dialed. It routes the call in less than a second, and typical customer savings are more than 50 percent.

Similarly, most auto insurance companies assume that consumers don't know much about insurance and rarely shop their policies around for a better rate. Progressive Insurance assumes no such thing. When a consumer calls its 800 number or links to its Web site to get an Express Quote, Progressive gives its own rate and the current rates of up to three leading competitors.

The company, based in Mayfield Village, Ohio, has substituted education and information for presumed ignorance and slick sales pitches. Its approach sends a different signal to consumers, many of whom buy from Progressive even if the rate is higher.

Progressive's migration to a customer-focused business model began in 1988 when California voters passed Proposition 103, freezing insurance rates and mandating good driver discounts. According to Leslie Kolleda, a public relations person at Progressive, "Proposition 103 was our wake-up call. Consumers were mad as hell and not going to take it anymore. We could continue to do things the way we always did or we could create a consumer-friendly experience."

Like Progressive, Charles Schwab also has developed a business model based on empowering the customer. While conventional financial planners often act as prophets or wisemen and sell only proprietary funds, Schwab emphasizes objective information and financial education to help customers identify their financial goals and make decisions that are right for them. Schwab's "One Source" guide covers hundreds of funds that are not offered by the company. It is available to customers and noncustomers alike. According to a senior executive at Charles Schwab: "We presume that our customers are really, really smart and we don't think we can fool them."

In the auto industry, salespeople used to intimidate customers who had little information by playing a game of hocus-pocus about the actual cost of a vehicle. Today, car buyers walk into dealerships armed with spec sheets downloaded from Internet sites, such as Microsoft's CarPoint or Edmunds.com, that tell them the dealer's own invoice. Jack Gifford, professor of marketing at Miami University in Oxford, Ohio, observes that "consumers shopping for cars are negotiating not on price, but on how much profit margin the dealer will make. It's a very different kind of negotiation than in the past." Retailers that do not empower customers will find that they empower themselves. Web sites such as bottomdollar.com or comparenet.com allow consumers to instantly compare the prices and features of virtually any product. These services dramatically reduce the cost of finding the best deal. By incorporating such services into their business models, retailers build trusting, informed relationships with customers and make their lives easier.

Personalize Your Offering

The empowered consumer wants it all: customized products and attentive service without the luxury prices that usually accompany them. In sectors as diverse as computers, clothing and vitamins, manufacturers and retailers are deploying new technologies and business models to provide custom-made products and personalized experiences at competitive prices.

Dell Computer and Gateway 2000, for example, manufacture each computer as orders come in, assembling components according to customers' exact specifications. Customers don't have to choose from a limited, off-the-shelf selection or wait a long time for delivery. Instead, the all-powerful consumer configures his own machine, which is custom-made, shipped and delivered in a matter of days.

TC2, a clothes manufacturing consortium, has begun testing a new sales method that takes the concept of "tailor-made" to a whole new level. A customer walks into a booth located at a demonstration center in North Carolina, and either strips to his underwear or puts on tight-fitting stretch clothing. Six cameras take 48 snapshots of his body, which a computer then combines into a 300,000-point, three-dimensional map. More than 100 key measurements are extracted from that data and transmitted electronically to a plant. A customer can watch his garment being made and get it in minutes. TC2 has sold its first two booths (to a jeans manufacturer and a startup company), and Brooks Brothers has announced that it will put one in its New York store in early 1999. Initially, Brooks Brothers will manufacture only shirts and provide express shipments to consumers—but the expansion to other garments and multiple stores is easy to imagine. As for TC2, it is now refining the "virtual try on"—a system where the customer "sees" himself wearing the garment and can adjust the fit accordingly. It expects the technology to be perfected within three years.

Similar fitting technologies are being used by Custom Foot and Digitoe to create custom footware at mass-production prices. But personalization doesn't necessarily mean high tech. Vitamin companies such as GNC, Green-Tree and Ideal Health are creating customized vita-packs to meet customers' individual nutritional requirements. And a simple system from Colorlab lets customers create custom-blended lipstick in minutes at any cosmetics counter.

Abandon Artificial Boundaries

Here's a little secret for retailers: Consumers don't care what industry you are in. And they don't care if you are a manufacturer, wholesaler or retailer. They just want you to give them what they want—which, in a word, is convenience.

As a result, retailers are crossing industry boundaries to help consumers consolidate their shopping trips. In Europe, supermarkets realized years ago that customers wanted the convenience of filling up their cars with gas when they shopped for food. In France, for example, 60 percent of all gasoline is now sold at supermarkets. In Britain, supermarkets will sell more gas than Shell Oil this year.

Convenience also means having a single trusted source. Why have four separate companies to finance your car, insure it, issue an extended warranty and provide roadside assistance? Allstate Insurance in Northbrook, Illinois, is developing a complete package for automotive care that covers all of these categories. According to Mary Beth Shea, responsible for brand and product development at Allstate, "We feel our business is protection, not just insurance policies. For example, we can provide a full circle of protection around two of the most important assets our customers own: their home and their car. Our goal is to maximize the use and enjoyment of these assets and minimize the risks." Since consumers want it all, retailers are blurring industry boundaries to remove trade-offs. In the food business, for example, customers traditionally were forced to choose between the quality of restaurant food and the convenience of prepared foods. EatZi's, a chain based in Dallas, Texas, is a cross between a restaurant and a gourmet fast-food stop. Thirty-five chefs prepare a full variety of high-quality meals for discriminating shoppers who have little time to cook, but no patience for second-rate fare.

Consumers also want shopping to be a rewarding and pleasurable experience. In response, retailers skilled at creating such experiences in a limited product offering are moving into new areas.

Nordstrom will soon bring its renowned customer service in clothing to financial services by offering home-equity loans and money-market checking. Virgin Group is bringing the adventurous spirit of its airline and media stores to the passenger rail industry through its recent acquisition of British Rail. Disney has extended the wholesome fun of its theme parks and movies to cruise lines, community planning and adult education.

Successful companies are not only expanding "horizontally" into new fields, but also making a mockery of the old "value chain," where the manufacturer sold to a wholesaler, who sold to a retailer, who sold to the consumer. Are Dell Computer and Gateway, which manufacture computers to order and sell directly to consumers, manufacturers or retailers? Are Sam's Club and Costco, which sell to consumers at wholesale prices in warehouse-like stores, retailers or wholesalers? Who will be the retailer in the virtual supermarket of the future, when one company runs the online ordering service, another runs the express delivery service and another the regional warehouse?

Traditional labels are rapidly becoming meaningless, and a company must look for ways to break out of the artificial horizontal and vertical boundaries of "its industry." But do so with an understanding of what you bring to the party. It's not enough to identify a potential market or customer benefit; you will need the necessary core competencies and strategic assets as well.

Without them, you will either fail to execute your vision or lose share to imitators. If you don't have the right portfolio of competencies and assets, acquire them or ally with companies that do.

When moving outside your traditional industry, your best bet is usually to move along your existing value chain or into "adjacent" value chains that share a unique core competence or a rare strategic asset. Prime retail locations were strategic assets that enabled supermarkets to sell gasoline—and, conversely, for gas stations to open convenience stores. A core competence in complex billing systems is what enabled AT&T to move into the credit card business a few years ago. More recently, it leveraged its national presence (a strategic asset) to create one of the first nationwide cellular phone networks.

Remember: consumers don't care what industry you are in—as long as you create value and make their lives easier.

Provide Solutions

Access to information is making some consumers almost as knowledgeable about retailers' businesses as their accountants. When consumers know the wholesale price of an item, products become commodities. The traditional model of offering a broad selection of products and marking up each item doesn't work today.

In their search for new business models, retailers are taking a lesson from the business-to-business market where companies have wrestled with commoditization for years. That lesson is to focus on solutions beyond products and services.

Jack Welch, CEO of GE, describes the company as a "global solution service provider," a label that applies to mundane businesses such as locomotives, domestic appliances and jet engines every bit as much as it does to GE Capital.

According to Jeet Singh, CEO of the Art Technology Group, a software company in Boston that develops platforms for personalizing e-commerce sites, "Offerings have become much less commodity like in the business-to-business market because so much is wrapped around the product—specialization, services and volume or repeat discounts—all designed to solve a customer problem."

In response to consumer power, retailers are wrapping commodity products into profitable packages that make customers' lives easier. For example, consumers are increasingly turning to meal solutions rather than meal ingredients. Salad bars, precooked chickens, and prewashed, precut and prepackaged lettuce are now standard items in most supermarkets.

In fact, customer service and execution are critical ways of differentiating products that otherwise are commodities. According to Singh, "A shoe from Neiman-Marcus or Nordstrom's is not the same as from another department store because it can be returned no-questions-asked. And computers purchased from some catalogs or Web sites are different because they can ship the package that very day for next-day delivery. Other sites take two or three days to get the package ready for shipment."

Home Depot is one retailer that has embraced a solutions-oriented business model. The company started by providing do-it-yourselfers with everything they need for home repair at low prices. Recently it began moving to services and solutions. Do-it-yourselfers can now take classes in home repair or have Home Depot arrange complete installation services.

TravelFest is another company packaging products and services into solutions. In fact, Gary Hoover, the founder of TravelFest, has said, "We want to be the Home Depot of travel." At the five Texas-based TravelFest stores, you can do research on a country you want to visit, make plane and hotel reservations to get you there, buy clothes, guide books, maps and luggage, take foreign language classes, exchange money and get help obtaining a visa.

Find a New Economic Engine

The rise of consumer power means that your economic engine—where and how you make money—may need an overhaul. Once-reliable sources of profit may shrink or disappear. In their place, you will need to find related products or entirely new pricing structures to give consumers control, convenience and rewarding experiences.

One route to a new economic engine is to take the well-known concept of a "loss leader" a step further, from the level of the product to the level of the business model. For many years, AMR (the parent company of American Airlines) made far more money from its Sabre reservation system than from flying airplanes.

Movie theaters and amusement parks make most of their money on food and beverages, not admission tickets. The majority of profits at insurance companies come from investing the premiums paid by customers, not from the difference between premiums and payouts for claims. Even on the Internet, where most companies measure their age in months, retailers have had to re-think their economic engines. Online services such as America Online initially thought membership fees would drive profits, but have since migrated to business models based on advertising.

Another option is to change to an auction-based pricing structure. Consumers are flocking to online auction sites, drawn by information about demand for a product, control over how much they bid and the excitement of competing for a bargain. Priceline.com uses a reverse auction to let consumers set their own prices for airline seats, hotel rooms and new cars. Consumers tell Priceline.com what they are willing to pay for a specific flight, room or car model. Airlines, hotels and car dealers looking to fill an empty seat or vacant room or make space for a new car shipment can accept the best offers of these consumers. Retailers selling time-sensitive products that disappear, such as airline seats, or that have difficulty judging demand and regularly discount items, such as clothing or cars, should consider reverse auctions in their search for a new business model.

Web sites such as eBay and ONSALE use a traditional auction in which customers bid for products listed online. Although these sites are filled with collectibles such as beanie babies, a growing number of small retailers are selling new products in much the same way. These retailers typically set a minimum bid equal to their cost of goods to make sure they break even.

When demand is high, prices are bid up and they make a healthy profit. When demand is low, they don't waste time wondering whether and how much to mark the price down.

Established retailers also are incorporating auction-like pricing in the form of automatic markdowns. L.L. Bean has adapted a business model from

Filene's Basement, a discount clothing store, to the world of e-commerce by automatically marking down certain items on its Web site until they sell. Customers can check the Web site anytime they want and don't have to wrestle with traffic (or other customers) for a bargain.

Rethinking Retail

Today's retailers must bring innovation to their tried-and-true business models or risk going the way of the five-and-dime.

Successful retailers will be those who see consumer power not as a threat, but as an opportunity. They will use data mining not to control the customer, but to empower and personalize. They will move across industry boundaries not for financial diversification, but to deliver products and services more conveniently to customers. They will package products and services not to cross-sell, but to solve customers' problems and make their lives easier. And they will develop new economic engines not to create a higher "share of wallet," but to deliver greater value to customers.

The bad news for retailers in the coming revolution is that competition will be fierce. The good news is that the customer is on your side.

Marcia Stepanek

Weblining

You may think that getting graded A, B, or C ended with graduate school. Try getting Sanwa Bank to waive its $20 fee on your bounced check. Customer reps are trained to treat everyone politely. But your luck will depend on a little letter that pops up on a screen as soon as your name is punched into a computer, or when your e-mail arrives at Sanwa's server. If that letter is a "C," customer reps don't exactly hustle on your behalf. That's because machines whirring at Net-speed have lumped you—often in seconds flat—with other customers whose accounts don't make much money for the bank. But if you score an "A," you're right up there with the cream: Customers who generate hefty profits get bounced-check waivers, no questions asked. And B's? They're harder calls. They actually get to negotiate with the rep before their case is decided.

At First Union Bank (FTU), it's a similar story. Its Web-aided computer system, called "Einstein," takes just 15 seconds to pull up the ranking on a customer. First Union won't describe the formula in any detail, other than to say that the ranking software takes stock of minimum balances, account activity, branch visits, and other variables. But the color-coding that appears in a little square on the screen offers a hint. Greens get more flexibility on credit card rates. Reds receive less—and may pay higher fees for some basic services.

Created unequal   What if the reds get mad and take their business elsewhere? Well, that's sort of the point, says Paul Rachal, who helps develop software for banks at Unisys Corp. "This idea about 'whatever the customer wants' is gone," says Rachal. "Now, it's whatever companies can afford to offer, based on each customer's worth. Not all customers are created equal."

Today, bank computers assign ranks based on your assets and your past behavior as a customer. But soon they'll have far more information to work with. Reams of personal details are flooding into thousands of databases across the Web—some of which exist for no other purpose than to sell data to others. Want to know who's Jewish and who's Japanese? You'll find guides to that in a catalog from Acxiom Corp. (ACXM), an information broker that stockpiles names, addresses, income, race, religious affiliations, and other data on 95 million American households.

Companies have long scrutinized their customers, both to spot those who are high-value and to weed out the money losers. But with the oceans of information available on the Net, plus ever faster computers and software, companies can maintain the equivalent of profit-and-loss statements on every customer. They can sort people into more categories and, in some cases, predict how they will behave.

All this slicing and dicing will go into hyperdrive as banks, insurers, credit-card companies, retailers, media concerns, and medical businesses move the bulk of their activities onto the Net. Forrester Research says some 23% of companies are beginning to use the Net to "micro-segment" customers. By this time next year, the number could swell to 60%.

That's good news for companies: The more finely they can dissect your data profile, the more closely they can tally what you are likely to cost them against the profits you bring—and cut you off if you don't add up nicely. But to many people this micro-segmentation raises serious questions. Left to evolve, says Forrester analyst Bob Chatham, this technology could lead to a commercial culture in which "high-value customers are bought and sold like derivative securities."

Call it Weblining, an Information Age version of that nasty old practice of redlining, where lenders and other businesses mark whole neighborhoods off-limits. Cyberspace doesn't have any real geography, but that's no impediment to Weblining. At its most benign, the practice could limit your choices in products or services, or force you to pay top dollar. In a more pernicious guise, Weblining may permanently close doors to you or your business.

Old-style redlining is unacceptable because it is based on geographic stereotypes, not concrete evidence that specific individuals are poor credit risks. Webliners may claim to have more evidence against the people they snub. But their classifications could also be based on irrelevant profiling data that marketing companies and others collect on the Web. How important to your mortgage status, say, is your taste in paperbacks, political discussion groups, or clothing? Yet all these far-flung threads are getting sewn into online profiles, where they are increasingly intertwined with data on your health, your education loans, and your credit history.

This confluence of many streams of personal information, unthinkable just four years ago, is rushing into uncharted canyons. Using technology known as neural networks, many companies believe they can predict your behavior based on all these scattered facts. Cardholders will never be shown their data. And scientists who devise these programs admit that they can't vouch for their accuracy, or even say how they reach a specific conclusion. Neither can the programs' designers, some of whom admit that the technology is dicey. "You've got to be really careful with this, so you don't start judging people on the wrong assumptions," says Tony Patterson, a director at HNC Software Inc. (HNCS) in San Diego, which sells this technology to banks and others. HNC has a new division, eHNC, which will market neural nets to a broader array of Internet businesses.

Are the stereotypes and segmentation that all this technology generates any less disturbing than geographic stereotypes? Lots of people are starting to ask that question. Says Ward A. Hanson, a marketing professor at Stanford University's Graduate School of Business: "It's your data profile that will determine if you get the best service, the best price, and the best access to new products and information."

If you do get Weblined, you may not even know it. For that, thank the wonders of "personalization" software, which quietly analyzes data and dishes up products or services seemingly tailored to you. On the surface, it might seem as if you are getting something really spiffy—a suggestion for a vanity checkbook, or a reminder of your daughter's birthday. In fact, somebody—or perhaps just a computer—has decided what you are fit to see, sample, or buy, based on sometimes-crude calculations of what you are worth to the firm. "Companies can segment without being very obvious about it," says Forrester's Chatham. "But just because it's personalized doesn't mean that what you're seeing and getting is first-class."

And if you peek into the machinery of personalization, you may not like everything you see. Here's how personal it's getting on the Net: Data broker Acxiom offers a new service called InfoBase Ethnicity System, described in a 1999 marketing catalog as a "broad and precise breakdown of ethnic, religious, and minority classifications." The service can, in seconds, match names against housing, income, education, and other demographic data—and identify individual or group ethnicity, designated by "B" for black, "J" for Jewish, "W" for white, "N" for "Nipponese" (meaning Japanese), and so on. Prices for blocks of such information start at $1,500. You can request the full names, addresses, and ages of pre-school children, or "select parents and children by age, gender, and declared religious affiliation." If you have a product you would like to target to "full-figured African American women," as the catalog puts it, you can get it from Acxiom—which serves a cross-section of companies from Lands' End to Conseco Insurance.

Mother lode   This spring, the company plans to move all this information into a new Net-enabled service—AbiliTec—that helps companies consolidate the information they have collected about customers and, for an extra fee, combine it with details from the data mother lode, called Acxiom Data Network. ADN, in turn, has been integrated into popular Web software programs from the likes of E.piphany, which make Acxiom's information instantly available to many more companies.

Acxiom is hardly alone. Naviant Technologies Inc. processes online product registrations for other companies such as IBM. In the process, it has gathered real-world data on more than 17 million households. Another data broker, HotData, helps its client companies link their in-house customer-tracking software with databases from credit watcher Experian and others.

The data collectors don't see any real harm in all this. John Carter, Acxiom's chief of Target Market Applications, says these indexes are just another tool to help marketers get personal with customers. Airlines, credit-card issuers, and mail-order companies have a long tradition of favoring their "good" customers with an arsenal of frequent-flier programs, Platinum cards, and premier rankings.

The good stuff   Indeed, segmentation can make smart business sense. The more a company knows about you, the better chance it has of persuading you to stay loyal when you are courted by a competitor. Levi Strauss & Co. says it has sold 33% more jeans—and hiked repeat-visitor traffic on its Web site by 225%—since it started using personalization and segmentation software. What's more, companies can boost efficiency by treating customers according to a ranking system—one that gives them a level of service in sync with their value to the company. Sanwa Bank estimates that its customer-service operation increased productivity by 14% last year by showering its resources on "A" customers, who bring the most value to the bank. At First Union, the use of such software contributed to an 18% increase in service productivity during the first two years that it was used, says Steve Boehm, general manager of First Union Direct. Such gains are especially critical at busy Web commerce sites. "You can't offer the good stuff to everyone, because it would bring the site to its knees," says Richard Rovner, a senior manager at software maker SAS Institute.

Even the pruning of certain customers may be justified by efficiency gains. Before the Internet, Weyerhaueser's Wisconsin door factory had no idea which distributors were costing the company money and which were bringing in value. Now, Net-based software that handles orders is tied to ranking software, which spots distributors Weyerhaueser (WY) can afford to lose. "The machine is smarter than we are," says Lee Kirchman, the plant's marketing chief. Since it implemented these programs, the company has shed roughly half its customers. But it has doubled orders to more than 800,000 doors last year.

The question is, are the results of segmentation equitable and just? It depends on which marketing basket you land in. "For some people it's fair, and for some it's not," says Roger Siboni, CEO of E.piphany (EPNY), a Silicon Valley maker of e-commerce software, including segmenting programs. Marketing expert Donna Hoffman calls it good old-fashioned cherry-picking, the wooing of only the juiciest customers. "The danger for abuse, for digital redlining, is extremely high," says Hoffman, an associate professor at Vanderbilt University in Nashville.

Companies that promote personalization and segmentation say that consumers get products that are appropriate to their tastes and means. But some sociologists argue that Weblining systematically limits the cultural and economic choices presented to different groups. "There's an anti-democratic nuance to all of this," says New York University Sociologist Marshall Blonsky. "If I am Weblined and judged to be of minimal value, I will never have the products and services channeled to me—or the economic opportunities—that flow to others over the Net."

It would almost be better if the decisions about who sees what were less narrow. In fact, segmenting decisions spring from businesses' desires to forge more orderly markets. What's more, the mathematical algorithms that funnel individuals and groups of people into narrow categories aren't remotely scientific. They may incorporate the biases and intellectual limitations of the software's designers and users. Not all lower- and middle-income consumers crave a steady diet of action films. But if that's what gets served up at a local theater, that's where much of the traffic will flow.

Sure enough, Hollywood studios are starting to use the Net and sophisticated box-office data-tracking technology to speed up decisions about who gets to see which movies, which stars, and even which plot lines. Twentieth Century Fox relies on a Web-powered database, called Project Eight Ball, to place films in 30,000 theaters. The system purports to tell you which crowds prefer Wesley Snipes to Nicolas Cage.

Scientific or not, high-powered computing increases the incentive for businesses to Webline customers by making human behavior appear predictable. Visa International, for example, is using neural networks to build up elaborate behavioral profiles. Over months, these systems—which emulate the learning power of the brain—track a person's behavior online and off, then match it against models of similar personality and behavior types to predict how people will act in the future. The initial incentive was to recognize and thwart fraud. Now Visa is testing the software with 12 member banks in an effort to anticipate loan defaults. "This gives us smarter data, and with Web-based technology, we can get that to our member banks in real time," says Martin Izenson, a director in Visa's risk management and security group.

Black box   The military developed much of this technology to help radar systems, for example, distinguish missiles from birds. Joel R. Reidenberg, a law professor at Fordham University in New York, thinks the technology has outpaced our ability to assess its performance or its impact. "Neural networks are a black box," he says. In a period of just weeks or months, the value assumptions in the networks evolve and can no longer be analyzed with precision, even by the developers. Think what that says about the micro-profiles that are generated. "Some of this really crosses the line into offensiveness," says Reidenberg.

Customers often appreciate the personalization on a Web site, or in a store. But they bristle when they learn about the rankings that go with it. Last summer, Nob Hill Foods, a supermarket chain in Gilroy, Calif., and Wild Oats Markets Inc., a health-food chain in Boulder, Colo., halted their so-called loyalty card programs, which gave cardholders discounts that others didn't get. Customers were complaining that it smacked of discrimination, and some shoppers were threatening a boycott. "Mostly, people resented the snob factor," says Wild Oats spokesman Dan Hall.

In their zeal to collect more data to feed into their computer systems, some businesses that deal with customers face-to-face are forgetting their manners. Driving home from work last fall, Seattle City Planner Terry Whittman stopped at a West Seattle Pizza Hut to pick up dinner, but before she could pay, a register clerk asked for her name, address, phone number, and pizza-topping preferences. When Whittman declined, the clerk refused to fill her order. No data, no pizza. "It was absurd," says Whittman, who had offered to pay cash. Pizza Hut acknowledges the incident, explaining that the "surveys" were aimed at building up a database of online and offline customers. Even so, Pizza Hut admits clerks overstepped company policies.

Stanford computer-science professor Eric S. Roberts says that many of the designers of the new segmenting technology didn't think of the social implications when they invented it. The moral of the story, says Tara Lemmey, president of the Electronic Frontier Foundation: "Just because technology lets you segment more tightly doesn't mean you should."

As Weblining evolves, will we end up constructing a more menacing marketplace? Maybe so. It could be that people who are able to pay more will be prodded to do so by segmentation software. But it is far more likely, as competition for high-value consumers increases, that people with the best profiles could also get the best prices and the best service—locking out the also-rans. Small businesses could face similar Weblining. Some of Weyerhaueser's small distributors, for example, are grumbling about the shabby way they've been treated.

It would be one thing if flexibility were built into this system. But your digital profiles and rankings never go away. Nor can you review them for errors. At the click of a mouse, your e-dossier may be available to other businesses that are keen on segmenting you even more precisely. And because the Internet is still evolving, the whole process of sorting customers will get faster, cheaper, and more subtle at every turn. The Net may be advancing at the speed of light, but it's going to start feeling more and more cramped inside the pigeonhole.

POSTSCRIPT

The New Marketing Paradigm Shift: Are Consumers Dominating the Balance of Power in the Marketplace?

What I want, where I want it, when I want it"has become the wake-up call to marketers recognizing the newfound impact of empowered consumers, according to Loewe and Bonchek. Both as individuals and *collective brand* communities, consumers can now assert their demands for customer-delivered value with authority. Consumers have the power because competition is only a few clicks away. They can patrol for prices or, even better, have "search robots" patrol for them. Almost every major industry from health care to telecommunications is adjusting to accommodate these changes in the marketplace.

Stephen Greyser, an emeritus professor at Harvard University, refers to this paradigm change as the "Copernican Revolution." Copernicus challenged the orthodoxy of sixteenth-century European scientists who until then believed the Earth (not the sun) to be the center of the universe. Now enlightened consumer behavioralists profess the customer is at the center of our new marketing universe (not the company). The Internet makes it possible for consumers to reach providers in new ways. Companies can use it to offer previously unimaginable interactive experiences. Consumers actually become product developers. This "co-opting of consumers" is done on a large scale. For example, more than 650,000 Microsoft customers tested a trial version of Windows 2000 before it was finally commercialized.

Stepanek contends that our privacy may be compromised by interacting with companies on the Internet. Because of superior technology and sophisticated marketing databases, the public finds its personal space and freedom under attack. Authors such as Charles J. Sykes and Amitai Etzioni offer suggestions by which we can recover the territory that we have lost—"our fundamental right to our own lives." Smarting from a consumer privacy backlash, 26 leading companies that collect consumer data, including DoubleClick, American Airlines, and PriceWaterhouseCoopers, have formed a "personalization consortium," an industry group that plans to develop guidelines for using personal information when marketing to individuals. They promise to let consumers access information gathered about them and to allow them to edit it.

The concept of the *digital divide* is of equal concern to many public policy advocates. Critics estimate that by 2020, 40 percent of America will still be offline. From the global perspective, many nations face problems of infrastructure, politics, and cultural barriers, which preclude the benefit and opportunities of e-commerce. Entering the new millennium, less than 1.5 percent of the population of Russia and 1 percent of the population in both China and India have access to the Internet. The social interaction of face-to-face contact for many shoppers will likely never be replaced as we live in a real world of travel, exercise, and the physical dimensions outside the cyberworld.

This customer may be in the "driver's seat" but the marketer may remain the final decision maker. Clearly, both marketers and consumers have become "reinvented" as a result of advancements in information and connection technology. Shopping malls and offline companies will continue to scramble in an effort to remain competitive. Many are complementing and coordinating their Internet efforts, with others seeking new ways to entertain and retain customers.

Suggested Readings

Amitai Etzioni, *The Limits of Privacy* (Basic Books, 1999)

Jay R. Kingley and Barry Uphoff, "IT and the Internet May Threaten Health Insurer Profits," *National Underwriter* (November 9, 1998)

Noreen O'Leary, "Power to the People," *Adweek* (January 10, 2000)

Karen Pallarito, "Do-It-Yourself Health Insurance," *Modern Healthcare* (September 27, 1999)

C. K. Prahalad and Gary Hamel, *Competing for the Future* (Harvard Business School Press, 2000)

C. K. Prahalad and Venkatram Ramaswamy, "Co-Opting Customer Competence," *Harvard Business Review* (January–February 2000)

Charles Sirois, "Telecom in the New Millennium: A Shift of Power," *Telecommunications* (May 1999)

Charles J. Sykes, *The End of Privacy: Personal Rights in the Surveillance Society* (St. Martin's Press, 1999)

bottomdollar.com. `http://www.bottomdollar.com`

buy.com. `http://www.buy.com`

Egghead.com. `http://www.onsale.com`

Epinions.com. `http://www.epinions.com`

DoubleClick: The Global Internet Advertising Solutions Company. `http://www.doubleclick.com`

ISSUE 11

Is the Traditional Development of Brand Loyalty Dying?

YES: Evan I. Schwartz, from *Digital Darwinism: Seven Breakthrough Business Strategies for Surviving in the Cultural Web Economy* (Broadway Books, 1999)

NO: Rebecca Piirto Heath, from "The Once and Future King," *Marketing Tools* (March 1, 1998)

ISSUE SUMMARY

YES: Writer Evan I. Schwartz explains how building brands is accomplished by using the interactive attributes of the Internet. He concludes that emotional branding does not work well on the Internet, so mass media and interactive media should reinforce one another.

NO: Writer Rebecca Piirto Heath makes a case for the importance of a known and trusted brand as a primary influence on a purchase decision. Building a strong brand image strikes an emotional bond with the consumer through brand character and memorability, she asserts.

Due to the confluence of several factors—including the "sophisticated" information-rich consumers, these consumers' real-time demands, and the endless stream of new providers with access to consumers over the Internet—the proliferation of narrow-cost media has raised major questions concerning several dimensions of brands. The specific debate questions relate to brand meaning and importance, the general level of loyalty in the information age, and the traditional formulas for developing brand loyalty. Some see brands as symbols that evoke a unique set of product attributes and reflect the character of the product or company. According to David Aaker in *Building Strong Brands* (Free Press, 1996), a brand is "a set of differentiated promises that link a product or service to its customers."

The world's first brand names derived from the practice of ancient Egyptian shepherds putting name tags on their sheep. Then came the practice of using branding irons to burnish a "badge" on the hide of a bull, which became a symbol of the Texas cattle culture's ownership, pride, and prestige. When mass-circulated newspapers arrived in the late 1800s, companies used brands to introduce national advertisements and identify the source of manufacturing. The first multimillion-dollar campaign was for Nabisco's Uneeda biscuit in 1889. Soon others followed, like Prudential's life insurance and Proctor & Gamble's (P&G's) Ivory soap, with its slogan "99-44/100% Pure: It Floats." This became the first point of differentiation from other products.

Radio and television brought branding into a new world of dominating the mass media with one-way advertising, which targeted millions of consumers, then later segmented audiences with "extended" brands, e.g., Diet Coke. This brief historical perspective is essential to appreciate the significance of what Evan I. Schwartz describes as *Webonomics.* He sees the distinguishing feature between one-way media and two-way, or interactive, media as a simple matter of control. He asserts that in traditional media advertising is intrusive. The marketer purchases space and has complete control over what goes in that space. If one repeats the slogan enough, using an emotional rather than a rational appeal, one ends up with a brand image.

But *rational* branding has become the buzzword for Internet marketers. This media is different due to two major factors: First, it provides comparative product information on salient attributes; second, it affords the interactivity so unique to the online consumer. The critical distinction is that old economy brands, which rely primarily on the mass media, solved problems for sellers, not consumers. Proctor & Gamble, General Foods, and Kellogg's spent billions of dollars trying to differentiate their brands and build focused identities through emotion, repetition, and unique selling propositions.

The key change is a shift in emphasis from the product domain to a solution brand. The new orientation is derived from the concept of "cost transparency" and the opportunity to determine which provider truly solves a problem for the consumer. Schwartz contends that the new perception of brands is moving from the mass media emotional connection to a relevant and rational appeal, which asks, What will the brand do for me? Brands do not exist on the shelves of stores but only in the minds of consumers, he concludes.

The controversy over general levels of brand loyalty is strongly divided. Some critics believe that the Internet will devastate the traditional giant offline brands such as Coke, Campbell's Soup, and Ivory. They contend that there has been an explosive success of the most recognized brands—predominantly dot.com companies—most of which did not exist less than a decade ago.

Rebecca Piirto Heath, however, suggests that brand loyalty has never been higher. She argues that as far as the Internet is concerned, when consumers are unable to see or feel a product, a familiar brand can allay their fears. Furthermore, when information overload makes product choice a complex and imposing task, again consumers are likely to rely on the confidence of an established brand. This is especially true on the Internet, where the number of choices can be overwhelming. The recognized brand becomes a "safety net" for consumers.

 **YES**

Build a Brand That Stands
for Solving Problems

Why Web Branding Is Different

Brands may not be what you think they are. Brands don't exist on store shelves, in TV commercials, or even on Web sites. They exist solely in the minds of consumers, making brand strategy a form of psychological warfare. Branding is also about far more than awareness. Like a neglected house, some world-famous brands that everyone knows can fall into a state of disrepair (remember what happened to Woolworth's), while some of the world's strongest brands don't even ring a bell with most people (such as Callaway golf clubs, the Rolls Royce of golf equipment).

A brand isn't just a famous name. Says Stuart Agres, a top executive with global advertising powerhouse Young & Rubicam (Y&R): "A brand is a set of differentiating promises that link a product or a service to its customers."

Today's concept of branding has been built up in stages over time. It all began in ancient Egypt when shepherds started putting name tags on their livestock. ("Hello, my name is Omar the Ibex. If found, please return me to Achmed.") Shepherds thus became the world's first known brands. The practice of branding livestock endured, eventually spreading to the early American West, which was overrun with wild cattle. Using a branding iron to burnish a badge on a bull's behind became a prime pastime of Texas cattle culture. Cattle ranch brands such as Alamo and Austin became known throughout the land as symbols of ownership, pride and prestige.

A more sophisticated use of branding developed in medieval Europe. Plagues were a major ordeal at the time, and people were becoming ill from drinking brews infested with germs and nasty vermin. The German purity law of 1516 was a hugely successful attempt to change that. And so beer brands sprang up to tell the drinker that these lagers were brewed in accordance with the regulation. From then on, brands were used to confer quality. And people would pay more if they were assured higher quality.

Or some other sort of distinct attribute. Following the lead of the German brewers, whiskey distillers began shipping their concoctions all over the known world—in wooden barrels with the producer's name burned onto them. In 1835, a band of bootleggers introduced "Old Smuggler," a brand of Scotch made using a special distillation process. Branding now had a new role: product differentiation, as well as ownership and quality.

Initially, these attributes had to travel largely by word of mouth, as mass media hadn't yet evolved. When mass-circulation newspapers appeared in the late 1800s, several companies seized the opportunity and introduced national advertisements. The first national, multimillion dollar advertising campaign was for Nabisco's Uneeda biscuits in 1889. Other early national brands included Prudential's life insurance and Procter & Gamble's Ivory soap ("It floats!" and "99 and 44/100% pure" became their points of differentiation.) Mass marketing had begun, and branding was its most potent tool. By 1922, according to Webster's, brand-name was accepted as an adjective, as in "brand-name car" or "brand-name cracker."

With the advent of radio and then television, branding became somewhat of a weird science and a black art at the same time. But if you think about many of the dominant brands established in the mass media, they are different from the most valuable brands established on the Web. To understand why, we have to go back to a distinction introduced in [the book] *Webonomics:*

The distinguishing factor between one-way media and two-way, or interactive media, is the simple matter of control. In traditional media, advertising is intrusive. The marketer purchases space and has complete control over what goes in that space. The viewer or reader has to look at that ad as the marketer intended it. The only recourse is turning the page or changing the channel. As a result, the advertisers can say whatever they want. And they sometimes take this paid-for privilege to absurd heights. Does anybody honestly believe, for instance, that drinking Slim-Fast shakes twice a day amounts to "balanced nutrition for a healthy life," as the company's slogan says? Probably not. But if you repeat it often enough using an emotional rather than a rational appeal, you end up with a brand image.

Rational branding has become a new buzzword among Web marketers. "Rational branding strives both to move and to help the online consumer at the same time," says *BusinessWeek* in an article on the topic. "But the tactic poses a real challenge to makers of consumer products. There are frighteningly few ways to make soap or soda useful in the virtual world. Indeed, of the top five buyers [of] TV advertising, most are nearly invisible online."

It's indeed telling that there have been no new soft drinks or beers, no new soaps and detergents, no new cereals or frozen entrees, no new makes of cars and trucks that have established new brands solely on the Web. Consider brands such as Tide detergent, AT&T long distance, Disney films, Ford trucks, Miller beer, Kellogg's cereals, Coca-cola and so on. Yes, they are all products and services with famous, valuable brand names. The makers of these products typically spend hundreds of millions of dollars, if not billions, every year on ads that try to differentiate their offerings from competing ones. Yes, Coke will quench your thirst and Tide will clean your clothes. But none are really aimed at intricate multi-step problem domains, like many of the emerging brands on the Web. These mass media brands were created to solve the problems of sellers, not consumers.

Those products use emotion to try to forge identity. And on the Web, consumers do not have to endure emotion-laden advertisements. They spend their time doing things, finding things, getting chores done—and sidestepping ads. The most valuable Web brands—including Yahoo, Amazon.com, and E*Trade—are not product brands. They are brands for a complex set of services—solutions—that help people cut through the clutter and perform a series of tasks.

"Consumers are not looking for more choice," says Mark Dempster, director of brand strategy for USWeb/CKS, a Silicon Valley marketing strategy agency. They have enough product choice already. "Rather, they are looking for 'made-for-me' solutions." Unlike mass media, the interactive, personal media such as the Web simply aren't good at burnishing an emotionally-charged message into the minds of millions. The Web is adept at taking a user through a series of screens, a step-by-step process with an end result in mind. Consumers can actually use the Web as a tool to accomplish a particular objective.

Solution branding may not be entirely new. (High-tech service firms, from IBM to EDS, are among those that have been touting for years the idea that "we sell solutions.") What is new is the rise of interactive solution services and how the new brands in this domain are already beginning to rival the prestige of venerable mass media brands.

What Makes for a Strong Brand?

Still, Web-based businesses can learn a lot from the past. Emotion-based product brands such as Coke and Pepsi have showed the world that if branding isn't everything, it's sure damn close. Countless studies have shown that there's nothing like a strong brand for juicing both your net income and stock price. Coca-Cola's brand names, for instance, are worth a staggering $167 billion (the difference between its physical assets of $15 billion and its recent stock market capitalization of $182 billion). Such brand equity is no doubt one of the most stunning achievements in modern business. By repeating the emotional attributes and sheer sensibilities of sweetened fizzy water enough times in advertisements and promotions, Coke has become the world's most ubiquitous brand.

Many of the same tactics and techniques pioneered by the product brands we all know transcend media and are still critical for creating these new solution brands. According to Y&R, the process of building any strong brand must begin with brand differentiation, which is "the perceived distinctiveness" of the product or service. "Differentiation gives birth to the brand," says Y&R's Agres, who leads an ongoing research project called the Brand Asset Valuator, an assessment of 8,500 brands that involves interviewing tens of thousands of consumers in 24 countries.

The first question that emerging Internet businesses need to ask is: "What makes this brand stand apart?" Coca-Cola and Disney, for instance, still maintain their differentiation, while TWA and Greyhound do not, according to the study. The winners have been adept at innovating what their products were about, identifying and attaching new attributes themselves. Among Web brands, CDnow and Music Boulevard seemed to struggle to stand apart from one another, thus explaining, in part, why they rushed into each others' arms and merged. No one seemed to know why one online music store was better or worse than the other.

The second pillar of building brand equity is establishing brand relevance. Customers are always subconsciously asking: "Does this brand speak to me?" This is the so-called personal appropriateness of the brand. You can be extremely aware of what a brand stands for without being personally interested in making the brand a part of your life. Think of Ferrari and Victoria's Secret. Many people know exactly what makes these brands different, yet they only address the real needs of a certain few. You can become a market leader with high differentiation but low relevance, but it will ultimately reach a very targeted market. On the flip side, you can be relevant to many people but not differentiated. Witness the dozens of low-cost online stock brokerage services on the Web that have failed to establish leadership in their category.

The third factor is brand esteem, which is a measure of how highly consumers regard the brand. This is closely related to perceived feelings of popularity or high perceived quality on the part of consumers. Global brands with the highest esteem ratings due to perceived quality include Hallmark and Kodak. Those with high esteem ratings due to a widespread sense of popularity—brands that are in a sense vague—may include Yahoo and Amazon.com.

Finally, the fourth factor, brand knowledge, measures the consumer's understanding of the brand's inner workings. High brand knowledge suggests acute customer intimacy or proof that consumers are experienced with how your product or service works for them—for better and for worse. Y&R considers this the culmination of any branding effort.

Yes, strong brands need both high esteem and knowledge. But brands with high knowledge and low esteem tend to be desperately discounting their products to avoid losing market share or serving a market with polarized opinion about them. People may know a lot about them, but not hold a high opinion. An example of such brands, according to the Y&R study, include McDonald's and the National Rifle Association.

Conversely, brands with high esteem and low knowledge tend to be newer, expanding, and possessing some sort of unrealized potential. That's the perfect description for many of the newer Web brands. The danger, of course, is that these names can take on the aura of a passing fad. "Consumers want to be seen going with the winner," says Agres. But if the perceived popularity drops, if the fad fades, then there is nothing left propping it up. That's why brands that only have esteem going for them and neglect the other three pillars can be in grave danger.

Although the Brand Asset Valuator was originally developed to measure mass-media brand names, these four pillars of building brand equity also apply to the millions of domain names in the emerging Web economy. And most Web-based brands have yet to take the leap into this more sophisticated realm of thinking. As a result, so many young companies make the mistake of equating brand strength with simplistic awareness, a mistake that may lead to brand death.

"The battle can't solely be for people's attention," Agres says. It's not just about people knowing your name, but what your name stands for, whether it speaks to people's real needs, whether people hold it in high regard, and whether your promises are delivered upon when consumers finally have real, first hand experience with it. In general, he says, growing, thriving, profitable brands should have higher ratings for differentiation than relevance, and higher ratings for esteem than knowledge.

Solution brands have to leap especially high barriers en route to these goals. Let's bring it back to the online grocery services. "It shouldn't just be online retail," Agres concludes. "Online retail is besides the point. It has to be more than the superficial: we'll-deliver-your-groceries message. It has to be: What is the brand doing for me? How do I benefit? Communicate the promise." And deliver the promise as well as the groceries.

Keeping Your Solution Brand Alive

Brands exist in a larger, overall context, which is constantly shifting. The surrounding environment comprises many elements, including the changing expectations of customers, what your competitors are doing, how investors perceive your market segment, and new technological developments.

The fact that the larger market conditions can unexpectedly mutate is well-known in the traditional world of branding. "The sands constantly shift," says Mark Dempster, the CKS brand strategist. "CEOs that don't pay attention will have the context of their brand change right under them."

As a result, brands that seem dominant one minute can lose their footing the next. And on the Web, that can happen by the next time you upgrade your browser. The Netscape brand name, for instance, was practically synonymous with the Web's early, we've-just-discovered-a-new-planet sensibility. Customers, competitors and investors were euphoric over it. It exhibited enormously high differentiation and esteem.

Then the context shifted. "When we started Netscape, we thought we were a software company," says co-founder Marc Andreessen, the chief developer of the first commercial Web browser. "What do software companies do? They create software and sell it. Turns out, that's not the business model that made sense for us. People already have more software than they know what to do with, and we had to keep giving away the software just to get people to use it." Obviously, with Microsoft's entrance into Netscape's core market, the competitive landscape was altered enormously and permanently.

Netscape's business then shifted toward selling software for corporate Intranets. Consumers might not pay for browser software, they thought, but corporations would pay for industrial-strength network management software and related services. This new sector rapidly became the company's biggest source of revenue. But as Netscape was battling Microsoft in those markets, too, and concentrating on corporate software, the context was mutating yet again.

Yahoo and other Web search services were paying Netscape about $5 million per year for choice spots on Netscape's home page, which happened to be the default home page for tens of millions of Web surfers worldwide. Directed properly, the attention of these people was worth far more than that. Yahoo parlayed that aggregation of attention into a market valuation topping $20 billion, while Netscape's market value was stagnating. By early 1998, Netscape was forced to shift its focus to take advantage of this key opportunity, this time to developing its Netcenter homepage into a major "portal," a navigation service that tries to cut through the choice and complexity for the user. Netscape was now in competition with one of its main business partners.

But Netscape's portal lacked differentiation. While Yahoo was evolving its Web experience brand in many new ways, Netscape was forced into a perpetual game of catch-up. By the time it was swallowed by America Online, Netscape's NetCenter had plenty of traffic, but it trailed that of Yahoo. And more importantly, it offered little in the way of unique solutions or features. Its stock market valuation and behavior reflected that.

Toward the end of its existence as an independant entity, Netscape was lashing out ferociously at its competitors, sometimes in defensive terror. It finally fetched $4.2 billion—approximately the same valuation that it had shortly after going public three years earlier. In an e-mail message unearthed in the landmark government trial against Microsoft, Netscape's co-founder Marc Andreessen urged America Online chairman Steve Case to combine forces against a larger predator. "We must use our unique strengths to kick the [expletive] out of the Beast from Redmond that wants to see us both dead," Andreessen wrote.

The longer you let your brand drift, the longer you let your competitors define what the new context is, the harder it becomes to reposition the brand in the new context. This is true across every industry.

The Howard Johnson's hotel chain is a case in point. "HoJo is a venerable brand that has gone stale," Dempster says. "You think of those wonderful family car trips in a station wagon in the '50s and '60s. But it has lost its footing in an age when Hyatt and Hilton have become more like high-tech corporate offices than hotels." The entire context of what a hotel should be had been transformed. But HoJo's properties and image were still the same. It had high brand knowledge and low esteem. Everyone seemed to know and understand the brand, but they didn't think too highly of it compared to competitors.

These days, the top manager of the HoJo brand happens to be Wall Street financial whiz Henry Silverman, the CEO of marketing giant Cendant. Silverman had purchased HoJo along with Ramada (another high knowledge, low esteem brand) for $170 million in the early 1990s, then proceeded to kick 150 hotels out of the Howard Johnson's system. He also forced others to upgrade their facilities and quality of service—all aimed at rebuilding brand esteem. But whether he succeeds in reconnecting consumers with HoJo, creating a new promise for the brand, remains to be seen.

Rebuilding such a brand, according to David Aaker, a brand strategy expert at University of California at Berkeley, is usually a long, tough slog. "Schlitz Beer tried to rebuild its brand and failed," Aaker says, "Toyota and Nissan did it, but it took them 15 years." In the new Web economy, no one has that kind of time. The brand manager of the future is like an air traffic controller," Dempster says. "It's all happening in real time."

Shift happens! That's why Yahoo doesn't just react to but actively goes about causing such shifts. As a result, Yahoo often seems as if it is a solution brand that is constantly in frantic search of new problems to solve. It seems to be reinventing its brand every 90 days. The site may have started as a Website directory but it quickly moved to add a keyword search engine, then a personalized news service, then a virtual community with bulletin boards and chat, then a free e-mail service, then a series of city guides for major U.S., European and Asian destinations, then a travel guide, then a personal finance service, then a complete e-shopping guide sponsored by Visa. Then it acquired its way into the business of opening and hosting low-cost Web storefronts for budding merchants.

As it keeps forcing shifts in the market, Yahoo has managed to maintain the single largest daily audience of any Web site, attract the largest share of advertising and sponsorship revenue, and incidentally, turn a respectable profit at a time when profitable e-commerce companies are scarce.

All this activity has mesmerized investors and has had the potential to confuse users of the service. They may never have high brand knowledge of all of Yahoo's many services, but Yahoo has succeeded in differentiating itself from the pack and boosting its brand esteem, its perceived popularity. Yes, the site has been in a constant state of flux since its launch. But co-founder Jerry Yang argues that customers have come to expect this. "We're a Web experience brand," Yang says. "And I think our customers understand that."

Yet Yahoo also seems to be scrambling, getting itself into the features game, without a clear message that it all adds up to some sort of meaningful solution to a specific set of problems. "We want to be the only place that anyone has to go to—to find and get connected to anything or anybody," says Yahoo CEO Timothy Koogle. That, in a nutshell, is what Yahoo is all about, he says. Can he be a little more vague?

Luckily, Yahoo's rivals in the Internet portal race seem to be scrambling even more frantically to develop the ultimate, overarching Web experience solution. That's the nature of business on the Web. Still, danger always lurks. At any point, some other brand could appear out of nowhere and shift the context of the digital landscape right out front of all of us.

NO

Rebecca Piirto Heath

The Once and Future King

What is in a brand? If you took the Nike name off the sneaker, would it carry the same cachet? Would a Godiva chocolate by any other name taste just as sweet? If your boss asked for a Coke, would you just grab the no-name cola from the end display, or would you look a little farther down the aisle to find The Real Thing?

Answers: No, no, and Always Coca-Cola. There was a time when Americans proudly declared their independence from the ineffable appeal of "name brands" in favor of the hard-nosed practicality of generics and private labels, but those days are over. The 1997 Yankelovich Monitor survey of American consumers shows that a known/trusted brand name is a strong influence on purchase decisions for 63 percent of respondents, up from 51 percent in 1994. By contrast, "low price" was a strong influence for 61 percent of [1997] respondents. [Recently] the editors of Roper Reports announced that for the first time in almost 10 years, growing numbers of Americans perceive "a great deal of difference" between brands. Respondents were most discriminating when it came to automobiles—62 percent say there's a lot of difference between car makers —but they also look for the right labels on personal computers (35 percent), televisions (34 percent), and even small-ticket items like coffee, cola, and facial tissues (33 percent, 32 percent, and 23 percent, respectively). More than half of the 1997 respondents (54 percent) agreed strongly with the statement, "Once I find a brand that satisfies me, I usually don't experiment with new ones," compared to 46 percent in 1995. Roper Starch also found a high level of agreement with the statement, "Some makes are worth paying more for" in categories like luxury cars (58 percent, compared to 47 percent in 1994), PCs (51 percent, up from 38 percent in 1994), TVs (50 percent, up 3 percent since 1994), and stereo equipment (49 percent, up from 41 percent in 1994).

The renewed revenue-generating power of brands is rocking the corner offices of corporate America. "Companies are beginning to understand that creating, reinforcing, and growing brand loyalty is the basis for enduring profitability growth," says Larry Light, a branding guru and president of Arcature, Inc. of Stamford, Connecticut.

Brands now have equity—a recognized bottom line value apart from product sales revenues. A brand's equity is the added value that lets Absolut vodka charge a higher price for its product than the no-name alternative. The most dynamic brand names—Microsoft, Nike, Coca-Cola, McDonald's—evoke an image that goes far beyond the products the company makes. According to Financial World magazine, Coca-Cola's brand was worth an estimated $39 billion in 1995. The value of the Marlboro name was set at $38.7 billion, Microsoft was worth $11.7 billion, and IBM and Intel logged on at $7.1 billion and $9.7 billion, respectively.

Name recognition has become so valuable an asset that some companies have outsourced the actual manufacturing process so they can devote all their attention to nurturing the brand. Nike doesn't own sneaker factories anymore. Sara Lee, which controls the Champion, Playtex, Hanes, and Hillshire Farms brands, recently made headlines by selling off many of its bakeries, meat-processing plants, and textile factories to become a "virtual" corporation that puts its name on things it no longer produces. "Slaughtering hogs and running knitting machines are businesses of yesterday," explained CEO John Bryan when announcing the first round of manufacturing assets sales. At the close of the 20th century, even manufacturing firms are moving from the industrial age to the information age.

A Wake-Up Call

The idea that brands have value in and of themselves represents a revolutionary change in American business thinking, says Light. In the mid-1980s, the whole discipline of marketing was in disrepute. With generics and private labels at the peak of their popularity, branding was widely perceived as a dead-end strategy. In a panic, brand marketers resorted to fevered rounds of price deals and couponing.

This was a curious state of affairs, considering that the rest of the world has long associated America with brand names like Coke, Pepsi, and McDonalds. But then, American companies have typically relegated brand maintenance to their marketing and advertising functions, placing greater importance on tangible assets like products and machinery. Europeans, on the other hand, have traditionally placed a higher value on intangible assets, like a tradesman's reputation and a customer' s goodwill.

Light, who served as the former chairperson of the Coalition for Brand Equity (a research group formed by ten trade associations) says there are historical reasons for this disparity. The modern concept of trademark was developed in medieval times by the Vatican. "The Vatican identified two forms of intellectual property," Light says, "the design of a product or the product itself, and the reputation of the person who designed or made the product." There were two courts for handling disputes arising from trademark conflicts: the court of law, run by lawyers, to try trademark infringements, and the court of equity, run by the church, to handle issues of reputation. Besmirching a business's reputation was viewed as a high sin.

"They recognized even then that the source of the product, your image, your reputation, your goodwill was more valuable than the product," observes Light. The Anglican church condoned the practice of treating goodwill as an asset on a balance sheet. "We got our trademark law from the UK. What didn't come over to the U.S. was the idea that goodwill is a very valuable asset," Light says. "That's why the whole concept of brand equity came from Europe, and the concept of brand valuation was born in London, not in New York."

By the 1990s, American executives had begun to adopt a more European view of brands, but the marketing community lagged behind. "This was the big lie of marketing," recalls Light. "I knew that brands were not going to die; they were going to be stronger than ever. What needed to be murdered was the mismanagement of brands. We had board rooms saying brands are valuable assets, while the marketing community was killing the assets that were most valuable and turning brand-loyal customers into deal-loyal customers."

The turning point came on April 2, 1993, when Marlboro—one of the world's strongest brands—cut its price. The move was widely regarded as confirmation that brands were extinct. But the following Monday, the stock-market value of packaged-goods companies fell $25 billion.

"Thank God for Marlboro Friday," says Light. "On that day, we learned some very significant lessons." The message was that the financial community cared about brands, and that strong brands were worth billions.

The Other Side of the Ledger

Besides, the last decade has seen massive corporate downsizing. Companies adopted total quality management to increase efficiency, and fine-tuned business processes to cut costs to the bone.

"Now they're looking at the revenue side of the balance sheet: selling more product, increasing margins and profits," says Alan Bergstrom, president of The Brand Consultancy in Atlanta, Georgia. "Brands can do all those things. If I can position my brand to appeal to a broader customer base, attract a new customer set, I'll sell more products. If I position my brand right, I can also extract a higher price. Branding is on the radar scope of so many senior executives now because for the first time, they see brands not as a marketing/advertising expense, but as a revenue generator."

Don Schultz, author of Measuring Brand Communication Return on Investment and president of Agora Inc. in Illinois, takes an even more radical view of the situation. "Twenty-first century organizations have to compete on brands because they have nothing left," he asserts. "They can't get product differentiation, they can't get superior pricing, distribution, or promotion, so branding strategy is it."

The brands have been delivering. Brand cachet is the reason consumers with means don't mind paying $89,000 for a Humvee or $1,700 for a bottle of Chateau Margaux. What's the difference between the line drawn by a Montblanc pen and one drawn by a Bic? "The difference is 120 bucks," Bergstrom shrugs. "The Montblanc name is what gives Montblanc that price premium. It represents quality—the way it looks, the way it feels in your hand." Even commodity products can get a price premium from branding. When given a choice, 60 percent of consumers in grocery stores will choose Sunkist oranges over an unbranded variety. Why? "Because they see Sunkist as a brand that stands for something they're willing to pay extra for," says Bergstrom.

More Than a Trademark

A strong brand has a big advantage in today's marketplace, where more and more products vie for consideration by customers with less and less time to make choices. "Branding helps people simplify their decision-making process about what product or service to buy, Bergstrom says. "It's almost like a handle for them. If it's got that brand, it stands for something that's relevant to me. I trust it; therefore, I buy it."

As Light sees it, the secret to all successful brands is that they stand for something. "Brands are much more than simply trademarks or logos," he says. "A brand is a promise to the customer." A brand differentiates the product that makes that pledge from the rest of a crowded field of competitors. Tide is not just a brand of powdered detergent: It's the assurance of powerfully clean clothes. Crest is not simply a brand of fluoride toothpaste. "Crest promises that you will die with your own natural teeth in your head," Light says. If Crest represents healthy teeth, Procter & Gamble can reinforce its promise with Crest mouthwashes, toothbrushes, and a whole spectrum of other products promoting dazzling dentition.

The idea of brand promise goes far beyond the mere experience of a product or service. It encompasses the entire spectrum of a consumer's awareness of the company behind the brand, says Bergstrom. "To fully leverage the power of brands, you must look at the brand from the customer's perspective," he says. "It represents the sum of all points of encounter, including not just the product and service and advertising, but distribution, delivery, point of sale, and customer service."

Brands that keep faith with their customers allow their companies to enter new markets and extend the promise into new categories. But line extensions and forays into new markets carry significant risks, and they can be disastrous for companies that fail to do their homework. It's not just a matter of losing money on a product that goes nowhere; it's the possibility that the clinker will take the brand name down with it, by losing the trust of loyal customers. "The most important thing about a line extension is to recognize that brand management is about promise management," says Light.

Keeping the Promise

A viable brand promise requires three things. First, it must be relevant to the customer. That is, it must be about something the customer cares about. Second, it must be distinctive and specific, separating the product or service from the rest of the market. Finally, it must be trustworthy or credible. "The customer has to have confidence that you will deliver on your promise," Light says. "If you fail to deliver on the trust, you've broken the promise, and the brand loses its specialness." Arm and Hammer is one company that has had great success with line extensions, moving from baking soda to toothpastes.

"They've created brand equity based on freshness, all-natural ingredients, and good health," Light says. "Not only have they not broken people's trust, but they have reinforced the overall promise." Procter & Gamble's decision to come out with liquid Tide also represents a well-thought-out extension, Light says. Under the old way of thinking at P&G, liquid Tide would have been Era. The new P&G branding policy recognizes that Tide is the laundry product that does the best job of cleaning tough stains, whether it comes in a liquid or a powder. "The key is that you should not have gentle Tide," says Light. "That promise would be inconsistent, and actually belongs to Ivory."

On the other hand, Starbucks is a strong brand that has had mixed results with line extensions. "Starbucks stands for high quality, outstanding coffee. It's a nice warm experience that makes people feel good, so there's an emotional dimension to it," Bergstrom says. This promise translated well into the frozen desserts category when Starbucks began offering ice-cream products last year.

But Starbuck's foray into the airline food-service arena has been less successful, Bergstrom says. In an attempt to increase brand awareness and introduce the brand to new customer segments, Starbucks agreed in 1996 to supply coffee for United Airlines flights. "In theory, it made sense. In reality, it was a bad decision," Bergstrom says.

His explanation: The key reason for Starbuck's success as a brand was that it rigorously controlled the quality of its product. Then it turned over a chief attribute—quality control—to an airline, whose primary concern is transporting people, not serving premium coffee. In doing so, Starbucks began to chip away at its covenant with consumers. "If this is my first impression of Starbucks and I have a cup of coffee on a UA flight that's terrible, what are my chances of choosing Starbucks again?" Bergstrom asks.

Measuring the Promise

Such missteps can be avoided if companies take the time to fully understand all the attributes—both tangible and intangible—that make up the brand's promise, says Don Dietrich, vice president of Chilton Research Services. The Radnor, Pennsylvania, firm does diagnostic brand-equity modeling to identify the key attributes of brand promise.

"We identify the chain of reasons that customers make a choice," Dietrich explains. "The typical process starts with tangible attributes, moves to benefits and emotional or self-expressive benefits, then to values that are fulfilled by the benefits." The idea is to encourage customers to think about their reasons for choosing one alternative over another, and to uncover the whole range of reasons underlying consumer choice.

For example, the Jaguar brand promises self-expressive imagery and intangibles: the distinguished, European, rich, sporty driving experience that goes with the country British racing gentleman archetype. Cheerios, on the other hand, promises the tangible attribute of crunchiness. One key attribute of brands like McDonald's and Coke is the ubiquitousness of the product, with an outlet around every corner.

By understanding the composite pieces of a brand's promise at the attribute level, companies can discover the degree to which the attributes will translate to a new category or line extension. Chilton uses statistical modeling, laddering techniques, and in-depth interviews to identify the attributes that resonate most with customers, then tests the degree to which each attribute makes individual customers willing to pay more for the brand.

Dietrich says a lot of companies go awry when they fail to fully explore the leveragable attributes in the new category. "The existence of competitors means that someone has done a lot of work in the category, and if you want to get a piece of their pie, you better be prepared to catch up in consumer understanding," he warns.

For example, a fruit-juice manufacturer introducing a new brand of frozen juice bars has to understand what the original product represents for consumers, and how those attributes translate to the new category. The main attributes of juice—wholesomeness and nutritional value—may not fly with consumers in the frozen bar category. "If sweetness is very important in the new category and you're strong on sweetness, that's the thing to emphasize in all your communication as you move forward and enhance your position in that attribute," advises Dietrich.

Measuring Brand Equity

A number of firms have developed ways to quantify and isolate the elements of brand equity. "By understanding brand equity, a company can chart an aggressive brand strategy that powers growth and boosts the bottom line," says Eric Almquist, vice president of Management Consulting Inc. of Lexington, Massachusetts. Mercer has used its proprietary method, Strategic Choice Analysis, for clients ranging from large online services to airlines and financial institutions.

"Companies do not own the equity in their brands," Almquist says. "The equity is in the customer's mind. Companies can only indirectly manage that brand equity." Mercer measures the relative value of brand equity by customer segment for the client and its competitors by identifying the positive and negative equity elements that are actually shifting market share. Mercer recently worked with a large high-tech company to help understand its more than 100 different brands with overlapping customer segments. The results showed that while the brands were individually strong, the overlap confused customers and eroded the company's overall brand equity. By consolidating many of its brands and aligning them better with its sales channels, the company was able to increase revenue by 15 percent while reducing marketing expenses. "We estimated that improving three of their brand equity dimensions would yield $6 billion in sales," Almquist says. "While that hasn't happened yet, it shows the power of brand equity measuring."

Don Schultz believes strongly that in order to compete, today's companies must precisely measure the return on their brands' equity. "If in the 21st century brands are the only thing you've got, then you had better figure out how to develop them, spend against them, and how to measure the return on them," he says. Schultz has developed a method to measure brand return on investment that quantifies the bottom-line value to the corporation of each customer segment and calculates the cost of retaining or investing to get more business from a segment.

All customers are not created equal. If two customer groups each generate $10,000 a year for a company, but the brand attracts 90 percent of the business of one and only 25 percent of the business of the other, the more loyal group is worth more today. But the less loyal group may represent significant future income. "The first thing you have to understand is the value of your customers," Schultz says. "We can place differing values on each based on their behavioral patterns, the kind of income flow they generate, and what the costs are for retaining or investing in future income flows."

Beyond Brand Preference

Light cautions that cultivating brand preference is not enough to grow profits. "We have to move beyond brand preference to create brand enthusiasm," he says. "These are the customers who are not only satisfied, they're so enthusiastic they will repeat; they will advocate. Even when all things are unequal, they will buy your brand." Light agrees that a brand-loyal customer is eight to ten times as profitable as a brand-disloyal customer, and that marketers have to be choosy about where they invest their resources. One company found that 60 percent of its marketing dollars were directed at its least loyal customers, in effect rewarding them for disloyalty. "By spending marketing dollars carelessly, they were inadvertently educating consumers to move down the loyalty ladder, not up," Light says.

Another study, for National Purchase Diary, illustrates the danger of taking loyal customers for granted. The study gauged the subjects' brand loyalty from year to year. Among those who exhibited low brand loyalty, 87 percent were still disloyal the next year. More importantly, of those who exhibited high loyalty, 47 percent were not loyal the following year. "Taking a loyalist for granted is a drastic mistake, " Light says.

Yet, few companies invest adequately in reinforcing the behavior of the most loyal customers. "We forget about the customer after they purchase from us," Light says, "but what we really need to do to maximize brand enthusiasm is to get to them right after they make a purchase, and form a relationship with them." Light's research shows that a 5 percent improvement in the loyal customer base will produce a 25 percent improvement in profits.

In truth, despite all the talk of brand valuation, brand equity, and the importance of building *brand* loyalty, many branding experts feel that companies still have a long way to go before they tap into the full power of brands.

One shining exception—and everyone's favorite example of excellence in brand management—is the Disney Company. The Disney brand promise is to keep alive the magic of childhood, a promise that has been extended and reinforced in categories as diverse as CDs, films, clothing, toys, books and theme parks. "A dynamic brand doesn't sit still—you have to position the brand on a trajectory of where the market's going to be in five years or longer," Bergstrom says. "Disney's done that probably better than anyone."

"Disney is a family thing, a set of constant expectations in the public's mind... a certain quality, a certain type of entertainment," says a company spokesman. "Our job is to be protective of that Disney thing." What's surprising about that statement is that it was made by Walt Disney in 1938.

"It is still reflected and maintained at every level of the organization today," Bergstrom says. "That Disney thing" created a category of family entertainment that hadn't previously existed. "That's the true power of a brand," Bergstrom says. "If you can get the entire organization to rally 'round it and communicate it to the customer in everything they do, it really does become the corporation's most valuable asset."

POSTSCRIPT

Is the Traditional Development of Brand Loyalty Dying?

Brand building on the Internet provides interesting contradictions. For example, if there are thousands of companies selling books on the Internet, why are most people still buying from Amazon.com or Barnesandnoble.com? Perhaps these brand names do indeed lower the perceived risk of the transaction. On the other hand, consider the success of another Internet company, Priceline.com, which basically renders the brand invisible and insignificant to buyers. How about eBay, where the above two models literally converge, since both price and brand are equally important?

Is word of mouth likely to be important in brand building? Companies like Epinions.com allow people to compare features and read reviews by actual owners. That may or may not be beneficial for all companies. Brand equities are likely to be built as well as destroyed much faster.

How about the longevity of the brands? Some well-established Internet brands like Drkoop.com (medical advice) and ivillage.com (for women) are currently running into rough weather. A recent prediction by Forrester Research forecasts a grim future for online retailers. Researchers contend that most e-tailers will be gone in one year.

Branding is highly unlikely to become obsolete. It is difficult to imagine Rolex watches, Nokia phones, and Volvo cars diminishing in value. On the other hand, with the Internet acting as a global conduit for fads and hype, is the importance of brands as image signifiers likely to grow? How should we value and evaluate e-business brands?

Suggested Readings

David Aaker and Erich Joachimsthaler, *Brand Leadership: Building Assets in the Information Society* (Free Press, 2000)

"AOL, Yahoo! Top E-Brand List," *Business Communications* (March 2000)

Phil Carpenter, *E-Brands* (Harvard Business Press, 2000)

Gil McWilliam, "Building Stronger Brands Through Online Communities," *Sloan Management Review* (Spring 2000)

Frederick Newell, *Loyalty.com* (McGraw-Hill, 2000)

Agnieszka Winter, *Warp-Speed Branding: The Impact of Technology on Marketing* (John Wiley, 1999)

ISSUE 12

Is "Extreme Sports" Marketing Risk and Thrill Seeking to Society?

YES: Karl Taro Greenfeld, from "Life on the Edge: Is Everyday Life Too Dull? Why Else Would Americans Seek Risk As Never Before?" *Time* (September 6, 1999)

NO: Myra Stark, from "The Extreme Generation," *Brandweek* (September 1, 1997)

ISSUE SUMMARY

YES: Karl Taro Greenfeld, a business issues writer, asserts that "extreme sports," such as snowboarding and mountain biking, have enjoyed incredible growth in contrast to the demise of baseball, touch football, and aerobics. He offers evidence to illustrate parallel behavior for risk taking and thrill seeking in many aspects of other national behaviors.

NO: Myra Stark, director of knowledge and management insight at Saatchi and Saatchi, highlights the appeal of extreme sports to its target market, emphasizing the quest for individualism and self-expression. Competitiveness and the development mindset are also derivatives of these unique recreational challenges, maintains Stark.

Two basic components are relevant to this marketing issue. First is the direct impact of marketing on the participants of extreme sporting activities, such as snowboarding; bungee jumping; paragliding; Buildings, Antennae, Span bridges, and Earth cliffs (BASE) jumping; and mountain biking. Second is the impact on society, or the view of extreme sports, as a recent *Time* article put it, as "a collection of attitudes, lifestyles and trends that symbolize these sporting participants, and directly influence our culture, representing a vivid manifestation of a new national behavior."

Extreme sports emerged into the X-Games when ESPN accountant/programmer Ron Semiaco decided that demand existed for a TV event featuring athletes whose lifestyles and culture reflected their passion for extreme sports. The past five years have witnessed a steady increase in the popularity of "extreme games" in many areas of the United States. The growth of this phenomenon has been incredible. Currently referred to as the "X-Games," alternative sports have reached at least 155 million homes in 175 countries broadcast by ESPN, ESPN2, ESPN International, and *ABC's Wide World of Sports*. Its popularity is reflected in the estimated over 7 million bungee jumps that occurred in the 1990s and the fact that the number of climbers attempting Mount McKinley (the tallest peak in North America) has almost doubled in the last few years. Fueled by promotional tie-ins, sponsorships, licensing agreements, and road trip promotions, X-Games Gold sponsors were paying over $2 million for advertising privileges. And extreme sporting equipment alone reaped an estimated $4 billion in 1998.

Certainly much of "extreme" has become "mainstream," appealing to a wide range of athletes, both men and women, from teens to 30-somethings. However, while most skydivers are younger, parachute associations report that their fastest-growing membership segment is the over-40 age group. Some consumer theorists believe that the appearance of "living on the edge" and the perceived danger of extreme sports is a significant motivator that attracts many.

Aside from the adventurer "wanna be's" are the true "adrenaline junkies." These are the people who thrive on pushing the limits, breaking the rules, and transcending the boundaries of society's expectations. One-third of the 18- to 34-year-olds belong to this category of "experiencers," as classified by the Values and Lifestyles Psychographic Segmentation (VALS) method of segmentation. Understandably, they represent a popular target for marketers to the inherited prospects of generation Y.

But what are the tradeoffs for the success and profits derived from marketing extreme sports? First is the chilling number of deaths and injuries associated with a sporting industry synonymous with danger and risk. BASE jumping has the world's highest fatality rate with close to 50 deaths in less than 20 years. The National Park Services are concerned with the rise in accidents and rescue costs, and the Economic Product Safety Commission has reported that over 48,000 emergency room injuries were related to skateboarding alone.

Are marketers, industry sponsors, and the sports media putting lives in danger by glorifying a steady pipeline of increasingly dangerous stunts? Is there a correlation between the level of risk/danger and marketing success? Some critics suggest that the preoccupation of the "self" in extreme sports erodes the appreciation of teamwork and celebrates showboating. Is there a "lack of moral structure that binds people together in a meaningful way"? How much has society been influenced by the extreme marketing phenomenon? Karl Taro Greenfeld notes as examples the trend toward e-trading and investments in high-risk Internet stocks. The marked increase in gambling and lotteries, the use of hard drugs, and even unprotected sex have been linked to extreme sports.

Myra Stark suggests, however, that the characteristics of extreme sports encourage an entrepreneurial spirit and provides a driving force for individual achievements. Many other variables may be relevant to the high-risk social behavior of American culture. Is the behavior a reaction to economic prosperity, longer life, and the absence of a major ground war? The influence of "real time" and immediate gratification may also be at work.

 **YES**

Life on the Edge

Five... four... three... two... one... see ya!" And Chance McGuire, 25, is airborne off a 650-ft. concrete dam in Northern California. In one second he falls 16 ft., in two seconds 63 ft., and after three seconds and 137 ft. he is flying at 65 m.p.h. He prays that his parachute will open facing away from the dam, that his canopy won't collapse, that his toggles will be handy and that no ill wind will slam him back into the cold concrete. The chute snaps open, the sound ricocheting through the gorge like a gunshot, and McGuire is soaring, carving S turns into the air, swooping over a winding creek. When he lands, he is a speck on a path along the creek. He hurriedly packs his chute and then, clearly audible above the rushing water, lets out a war whoop that rises past those mortals still perched on the dam, past the commuters puttering by on the roadway, past even the hawks who circle the ravine. It is a cry of defiance, thanks and victory; he has survived another BASE jump.

McGuire is a practitioner of what he calls the king of all extreme sports. BASE—an acronym for building, antenna, span (bridge) and earth (cliffs)—jumping has one of the sporting world's highest fatality rates: in its 18-year history, 46 participants have been killed. Yet the sport has never been more popular, with more than a thousand jumpers in the U.S. and more seeking to get into it every day. It is an activity without margin for error. If your chute malfunctions, don't bother reaching for a reserve—there isn't time. There are no second chances.

Still, the sport's stark metaphor—a human leaving safety behind to leap into the void—may be a perfect fit with our times. As extreme a risk taker as McGuire seems, we may all have more in common with him than we know or care to admit. Heading into the millennium, America has embarked on a national orgy of thrill seeking and risk taking. The rise of adventure and extreme sports like BASE jumping, snowboarding, ice climbing, skateboarding and paragliding is merely the most vivid manifestation of this new national behavior. Investors once content to buy stocks and hold them quit their day jobs to become day traders, making volatile careers of risk taking. Even our social behavior has tilted toward the treacherous, with unprotected sex on the upswing and hard drugs like heroin the choice of the chic as well as the junkies. In ways many of us take for granted, we engage in risks our parents would have shunned and our grandparents would have dismissed as just plain stupid.

⊷⟨◉⟩⊷

More than 30% of U.S. households own stocks of some form or another, whether in investment accounts, mutual funds or retirement plans, up from 12% just 10 years ago. While an ongoing bull market has lulled us into a sense of security about investing, the reality is we are taking greater risks with our money than any other generation in American history. Many of us even take this a step further, buying "speculative growth," i.e., highly risky Internet and technology stocks, breezily ignoring the potentially precipitous downside.

We change jobs, leaping into the employment void, imagining rich opportunities everywhere. The quit rate, a measure of those who voluntarily left their most recent job, is at 14.5%, the highest in a decade. Even among those schooled in risk management, hotshot M.B.A.s who previously would have headed to Wall Street or Main Street, there is a predilection to spurn Goldman Sachs and Procter & Gamble in order to take a flyer on striking it rich quickly in dot.com land. "I didn't want someone in 20 years to ask me where I was when the Internet took off," says Greg Schoeny, a recent University of Denver M.B.A. who passed up opportunities with established technology firms like Lucent to work at an Internet start-up called STS Communications. Schoeny is a double-dare sort who also likes to ski in the Rockies' dangerous, unpatrolled backcountry.

A full 30% of this year's Harvard Business School graduates are joining venture-capital or high-tech firms, up from 12% just four years ago. "The extended period of prosperity has encouraged people to behave in ways they didn't behave in other times—the way people spend money, change jobs, the quit rate, day trading, and people really thinking they know more about the market than anyone else," says Peter Bernstein, an economic consultant and author of the best-selling *Against the Gods: The Remarkable Story of Risk.* "It takes a particular kind of environment for all these things to happen." That environment—unprecedented prosperity and almost a decade without a major ground war—may be what causes Americans to express some inveterate need to take risks.

There is a certain logic to it: at the end of a decade of American triumphalism abroad and prosperity at home, we could be seeking to upsize our personalities, our sense of ourselves. Perhaps we as a people are acting out our success as a nation, in a manner unfelt since the postwar era.

The rising popularity of extreme sports bespeaks an eagerness on the part of millions of Americans to participate in activities closer to the metaphorical edge, where danger, skill and fear combine to give weekend warriors and professional athletes alike a sense of pushing out personal boundaries. According to American Sports Data Inc., a consulting firm, participation in so-called extreme sports is way up. Snowboarding has grown 113% in five years and now boasts nearly 5.5 million participants. Mountain biking, skateboarding, scuba diving, you name the adventure sport—the growth curves reveal a nation that loves to play with danger. Contrast that with activities like baseball, touch football and aerobics, all of which have been in steady decline throughout the '90s.

The pursuits that are becoming more popular have one thing in common: the perception that they are somehow more challenging than a game of touch football. "Every human being with two legs, two arms is going to wonder how fast, how strong, how enduring he or she is," says Eric Perlman, a mountaineer and filmmaker specializing in extreme sports. "We are designed to experiment or die."

And to get hurt. More Americans than ever are injuring themselves while pushing their personal limits. In 1997 the U.S. Consumer Products Safety Commission reported that 48,000 Americans were admitted to hospital emergency rooms with skateboarding-related injuries. That's 33% more than the previous year. Snowboarding E.R. visits were up 31%; mountain climbing up 20%. By every statistical measure available, Americans are participating in and injuring themselves through adventure sports at an unprecedented rate.

Consider Mike Carr, an environmental engineer and paraglider pilot from Denver who last year survived a bad landing that smashed 10 ribs and collapsed his lung. Paraglider pilots use feathery nylon wings to take off from mountaintops and float on thermal wind currents—a completely unpredictable ride. Carr also mountain bikes and climbs rock faces. He walked away from a 1,500-ft. fall in Peru in 1988. After his recovery, he returned to paragliding. "This has taken over many of our lives," he explains. "You float like a bird out there. You can go as high as 18,000 ft. and go for 200 miles. That's magic."

America has always been defined by risk; it may be our predominant national characteristic. It's a country founded by risk takers fed up with the English Crown and expanded by pioneers—a word that seems utterly American. Our heritage throws up heroes—Lewis and Clark, Thomas Edison, Frederick Douglass, Teddy Roosevelt, Henry Ford, Amelia Earhart—who bucked the odds, taking perilous chances.

Previous generations didn't need to seek out risk; it showed up uninvited and regularly: global wars, childbirth complications, diseases and pandemics from the flu to polio, dangerous products and even the omnipresent cold war threat of mutually assured destruction. "I just don't think extreme sports would have been popular in a ground-war era," says Dan Cady, professor of popular culture at California State University at Fullerton. "Coming back from a war and getting onto a skateboard would not seem so extreme."

But for recent generations, many of those traditional risks have been reduced by science, government or legions of personal-injury lawyers, leaving boomers and Generations X and Y to face less real risk. Life expectancy has increased. Violent crime is down. You are 57% less likely to die of heart disease than your parents; smallpox, measles and polio have virtually been eradicated.

Combat survivors speak of the terror and the excitement of playing in a death match. Are we somehow incomplete as people if we do not taste that terror and excitement on the brink? "People are [taking risks] because everyday risk is minimized and people want to be challenged," says Joy Marr, 43, an adventure racer who was the only woman member of a five-person team that finished the 1998 Raid Gauloises, the granddaddy of all adventure races. This is a sport that requires several days of nonstop slogging, climbing, rappelling, rafting and surviving through some of the roughest terrain in the world. Says fellow adventure racer and former Army Ranger Jonathan Senk, 35: "Our society is so surgically sterile. It's almost like our socialization just desensitizes us. Every time I'm out doing this I'm searching my soul. It's the Lewis and Clark gene, to venture out, to find what your limitations are."

That idea of feeling bracingly alive through high-risk endeavor is commonly echoed by athletes, day traders and other risk takers. Indeed, many Silicon Valley entrepreneurs are extreme-sports junkies. Mike McCue, 32, CEO and chairman of Tellme Networks, walked away from millions of dollars at his previous job to get his new company off the ground. It's his third start-up, and each time he has risked everything. In his spare time, McCue gets himself off the ground. He's also an avid rock climber. "I like to feel self-reliant and independent," he says. "And when I'm up there, I know if I make a knot wrong, I die."

Even at ground level, the Valley is a preserve of fearless entrepreneurs. Nirav Tolia passed up $10 million in Yahoo stock options to start *epinions.com,* a shopping-guide website. "I don't know if I would call it living dangerously," he says. "At Yahoo I realized that money was not the driver for me. It's the sense of adventure."

Psychologist Frank Farley of Temple University believes that taking conscious risk involves overcoming our instincts. He points out that no other animal intentionally puts itself in peril. "The human race is particularly risk taking compared with other species," he says. He describes risk takers as the Type T personality, and the U.S. as a Type T nation, as opposed to what Farley considers more risk-averse nations like Japan. He breaks it down further, into Type T physical (extreme athletes) and Type T intellectual (Albert Einstein, Galileo). He warns there is also Type T negative, that is, those who are drawn to delinquency, crime, experimentation with drugs, unprotected sex and a whole litany of destructive behaviors.

All these Type Ts are related, and perhaps even different aspects of the same character trait. There is, says Farley, a direct link between Einstein and BASE jumper Chance McGuire. They are different manifestations of the thrill-seeking component of our characters: Einstein was thrilled by his mental life, and McGuire—well, Chance jumps off buildings.

ᴄ₄◉⋗

McGuire, at the moment, is driving from Hollister to another California town, Auburn, where he is planning another BASE jump from a bridge. Riding with him is Adam Fillipino, president of Consolidated Rigging, a company that manufactures parachutes and gear for BASE jumpers. McGuire talks about the leap ahead, about his feelings when he is at the exit point, and how at that moment, looking down at the ground, what goes through his mind is that this is not something a human being should be doing. But that's exactly what makes him take that leap: that sense of overcoming his inhibitions and winning what he calls the gravity game. "Football is for pansies," says McGuire. "What do you need all those pads for? This sport [BASE jumping] is pushing all the limits. I have a friend who calls it suicide with a kick."

When a BASE jumper dies, other BASE jumpers say he has "gone in," as in gone into the ground or gone into a wall. "I'm sick of people going in," says Fillipino. "In the past year, a friend went in on a skydive, another drowned as a result of a BASE jump, another friend went in on a jump, another died in a skydiving-plane crash. You can't escape death, but you don't want to flirt with it either." It may be the need to flirt with death, or at least take extreme chances, that has his business growing at a rate of 50% a year.

The jump today from the Auburn bridge, which Fillipino has done dozens of times, is about as routine as BASE jumping can be. But Fillipino is a veteran with 450 BASE jumps to his credit. For McGuire, who has just 45, every jump is still a challenge. And at dawn, as he gets his gear ready, stuffing his chute and rig into a backpack so it won't be conspicuous as he climbs the trestles beneath the bridge (jumping from this bridge, as from many other public and private structures, is illegal) he has entered into a tranquil state, as if he were silently preparing himself for the upcoming risk.

When our Type T traits turn negative, though, there is a disturbing, less serene element to America's being the risk nation. One chilling development is the trend of "barebacking," a practice in which gay men have unprotected sex with multiple partners. Jack, an avid proponent of barebacking, argues that the risk of becoming HIV positive is outweighed by the rush of latex-free passion —especially in an era when, in his view, protease inhibitors are on the verge of turning AIDS from a fatal disease into a chronic illness. "It's the bad boy in me getting off," he admits. "One thing that barebacking allows is a certain amount of control over the risk. In sex, we have the ability to face the risk and look it in the eye."

The Stop AIDS Foundation surveyed some 22,000 gay men in San Francisco between 1994 and 1997, and during this period, the number of men who reported they always used condoms fell from 70% to 61%. "For some gay men, there is a sense of inevitability of becoming infected," says Michael Scarce, 29, a doctoral student in medical sociology who has been researching the barebacking phenomenon for the past two years. Scarce says that rather than living in fear and wondering when their next HIV test is going to return positive, some men create an infection ritual. "It really is a lifestyle choice," he says. "It comes down to quality of life vs. quantity of life."

This consequences-be-damned attitude may also be behind some disquieting trends that surfaced in a report issued [recently] by the Substance Abuse and Mental Health Services Administration stating that the number of Americans entering treatment centers for heroin surged 29% between 1992 and 1997. "I'm seeking the widest possible range of human experience," says a recent Ivy League graduate about his heroin use.

The most notorious example of negative thrill seeking may have been when the Risk Taker in Chief, Bill Clinton, engaged in unprotected sex in the

Oval Office. Experts point out that many people were forgiving of Clinton in part because they could identify with his impulsiveness. "Risky behavior has been elevated to new heights," argues Cal State's Cady. "There was never so much value put upon risk as there is now."

The question is, How much is enough? Without some expression of risk, we may never know our limits and therefore who we are as individuals. "If you don't assume a certain amount of risk," says paraglider pilot Wade Ellet, 51, "you're missing a certain amount of life." And it is by taking risks that we may flirt with greatness. "We create technologies, we make new discoveries, but in order to do that, we have to push beyond the set of rules that are governing us at that time," says psychologist Farley.

That's certainly what's driving McGuire and Fillipino as they position themselves on the Auburn bridge. It's dawn again, barely light, and they appear as shadows moving on the catwalk beneath the roadway. As they survey the drop zone, they compute a series of risk assessments. "It's a matter of weighing the variables," Fillipino says, pointing out that the wind, about 15 m.p.h. out of the northwest, has picked up a little more than he would like. Still, it's a clear morning, and they've climbed all the way up here. McGuire is eager to jump. But Fillipino continues to scan the valley below them, the Sacramento River rushing through the gorge.

Then a white parks-department SUV pulls up on an access road that winds alongside the river. Park Rangers are a notorious scourge of BASE jumpers, confiscating equipment and prosecuting for trespassing. Fillipino contemplates what would happen if the president of a BASE rig company were busted for an illegal jump. He foresees trouble with his bankers, he imagines the bad publicity his business would garner, and he says he's not going. There are some risks he is simply not willing to take.

Myra Stark  **NO**

The Extreme Generation

First there was bungee jumping, mountain-biking and snowboarding. Now we have sky surfing, street luging, river running, riversurfing, BASE [building, antenna, span, and earth] jumping, downhill mountain biking at speeds as high as 60 mph and extreme fighting. What these activities cum "extreme sports" have in common is that they involve high risk for injury and even death, and are extremely attractive to men 18 to 34, the most elusive and difficult demographic for marketers and advertisers.

Given the extreme nature of these sports, the question of how widespread they are naturally presents itself. True, snowboarding and freestyle skiing have been added to the Winter Olympic Games, and ESPN covers extreme sports extensively in its biannual X Games. But looking for data to substantiate the numbers of participants and spectators is really almost an irrelevant endeavor.

What is crucial for marketers to see is that these sports have become the "coolest" sports among kids, teens and Gen Xers, and therefore are a fast growing outlet for fantasy among boys and young men, and a smaller but growing number of women.

The real significance of extreme sports for marketers and advertisers, however, lies in the insight they offer into the psyche of this segment and of their generation as a whole. It's not hard to understand the appeal of extreme sports to young men. In most societies, young men are attracted to feats of daring and physical challenge as ways to prove their worth and display their testosterone. The risk, or peril, involved in these activities is an integral part of their appeal. Whether they involve hunting with bows and arrows, as was true of Native American coming-of-age rituals, or guns, liquor and cars, they are viewed by males as initiation rites into manhood. Various explanations have been offered about why extreme sports have emerged as one of our rites of passage in the '90s. Perhaps it is because this age group has not had to go to war, the ultimate proving ground for men. Perhaps the appeal is a byproduct of living in a risk-averse time in America—safe sex, controlled drinking, avoidance of smoking. Then there are those who see extreme sports as just the '90s equivalent of the competitiveness, adventurousness and independence inherent in the American character, or maybe even just the fringe edge of the outdoor adventure vacation trend.

Whatever the reason for its rapid rise, extreme sports, sometimes referred to as "alternative sports," also offers valuable insights into the nature of this generation of twentysomethings, as well as the teens that aspire older and the thirtysomethings who aspire younger. It's been clear since we first began to define the mindset of this generation that individuality was one of its hallmarks. This is the generation, after all, that helped create the individualistic micro-beer phenomenon. And one of the strongest appeals of extreme sports is their individual nature. They are not team sports; they are not organized or regulated. There are no official uniforms. In fact, many of the folk heros of these sports also express their individuality through clothing and hairstyle; Missy Giove, the mountain biker, for example, who sports a Mohawk topknot with shaved hair on the sides, sometimes silver, sometimes purple, along with tattoos and body piercing. The athletes in ESPN's X Games are also likely to have blue hair and pierced eyebrows, looking more like Dennis Rodman than Tiger Woods.

But what's become clear only recently, though, is that contrary to our early image of this generation—one of slackers or dropouts alienated from the system—these young consumers are, in fact, very competitive. They are now being seen as the most entrepreneurial and driven of generations. A survey released by the Center For Policy Alternatives makes it clear that a majority of 18- to 24-year-olds see themselves as "focused, determined and independent," even though older generations view them as lazy, confused and unfocused—owing in large part to a generational divide concerning computers and music. Extreme Sports, with their individualistic, one-to-one competitiveness, appeal to the entrepreneurial spirit of this generation.

So these sports should be read as a generational signpost as well as a sign of our times. The problem is that they are already becoming an advertising cliche. We are already beginning to expect the sight of flying bodies on skateboards and snowboards or skydivers when a product aimed at this audience is advertised. The strategic and creative challenge for marketers and advertisers then is to tap into the powerful cultural resonance these sports have for this generation while avoiding the cliched-presentation they now receive.

POSTSCRIPT

Is "Extreme Sports" Marketing Risk and Thrill Seeking to Society?

The nation's largest sporting goods trade show of the new millennium revealed the accelerated growth and influence of extreme sports. Kids seem to be more influenced by ESPN2 than the NBA, and many prefer the X-Games to the World Series. This is a major shift, with incredible implications for the future of sports marketing. Industry giants that focus on traditional sports are losing ground to the smaller companies that are seemingly more in touch with unique appeals to "extreme" teens. Snowboarding is now gaining legitimacy as an Olympic sport. The "X-attitude" has directly influenced advertising with the "MTVesque" in-your-face, fast-paced creative techniques.

Another issue associated with several sports is violence as a commodity and a form of "aggression marketing." While the critique of violence as an appeal for sports marketing has its origins in America, it has become a global issue and the central theme of promotions in several countries. The success of the World Wrestling Federation (WWF) was the subject of a cover story in the February 2000 issue of *Time*, which asked, "Should your kids be watching?" The WWF was number one in book, cable, and video sales in the United States.

Sports celebrities and their responsibilities as role models has surfaced as a contemporary marketing issue. The preoccupation with money and endorsements is often the subject of public scrutiny. In extreme sports, critics have focused on the reckless, self-oriented, break-the-rules image of many celebrities who publicly decry safe sex and seem obsessed with the adrenaline rush lifestyle. Others suggest that extreme sports offer rewarding opportunities for thousands who are unable to gain access to professional sports.

Many believe that the real significance of extreme sports is the reflection on attitudes and the psyche of both current and upcoming generations. The quest for thrills and individuality are hallmarks of this generation, and the linkages to consumer behavior are invaluable. But is the promotion of extreme sports sacrificing safety for profits by equating levels of risk with the challenge of success? Critics feel it is irresponsible of sponsors to allow such sporting activities to become increasingly fraught with peril. While the evidence is arguable, supporters claim more injuries are incurred but less reported than with traditional sports. What should the limits of responsibility be for marketers of extreme sports?

Sociologists suggest the focus on individuality erodes the development of teamwork and celebrates "showboating." They also suggest that the hard work and practice in developing sporting skills are sacrificed for the short-range high of the adrenaline rush. Furtherore, the "No Fear" attitude undermines the notion of the work ethic, comradery and sportsmanship. Instead, sociologists contend that the quest for instant gratification inherently ordains a reckless, self-indulgent lifestyle that carries over into other social activities.

A final issue is the question of "extreme transference"—applying the extreme attitude of risk-taking, breaking the rules, the adrenaline rush, and thrill-seeking to the marketing of other products and services. For example, the media has become emboldened with dramatic television programming, like *Jerry Springer* and *Who Wants to Marry a Multi-Millionaire?* The Xtreme Football League (XFL) promises a wilder and less refereed version of professional football. It is likely to be influenced by the violence and glitter of the WWF. Will this repel viewers and allow the pendulum to swing back to the broadcasting of more traditional organized sports, or will television continue to strive for even more dramatic and shocking programming?

Suggested Readings

Devin Gordon, "Up, Up and Away, Dude!" *Newsweek* (January 1, 2000)

"Extreme Sports Rule Sporting Goods Industries," *The Wall Street Journal* (February 14, 2000)

Rebecca Piirto Heath, "You Can Buy a Thrill: Chasing the Ultimate Rush," *American Demographics* (June 1997)

Paul Hochman, "Street Lugers, Stunt Bikers, and Colgate-Palmolive!" *Fortune* (November 22, 1999)

Ann Marie Kerwin, "Times Mirror Takes Extreme 'Stance,'" *Advertising Age* (November 8, 1999)

Scott Lajoie, "Let the Games Begin," *Forbes* (February 21, 2000)

Alex Salkener, "When Sports Become Too Extreme," *Christian Science Monitor* (March 24, 1998)

"United States: Thrilled to Death," *The Economist* (November 13, 1999)

Xtreme Scene. `http://www.xtremescene.com`

eXtremeLinks. `http://www.extremelinks.com`

Violence Memphis Working Paper. `http://www.hmse.memphis.edu/WPSLC/sjackson.htm`

ISSUE 13

Should Classrooms Be Commercial-Free Zones?

YES: Peter Ferrara, from "The Clear Benefits of Channel One," *Americans for Tax Reform Policy Brief* (May 19, 1999)

NO: Peggy J. Farber, from "Schools for Sale," *Advertising Age* (October 25, 1999)

ISSUE SUMMARY

YES: Peter Ferrara, general counsel and chief economist for Americans for Tax Reform, defends Channel One as a much-needed 12-minute documentary news program designed to educate students about current events, social studies, economics, and history.

NO: Peggy J. Farber contends that the outrage over commercialism in American classrooms is intensifying, as the private sector becomes inventive with sophisticated techniques and innovative ways of marketing to students in schools. She offers large-scale marketing research, exclusive contracts, and computer ads as current examples of marketing that has been spawned from the origins of Channel One.

Since the late 1980s, there has been a strongly divided debate over the appropriate relationship between schools and business. The "cola wars" have long been waged in school hallways. Donating scoreboards often meant the strategic placement of vending machines. School endorsements of several educational programs have long existed, such as Pizza Hut's "Book It" program, reaching over 15 million kids, awarding pizzas for those completing reading assignments. Now market research is done in classrooms, and product placement is used in school textbooks.

The issue became besieged with controversy, however, when Whittle Communications launched its venture Channel One in March 1989. This original daily news program was created expressly for teens and is beamed by satellite to about 12,000 middle and high schools and 8.1 million students. It is financed by 2 minutes of commercial time out of each daily 12-minute news program.

Reaction among administrators and teachers was originally mixed and may still be conjecture. While there was strong support for news program broadcasts in public schools, the nearly 85 percent support for the program dropped to less than half (37 percent) when advertising became part of the package. Student reaction has been positive, as many find the program informative and influential enough to spark interest in watching news at home.

Both sides of the Channel One debate present strong arguments. Supporters point to the numerous other commercial ventures involving computer donations, exclusive beverage arrangements, research projects, and book cover promotions. They also tout the test results that show a high level of attention and learning, often stimulating interest and incentives to explore the news. Paul Folkner, vice president at Channel One, defends the program by pointing out that most educators find it useful and that the 2,000 middle and high schools that show it renew their contracts at a 99 percent rate.

Are certain business ventures in public schools a form of commercial exploitation of a captive market? Are we sending a message to students that they are each part of a market, for sale to the highest commercial bidder? And do the kids perceive the commercial products as being endorsed and promoted by the school? The Channel One controversy has actually resulted in a Senate Committee hearing where Ralph Nader charged parental neglect and delinquency of school boards.

The reality is that resistance to such programs is waning. As marketers have developed more sophisticated methods of delivering value and developing creative partnerships with public schools, critics of Channel One will likely be outraged over newer, more intrusive commercial arrangements such as "Zap Me," which offers free computers to 6,000 preselected schools and access to over 11,000 Internet connections. It also exposes kids to banner ads for four hours a day. Is this arrangement a more serious issue than Channel One in the classroom? The school population represents the largest market segment in America today. As taxpayers continue their reluctance to support school budgets, administrators are quick to oblige when marketers provide tenable solutions.

Still, the notion of treating school kids like *consumers* rather than *learners* poses a sensitive issue. But equally relevant is the integrity and importance of corporate America and marketing as an essential economic institution and a pillar of American culture. Is there an inherent prejudice against marketing displayed by public school educators? Is the marketplace not a "mirror of society," reflecting lifestyles and values of American culture? Should students not be exposed to brand products and the institution of marketing as an essential foundation of the American way of life? In Canada, most educators have endorsed Cable in the Classroom (CITC), a public service initiative by the Canadian federal government that provides free cable connection and over 540 hours per month of commercial-free educational programming to schools across the country. This has successfully replaced the privatized Youth News Network (YNN), which required compulsory viewing of commercials as well as single bias news broadcasts produced by unknown sources. Should the U.S. government take similar initiatives?

Peter Ferrara  **YES**

The Clear Benefits of Channel One

In a 1998 study, Max Sawicky and Alex Molnar concluded that Channel One costs taxpayers across the country $1.8 billion each year. This study, however, was deeply flawed methodologically and its conclusions, therefore, are incorrect.

The truth is that Channel One involves no costs to taxpayers. It is a free service financed by 2 minutes of paid commercials during each daily 12 minute news program.

Indeed, taxpayers receive considerable net benefits from Channel One. First, the daily news program is used to educate students about current events, social studies, economics, geography, history and other subjects. Teachers and school administrators have heavily praised the program for its educational value, and it has won numerous prestigious awards.

Moreover, Channel One also offers subscribers several hours of optional, free educational videos each week covering a wide range of subjects and these videos are also heavily used by the schools. In addition, Channel One provides each subscribing school, also free of charge, with its own telecommunications equipment to receive and transmit the news program and educational videos. This equipment can then be used by the school for any other broadcast, video, or student activity it chooses.

This arrangement, therefore, greatly benefits taxpayers as well as students. As we will discuss, the value of the full range of benefits provided by Channel One is at least $425 million for the public schools alone. In fact, taxpayers should question schools that do not have Channel One as to why they have not taken advantage of the windfall from this market innovation.

These issues will be thoroughly discussed in this report. We will begin by first discussing in more detail Channel One and the service it provides. Then we will discuss the findings of Sawicky and Molnar, and why their analysis is flawed and their conclusions incorrect. In the process, we will analyze the true costs and benefits of Channel One.

What Is Channel One?

Channel One provides a daily 12 minute news program for middle and high school students in about 12,000 middle and high schools across the country, including public, private and parochial schools. This covers about 40% of all middle and high schools in the country.

The news program is entirely original, produced by Channel One's own staff and reporters on location around the world. The program is written and designed specifically to interest teenagers. It is beamed by satellite each night to the subscribing schools, and then shown on TV monitors in each classroom the next day. The daily audience includes about 8.1 million students, which is close to the daily audience of the major network evening news shows. Indeed, Channel One reaches 5 times as many teenagers each day as the news shows on ABC, CBS, NBC, and CNN combined.

No one is forced to watch Channel One. The program is available for pre-screening each morning by school administrators and teachers. If the school considers the program inappropriate in any way, it doesn't have to air it for students. If an individual teacher doesn't want to use the program in their class-rooms that day, they can opt their class out as well. If an individual student's parents don't want their child watching Channel One for any reason, they can choose to have their child opt out as well. In about 10 years of Channel One broadcasts, however, any such opting out has been negligible.

Each school that subscribes to Channel One receives about $25,000 worth of telecommunications equipment, so that it can receive and broadcast the daily news program to its students. This equipment includes a fixed KU band satellite dish, an addressable receiver, 19 or 25 inch color TVs in every class-room, VCRs, and internal wiring with complete maintenance by Channel One. Apart from Channel One's daily news program, the school can use this telecom-munications network for any other educational, training, or student program-ming it chooses.

In fact, Channel One provides hours of additional, optional, educational programming every day, including historical documentaries, biographies, and programs on mathematics, science, and art. This adds up to over 250 hours and more than 400 separate programs each year. In schools subscribing to Channel One, 97% of teachers report that they have used these videos, and two-thirds (66%) say they do so frequently. Buying the library of educational videos themselves would cost each school about $36,000 per year.

Students, teachers and administrators report a high level of satisfaction with Channel One. Remarkably, 99% of schools subscribing to the service renew their contracts each year. A 1994 study by the Institute for Social Research at the University of Michigan found 93% of teachers in schools using Channel One would recommend it to other schools. A more recent, 1999 study by Applied Research Consulting (ARC) found that after 10 years of operation now 98% of teachers in Channel One schools would recommend it. The same proportion, 98%, also wanted their schools to continue to receive Channel One. Channel One is now seen by over 400,000 teachers every day.

The study also found that 91% of these teachers think Channel One is valuable in informing their students about current events. In addition, 89% believe students learn more from Channel One than from news seen at home, and 80% regularly discuss the shows in their classes. Over 90% of the teachers also report that Channel One programs are appropriate for teenagers, interesting to teens, and driven by positive values. And 94% report that they believe Channel One reporters were good role models for their students.

Among students, the ARC study found that 85% wanted their school to keep Channel One. The students reported that Channel One was educational, interesting, and their "No. 1 source of news." Over three-fourths of students also report that the information they learn from watching Channel One is as valuable or even more valuable than the other things they learn in school. A Gallup poll also found that 86% of teenagers thought Channel One was an "Excellent" or "Good" idea for their schools.

In the 1997–98 school year, Channel One correspondents broadcast original news segments from nearly 2 dozen countries around the world. Original interviews have recently included General Colin Powell, Newt Gingrich, Walter Cronkite, Mikhail Gorbachev, and House Speaker Dennis Hastert, who gave his only interview on his first day as Speaker to Channel One.

Channel One coverage focuses on aspects of stories that would be particularly interesting to teenagers. For example, the coverage of the death of Jordan's King Hussein discussed the challenges Hussein faced when he became King as a teenager. The segment was also able to devote time to the history of Jordan, providing educational information to teenagers that helps them put the story in context. This would not be included in the more rushed network newscasts.

Channel One stories also cover positive role models for teenagers. One story discussed a young man who climbed out of poverty and ended up at the U.S. Naval Academy. Another discussed a high school student who spent the summer doing volunteer work for Mother Theresa.

The philosophy of Channel One is to emphasize facts and in-depth coverage and avoid the sensationalism of much of TV news. *TIME* magazine reports,

> "Perhaps most impressive is Channel One's coverage of world affairs. At a time when the broadcast networks are cutting back on their overseas coverage, Channel One has sent its correspondents to Haiti, Rwanda, Bosnia and other global hot spots. Their stories often run three or four minutes —enormous by network news standards—and have an immediacy young audiences can relate to."

Similarly, in a story entitled "Day v. Night," *Brill's Content Magazine* last fall compared Channel One's coverage of major news events quite favorably to the *NBC Nightly News*. Among other issues, the article noted Channel One's sensitive treatment of the school shootings in Jonesboro, Ark. Afraid that extensive coverage might produce copycat shootings, Channel One delayed coverage while it consulted with teachers nationwide. Its coverage then focused on how some students had heard of the shooting plot and failed to report it. The segment encouraged students to look out for signs of danger and report potential trouble. Channel One was also praised for its sensitive handling of the Clinton/ Lewinsky story.

Channel One now has a formal cooperative arrangement with *ABC News,* sharing news coverage and resources. As a result, Channel One reporters have appeared on *ABC News* broadcasts, and Peter Jennings and Ted Koppel have co-anchored Channel One programs. Channel One has also worked cooperatively on news stories with *Time* magazine, *U.S. News and World Report,* and *USA Weekend.*

Channel One's President of Programming is Andrew Hill, who holds a master's degree in education and was formerly President of CBS Productions. In that capacity, he produced some of the best and most widely proclaimed family programs on television, including *Touched by an Angel, Promised Land,* and *Dr. Quinn Medicine Woman.* The Channel One staff includes several other former major network news journalists and senior educators.

Channel One provides teachers with guides, calendars, lesson plans, academic resources, and other materials to help them integrate the news program and optional videos into their curriculum. A daily Educator's Guide offers suggestions regarding how to incorporate upcoming news programs and educational videos into teachers' lesson plans. It includes discussion questions relating to the newscast and the videos to promote classroom analysis after the programs are shown.

The Channel One service also includes a website for teachers offering daily lesson plans, academic resources, and discussion groups with other teachers around the country. It also provides analysis and sequencing questions to help develop critical thinking skills, and a daily writing assignment for students so teachers can use the news program to help develop composition skills. Another section helps teachers instruct students regarding vocabulary words used in broadcasts.

Teachers consequently do use the Channel One newscast as a starting off point for classroom discussions and instruction. It is obviously useful in this regard in Current Events and Social Studies classes. But it can also be useful in teaching geography, English, science and math. The educational videos, of course, are directly instructional in almost every subject.

Bruce Hunter, Principal of Washington Middle School in Seattle, Wash. explains how and why his teachers use Channel One:

> "We feel middle-school students don't get enough information about the news ... [Channel One] is an opportunity for us to give them that experience each day and use it as an opportunity to discuss current events."

Similarly, Jake Summerall, a teacher at Nazareth Academy in La Grange Park, Ill. writes,

> "I teach a Current Events class and let me tell you, my students really enjoy watching the program every morning. Most of our class discussions are based on your cover stories that we watch and learn about every morning. It's a pleasure to view your show and I would like to say, keep up the excellent job that is being done."

From Phoenix City Middle School in Phoenix City, Alabama, teacher Nikki Robertson writes,

> "My sixth grade Social Studies classes love to watch Channel One every day! The students keep a Channel One journal in which they write about the stories they view on Channel One each day. They also locate, mark, and write the latitude and longitude of locations discussed in Channel One stories each day. Not only do the students get a daily dose of map skills, they also stay current on daily events. I feel that through the use of Channel One in my classroom my students are more prepared for life in the real world."

Cheryl Huddleston, a teacher in Hot Springs High School in Hot Springs, South Dakota also writes, "almost all of your topics have been relevant jumping off points for other discussions in my class."

Catholic schools have found Channel One highly beneficial as well. Monsignor John Jordan of the National Catholic Education Association writes,

> "Channel One is a valued part of daily education in 1100 of our Catholic schools. Channel One is viewed daily by thousands of religious and lay teachers who monitor your programming. The traditional values you espouse are highly consistent with those we teach."

Jordan also writes,

> "The Channel One network helps to deliver our training programs to the thousands of teachers in our Catholic secondary and middle schools throughout North America. The Channel One Network, as a medium for this project, has opened up avenues for teachers to receive theology courses via live interactive television. Reaching over 1100 Catholic schools just through Channel One is ... a real gold mine for Catholic schools."

The daily Channel One news show has now won over 200 journalism awards after just 10 years of broadcasts. These include the prestigious George Foster Peabody award, the Edward R. Murrow Responsibility in Television Award, the Faith and Values Award, the Christopher Award, and the Catholic Julian Award. For years, the Armed Forces Radio and Television Service has also broadcast Channel One's daily news show to American personnel stationed in 156 countries around the world, including Germany, Italy, Turkey, Panama, the Azores, Japan, the Philippines, Australia, Korea, Cuba, Iceland, Spain, Greece, the Indian Ocean, and the Marshall Islands.

Some have criticized Channel One for the two minutes of advertising on its daily newscast, which finances the entire service—the news program, the educational videos, and the telecommunications equipment. But every newspaper and magazine used in a classroom contains numerous ads, as does the Internet, now used in schools as well. Ads are also found in student newspapers and yearbooks, at school sporting events, and on educational software.

The Channel One ads are standard network fare that students would generally have seen at home. Indeed, Channel One rejects as inappropriate some ads that are run on national TV. Channel One will not accept ads regarding tobacco products, alcoholic beverages, abortion, contraception, firearms, movies not rated G or PG, politics, prescription drugs, gambling, and others. Over the years, moreover, Channel One has run over $100 million worth of public service ads free of charge, for such causes as the Partnership for a Drug Free America, the Centers for Disease Control, the American Cancer Society, the Points of Light Foundation, the Center for Gang Violence, Mothers Against Drunk Driving, and the National Center for Missing and Exploited Children.

Most importantly, a study of this advertising issue by researchers at Boston University and Santa Clara University found that students understand that the commercials pay for the educational programs and that the school is not endorsing the products advertised. The students recognize this in regard to Channel One just as they do for ads in newspapers and magazines distributed in class, or in their student and hometown newspapers.

Educators generally seem to reach the same conclusion on this issue as the staff of the Kansas State Board of Education, which found,

> American students benefit educationally from well-designed, well produced, and informative daily news programs designed especially for them. Such programming is technologically possible and economically feasible only through commercial marketing. It would be shortsighted to deny this opportunity.

The True Costs of Channel One

Even though Channel One is provided to schools free of charge, Sawicky and Molnar conclude that "The twelve minute Channel One program costs American taxpayers $1.8 billion annually." This conclusion is completely erroneous. For while the authors prove adept at arithmetic, the data they have worked with have nothing to do with costs incurred by or for Channel One.

Sawicky and Molnar start with data on each state's current annual expenditures for all public elementary and secondary schools. They then use data on average daily school attendance in each state to calculate an average annual expenditure per student. Then using data on the average length of a school day in each state, they determine what proportion of school time each day and then each year is used by Channel One's daily 12 minute newscast. They then multiply this proportion by the average annual education expenditure per student in each state to determine a cost per student in each state for Channel One.

From this data, they then calculate a national average annual cost per student for Channel One of $229. They then multiply this by an estimate of the total number of public school students that view Channel One daily to reach a total annual public school cost for Channel One of $1.8 billion.

What Sawicky and Molnar have calculated is the proportion of total annual expenditures for the public schools that use Channel One equal to the proportion of annual class time in those schools represented by Channel One's daily 12 minute newscast. This is a completely meaningless statistic. To say that it reflects the costs to taxpayers of Channel One is thoroughly fallacious as a matter of basic economics.

The costs that Sawicky and Molnar calculate are not variable or marginal costs incurred for or because of Channel One. They are fixed costs independent of Channel One that the schools have decided to incur whether or not they subscribe to Channel One. In other words, the costs that Sawicky and Molnar identify have nothing to do with Channel One. They are costs for teacher and administrator salaries, school supplies, books, and general school operations.

A valid economic analysis of the costs to schools of Channel One would focus on the variable or marginal costs for the school created by Channel One, not the fixed, general, aggregate costs the school will incur regardless of whether it subsidizes Channel One. The variable or marginal costs to schools for Channel One are zero. Again, Channel One charges schools no fee for its service. It also pays for, installs, and maintains all the necessary equipment to receive Channel One broadcasts. The schools have to incur no new costs to accommodate or receive Channel One. Therefore, the true economic cost to taxpayers of Channel One is zero.

The same analysis applies to the 2 minutes of advertising on each 12 minute Channel One newscast. Sawicky and Molnar calculate that this portion of the newscast costs taxpayers $300 million each year out of the supposed total $1.8 billion Channel One cost. They determine this by just multiplying the supposed $1.8 billion total cost by the proportion of Channel One's 12 minute broadcast devoted to commercials—one-sixth.

But this $300 million is just again the fixed costs of general school operations independent of Channel One, not any marginal or variable costs incurred as a result of Channel One. Schools across the country are not spending $300 million per year as a result of Channel One commercials. The marginal or variable costs to schools for Channel One commercials are again zero.

Sawicky and Molnar try to argue for their analysis by saying that time is money. But this nonanalytical slogan does not justify the economic fallacy of counting the general fixed costs of school operations independent of Channel One as the costs of Channel One. As a matter of economic analysis, the costs of Channel One to schools are the marginal or variable costs schools have to bear as a result of Channel One. As shown above, these costs to the school are zero. Therefore, the true economic cost to schools of Channel One is zero. To tell the public that costs for teacher and principal salaries, school supplies, books, and other general school operations incurred independently of Channel One are somehow the costs of Channel One is quite simply misleading propaganda.

If it could be shown that the Channel One broadcast has no educational value and is a complete waste of time, then the numbers that Sawicky and Molnar calculate could be considered a rough approximation of the economic value of that lost time. But Sawicky and Molnar expressly disavow any effort to make this argument, saying at the outset "appraising the educational value of Channel One is beyond the scope of this analysis" and later "We make no judgment on the educational value of Channel One."

Indeed, any such argument would be foolhardy, for the considerable evidence discussed above regarding the educational value of Channel One just scratches the surface of the available evidence. The 2 minutes of daily ads in the newscast have inspired some ideological opposition to Channel One on the grounds that it "commercializes" education. But no credible, qualified source raises any serious doubt that Channel One offers at least as much educational value as any other educational materials that might be used during those 12 minutes each day.

In fact, the real market evidence we have as to the educational value of Channel One is that 12,000 schools, with 400,000 teachers, representing about 40% of all secondary schools, have decided that the educational value of Channel One is well worth the 12 minutes of time each day devoted to it. In other words, a large and still growing number of the people who are in charge in the schools of deciding what has educational value have concluded that the educational value of Channel One warrants the time devoted to its use. To argue that Channel One has no educational value, Sawicky and Molnar would have to substitute their judgment for the judgment of all these professionals employed for their very expertise in making such decisions. There is no sound basis, as a matter of economics or otherwise, for such a substitution of judgment.

Might the 2 minutes of advertising included in the Channel One newscast at least be considered as lacking any educational value? These 2 minutes are an integral part of the Channel One service; indeed, they are the key part that finances everything else. They cannot be separated from the rest of the service and considered in isolation. The question that educators must consider is whether the educational value of the Channel One service is worth the 12 minutes each day devoted to the newscast as a whole. A huge and increasing number of professional educators employed to make precisely that decision are saying yes.

The two minutes of advertising on the Channel One newscast are analogous to the ads in newspapers and magazines that might be used in class, or the ads seen on the Internet or on educational software, or the credits on educational films. Students utilizing these resources may spend some time reading the ads or credits. But educators consider the time so spent to be de minimis, and to not deprive the materials overall of sufficient educational value for the time devoted to them. The same point applies to Channel One.

Indeed, any private news source must include some advertisements in order to pay the bills. To say that all such ads are to be banned from schools as not educational would amount to a ban on all private news sources in schools, as well as all student newspapers. The only source of news broadcasts or materials in classes would then be the government. This would not be desirable in a free, pluralistic, democratic society.

The True Benefits of Channel One

While Channel One involves no actual costs for taxpayers, it provides them with several clear benefits. First is the 12 minute daily newscast itself. As the discussion above indicates, this newscast has substantial educational value. Teachers use the newscast to teach current events and social studies, as well as economics, history, geography, and vocabulary. A large and growing proportion of professional educators charged with deciding what has educational value has determined that Channel One is well worthwhile. The newscast has won over 200 awards for its content, which is developed by top media professionals with network experience. While it is hard to put a number on the educational value of Channel One, that value is clearly substantial. It would cost schools across the country close to $15 million to replicate the daily news show. And that cost would not measure the full value of the programming to students.

Yet, while Sawicky and Molnar repeatedly state that they make no judgment or appraisal of Channel One's value, in a discussion of the costs and benefits of Channel One, they assert that "the logical market value of Channel One's programming is zero." Their discussion, then, credits no value to the Channel One newscast.

The authors reach this intellectual dead end by arguing that an alternative to Channel One is offered to schools by *CNN: Newsroom-World View.* Since this alternative is offered at no charge to schools, the authors conclude that the market value of the newscast provided by Channel One is zero. They conclude from this reasoning that there is no value of the Channel One newscast to weigh against their alleged costs of the program.

On this fallacious excuse for economic reasoning, there would be no value to the CNN newscast as well. Consequently, there would be no reason for schools to ever broadcast either news program. Indeed, on this reasoning, the "logical market value" of all cable and satellite TV services to homes would be zero, since a free alternative is available—the standard, over-the-air, broadcast networks and local TV stations. If Sawicky and Molnar had been advising Ted Turner, he would never have started *CNN.*

Moreover, the *CNN* newsfeed is not at all comparable to Channel One. *CNN* just splices together segments of its standard, daily, adult broadcast. It does not involve original programming designed to interest and inform teens. Nor does it involve accompanying materials to integrate the broadcast into the curriculum and assist in using it to educate, as Channel One does. It also, by the way, amounts to an advertisement for *CNN*, and is part of the company's marketing strategy.

A thought experiment will clarify the issue quite succinctly. Suppose Alex Molnar offered to play first base for the St. Louis Cardinals for free next season. Would that mean that the "logical market value" of Mark McGwire as a baseball player would fall to zero?

Another major benefit of Channel One is the several hours per week, amounting to 250 hours per year, of free educational videos that Channel One subscribers can choose to receive from Channel One. These are purely educational videos covering a wide range of subjects. If a school were to purchase the 400 different videos Channel One offers each year, it would cost roughly $36,000. Alex Molnar's own school, the University of Wisconsin, in fact spends thousands of taxpayer dollars each year buying many of the same videos Channel One offers for free, or videos from the same educational service and catalog that supplies Channel One. Over the 12,000 schools using Channel One, the yearly value of these videos would be over $400 million. For just the public schools using Channel One the value would be $360 million. Sawicky and Molnar completely ignore these educational videos in their study, and consequently, their analysis is incomplete and inadequate.

Finally, Channel One provides each school free of charge a full telecommunications network, including satellite dish, addressable receiver, TV monitors for each classroom, VCRs, internal wiring, and all necessary maintenance. Apart from the daily 12 minute Channel One program, this network is then fully available to the school for whatever use it chooses. Thousands of schools have taken advantage of the system to create in-house journalism programs. The market value of this telecommunications network is about $25,000. For the 12,000 schools that use Channel One, the total value of these systems is $300 million. For the public schools alone, the value is $250 million. Indeed, schools could not get this equipment and maintain it as inexpensively as Channel One, with its bulk buying and developed maintenance expertise. The *CNN* service touted by Sawicky and Molnar, by the way, provides no equipment to schools.

Sawicky and Molnar insist that an economic analysis must consider only the rental value of this equipment. But that would not change the analysis in any significant way. The present discounted value of proper rental charges will just equal the market purchase price anyway. Providing and maintaining the entire telecommunications network for free is a major benefit whether considering the purchase price or economically equivalent rental price of the equipment.

Consequently, while Channel One is provided at no cost to schools or taxpayers, it provides them with several major benefits. These benefits overall are worth at least $425 million for the public schools alone, providing a large savings for taxpayers. Channel One is quite simply a brilliant market innovation that greatly benefits schools, students, and taxpayers. Indeed, where schools are not using Channel One, taxpayers should question them as to why they are not taking advantage of this market windfall.

Conclusion

The true cost of Channel One to taxpayers is zero. Sawicky and Molnar's cost estimate is thoroughly in error because it attributes independent costs of school operations, such as teacher salaries, administration, school supplies, etc, to Channel One, even though those costs are not incurred to accommodate Channel One and would be incurred regardless of whether the school subscribes to Channel One. That is not valid economic analysis.

While Channel One imposes no costs on taxpayers, it offers important benefits for taxpayers, students, and schools. It provides an original, daily, newscast that aids in the education of students on a broad range of topics. It provides a wide array of free educational videos that are heavily used as well. And it provides each school with a free telecommunications network that it can use as it chooses apart from the Channel One broadcast. The total value to the public schools alone of these benefits is at least $425 million.

As a result, Channel One is so beneficial that taxpayers whose schools are not using it should question them as to why they are losing out on the windfall benefits from this major market innovation.

Schools for Sale

Pop quiz:
Companies selling products to children can

A) Conduct large-scale market research projects inside schools
B) Expect to pay high fees for exclusive marketing contracts with school districts
C) Reach teen-agers who are using school computers with hip 30-second TV commercials
D) All of the above

The correct answer is D.

In the 10 years since Christopher Whittle and his Channel One newscasts stirred national controversy by introducing TV advertising into schools, marketers and school administrators have grown more savvy in their dealings with each other. School leaders have discovered their negotiating muscle, forcing beverage manufacturers to boost their fees by as much as 1,000% for the right to shut the competition out of a school district. And companies have become smarter about tailoring their activities to educational environments.

All of this has created some extraordinary opportunities for businesses to reach a market that was entirely off-limits just a decade ago. It has also raised alarms among state and federal officials about the extent of commercial penetration of the nation's schools. In late September [1999], U.S. Rep. George Miller, (D., Calif.), introduced legislation calling for a nationwide study to determine how widespread advertising in schools is, and California enacted two powerful laws to slow school commercialization.

"Students should go to school to learn, not to provide companies an edge on the hotly contested youth market," Rep. Miller said as he introduced his legislation.

More Sophisticated Methods

Yet even as the outrage continues to intensify, so does the level of sophistication of in-school marketing. Within the last few years, several upstart companies have cracked the code for entry into U.S. schools. Education Market Resources, a young Kansas City, Kansas, market research company, has escorted dozens of the nation's largest companies—Walt Disney Co., Kellogg Co., Mattel, McDonald's Corp. and Pizza Hut—into several hundred elementary and secondary schools in 90 cities to conduct focus groups on kids' reactions to new flavors, toys and ad campaigns.... Cover Concepts Marketing Services has quietly maneuvered corporate giants such as Nike, Calvin Klein, and Quaker Oats Co., into classrooms in 31,000 schools via free textbook covers sporting trendy ads. [Recently] ZapMe!, a year-old Internet company developed expressly to deliver ads to students, went public, selling shares on Nasdaq.

"There are a couple of reasons why commercial interest in kids and schools has intensified," says David Walsh, president of the National Institute on Media & the Family, a non-profit group in Minneapolis that studies the impact of media on children. "One is the size of the market. Basically, the school population right now is the largest market segment in America. And this is the only market segment where there is an institution where they are held as a captive audience for 6 hours a day."

◈

Corporate America has found enterprising ways to reach this huge, stationary market. ZapMe!, for instance, has a deal educators find hard to resist: schools get free high-end computers—high-speed, broad-band Internet connections, and a network of 11,000 pre-selected education Web sites—in exchange for a promise to use the computers at least 4 hours a day. ZapMe! gets a guaranteed teen and pre-teen audience for the commercials that run continuously on the lower left-hand corner of the screen, and permission to monitor the students' Web browsing habits, breaking the data down by age, sex and ZIP code.

None of this bothers Kathy Reinheimer, head librarian at Egg Harbor Township High School, in Egg Harbor, N.J., a school that has had 15 ZapMe! computers up and running since last spring.

"The students love it," says Ms. Reinheimer. "We had a class in here yesterday doing research on the pyramids in Egypt. And they were able to get to the PBS Nova Web site through ZapMe! And it was wonderful... they got all kinds of archaeological information."

Ms. Reinheimer and her colleague Michael Sweeder brush off concerns about the presence of ads, comparing ZapMe! to its competitors. "To me, if kids are going to computer labs anyhow, they're getting on GeoCities, AOL and Hotbot, where there is more advertising that is more overt and more intrusive than anything on the ZapMe! space," Mr. Sweeder says. "And ZapMe! gives you 11,000 education sites right there. So kids might not even have to go beyond that to do average, basic research."

Regular Commercials

The ZapMe! ad space, however, is not the static banner Web browsers are used to. Because of its high-quality Internet connections, ZapMe! can run regular commercials in the space. When students click on the ZapMe! ad space, an expanded version of the commercial fills the screen. By clicking on the expanded version, students can go directly to the advertiser's home page.

The appeal of ZapMe! for advertisers is that it marries two things that are very powerful, the Internet and the in-school experience, says Julie Halpin, CEO of Geppetto Group, WPP Group's 2-year-old New York ad shop specializing in the children's market. Schools are powerful, Ms. Halpin says, "because there's no clutter. It's not like a magazine, or TV, where you're with a thousand other ads."

Students at the ZapMe! computer lab in Egg Harbor Township High School were a little less bowled over than the ad executives, though. "I don't really see them," one ninth-grader says of the continuous ads on the corner of her screen. "I don't see, like, stuff to buy."

"Ugh," said another when he was asked to click open the Arizona Jean ad. "I hate these commercials."

ZapMe! says it has signed up 6,000 schools in the last 12 months, but, at least on the East Coast, the company is struggling to get its network up and running. Schools in Philadelphia and New Jersey that signed contracts [in] February [1999] are still waiting for ZapMe! to install systems that were promised for [the] spring.

Channel One, the pioneer in school advertising, meanwhile, is still going strong. In 1994, Mr. Whittle averted personal financial disaster by selling Channel One to K-III Communications (now Primedia), but operations were unaffected by the sale.

Almost half the nation's high schools are wired for Channel One's daily 12-minute newscast and commercials. In exchange, schools get free TV sets for every classroom and a satellite hookup. Some 8.3 million teen-agers watch the newscast and commercials every day; 30-second spots go for up to $200,000 and the venture nets about $30 million a year.

๛๏๛

Business executives are not the only ones who have wised up to the in-school marketplace. In the last few years, school superintendents, too, have received an education in Business Negotiations 101. In Colorado Springs, Colo.—ground zero of the marketing explosion, where businesses can sponsor spelling bees and hang posters promoting teen products in the halls—school officials have extracted a 10-year, $8 million contract from bottler Coca-Cola Enterprises.

In the last 18 months alone, the number of exclusive soda contracts in school districts has increased nationwide 300%, to 150. Like many others, Colorado Spring's $8 million deal was brokered by Dan DeRose, head of DD Marketing in Pueblo, Colo., a company that has single-handedly changed the financial equation for schools and beverage companies around the country. This month, the San Jose, Calif., school district and Pepsi Bottling Group officials are expected to sign a DD-brokered deal that will raise per-pupil soda revenues for the schools from $2 a bottle to $26.

"For the last 20 years, Coke and Pepsi have gotten into schools for the cost of providing a scoreboard and a plastic cooler for the football team," says Mr. DeRose. "And we come in and say that's not going to happen anymore."

"Schools are pressed from all sides for funding," he adds. "Taxpayers are asking schools to be creative and innovative, to exhaust their resources before going back to the taxpayers."

Corporate Paraphernalia

Schools with exclusive beverage contracts sometimes find themselves inundated with corporate paraphernalia. Ryan Crockett, a senior at Doherty High School in Colorado Springs who protects his calculus book with a Coke book cover, says the proliferation of Coke products in his school doesn't bother him—except when school officials start pushing students to drink more Coke.

"Apparently we don't buy enough of their product to be worth the deal," he says. "At the junior high school my brother went to last year, the school stopped selling soft drinks at the dances from a stand. Students had to buy their sodas from the Coke machines."

While kids may chafe at pressure to buy soda, critics are concerned about more subtle coercion that commercial activity may exert on children. "Kids are in school to learn to read and write and how to think, not to learn to desire products," says Gary Ruskin, president of Commercial Alert, a consumer watchdog group.

Even those who approve of partnerships between businesses and schools are troubled by the increasingly sophisticated product advertising in schools. "Kids are so bombarded with commercial messages outside of school," says Mr. Walsh of the National Institute on Media & the Family. "The risk is that they will be treated increasingly as consumers in the one institution where they're supposed to be treated as learners."

Some Limits Imposed

Concerns like these are causing state and federal legislators to take action. A California law which goes into effect Jan. 1 [2000] bans exclusive soda and electronic contracts unless schools follow a set of strict procedures designed to ensure the public's chance to voice its objections. The legislation's sponsor, Democratic Assemblywoman Kerry Mazzoni, says she sympathizes with school leaders who are desperate for funding and high-quality resources. "But the reason school districts have gone to these contracts is because of funding problems we've had in California. That's not the right solution," Assemblywoman Mazzoni says.

Ms. Mazzoni also has shepherded a bill into state law this fall that bans the use of textbooks with brand names and company logos embedded in the material. That bill comes in response to complaints from a California parent about "Mathematics: Applications & Connections," a middle-school math book from McGraw-Hill that spices its word problems with references to Barbie, Oreos, Nike, and Sony PlayStations.

A McGraw-Hill spokesman says the company has revamped the book for California but has no intention of pulling it from other states. "This is the best-selling middle-school math book in the country. Teachers demand it."

Rep. Miller's bill, in addition to setting up a study of the extent of commercialism in schools, would prohibit ZapMe! and others from monitoring students' browsing habits and purchasing preferences unless parents give written permission. "He's not trying to usurp local school decision-making," says Daniel Weiss, a member of Rep. Miller's staff. "He realizes how strapped schools are. He just thinks we need to look at all the costs and benefits of these arrangements before we go much further down this road."

Now, though, there may be no turning back. In today's hyper-competitive business environment, consumers of all ages are inundated with marketing messages—adding new meaning to the term, "from the cradle to the grave." America's schools will never be the same.

POSTSCRIPT

Should Classrooms Be Commercial-Free Zones?

Are *services* provided by schools and school systems *products*, and should they be viewed in some ways like a business? The principles of cost effectiveness and the bottom line are in stark contrast to ideals of educators bent on the notion that schools and commercialism are dissonant and conflicting concepts. Are commercial interests and education quality mutually exclusive or inherently at odds with each other?

Major developments are undeniably positive signals for the future of marketing/business partnerships in education. The inordinate growth of online distance education and the emergence of for-profit schools are examples of this partnership. Colleges and universities are utilizing private firms to produce and market their for-profit, often autonomous educational packages. The trickledown effect of this burgeoning market will likely influence K–12 schools to be less resistant toward private sector partnerships. A marked trend has already begun.

The idea that schools should be culpable for delivering quality products (educated students) has never been more popular or clearer to many concerned parents seeking top standards for their children's education. Mandatory testing of teachers and the push for universal student access to the Internet are examples of this concern.

Suggested Readings

Margaret Atherton and Benet Middleton, "Commercial Materials in Schools: Parents' View," *Consumer Policy Review* (March–April 1999)

Deron Boyles, *American Education and Corporations: The Free Market Goes to School* (Garland, 1998)

"For-Profit Schools," *Business Week* (February 7, 2000)

Roy F. Fox and George Gerbner, *Harvesting Minds* (Praeger, 1996)

Rob Gray, "Perils of Sending Brands to School," *Marketing* (April 22, 1999)

Nadia Labi, "Classrooms for Sale," *Time* (April 19, 1999)

"Lobbyists Fear New Curbs As EC Probes Ads in Classrooms," *Campaign* (May 1, 1998)

Jill Wynns, "Yes: Selling Students to Advertisers Sends the Wrong Message in the Classroom," *Advertising Age* (June 7, 1999)

On the Internet . . .

Center for Media Education

Excerpts from *Web of Deception: Threats to Children from Online Marketing* by the Center for Media Education can be found at this site.

http://www.igc.apc.org/cme/kidadsreport.html

American Demographics

This is the home page of the magazine *American Demographics*, which has examined demographic trends over the last 20 years.

http://www.americandemographics.com

Official MBA Guide

This Web site offers a searchable database of vital information for prospective MBA students on MBA programs or business schools. Students can conduct research to find out what programs best meet their graduate education needs and rank programs on criteria they consider important.

http://www.unicorn.us.com/guide

PART 4

Segmentation, Positioning, and Target Marketing

*D*o *you carry a credit card, chew tobacco, pass by billboards advertising malt liquor, or have an eating disorder? If so, you may belong to a vulnerable group, depending on your personal consumer situation. All of the above are issues relating to certain "sensitive," or vulnerable, groups that many believe have been exploited by questionable marketing practices. What are the parameters for determining which marketing techniques are acceptable under these special circumstances? Who should decide where, when, how, and to whom legal products and services can be sold?*

How do we classify groups of consumers? Certainly age is considered by many to be the greatest common denominator for understanding consumer behavior. Generations share unique cultural backgrounds and shared experiences that galvanize their values and consumer behaviors. "Cohort segmentation" takes a narrow view of age analysis, and many new dimensions of the cohort concept truly enrich the understanding of the segmentation process.

A new development in education is the "distance learning" segment of college students. Total online providers are translating communications technology into new opportunities, particularly for nontraditional students who previously had no access to college classes. How will this development affect traditional educational institutions and their "brand equity"? What will be the impact of the "digital divide" on segmentation strategy?

- Should Marketers Target Vulnerable Groups?

- Is Generational Segmentation an Effective Marketing Strategy?

- Is the Marketing of Online Degree Programs a Threat to Traditional Education?

ISSUE 14

Should Marketers Target Vulnerable Groups?

YES: Barton Macchiette and Abhijit Roy, from "Sensitive Groups and Social Issues: Are You Marketing Correct?" *Journal of Consumer Marketing* (vol. 11, no. 4, 1994)

NO: Marcy Gordon, from "Collegiate Credit Junkies: Critics Allege Credit Card Companies Try to Hook Students," *ABCNEWS. com,* <http://abcnews.go.com/sections/business/DailyNews/credit990608.html> (June 8, 1999)

ISSUE SUMMARY

YES: Professor of marketing Barton Macchiette and Abhijit Roy, a doctoral student in marketing, contend that marketers should target all prospects who might benefit from their product or service. However, they must be particularly conscious when targeting sensitive or vulnerable groups, such as children, women, minorities, and gay males and lesbians.

NO: Writer Marcy Gordon presents several arguments against the marketing of credit cards to college students. She sees the problem to be at least commensurate to alcohol abuse or sexually transmitted disease and suggests that marketers are aggressively promoting addiction to credit.

Vulnerable groups are consumers who, due to personal or situational influences, may be unable to make prudent purchasing decisions. There are hundreds of cases relating to the issue of appropriate boundaries in targeting sensitive groups. While each case warrants independent scrutiny, many argue that managers must employ guidelines in order to make ethical judgments that enable them to "market correct."

With regard to "sin" products, such as tobacco, alcohol, and gambling, most agree that marketers should exercise particular caution in areas of targeting and promotion. However, situational influences can create ethical questions in marketing completely legitimate products, such as credit cards. Consider the practice of the life insurance salesman who solicits the neighbors of families recently victimized by drive-by shootings and capitalizes on their fear by showing gruesome pictures of the deceased. Such practices blemish the reputation of the life insurance firm, as well as the reputation of marketing in general.

Several recent issues have centered upon promoting inherently damaging products, such as marketing malt liquors in minority neighborhoods fraught with rampant crime and drug addiction. Critics contend that marketers should exclude these locations and avoid the use of billboards promoting cigarettes, alcohol, and even lottery tickets. Similar criticisms of Uptown and Dakota cigarette brands, which were originally conceived to target African Americans and single, blue-collar working women, respectively, were doomed as "damned brands" and were never launched in the marketplace.

Credit cards, however, are an accepted if not an essential product for transacting personal business and for validating identification. The average adult American carries at least four credit cards. Credit card marketers visiting college campuses secure 24 percent of first-time card users. Now there is a dramatic trend to disallow these representatives on campus.

The basic question that drives this issue is the policy of *selective exclusion* —purposely ignoring potential target markets because of group sensitivity or a politically charged situation. Some critics object to the idea that marketers should ignore various minority markets due to their alleged vulnerability. They argue that their rights of consumer choice and sovereignty are compromised. Critics ask, Why should these minority consumers be arbitrarily excluded from products differentiated to their unique preferences? Could this be interpreted as a means of discrimination? Some marketers object to the inference that certain vulnerable groups are less capable of making purchase decisions and should be denied equal opportunities of brand choice. The argument for selective exclusion is also contradictory to the long-standing charge that minorities are underrepresented in American advertising, neglected as a viable market segment in many product categories, and portrayed in stereotypical ads that are insensitive to the nuances of their subculture.

The use and legitimacy of marketing's most fundamental tools—targeting, positioning, and segmentation—are at the core of this debate. From advertising to children on the Internet and in the classroom to promoting sweepstakes to the elderly, marketing to vulnerable groups requires a serious analysis of the current political environment and the balance between social responsibility and consumer rights.

Marcy Gordon challenges the marketing of credit cards to college students in a case against the aggressive marketing of "addiction to debt." She finds the statistics on their abuse appalling and argues that the resulting ramifications are clear. But marketers assert that most students use credit cards responsibly and find them essential to establishing a credit history. Should college students, many of whom are underaged and living away from home for the first time, be considered a vulnerable group? Should marketers be denied the right to promote credit cards to students because some students abuse them?

Barton Macchiette and Abhijit Roy  **YES**

Sensitive Groups and Social Issues: Are You Marketing Correct?

The Nature of Sensitive Groups

The term "sensitive group",... refers to a segment of the population generally perceived as being disadvantaged, vulnerable, discriminated against, or involved in social issues which consequently influence their consumer behavior. Admittedly, the concept is provocative, subjective and often influenced by contemporary media events which popularize a particular issue and bring national attention to the sensitive group. Thus, the degree of sensitivity is affected by the extent of media attention generated from consumer advocates, regulatory agencies, support groups, and the public at large. For example, recent concern about gays in the military has been translated into a focus on this group as a viable market segment and created ethical debates associated with targeting this group.

Problems of Group Isolation and Mutual Exclusivity

A strong argument can be made to suggest that all consumers, at some point, are members of a sensitive group. This is either by choice of lifestyle, situational circumstance, life cycle, or demographics. For example, one might be born into an impoverished community or with a physical disadvantage. Children are categorically "sensitive", due to their lack of information-processing skills and lack of maturity. Middle age may bring divorce, loss of loved ones, unemployment, or disability. Elderly consumers face debilitating health and vulnerability to being overly trustful to marketing ploys. This perspective also suggests that a large variance of intensity exists in terms of group sensitivity. This is a function of the consumer's situation and the marketing environment at a particular point in time.

Group Sensitivity Is Product Related

In a marketing context, sensitive groups may also be product related. For example, an elderly consumer may have extreme competence in discerning

Adapted from Barton Macchiette and Abhijit Roy, "Sensitive Groups and Social Issues: Are You Marketing Correct?" *Journal of Consumer Marketing*, vol. 11, no. 4 (1994). Copyright © 1994 by MCB University Press. Reprinted by permission. References omitted.

product categories with which she or he has had a life's worth of vocational consumption experience. Yet, the same person may be vulnerable to life-saving communication beepers which may use high-powered fear appeals through telemarketing, and may be unscrupulously overpriced. Thus, products considered to be legitimate when targeting one group, may not be perceived as being socially responsible when targeting other sensitive groups. The question of promoting cigarettes to children is another case in point.

Sensitive Groups May Have Life Cycles

This hypothesis can be construed in two ways. The first view is that people transcend group sensitivity merely by living out normal life spans. Thus, there is an important temporal dimension to the concept of sensitivity. For example, permanently disabled individuals will face their inevitable problems longer than those facing temporary unemployment.

The second view is that some sensitive groups and social issues experience a life cycle. This results from the media collectively popularizing a particular group and social issue. Often, national talk shows, newspaper and other media events will focus on a specific social issue related to a sensitive group. Eventually, a new issue will engage the public's attention and the cycle may repeat.

Proposed Typology of Sensitive Groups

Despite the lack of mutual exclusivity, it is important to provide a general means of categorizing the source and nature of various sensitive groups. The following typology identifies the primary sources from which groups derive their sensitivity.

In examining these groups, one should not only consider the perceptions of sensitive group members, but also attitudes of the public at large concerning related social issues. This most often exerts the real pressure on marketers for social responsibility and remedial action.

Culturally Dictated Sensitive Groups

These groups elicit a high impact media profile and, despite fluctuations in the intensity of public awareness, have captured the nation's attention and invite public scrutiny for an *enduring* period of time. They are usually associated with specific social issues.

In the last decade, the nation has embraced such sensitive groups as abused children, starvation in the Third World, subjects of sexual abuse, and victims of terminal illness. More recently, the homeless, gays and sexually harassed women have received acknowledgment from the general public, which has a heightened awareness of such issues.

Situationally Influenced Sensitive Groups

These groups result from *temporary* environmental or personal circumstances which place the consumer in a sensitive group for a period of time. Divorce, temporary unemployment, family death or other circumstances can create a situation of consumer vulnerability. An example would be the controversy surrounding the "Smoking Joe" cartoon character. Many critics feel that he is easily recognized by children which may motivate them to start smoking. Similar allegations have been made against malt liquor marketers targeting low income African-Americans.

Marketing-Generated Sensitive Groups

This term refers to groups that become vulnerable as the result of promotional strategies conceived and executed by marketers. Those groups are usually created through marketing innovation. Children are a particularly vulnerable population. Cartoon characters such as Little Mermaid, Smurfs and Ninja Turtles are examples of marketing-generated products that have translated into segments of young consumers who are very brand loyal to these promotionally conceived characters. The controversy surrounding [the] "Barbie" doll as a role model for pre-teen girls falls into this category (Leo, 1992). Licensing agreements allow thousands of manufacturers to utilize the characters as promotional leverage for selling a wide array of products. "Product-based programming" is an example of an ethical issue for marketing-generated sensitive groups. This refers to the notion that children may not distinguish actual programming from product-related ads that sponsor the show; i.e. ads for Ninja Turtle dolls, embedded in the Ninja Turtle TV program.

Issue-Driven Sensitive Groups

Unlike the above-mentioned categories, these consumers need only to be sympathetic to cause-related or social issues, rather than being an actual member of a vulnerable group. These are defined as groups of consumers responding to social issues through observable changes in their purchasing behavior. "True-blue" green consumers, rain forest advocates, and members of other cause-related marketing groups are suitable examples.

College Students As Vulnerable Groups— The Case of Credit Cards

The Situation

Colleges and universities are denying access to third party credit card marketers in increasing numbers. There were 22 campuses that disallowed the practice in 1988. That number has increased dramatically and is expected to cross 400 in the next couple of years. Private sources that monitor college credit card marketing (*College Marketing Intelligence*) contend that the number is much higher, estimating that 750 to 1000 college campuses have already banned on-campus credit card marketing. Are college students so vulnerable they should be selectively excluded from the credit card market?

Historical Perspective

In the 1970s, it was rare that a student would be able to secure a credit card without the backing of a cosigner (i.e., mom or dad). But [due to] the necessity of their use in today's society and our credit-driven economy, demand has caused credit card companies to bring their services to college students on campus. This has successfully resulted in providing close to 25% with their first credit card. Due to broader financing options and larger interest rate spreads, lenders are more comfortable taking risks with many more segments of our current population.

Why They Target College Students on Campus

College students throughout the United States spend $90 billion annually, and they are likely to be big spenders once they enter professional life. This is a greater amount than the GNP [gross national product] of several countries in the world. As a result, advertisers spend more than $140 million annually to appeal to college students. This makes credit card companies the biggest spenders in advertising, replacing beer marketers who have reduced their presence in the college market due to political and social pressures.

College students are hard to reach through conventional media and thus pose a special challenge. They watch less television than other adults and when they do watch it is usually very late at night. They read newspapers less frequently. Also, credit cards need to be explained and lend themselves more to a personalized sales format. Recognizing the importance of building long term customer relationships, credit card marketers strive to provide appropriate information and differentiate their product offerings through face to face communications.

The Education Resources Institute (TERI) is a nonprofit Washington DC based Institute for Higher Education Policy. According to a recent (1999) study by them, almost 2/3 of the college students pay off the balances immediately and over 80% have balances of only $1,000 or less. Another survey by the *US Public Research Group* revealed that the average balance was $968 for students with a credit card in their name.

Benefits to the College and Students

Many colleges are benefiting enormously through the use of *affinity credit cards*. These cards with college logos are very popular among both students and alumni, generating a great deal of publicity and group cohesiveness among participating stakeholders. Many schools reap a handsome profit from the percentage returned to the institution for participating in the affinity program.

Ironically, 20% of college students pay their tuition and fees with credit cards. Better than half of these students get their cards to build a credit history essential for investments and financing throughout their lives. They usually become the best and most loyal customers and develop long standing relationships with the credit card providers. *Mastercard* found that 75% of college card holders retained them for at least fifteen years. The delinquent and charge-off rates for these card holders are no worse, and in many cases better, than those of the general population.

Proactive Measures to Deal With Student Debt

Rather than prohibit credit card marketers, colleges should encourage their accountability by working with them, emphasizing educational objectives of credit card use. Student government and relevant organizations can become involved. *Purdue University*, for example, requires credit card companies be sponsored by a student organization. Implementing the use of *debit-cards* and reporting defaulters to the college are tenable policies. Limiting pre-approved credit card offerings can also be helpful in a mutually beneficial effort to eliminate card abuse.

It is ludicrous to believe that prohibiting credit card reps on campus will prevent students from acquiring the service through other less interactive and informative promotional methods. So why not approach the real problem of credit card abuse through mutually acceptable pro-active methods?

Dilemmas in Defining Vulnerability

This issue raises interesting questions in reference to the boundaries and de-terminants of *vulnerable/sensitive groups*. Recently several banks in the mid-west were acknowledged for initiating savings and checking accounts for elemen-tary students (under the auspices of parents) as an educational program. Yet, college students are denied access to credit card providers on campus. Most of these students are now non-traditional, working part-time and certainly old enough to legally drink alcohol and vote. Should our most gifted minds and fu-ture professionals be denied the same rights afforded consumers of the general population? This is not only a legal product, but a necessity of normal life, and a pillar of American culture. The average adult carries approximately four credit cards and would be hard pressed to travel or function as a consumer without at least owning one.

There seems to be little resistance from students to this policy of *selective exclusion*. Credit card companies are quietly finding new means for reaching potential students such as marketing on the internet. But have their constitu-tional rights to freedom of speech been infringed upon? Does the policy of selective exclusion send a terribly humiliating message to those denied their consumer sovereignty? In this case are administrators saying "Since you are so financially irresponsible, we must protect you from these pernicious credit card marketers"?

It is a long established tradition to have Marine Corp and Armed Service booths to recruit students to possibly "die for their country", but don't let them sell the right to function in the U.S. economy. When it comes to those credit card marketers, *Just Say No!*

Would members of a blue-collar Labor Union, elderly folks in a retire-ment community, *The Audubon Society*, or the *Harley Davidson Association* be any less vulnerable than college students? Perhaps *college administrators* should be the only viable target for socially responsible credit card companies trying to avoid exploiting the "fiscally challenged" segments of the market.

Dangers of Dictating Vulnerability

Who should determine the question of vulnerability? What are the criteria for a policy of selective exclusion? Should the responsibility rest with the marketer, the government or community and organization leaders?

The inherent danger is that more frequently, self appointed "gate-keepers" can control the access of legal products and services to consumers over whom they exert influence. Depriving the fundamental rights of product choice that others freely enjoy should require solid evidence that seriously and irrefutably warrants infringing upon consumer control over their own purchase decisions. Obviously, cigarettes, alcohol, and other *inherently damaging* products should not be promoted to children. Each sensitive situation should be carefully analyzed in the context of social responsibility. But the insidious nature of selective exclusion can threaten the most fundamental of democratic principles.

For example, the logical extension of prohibiting credit card reps from campus is to ban mail to students from these companies. Then, perhaps *Guns and Ammo* magazine can be arguably dangerous for college students. Thousands of questionable products and services can be arbitrarily and capriciously dissected by those empowered to control access to the marketplace.

Harsher critics have coined the term "Social Nazis" to describe those who believe their enlightened knowledge of what is justifiable for others imbues them with the right of controlling the marketplace. Who has the wisdom to make such determinations? But those weekend, late night pizza consumers are surely doing themselves harm. Let's at least keep those delivery guys off-campus!

Managerial Implications

The New Marketing Culture

The current cultural milieu accenting political correctness has become a critical factor in marketing management. Recent evidence suggests that marketers take great risk by ignoring the potential reactions caused by various interpretations of their marketing actions by concerned publics. Not only have boycotts increased dramatically in the last few years, but also other means of collective action to deter and publicly damage incorrect or socially irresponsible marketers have arisen. These actions can depreciate a brand's equity and tarnish a well-established corporate image.

Consequences of Ignoring Social Responsibility: Damned Brands

If adequate analysis and foresight is absent from the marketing plan, the result may well be a "damned brand". This is a brand that, owing to a lack of foreseeing social response from a sensitive group, has received such negative publicity that the product is dropped for the sake of preserving brand equity and corporate image. Such adverse public reaction can arise from social issues relating to questionable products and promotional techniques, which are interpreted as exploitation of a particular sensitive group.

Given the adversarial climate towards marketers, caution should be taken to pre-empt the launching of a "damned brand", or initiating a new promotional campaign that might create a negative public image. Certain products invite public scrutiny because of their inherently injurious nature or ethical controversies may surround marketing campaigns targeting sensitive groups. Companies have been forced to "bail out" and abandon their efforts when such negative publicity (regardless of its legitimacy) has surfaced. Brands such as Uptown and Dakota cigarettes and Power Master malt liquor became "damned" by the allegations of exploitation in reference to African-American consumers.

What Is Marketing Correctness?

In [recent] years, the national debate over "political correctness" has emerged from college campuses and has migrated into the business environment. The central focus encompassed issues relating to vulnerable populations, multiculturalism and speech codes as they relate to gender, race and class. Primarily, the movement involved challenging traditional views and social norms as related to these groups. Soon these principles were applied to the corporate world, concentrating mostly on environmental issues and marketing to sensitive groups.

Thus, the term "marketing correct" refers to the process of establishing a social responsibility policy as a fully integrated, systematic component of the marketing program, carefully incorporated into each promotional plan. Inherent in the philosophy of marketing correctness is the idea that social responsibility has become a salient attribute and a fruitful means of product differentiation. It is not an arbitrary "give away" program, but should enhance profitability, build brand equity and more clearly define product positioning in the marketplace.

The level of commitment to social responsibility is dictated by several factors, including the nature of the product, target market, corporate culture and mission statement. Companies selling tobacco and alcohol through inner city billboards, or handguns to women, obviously must answer to a higher sense of social responsibility because of the inherent controversy surrounding these products and sensitivity to their target markets.

Ben and Jerry's and the Body Shop, for example, are totally committed to social responsibility, in that it is deeply embedded in their mission statements and is a significant component of their corporate image. This is not to imply that all companies should be totally consumed by the subject, but that they should strive for a new perspective. Marketing correctness implies an awareness of how social responsibility can be incorporated into the marketing mix.

Integrating Social Responsibility into the Marketing Program

The development of a social responsibility program requires research, sensitivity and commitment from all levels in the marketing team. It should be consumer driven. Cultural diversity implies not only differences in language and lifestyle, but also temperament, perceptions and values intimately linked to consumer behavior. Knowledge of these differences can provide rich insights for product development, positioning strategy and promotional appeals.

Concept testing, focus group studies and constant tracking of consumer attitudes is a critical component of social responsibility policy. Often with incredible haste, an issue can develop which draws a particular industry practice, promotional technique or product attribute into the limelight of public scrutiny. Companies devoid of a crisis management program and contingency plan are at great risk in this volatile marketing environment. It is prudent to be prepared for the unexpected with systematic alternative measures, a central source of communicators, and pre-established decision-making authority. Finally, it is wise to establish an interactive communications network and constructive liaison with opinion leaders of special interest groups representing the target markets that might react negatively to a particular market plan. Involving members of such groups in developing the plan, or alerting special interest group leaders concerning campaign concepts and the logic behind them, serves as an "inoculation effect", and can desensitize potentially damaging issues. Overall, a successful social policy program is predicated on awareness of cultural diversity, sensitive groups and their special interests; research on contemporary and potentially relevant social issues; a creative search for regional and cause-related marketing, preparedness for crisis; and common sense. Specific guidelines for proactive strategies are offered below:

1. Establish corporate social responsibility [CSR] as a component of a firm's marketing information system
2. Introduce sensitive group and social issue research in the earliest stages of the new product development process
3. Specifically, establish a model for tracking public attitudes and perceptions of relevant social issues and sensitive groups
4. Consider alternative means of utilizing social policy to build brand equity and enhance relationship marketing with sensitive groups
5. Utilize concept testing and focus groups among consumers representing targeted sensitive groups
6. Develop an ethical rationale and defensive strategies prior to the introduction of a marketing plan
7. Seek to gain endorsements from opinion leaders and respected celebrities within these groups
8. Have a crisis management program intact and consider the crucial linkages of public relations and publicity to corporate social responsibility programs
9. Consider optimizing the use of interactive marketing, and video news releases to enhance the use of CSR projects
10. Examine opportunities with sensitive groups for socially-oriented, cause-related marketing programs and environmental issues.

Conclusion

It is very probable that America's concern with social responsibility will continue to create problems and opportunities for marketers targeting sensitive groups. Anticipating and incorporating these issues into a systematic social responsibility program is essential for competing.... Social issues, cultural diversity, environmental concerns and cause-related marketing are becoming a central focus in many areas of consumer decision making. They represent great potential for product positioning and building brand equity among a growing number of socially responsible consumers. While product quality, value and service still reign supreme, the new era of competition asks—"Are You Marketing Correct?".

Collegiate Credit Junkies

University of Central Oklahoma freshman Mitzi Pool, $2,500 in debt, hanged herself in her dorm room, her checkbook and credit card bills spread out on her bed.

Consumer groups are citing the 1997 death to underscore their criticism of credit card companies, who they say are aggressively trying to get college students hooked on credit the way cigarette makers tried to get young people hooked on tobacco.

"Credit card companies are targeting America's children," Frank Torres, legislative counsel for Consumers Union, said today at a news conference organized by the Consumer Federation of America [CFA].

The CFA also released a study by Georgetown University sociologist Robert Manning showing that some students are forced to cut back on their courses or spend more time working to pay off their credit card debts.

About 70 percent of students at four-year colleges have at least one credit card, and revolving debt on these cards averages more than $2,000, Manning's study said. In the worst cases, students are forced to drop out of school and work full time.

At the news conference, Tricia Johnson of Enid, Okla. recounted how her daughter Mitzi had phoned her on a December night in 1997, crying because she had lost her part-time job and didn't know what to do. She already had maxed out three credit cards after 3½ months of college.

"I tried to assure her that . . . we would sit down and go over her bills and work some plan out," Ms. Johnson said. "This was my last conversation with my daughter." Later that night, she killed herself.

Companies Defend Marketing

Credit card companies such as Visa USA Inc. and MasterCard International have defended their college marketing practices, maintaining that most students use credit responsibly and appreciate getting the cards as a way to establish a credit history.

Referring to the suicides of Ms. Pool and Sean Moyer, a University of Oklahoma junior who had $10,000 in credit card debt when he killed himself in

1988, Visa said "The loss of a young person is tragic under any circumstances, and it is very troubling to hear of the loss these families suffered."

"Visa and its (member banks) feel a strong responsibility to educate college students about wisely managing their personal finances," the company said in a statement. "We see financial education as an important tool to prevent problems before they occur."

The consumer groups also criticized colleges and universities for allowing what they said was aggressive marketing of credit cards on campuses and benefiting financially from it.

Credit card companies pay colleges and universities fees to be able to sponsor school programs and student activities, to rent tables on campus used to solicit students to apply for cards, and for marketing agreements such as "affinity" cards linked to colleges, the groups said.

Lure Students With Giveaways

A study last fall by the U.S. Public Interest Research Group found that credit card companies lure students on campus with free T-shirts, Frisbees and other items if they apply for cards. It also found that students who obtain cards that way often end up with bigger unpaid balances and pay off their debts later than those who do not.

"The unrestricted marketing of credit cards on college campuses is so aggressive that it now poses a greater threat than alcohol or sexually transmitted diseases," said Manning. "Typically, students slide into debt through the extension (by credit card companies) of unaffordable credit lines."

His study, which was partially funded by the CFA, was based on interviews with and questionnaires completed by students at Georgetown University, American University and the University of Maryland, all in the Washington area.

Spokesmen for the American Council on Education, which represents college and university administrators, had no immediate comment. Officials at the three schools focused on in the study did not immediately respond to queries by the Associated Press.

The debate comes about a month after the House, seeking to stem an increase in personal bankruptcies, passed a bill sought by credit card companies that would make it tougher for people to erase their debts in bankruptcy court.

The bill was passed by a veto-proof 313–108 margin, getting solid support from Republicans but splitting Democrats. Parallel legislation is pending in the Senate.

Stephen Brobeck, executive director of the CFA, said . . . that Congress should adopt a measure requiring people under age 21 to get a parent's approval or demonstrate sufficient income before obtaining credit cards.

POSTSCRIPT

Should Marketers Target Vulnerable Groups?

$\mathbf{C}$lose to 400 colleges and universities are expected to "kick out" third-party credit card marketers, banning their tables and booths from college campuses. University representatives claim to be protecting students from their own potentially destructive credit habits. Are colleges justified in denying students access to credit cards through such means? Are college students indeed a vulnerable group? At what age do people become responsible for making their own choices, including the everyday decisions of how they will spend the money that they have earned—or borrow against the money they hope to earn in the future? Is it appropriate for colleges and universities to allow the U.S. Armed Services to recruit on campus but deny access to credit card marketers?

Macchiette and Roy provide guidelines for recognizing and dealing with the potential dangers of marketing in sensitive situations. However, the challenge of marketing to underage consumers encompasses perhaps the most egregious problems of vulnerability. Major issues of commercialism in the classroom, advertising of alcohol, and the influence of media violence on children are important issues to explore. The Internet poses a new frontier for privacy issues, pornography, and a host of other societal problems.

Suggested Readings

D. Kirk Davidson, "Mentally Disabled Vulnerable to Unethical Marketers," *Marketing News* (January 4, 1999)

John H. Menchinger, "Marketing Correctness: A Word for the Wise," *Broker World* (November 1998)

Cristina Merrill, "Making Media Sales Smart," *American Demographics* (September 1999)

Ross D. Petty, "Interactive Marketing and the Law: The Future Rise of Unfairness," *Journal of Interactive Marketing* (Summer 1998)

"Student Credit Card Debt," *Commercial Law Bulletin* (November–December 1998)

Lisa Toloken, "Turning the Tables on Campus," *Credit Card Management* (May 1999)

Marcia Vickers, "A Hard Lesson on Credit Cards," *Business Week* (March 15, 1999)

ISSUE 15

Is Generational Segmentation an Effective Marketing Strategy?

YES: J. Walker Smith and Ann Clurman, from *Rocking the Ages: The Yankelovich Report on Generational Marketing* (HarperBusiness, 1997)

NO: Charles D. Schewe and Geoffrey E. Meredith, from "Segmenting the Market by Cohorts: Age Really Matters—'Coming of Age' That Is!" An Original Essay Written for This Volume (2000)

ISSUE SUMMARY

YES: Authors J. Walker Smith and Ann Clurman see the three major consumer generations as the matures, boomers, and generation X'ers. They examine these groups' unique attitudes, motivations, lifestyles, values, and spending patterns. Smith and Clurman offer several examples to illustrate the cohesive consumer behavior of these groups.

NO: Professor of marketing Charles D. Schewe and Lifestage Matrix Marketing founder Geoffrey E. Meredith contend that the case for generational marketing is simply too broad and all-inclusive to be helpful in depicting meaningful differences in market segments.

Ever since the first advertising agencies recognized the benefits of tailoring their messages to different audiences, market segmentation has arguably been the most valuable tool of the marketing manager. When marketing managers are asked which singular means of segmentation is generally most important, if forced to choose *only* one, the most common response is age. This is the conceptual basis for generational marketing. The goal is to segment buyers primarily by age groups, core values, and shared experiences. This approach provides widely accepted "defining moments" for each generation, which in turn become the significant basis for designing the marketing plan—and more emphatically, the communications campaign. In their selection, J. Walker Smith and Ann Clurman construct a "blueprint" for a person's purchase behavior by linking people of the same generation together. Generations are usually considered to be 20 to 25 years in length, or the time it takes for a typical person to grow up and start a family. The focus is on shared life experiences in one's formative years, generally agreed to be between 17 and 21 years of age. Connecting these generation members are shared experiences like pop culture, music, economic conditions, world events, natural disasters, heroes and villains, and experiences that create memorable bonds. The life stage of the individual deals with physical and psychological aspects related to age. This is significant in terms of product/service requirements and responsibilities associated with life change. Current conditions, technologies, and parameters that are contemporary influences on generation members are also considered. Smith and Clurman depict three major generations as matures (born between 1909 and 1945), boomers (born between 1946 and 1964), and generation X'ers (born since 1965).

The key question defining this issue is the variances in time spans for delineating "generations." While Smith and Clurman use three generational segments in their approach, Charles D. Schewe and Geoffrey E. Meredith have delineated six American cohort groups, ranging from Depression cohorts (79 to 88 years) to generation X. He believes that smaller, more well-defined cohort groups add much richer insights into understanding these segments and their consumer behavior.

The Smith/Clurman generational approach is clearly significant for guiding marketing strategies and in choosing general appeals that are congruent with the values and norms that are the hallmarks of three broad segments. But the question of breadth becomes the object of conjecture. How large can a segment be without losing significant nuances and changes in consumer behavior reflected by constantly changing values and attitudes? The true value of targeting by age lies in categories that reflect current mindsets and values. These factors are changing much more rapidly in today's "real-time" environment. Clothing, music, food, entertainment, and financial markets are particularly relevant to "cohort sensitivity." These are often products/services that appear to be influenced by reference groups and referent individuals or celebrities who often serve as spokespersons for a particular cohort group.

Consumers are sensitive to their age cohorts and tend to conform to the lifestyles and brands associated with their peers. While Levi's Dockers found success marketing pants to younger baby boomers, they failed in appealing to generation X'ers, who did not want to wear the same pants their fathers wear. Levi Strauss & Co. has lost a considerable share of the market by not adequately reading the changing appeals of the fast-emerging generation Y and the echo generation of age 20 and younger.

Companies have incorporated cohort and generational segmentation theory into training their sales forces to be aware of the values and perceptual screens of varying age groups. More recently, new brands are targeting the unconventional Y generation, which has become somewhat disillusioned with celebrities like Michael Jordan and flagship giants like Nike, opting for more unique "niche" brands. As skateboarding goes mainstream, and the younger consumers continue to become trendsetters, marketers look toward the Y generation as a dynamic influence on the marketplace.

J. Walker Smith and Ann Clurman

 **YES**

The Power of Generations

There is an ancient proverb: "Men resemble the times more than they do their fathers." Within the wisdom of those words lie the seeds of generational marketing. Marketers who use the principles of generational marketing to understand the factors that influence the values and buying motivations of consumers stand a much better chance of spotting trends way ahead of the competition and reaching customers first in profitable new ways.

Members of a generation are linked through *the shared life experiences of their formative years*—things like pop culture, economic conditions, world events, natural disasters, heroes, villains, politics, and technology—experiences that create bonds tying the members of a generation together into what social scientists were the first to call "cohorts." Because of these shared experiences, cohorts develop and retain similar values and life skills as they learn what to hold dear and how to go about doing things. This affects everything from savings and sex to a good meal and a new car.

Generational Marketing

Generational marketing is a strategic business perspective that studies these cohort effects and highlights what's relevant for better business decision-making. Consider a couple of examples.

- When Betty Crocker introduced a line of completely ready-to-bake cake mixes in the 1950s, sales were disappointing. Those were the days of the stay-at-home mothers whom today we call the Matures. To Matures, who grew up in the Depression and sacrificed to achieve victory in World War II, hard work was a virtue. Anything too easy was suspect. Convenience seemed like cheating. Eventually, after applying this insight, Betty Crocker found success with a modified version that required adding an egg. This appealed to the Mature housewife's sense that a little work was a lot better.

- Seagram found sales of its whiskeys slipping in the early 1970s. The reason: Baby Boomers weren't drinking as much as their parents. Mainly, though, they were in a hurry. Boomers were too impatient to "learn" to enjoy liquor or to wait to develop a taste for scotch. After some trenchant marketing research determined that young people were looking for something easier to drink, Seagram responded by concentrating its marketing on a new line of white spirits, like vodka. These could be mixed with juices or sodas, and appealed to the Boomer demand for easy access to pleasure and enjoyment. Vodka did not demand an acquired taste.

As these examples illustrate, the marketplace always evolves in response to the different needs of each generation. The values, preferences, and behaviors of consumers can be understood—and shifts better predicted—by breaking down what accounts for them into three distinct elements: (1) Life stage, (2) Current social and economic conditions, and (3) Formative cohort experiences.

- *Life stage* is how old you are and, therefore, where you are in your life—physically or psychologically. We need different products and services as our responsibilities and requirements in life change.
- *Current conditions* are those events that affect what you can buy. Layoffs, recessions, import/export restrictions, political turmoil, technological innovations, taxes, and so forth, all set parameters within which consumers operate in the marketplace.
- Most influential, though, are the *formative cohort experiences* we all share as part of a generation. These create the habits that define and differentiate generations, the unifying experiences through which each of us views the world and participates in the marketplace. These formative experiences shared with your cohorts are the filter through which you interpret all subsequent experiences.

Every generation will pass through the same life stages—getting a driver's license, going through the joy and pain of parenthood, confronting the uncertainties of retirement. Similarly, no matter which generation we belong to, we all must deal with the same circumstances—economic downturns, wars, or World Series. But each generation—Matures, Boomers, and Xers—responds to these life stages and circumstances in ways determined by that critical third factor—the early shared experiences that helped form the values and life skills of their generational cohort.

We are certainly *not* suggesting that marketers ignore crucial factors like demographics, economics, or anything else with obvious impact on your business. But we do not believe that you can truly understand your customers without knowing what makes them tick—the generation they belong to is a big part of who they are.

When you develop a marketing strategy, it is important to understand how old your customers are and whether the economy is booming or not. But this is just not enough. Matures and Boomers have responded differently to economic

Figure 1

Generational Influences

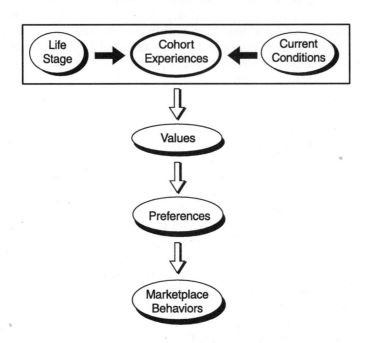

recessions over the last two decades, recessions they have both faced at the same time. Same economic pressures, different consumption patterns. As we'll see, Boomers will look nothing like Matures when they reach retirement; Xers today look nothing like the Boomers of twenty or thirty years ago. Same life stages, different consumers. Generational marketing won't explain everything, but it will explain a lot, and help us better understand the ways in which different individuals will react very differently to the very same marketplace.

Borrowing loosely from social science terminology, we call the events that define a generation "markers." Think of markers as the key set of collective experiences that shape a generation's values and attitudes. These set the tone for a generation, give it direction, provide it with whatever sense of cohesion it has.

For the older generation, the Matures, some of the most significant markers are the Depression, the New Deal, World War II, and the GI Bill. For Boomers they include the Great Society, general economic prosperity and the expansion of suburbia, Nixon, color TV, and sex, drugs, and rock 'n' roll. For the current crop of young people, Generation X, they include divorce, AIDS, Sesame Street, MTV, crack cocaine, Game Boy, and the PC.

Markers help us see why past is not prologue. You make a mistake if you assume that just because your customers are turning a certain age they will behave in the same ways as those who turned that age before them. As obvious as this may seem, it is one of the most common mistakes made in marketing planning.

For instance, a marketer who bases sales and advertising strategy strictly on demographic data, like age, might assume that Baby Boomers will abandon the Rolling Stones and switch from Coca-Cola as they pass their fiftieth birthdays in the years ahead. This would have major implications for the music and beverage industries. However, a smart marketer who considers generational cohorts knows that these deeply implanted preferences are sticking with Boomers as they pass through each life stage.

Don't assume that Boomers will behave like Matures when they reach fifty. Life stage is not everything. When the Boomers began to turn thirty-five, predictions were rife that they would begin to save and become more conservative, politically and socially, just like their parents. It didn't happen. The Boomers rolled right on past thirty-five, remaining true to their free-spending, free-spirited ways. The habits acquired and formed early in life continued to shape their behavior. They did change their consuming, of course, but always in ways consistent with the core values characteristic of their generation. Yuppies, for example, were, deep down, driven by the same core values of fulfillment and self-enrichment as hippies.

Another common mistake is something we call "generational myopia," or the shortsighted application of the values and attitudes of your own generation to the development of strategies for marketing to another generation. We've seen this happen a lot—a marketer will misjudge events and motivations by applying the perspective of his or her generation without truly understanding the unique generational experience of a different target group of consumers. This is a recipe for failure. Each generation is shaped by different markers; you must walk with them in their shoes, not walk on them in your shoes.

Matures, Boomers, and Xers

Consumers active in today's marketplace can be divided, for all practical purposes, into three broad generations—Matures, Boomers, and Xers. Indeed, empirically, our MONITOR data verify that these are cohesive groups of consumers.

The Matures, born between 1909 and 1945, came of age under the shadows of the Great Depression, World War II, Korea, and the Cold War. Their attitudes toward life and work were formed in the crucible of economic upheaval, common enemies, and America's role as an emerging superpower. Matures grew up in tough times, so they had a more constrained set of expectations. As a result, their core values are what we think of today as traditional values —discipline, self-denial, hard work, obedience to authority, and financial and social conservatism.

These values still determine the way in which Matures relate to the marketplace. They have been slow to embrace new products. They saved their money and saw retirement and leisure time as rewards for hard work. Products that fit their basic values have succeeded—and will continue to succeed—because these values grew out of their shared experiences and still guide their consumption.

Table 1

Generations at a Glance

	MATURES	BOOMERS	Xers
Defining idea.........	DUTY	INDIVIDUALITY	DIVERSITY
Celebrating............	Victory	Youth	Savvy
Success because......	Fought hard and won	Were born, therefore should be a winner	Have two jobs
Style......................	Team player	Self-absorbed	Entrepreneur
Rewards because....	You've earned it	You deserve it	You need it
Work is..................	An inevitable obligation	An exciting adventure	A difficult challenge
Surprises in life......	Some good, some bad	All good	Avoid it—all bad
Leisure is...............	Reward for hard work	The point of life	Relief
Education is...........	A dream	A birthright	A way to get ahead
Future....................	Rainy day to work for	"Now" is more important	Uncertain but manageable
Managing money..	Save	Spend	Hedge
"Program" means..	Social program	Cult de-programmers	Software programs
Go watch...............	*The Best Years of Our Lives*	*The Big Chill*	*Reality Bites*

Born between 1946 and 1964, Baby Boomers are the most populous and influential generation in America. Born to prosperity in a time of booming postwar economic expansion, Boomers enjoyed unprecedented employment and educational opportunities. They took this for granted, and the shared assumption of affluence shaped their values and embroiled them in the tumult of events that filled the sixties and seventies. The value system of Boomers, the "Me Generation," was built on the sense of entitlement created by their presumption of continued economic growth. With little else to worry about, Boomers were able to be more self-absorbed, pursuing personal goals and instant gratification.

Indeed, while Matures came of age expecting little because of the sacrifices demanded by wars and the Depression, the overriding marker for Boomers was the economic prosperity of the postwar years, a prosperity that was so internalized that it has shaped all Boomer attitudes about the marketplace. Boomers could, for example, more easily embrace an inclusive social perspective because they assumed there was prosperity enough to make everybody a winner. Boomers believed there would always be plenty to go around—lots now and more and more in the future—so why not share with everyone.

Central to the story of Boomers over the last decade has been that their ingrained sense of entitlement has been overtaken by unmet expectations. This is particularly true for Boomers born in the last years of their cohort, the so-called Trailing Boomers. In general, though, all Boomers have had to learn to do with less, and the impact of this on the marketplace will be continue to be felt for the next twenty years.

The next group, Generation X, or Xers, could be dubbed the "Why Me?" generation. Born in the wake of the dominant Boomers, they have been buffeted by tumultuous political and economic conditions. They are wary and uncertain about America's position in the world and about their own place in America. Yet, contrary to the image portrayed by the popular media, this is a savvy generation, enthusiastically ready, willing, and able to take on the challenges they face.

For Xers, hard work is a pragmatic necessity and they tend to be careful in planning for the future. In many ways, Xers are embracing some of the values of Matures because they too have lived through uncertain formative years. For this reason, Xers seem better able to deal with economic downturns than their Boomer predecessors....

"As Close to God As We Get"

Let's return to the proverb about men and their times. We know from social scientists that many early influences define how we think and behave. The key to understanding consumer behavior also lies in grasping the characteristics acquired when those consumers were young. Admittedly there are nuances within each generation—no individual person is their generation, lock, stock, and barrel. Some people change dramatically as they age, while others evolve less or remain the same. In addition, the interplay between generations can result in new needs that require new solutions. But the fundamental truth remains that marketers who recognize and seek to understand the impact of generationally based values on consumer habits will have an important competitive advantage over those who do not.

Indeed, it was a quest for understanding a new generation that contributed to the concept of generational marketing. Arthur White, one of the founders of Yankelovich Partners Inc., remembers the day in 1970 when he and Dan Yankelovich were summoned to Rockefeller Center by John D. Rockefeller III. Walking along the corridor on the fifty-sixth floor, he saw clouds swirling past the windows and, inside a grand office, one of the heirs to one of the greatest fortunes in American history. "This may be as close to God as we get," White whispered to Yankelovich.

But Rockefeller was not feeling very godlike that day. The previous summer he had seen a three-part documentary on CBS, called "Generations Apart."

And it had disturbed him very much. Like millions of others, Rockefeller watched as the reporter talked, in a sonorous voice, of a "widening generation gap on attitudes toward sex, religion, drugs, and money." That term—the generation gap—over the years has become a permanent part of the nation's lexicon, a defining idea about those times.

"All through America," continued the reporter, "all around the world, there are young people who want to make things happen.... To the older generation, it often seems the young lack a sense of history, lack a willingness or ability to recognize the great changes that have already taken place in our time. To the young, what has happened is irrelevant or inadequate. They see injustice remains; they're unsatisfied by justice gained.... To attack the old invites repression. The old control the instruments of power. But to ignore or repress the young will not make them silent any more, nor docile, nor will it soften their hard view of the adult world. This is Walter Cronkite, CBS News."

This groundbreaking documentary was based on a nationwide survey for CBS conducted by our firm. So Rockefeller had summoned Messrs. White and Yankelovich to his office to discuss this new generation gap and the attitudes exhibited by the upcoming generation of Rockefellers and their peers. When they left the meeting, Arthur and Dan had a new assignment: Find ways in which business leaders could interact with this rebellious new generation of American youth.

Table 2

Generational Remembrances

MATURES	BOOMERS	Xers
Orange juice	The Juice runs	The Juice walks
FDR	Nixon	Reagan
Flattops	*HAIR*	Skinheads
No more butter	No more war	No more ozone layer
Sunday drives	Drive-thrus	Drive-bys
Mom, Dad, Grandma, Granddad	Mom and Dad	Mom or Dad
Dr. Spock	Dr. Strangelove	Dr. Kevorkian

The immediate result was a detailed and provocative three-hundred-page report. A more lasting result, however, was its impact on the way marketers think about marketing.... We had built a bridge between the esoteric world of social science and the commercial world of business. Marketers could now learn to make better strategic decisions about their brands by adding to their understanding of the marketplace knowledge of the generationally driven changes in values and lifestyles that shape the ways consumers spend and save. A new sophistication in marketing method had been born.

The Payoff

Since the late sixties, and the Rockefeller study, this method has evolved and been refined. Over the years we have used generational marketing to help clients develop products and programs that are in tune with the present and poised for the future. In the early eighties, for example, we worked with a client, the publishers of a magazine called *Apartment Life,* to reposition the publication to catch the new wave of prosperous, independent Boomers. The country was emerging from the Reagan-era recession. Urban-oriented Boomers no longer wanted to live in cheap walk-ups, but neither were they ready to move to the suburbs. This had not been true of Matures before them, who had moved en masse into the newly created suburbs. To respond to this generationally driven shift, the magazine changed its name to *Metropolitan Home,* emphasizing a new luxuriousness and prestige in apartment living designed to appeal to this generation of newly prosperous Boomers.

About the same time, we worked with another client to market do-it-yourself furniture to these same prospering Boomers, an assignment that also involved identifying the generational differences between Matures and Boomers. To Matures, do-it-yourself projects saved money and thus appealed to the value they placed on saving. This was not a Boomer value. So as these younger consumers became potential customers for our client, we searched for a new way to reach them. We identified an opportunity to link an interest in the home as a showplace to the generational priority Boomers have to show off their successes. Assembling and finishing your own furniture became, in this client's revised advertising campaign, a measure of status and accomplishment instead of a sign of thrift.

By the mid-eighties, we predicted that Boomers would move away from brand names as symbols of status and look instead for products that were more functional and utilitarian. This portended a shift away from the more traditional brand loyalty that had always characterized Matures. Boomers differed because, as a generation, they were never as single-mindedly focused as Matures on material goods for their own sake. The desire for experience, not materialism, has always been the underlying motivator for Boomers. The need to express individuality in creative ways is generationally distinctive to Boomers, a trait rooted in their formative cohort experiences. Thus we foresaw that even though the importance of functionality would grow, Boomer consumers would still want to express an individualistic flair. One result of this was the idea that a brand of beer could create loyalty with a line of lite, dry, and regular brews tied together with an umbrella positioning that emphasized personal expression as the reason for sticking with the same brand for all types of beer purchases.

In the late eighties, we saw that consumer lifestyles had suddenly become too cluttered and complicated, particularly those of Xers. Broadly speaking, these consumers were uncomplicating their lives in ways that looked more toward economizing time than money. From a life-stage perspective, money was hardly an issue—they had little to economize to start with. But the generational issues were more fundamental and directly related to building brand relationships with consumers at early ages.

From a generational marketing perspective, it is clear that Xers have a very different sense of the pace and intensity of life. This resonates with other generations too, but not in the same fundamental way. For Xers an accelerated pace is not just a fact, it is a given; not just a circumstance of the times, but a basic condition of life. The tools they use to deal with this are things like time-shifting technologies and protean fashions and styles. Back then we saw a change coming in their definition of convenience—from the Matures' "do it quickly" and the Boomers' "do it efficiently" to their "eliminate the task." No longer, we forecasted, would consumers buy a different sneaker for every sport. Out of this shift in generationally driven values, cross-trainer athletic footwear was born.

Table 3

More Generational Remembrances

MATURES	BOOMERS	Xers
The Golden Rule	Do bees and don't bees	Just say no
Red Square	Berlin Wall	Chernobyl
Bathtub gin	Acid	Crack
Pan Am Clipper Fleet	Pam Am Shuttle	Lockerbie
How to Win Friends and Influence People	*I'm Okay, You're Okay*	*Men Are from Mars, Women Are from Venus*
"Are you now or have you ever been..."	"What's your sign?"	"Boxers or briefs?"

Refuse Not to Know

Your competition is already onto this. Yankelovich Partners was the pioneer of generational marketing, but others have used it over the years. Bill Backer, one of the greatest ad men of all time, was an early practitioner. Perhaps his greatest success was Coke's "Buy the World" ad campaign, featuring thousands of young people on a hillside in Italy singing, "I'd like to buy the world a Coke," an ad that the editors of *Advertising Age* recently voted as one of the fifty best TV spots in the history of advertising.

Many years later, Bill recalls that his goal in creating that ad was to improve Coke's approach to the market, which was at that time, in Bill's blunt opinion, simply "wrong." Its ads reflected "a view of the world held only by rich bottlers and stockholders," one that ignored the youth market because Coke's management felt it to be "a wasteland, degenerate and degrading." Moving the Coca-Cola Company into this market was a generational marketing undertaking that Bill says "nobody understood or wanted to learn." He recalls, though, with great satisfaction, how he undertook it, becoming in the process the "self-appointed Conrad who would take [Coke] into the heart of this jungle."

This perspective is still part of the practice at the agency that succeeded the shop Bill Backer helped launch years ago. Recently Bates USA restructured itself to match up its planning, creative, and account groups against consumer generational cohorts. A few savvy marketers got on top of this right away. As Bill Whitehead, the president and CEO, noted when announcing the completion of this restructuring, "We've seen it pay off in new business [for our agency] already." Indeed, Whitehead reminds us what his agency emphasizes to its clients —without an accurate view of generations, we are very likely to misinterpret what we see in the marketplace. "The popular view that the old are behaving younger is really misplaced," says Bill. "It's rather that the young are becoming older, and those habits are sticking with them."

You need to know all about generations. The consumer marketplace of today and tomorrow is no longer the homogeneous marketplace of the fifties and early sixties that was dominated by Matures. Bill Backer started helping Coke when the Baby Boomer generation was coming of age and complicating the marketplace. Today's Xers have roiled the waters even further. The generational mix in the marketplace is greater now than ever before. And all of these generations are smarter, craftier shoppers than the shoppers of twenty or thirty years ago.

Charles D. Schewe and
Geoffrey E. Meredith

 **NO**

Segmenting the Market by Cohorts: Age Really Matters—"Coming of Age" That Is!

Mark Twain once remarked that "Age is a thing of mind over matter. If you don't mind, it don't matter." Mark Twain was an unusually perceptive man—but he was primarily a writer, not a businessman. And for anyone in the world of business, age does indeed matter! And this article will show you how.

The age that matters is not old age but rather the time when one is emerging from youth and becoming an adult—the age from about seventeen to twenty-three. We have learned that at that particular time of late adolescence/ early adulthood we seem to shed our self and family-focused mental mindset, strap on a set of receptors and become far more involved in what is going on around us in our external environment. This is a particularly impressionable time, a time when core values are being formed. And the events that happen to us at that age forge those values in ways that do not change over our life's journey.

Some of these events are unique to each of us. For instance, we make a varsity athletic team in our freshman year and we are forever focused on sports. Or one of our parents is put out of work and we forever look for job security. But these events are individual events, felt by us and a few around us. However, there are other events that are shared with many, many others. We serve alongside millions of others and fight a world-wide common enemy in World War II. We thrill together to the words "one small step for man." We suffer through gas lines during the oil crisis of 1973. Or we find our lives meeting and merging digitally, as our lifestyles more and more integrate the Internet.

These kinds of shared major events can have an impact on one's life at any age. A man in his 30s who was drafted in 1943 had his career and life put on hold for at least two years; he was unquestionably impacted by World War II. But his core values had been formed a decade before, and he was basically the same person when he was discharged in 1945. However, a man who was drafted at age 18 in 1943 was a fundamentally different person on VJ-Day. His core values—and those of those who came of age with him during that time—

were formed and fixed by World War II. That group—that "cohort"—is forever bonded by the values created by that event.

It is those kinds of major, shared events, happening during the key coming-of-age years and forging groups of people with common value sets, that this segmentation approach is about.

We have learned that the most significant of these shared external events create values that stay with us throughout our entire lives, largely unchanged. These values are shaped by events that have two characteristics: the events must have social consequences; and they must be known and experienced by relatively large groups of people. These events are "defining moments"—and they become the glue that bonds different age groups together. They form distinct segments with a common thread—and provide the basis for "right-on" target marketing. We have borrowed the term "cohorts" from sociologists to define these age groups. And our cohort groups are aged not by decades or deciles but rather by the defining moments when that group was "coming of age" age.

Cohorts are the people we are born with, travel through our lives with, and experience similar events with, especially those events at the critical late adolescent/early adulthood years. At the core of the cohort concept is the idea that the events that are happening in the outside environment when we are coming of age—roughly between the ages of 17 and 23—imprint societal values that remain unchanged for the rest of our lives. These "defining moments"— the major events that happen as we are becoming an adult—can be huge, such as wars or the end of wars, or political dislocations, such as assassinations, or economic upheavals, such as depressions. They can also be major technological changes, for example the advancement from silent movies to talkies, or the rise of television, or the automobile.

Values also manifest themselves in very personal ways. As a generalization, each cohort tends to value most those things which it most lacked as it was coming of age. For example, people who came of age during the Great Depression still value financial security. And people who came of age following World War II, during the social change and uncertainty of the Cold War, the civil rights movement, and emerging female sexuality, an orderly world tops their list. Not surprisingly, they are still titillated by expressions of forbidden sexuality, such as Elvis, James Dean, and *Playboy*. Events that were happening when first becoming an "economic adult" affect life-long attitudes toward jobs, money, spending and saving, food and eating patterns, apparel, and much more. Events going on when one is becoming sexually mature and sexually active influence long-term core values about permissiveness, tolerance, and sexual behavior. In fact, sexual attitudes are the prototypical cohort effect! Some surveys have concluded that older people are becoming more tolerant of homosexuals, premarital sex, and other sexual alternatives. But rather than implying that people become more tolerant with age, it's fairer to say that tolerant people have become older, as liberal boomers enter the ranks of the 50+ crowd. Likewise, the kind of music that you listed to when you first fell in love is likely to be the preferred music format for the rest of your life. The Rolling Stones have enormous appeal today because the baby boomers liked the Stones when they were teens. Now that boomers have begun to turn 50, they haven't suddenly switched to Glenn

Miller. Cohort effects do not change with one's age or stage of life. That's why they can be such useful marketing tools.

The concept of cohorts was first articulated by the German philosopher and sociologist Karl Mannheim. Later, American sociologist Norman B. Ryder published *The Cohort as a Concept in the Study of Social Change* in the 1950s. Since that time, cohort analysis has been widely recognized and accepted in sociology. Human resource consultant Morris Massey, in his 1979 book *The People Puzzle* also used cohort analysis, to suggest how people of different age groups could learn to understand each other and get along better. Cohort effects are just as important for many marketers, but until now, cohort analysis has been almost totally ignored as a marketing tool.

The Power of Cohorts

The idea that different age groups are unique is not completely new to marketing. In fact, it is the essence of "generational marketing," which has received a lot of media attention in recent years as baby boomers have begun to cross the half-century mark. According to this theory, a new generation begins when a person has children, roughly in twenty-five year periods.

But we have found that popular generational breakdowns—Matures (55 and up), Boomers (36–54), and Xers (35 and under)—are really too broad to be useful as marketing targets. For example, if you are 55 today, how much do you really have in common with someone in their 80's? Not much, we suspect. And if you're 35, how similar are your buying habits to those of a 16-year-old? Again, we suspect not very. Cohort segmentation offers a much more focused approach than other marketing methods, and it gives marketers the precision they need to connect with target markets.

Defining Moments Create Ties That Bind

We all experience a wide range of events during our coming of age years. Not all are defining moments, however. Only those that are strong enough to have a lasting social consequence become defining moments. The death of President Kennedy was just such an event. It stole the enthusiasm and excitement for a new tomorrow that surrounded the "Camelot Days." The death of John Lennon, another event that shocked the world, however was not a defining moment since it had no lasting significant social consequences. Table 1 shows a comprehensive list of important historical events of the 20th Century. These were compiled in a recent study done by Stephanie Noble of the University of Massachusetts. Her results support earlier research into the lasting impact made by such defining moments.

These defining moments influence a cohort group's preferences, desires, attitudes, and buying behaviors in ways that remain with them virtually unchanged for the rest of their lives. This includes attitudes about everything from appropriate dress to family responsibilities to job satisfaction. Defining moments create cohort homogeneity that is missed in generational marketing. As a result, evoking strategic cohort words, symbols and memories can bring

Table 1

Important Historical Events

Time period events occurred	Events
1930–1939	Depression
	Implementation of Social Security
	Franklin Roosevelt's New Deal
	Social Reform
1940–1949	World War II
	Pearl Harbor
	D-Day Invasion
	GI Bill of Rights
	A-Bomb/Hiroshima
1950–1959	Korean War
	Equal Education Act
	Polio/Salk's Vaccine
	Rosa Parks
1960–1964	Social Change of '60s
	Cuban Missile Crisis
	John F. Kennedy Assassination
	Equal Rights/Civil Rights Act
1965–1969	Robert Kennedy Assassination
	Woodstock
	Stonewall Riots
	Man Walks on Moon
	Martin Luther King, Jr., Assassination
1965–1975	Vietnam
1970–1979	Oil Crisis
	'70s Inflation
	Kent State Riots
	Watergate/Nixon
	Women's Rights Movements
Throughout 1980s	'80s Recession
	Height of HIV/AIDS Scare
	Reagan's Terms
1985–1989	Challenger Explosion
	Fall of Berlin Wall
1990–1994	Gulf War
	Breakup of USSR
	President Clinton Elected
	World Trade Center Bombing
	Waco
1995–1999	Pope's Visit to U.S.
	Hong Kong Handover
	Princess Diana's Death
	Mother Theresa's Death
	President Clinton's Affair
	Kosovo
	John F. Kennedy, Jr.'s Death
	Columbine Shooting
	Oklahoma City Bombing
	OJ Simpson Trial
	Other Computers/Internet
	Advances in Medicine
	Ease of Travel
	Influence of Television

Source: Stephanie Noble, University of Massachusetts

substantial rewards for marketers. Using sociological research and the significant historical and social events of the last century as our guide, we have identified seven distinct American cohorts:

Seven Distinct American Cohorts

At the beginning of the 21st century, American adults can be divided into seven distinct cohorts:

Depression Cohort (Age 79–88):   This group's coming-of age experience consisted of economic strife, elevated unemployment rates and having to take menial jobs to survive. Financial security—what they most lacked when coming of age—rules their thinking.

World War II Cohort (Age 73–78):   Sacrifice for a common good was widely accepted among World War II cohorts, as evidenced by women working in factories for the war effort and men going off to fight. Overall, this cohort was focused on defeating a common enemy, and their members are more patriotic than those of other age cohorts.

Post-War Cohort (Age 55–72):   These individuals experienced a time of continuing economic growth and social tranquillity, a time of family togetherness, the Korean conflict, McCarthyism, school dress codes, and moving to the suburbs. Overall, this cohort participated in the rise of the middle class, felt a sense of security and stability in the United States, and expected prosperous times to continue indefinitely.

Leading-Edge Baby Boomer Cohort (Age 46–54):   This group remembers the assassinations of John and Robert Kennedy and Martin Luther King, Jr. It was the loss of JFK that largely shaped this cohort's values. They became adults during the Vietnam War and watched as the first man walked on the moon. Leading edge boomers were dichotomous: they championed causes (Greenpeace, civil rights, women's rights), yet were simultaneously hedonistic and self-indulgent (pot, "free love," sensuality).

Trailing-Edge Baby Boomer Cohort (Age 35–45):   This group witnessed the fall of Vietnam, Watergate, and Nixon's resignation. The oil embargo, and the consequent raging inflation rate led these individuals to be less optimistic about their financial fixture than the leading-edge boomers.

Generation X Cohort (Age 23–34):   These are the latchkey children of divorce and have received the most negative publicity. This cohort has delayed marriage and children, and they don't take those commitments lightly. More than other groups, this cohort accepts cultural diversity and puts quality of personal life ahead of work life. Despite a rocky start into adulthood, this group shows a spirit of entrepreneurship unmatched by any other cohort. Take a look at

many Internet start-ups, such as the search engine Yahoo!, and
you'll find successful Gen-Xers who did it their way.

N Generation Cohort (Age 23 and Under): We call the youngest cohort
"N Gen" because the advent of the Internet is a defining event for
them, and because they will be the "engine" of growth over the
next two decades. While still a work in progress, their core value
structure seems to be quite different from that of the Gen-Xers.
They are more idealistic and social-cause oriented, without the
cynical, "What's in it for me?" free agent mindset of many Xers.

But in using cohort marketing, you must be careful. If carried too far, age-
specific advertising can be deadly to a product, especially when it is aimed at
the mature market. Johnson & Johnson discovered this when it tried to market
Affinity shampoo as the product for "over-40 hair." This product quickly went
down the drain. So did Heinz's "Senior Singles—Soup for One." Explicitly positioning yourself as an old people's shampoo, soup, bank, or HMO is not a smart
move. However for younger cohorts, such as the N Gen, the exact opposite may
sometimes be true. They are often attracted by positioning that singles them
out and makes them feel special. With the judicious and subtle use of cohort
effects, a marketer can zero in on a specific age group without offending its
members. To show you what we mean, lets take a look at a case study. What'll
it Be? Coffee or Cola?

Imagine that you are a marketing executive for a company called General
Beverages. The company has two divisions: coffee and cola. Being the astute
marketer that you are, you know that over the last 40 years coffee consumption
has risen as people age. Even after age 60, coffee consumption remains high.
But in that same time frame, cola consumption has declined as people aged.

You also know that the first member of the baby boom generation turned
50 in 1996. Because of this, AARP [American Association of Retired Persons]
will gain a prospective new member every 8 seconds for the next 18 years. The
number of 18-to-34-year-olds will increase by only 11 million in the first decade
of the new millennium, while the number of adults aged 50 or older will grow
by almost 17 million.

Given these facts, which division has the brighter prospect for future
growth: coffee or cola?

You might use traditional cross-sectional age analysis and quickly conclude that coffee will remain king at General Beverages. Your conclusion would
likely be based on the premise that historic consumption rates by older age
groups will continue in the future. An aging population should boost the
demand for coffee and cut the demand for cola.

Unfortunately, it isn't that simple.

A cohort analysis of cola and coffee consumption yields the exact opposite outcome from an age analysis of the same problem! Younger, cola-intensive
cohorts will continue to consume soft drinks even as they age, according to
studies done by Joseph O. Rentz of the University of Tennessee. Meanwhile,
older, coffee-intensive groups will age and move out of the marketplace. They
will be replaced by baby boomers and younger consumers who drink less coffee

than older cohorts. In other words, people who grew up drinking cola—the baby boomers, Gen Xers, and N Gen—will most likely continue to do so later in life, thus cola consumption should increase as the younger population ages. This would indicate that despite an aging population, General Beverages should focus on its cola division for growing profits. In fact, the fastest growing beverage segment today is people who drink cola for breakfast!

This example shows the utility and validity of using cohort analysis to investigate consumption trends. But clearly all behavior is not cohort-driven. Societal roles, economic circumstances, or life events, among other factors, also influence marketplace behaviors. However, its usefullness is clear in many product categories and in the promotion of products. Automobiles [witness the new VW Beetle or the Plymouth Prowler], clothing [the resurgence of bell-bottoms and the difficulties besetting Levi's], food [beef stew on the Seniors' menu], and beverages as you saw above with coffee and cola are clearly cohort-related. Understanding cohorts can unlock to doors to successful marketing—in spite of the wisdom of Mark Twain.

POSTSCRIPT

Is Generational Segmentation an Effective Marketing Strategy?

Information technology is redefining marketing segmentation. It has become sophisticated to the point of profitably focusing on markets of one. It is also creating new frontiers for the power of cohort marketing by refining and correlating the significance of unique dimensions of increasingly well-defined age groups such as "tweens." Regional and global research now has the potential for unearthing appeals indigenous to cohort groups in specific cultures and geographic areas. Will this mean that traditional means of segmentation have to be totally redefined? Subcultures and minorities can be more effectively targeted by researching the varying levels of *sensitivity* specific cohort groups might exhibit to the same defining moments. Asian Americans, for example, were perhaps significantly influenced as a group by the image of a young student standing defiantly before an oncoming tank during the revolution at Tienanmen Square in Beijing, China. Psychographic dimensions can be correlated to age cohorts for mining richer correlations for promotional appeals.

The dramatic differences in perceptions of products by distinct cohort groups is often astounding, particularly for "value-laden products." These are products and services that reflect attitudes of cohort members, which might be termed the *generational-product clash*. An award-winning advertising campaign of the mid-1970s was "Should a Gentleman Offer a Lady a Tiparillo?" Cigarette smoking, a long-standing pillar of American culture and a social tool for ingratiating is now socially unacceptable and perceived as an obvious health risk. Watch the reaction of young generation Y'ers when a Depression cohort chain-smoker lights up in a crowded room! Watch videos of the Dean Martin celebrity roasts of the 1970s (now popular video infomercials) and try to find a nonsmoker or jokes that do not relate to drinking, ethnicity, or sex. Would the controversial TV show *All in the Family*, with all of its politically incorrect derogatory references to minorities, stand a chance today? If not for Nickelodeon, "oldies" radio stations, and the history channel, wouldn't American culture of the 1950s and 1960s be totally foreign to generation Y?

It is exhilarating to talk to the Depression cohorts, now ages 78 to 88, to truly fathom the dramatic differences in lifestyles, values, culture, and marketing environment of their generation as compared to today. Shifting marketing paradigms empowering consumers may be of paramount importance in targeting the savvy, high-tech teen cohorts. But will matures be flocking to this new technology? Will cultural icons, such as platform shoes, bell-bottoms, martinis, cigars, and swing music continue as an enduring fashion or become simply millennium retrofad?

ISSUE 16

Is the Marketing of Online Degree Programs a Threat to Traditional Education?

YES: Ted Marchese, from "Not-So-Distant Competitors: How New Providers Are Remaking the Postsecondary Marketplace," *AAHE Bulletin* (May 1998)

NO: David F. Noble, from "Digital Diploma Mills: The Automation of Higher Education," *First Monday: Peer-Reviewed Journal on the Internet,* <http://www.firstmonday.dk/issues/issue3_1/noble/index.html> (January 5, 1998)

ISSUE SUMMARY

YES: Ted Marchese, vice president of the American Association for Higher Education (AAHE), provides an overview of research that profiles an explosive array of colleges now providing online degree programs. He contends that there is a plethora of niche markets to render an optimistic future for online education.

NO: David F. Noble, a professor and historian, is critical of the high-tech transformation of education. He believes that it is implemented by top administrators and private sector commercial partners with little input from faculty and students.

Upon entering the millennium, well over 1 million students were enrolled in distance learning classes, mostly online, and this figure is expected to double by 2002. Freed from the physical parameters of the classroom, "cybereducation" is growing at an exponential rate despite the tremendous controversy currently raging primarily among stakeholders, such as faculty, administrators, students, and the private sector. Central to the debate is the perception that institutions of higher learning are transforming education into a standardized, for-profit commodity.

Historically, distance education evolved from "correspondence learning," with rural free delivery (RFD) mail and later broadcast media and interactive

TV with video and audiotapes. But the advent of the computer and the Internet have been the seminal forces in transitioning from the industrial age, when students came to campus, to the communications age, when the campus began coming to students. Today, a vast range of institutions have formed partnerships with major corporations, creating a mind-boggling array of online standardized courses and degree programs, which serve an unprecedented number of previously inaccessible market segments for distance learners.

The natural market for distance learning is the fastest-growing segment in an otherwise stagnant market, the nontraditional student of higher education. The working adults, almost half of all people enrolled in higher education in the United States, are part-time students. New York University's continuing studies program pulled in revenues of $92 million. Harvard's Extension School, serving 60,000 students, earned $150 million.

Distance learning partnerships are increasing at a remarkable rate. For example, Stanford University, the University of Chicago, the London School of Economics, Columbia, and Carnegie Mellon have all finalized deals with UNEXT.com, which, according to *The New Republic*, "provides state of the art learning engines and knowledge as rapidly as it is created at the world's most respected and distinguished educational institutions."

David F. Noble addresses many of the criticisms of distance learning mostly proposed by faculty, many of whom object to being forced to supply products for new business ventures of marketing online classes. Many feel it is pure profit motive that relegates their years of research into branded content, generating a steady stream of licensing and royalty fees for the university and their marketing partners. Noble argues that the online classes become "pedagogically meaningless." Moreover, most online classes are being taught by adjunct instructors rather than full-time faculty.

The issue of cost effectiveness portends a huge shift toward electronic classes. The accounting firm Price Waterhouse suggests that software will soon serve about 50 percent of the total student enrollment in community colleges and 35 percent in four-year institutions. Will students soon face a "tiered educational system," with traditional small face-to-face classes for the privileged few? The protection and copyright of intellectual material is another major issue to consider. Who owns the educational material that is faculty-generated and marketed through licensing agreements over the Internet?

The *commoditization* of the research function in universities has launched terms like *intellectual capital* and *knowledge based industries.* Will the increasing millions of online learners receiving degrees from "brand-name" universities damage the credibility and significance of the generic college degree? In general, does offering online education compromise academic standards? Is online education better suited to particular topics—like engineering and science—and less suited to learning interpersonal communications or clinical psychology?

Ted Marchese discusses the myriad of educational programs serving broad-based and niche markets that have been up and running in the last five years. He sees distance learning as a convenience. However, Noble fears that due to the development of distance learning, students of the future will be characterized as consumers rather than learners.

Ted Marchese  **YES**

Not-So-Distant Competitors

Quite suddenly, in just two or three years, American higher education has come face-to-face with an explosive array of new competitors. On campus, the surest conversation-stopper today is "University of Phoenix." To some academics, Phoenix looks like the first-sighted tip of an iceberg. But it probably won't be the one that sinks whole ships. Bigger bergs are forming. Charting them is difficult. To find these "new providers," we sought them out on the Web. Here's what we found.

The Convenience Market

By one light, Phoenix is just the most aggressive manifestation of a larger, branch-office trend that's at least a decade old. Dozens of private and regional-public colleges, for example, now offer degree programs in the Washington, DC, area. Wisconsin recently counted more than 100 out-of-state degree providers within its borders; there are 37 in Milwaukee alone. Last month I passed a busy intersection in Lake County, Illinois, where a former gas station had become a branch campus of Missouri's Columbia College. In the convenience end of the market, everybody goes after the other guy's lunch.

What's different about Phoenix is that it is explicitly for-profit, well capitalized, idea-driven, and national in ambition. From next to nothing a handful of years ago, Phoenix suddenly has 48,000 degree-credit students at 57 learning centers in 12 states. Its parent, the Apollo Group, recently reported quarterly profits of $12.8 million (before taxes) on sales of $86.5 million. Apollo also owns the College for Financial Planning (22,000 noncredit students), Western International University (1,800 students), and an Institute for Professional Development that provides contract services for "program development and management" at 19 colleges. Once-tiny Cardinal Stritch has parlayed the Phoenix formula into an enrollment of 5,300 students. Apollo's Phoenix division now has an online campus that offers computer-mediated distance education programs enrolling 3,750 students (up 53% from [1997]). Phoenix's phenomenal growth has been largely driven by niche programs at the BA-completion and master's-degree levels, especially in business, IT, and teacher education. It taps new and "left behind" markets: 97% of its students are adults who started earlier elsewhere; 57% are women, 37% minority.

At the undergraduate level, two long-established proprietary competitors have expanded aggressively. Chicago's DeVry Institute of Technology now has 15 campuses in the United States and Canada enrolling 48,000 students in business and technical programs; DeVry owns the well-regarded Keller Graduate School of Management (4,700 students). Indianapolis-based ITT Educational Services counts 25,800 students in its 62 institutes.

In the not-for-profit sector, dozens of existing universities and colleges have developed remote-site strategies. St. Louis-based Webster University now boasts 15,000 students in 64 U.S. locations plus six overseas. Chapman, National, Park, RIT, Ottawa, and Central Michigan also teach afar. The Maricopa district's Rio Salado Community College operates at 129 locations. The University of Maryland's University College teaches 35,000 students at hundreds of sites; it holds commencement ceremonies in College Park, Heidelberg, Tokyo, Okinawa, Seoul, Schwäbisch Gmünd, Irkutsk, and Vladivostok.

Courses at a Distance

If not "Phoenix," the scare words of choice are "Western Governors University." Again, though, distance education is not a new phenomenon: American universities offered correspondence courses a century ago. In 1995, according to a "flash estimate" released this spring by the U.S. Department of Education, fully a third of all institutions offered distance education courses, and another quarter planned to. But the way the field is moving, 1995 is distance education's olden days. WGU's founding back in 1996 created quite a stir, but it will fight for attention.... Nimble competitors have already come to market.

WGU's ambition, though, will be second to none. Its founders include 17 governors; its 14 "business partners" include IBM, Sun, AT&T, KPMG, Cisco, 3COM, Microsoft, and International Thomson. WGU won't employ teaching faculty, develop courses, or deal in credit hours: its online academic content will come from a range of qualifying providers (colleges or businesses, here or abroad), and all degrees will be competency-based. WGU's aim is to be the broker of choice within an academic common market that it helps create. Its "founding philosophies" are "partnerships" and "competition." Its business plan envisions 95,000 students by early next century... not just from the West (Indiana joined up in April). As courses are added from national universities, corporations, and publishers, Utah governor Mike Leavitt foresees WGU becoming the "New York Stock Exchange of technology-delivered courses."

A lot of other people have had variants of the same idea. California opted out of the WGU compact to create its own, more modest California Virtual University; CVU's catalog already lists 700 courses from 81 public and private institutions. SREB's Southern Regional Electronic Campus spans 15 participating states and aims to create a marketplace of courses offered by TV, the Internet, and otherwise; its online catalog now lists 100 mostly Web-based courses from 42 colleges. Colorado's community college system offers associate's degrees in business entirely over the Internet (for students anywhere) and coursework tailored for WGU; it got there fast by working with Denver-based Real Education, a firm that promises "to get your university online in 60 days." The Fort Collins-based National Technological University, a 14-year-old nonprofit, uses satellites to beam engineering coursework from 50 major universities to clients worldwide.

Several states—Georgia, Missouri, Indiana, Oklahoma, Minnesota, Utah, Virginia—are looking to gear up earlier investments in IT infrastructure for distance learning capability. The University of Wisconsin's system office partnered with Lotus to put together a Learning Innovation Center in Madison, with for-profit and not-for-profit arms, to vend UW courses and degrees worldwide; 565 courses are available. The University of Hawaii uses two-way video, cable, satellite, and the Internet to deliver 13 full degree programs to citizens statewide. The University of Nebraska chartered a for-profit entity to parlay its long history in distance learning into a worldwide operation. Penn State expects big things from its World Campus.

Individual schools are also making their moves. Two institutions with long histories of high-end continuing education, NYU and Boston University, have corporate partners that have helped them win impressive training contracts. Lansing Community College now has its own virtual college; SUNY's Empire State enrolls more than 6,000 students; Duke now offers a top-end Global Executive MBA; by plan, a fourth of all courses at Florida's new Gulf Coast University will be taken online. Established graduate-level players such as Walden, Fielding, Nova, the New School, and Arthur D. Little are looking to expand. Stanford's Office of Educational Ventures hopes to capitalize on the university's 30-year history of distance learning; UCLA and corporate partners launched the for-profit Home Education Network; UC-Berkeley's partner for online offerings will be UOL Publishing.

The Alfred P. Sloan Foundation has put $15 million into some 40 campus projects, looking for breakthroughs in access, pedagogy, and outcomes via asynchronous learning networks.

More Competitors

To Wall Street and entrepreneurs-at-large, the postsecondary education and training market looks huge and ripe for the picking ... an "addressable market opportunity at the dawn of a new paradigm," in the breathless words of Morgan Stanley Dean Witter. In dollar terms, close to $300 billion is spent a year on the function, $635 billion if grades P-12 are added in. Several Wall Street houses have set up "education industry" practices to attract investors. A report from NationsBanc Montgomery Securities characterizes the industry with words such as "inefficient," "cottage industry," "low tech," and "lack of professional management." It claims $1.7 billion has been raised on Wall Street since 1996 to finance new competitive ventures.

Alternative and distance providers claim just 2% of the postsecondary market today, but a combination of pent-up demand, changes in the tax law, and today's E-commerce boom could quickly balloon that market share by a factor of 10... at which point larger transformations could kick in. As unthinkable as this might seem to established higher education, Wall Street offers reminders that aggressive competitors cut the banking establishment's share of household financial assets from 90% in 1980 to 55% today.

Baltimore's Sylvan Learning Systems (1-800-EDUCATE), a Wall Street darling, aims to be the world's "leading provider of educational services to families, schools, and industry." Its five business areas are K-16 tutoring (700 sites), contracted services to schools, computer-based testing (Prometric), adult professional education, and English-language instruction around the world. In March, Sylvan and partner MCI spun off their Caliber Learning Network; Caliber successfully brought an $80 million initial public offering to market May 5th that will help build out its network beyond the present 48 shopping malls and business centers. Caliber's business goal is to offer brand-name professional education nationwide. It already has deals with Johns Hopkins (health) and Wharton (business) and agreements with other "medallions" (Berkeley, MIT, Georgetown) to offer brand-name courseware and degrees in other fields... at a mall near you.

Sylvan's revenues rose 35% last year, to $246.2 million. Total revenues for the quarter ending December 31, 1997, jumped 51%; the company reported net income of $11.8 million for that quarter on sales of $78.2 million. It is growth —and margins—like this that has investors chomping at the bit. ETS, with its ever-closer ties to Prometric, has taken a 1.4% ownership position in Sylvan, worth $22 million.

Jones Education Company (JEC), the brainchild of cable entrepreneur Glenn Jones ("Let's get the cost of real estate out of education!"), offers instruction via cable (Knowledge TV), courses and degrees from existing universities "anywhere, anytime" (College Connection), and self-paced video and CD-ROM learning products (Knowledge Store). JEC's College Connection online catalog offers six certificate and 11 degree programs from 14 partner universities, including Regis and George Washington Universities. The nonprofit Virtual Online University offers instruction from K through 16; its Internet-based Athena University uses MOO [an object-oriented programming language] technology to engage students in curricula spanning eight academic divisions, each headed by a dean. The Electronic University Network, started in 1983 and a feature of America Online since 1992, has launched the World Learning Network, whose "learning community" software aims to end "the isolation of the distant learner." In January it was acquired by Santa Barbara-based Durand Communications.

Specialty for-profit higher education companies include Fairfax, VA-based Computer Learning Centers (computer, IT training; 1997 sales of $64 million, 1998 of $97 million); Pittsburgh's Education Management Corp. (arts, culinary; $183 million); and Educational Medical of Rosewell, GA ($49 million). CLC's high-flying stock plunged 46% in March when Illinois sued the firm for false claims of job placement. In early May, Illinois reinstated CLC's permission to operate.

A recurring problem for proprietary providers like these is that employer reimbursement often hinges on the award of college credit. As an example of how that problem is solved, students taking Microsoft or Novell certification courses—which can cost more than $10,000—in any of 100 authorized ITCAP centers around the country get the credits they need through Tucson's Pima County Community College.

Want to learn HTML? Learn It Online, a new service from publisher Ziff-Davis, offers the course you need, with chat group, for $29.95.

A host of new providers hope to be the broker of choice for the flood of courseware hitting the Web. CASO's Internet University, essentially an indexing service, points the way to 2,440 courses. World Lecture Hall, at the University of Texas, lists thousands of courses in 95 disciplines. The Global Network Academy, a Texas nonprofit, lists 250 providers, 770 programs, and 10,000 online courses. Extensive listings also exist on websites at the Universities of North Carolina and Houston ("archive.edu"). Virtual University Enterprises (acquired by National Computing Systems) concentrates on listing corporate education programs, worldwide. A Web-based consumer's guide to distance education is maintained by the Western Cooperative for Educational Telecommunications.

More Niches

One of the most closely watched start-ups is the Michigan Virtual Automotive College (MVAC), a creation of the state of Michigan, the Big Three automakers, the United Auto Workers, and the state's two flagships, Michigan and Michigan State. Its president is former Michigan president Jim Duderstadt; MSU president Peter McPherson chairs the executive committee. MVAC's mission is to become the essential hub for auto industry education and training—to offer the best courses from any provider anywhere to corporate employees, be they on assembly lines, at drafting boards, or in executive suites. If engineers need the latest course in computer-aided design, MVAC can locate best experts in the subject, design the course, custom deliver it on-site or elsewhere, evaluate and continuously improve it... and ultimately vend it to the 27 major auto companies and 5 million auto industry workers worldwide. MVAC's watchwords include customer-driven, competency-based, and standards for delivery. In its first 16 months of operation, it has put together some 115 courses with professors or units from 27 universities (including Phoenix); 300 students are now enrolled, 2,000 set for fall. When suppliers, dealers, repair shops, and retail outlets are taken as part of the auto industry, enrollment projections soar to six and seven figures.

The essential idea behind MVAC—that an industry group can combine to produce its own education enterprise, entry-level through lifelong learning, and cease reliance on a "cottage industry" of existing campuses—has strong appeal among corporate execs, especially where dissatisfaction with traditional higher education is high. In the face of such a combine (and such course quality), observers feel, few colleges could maintain competitive offerings, on campus or off. Already the money has come together for like-minded start-ups in plastics, furniture, and tourism. Could health care, teacher education, accounting, or information technology be next?

An Industry Forms

With all the interest in creating online instructional materials, a new industry has emerged to provide the necessary consulting, marketing, and tools. Any recent *Chronicle* carries prominent display ads from would-be vendors: Cisco Systems, SCT, Collegis, Lotus, and the like, plus repeated "executive briefings" in 24 cities around the country from a Microsoft-Simon & Schuster-Real Education combine.

The IBM Global Campus offers a sophisticated set of interrelated tools and services for distributed learning environments and distance education. Products from IBM's Lotus division, including Notes and LearningSpace, promise enhanced forms of distance learning. Some 30 campuses, including the Wisconsin and California State University systems, use Global Campus services. SCT claims 1,100 collegiate customers; last fall it partnered with Asymetrix to offer a "total solution" for online learning. Microsoft teams with San Francisco's Convene International to provide an Exchange Server-based distance learning system for universities and businesses; Phoenix, Golden Gate, and UCLA Extension are among its customers. On April 29th, Educom's Instructional Management Systems project—a consortium of 29 software makers and universities—released technical standards that will allow learning materials and distance education systems from different vendors to "interoperate."

The trade journals are full of ads, too, for authoring software and templates that help individual professors and IT centers put courses on the Web. At a more elaborate level of presentation, MVAC officials budget $10,000-$12,000 per instructional hour to prepare the courses they offer. At a higher level still, for mass-market courses put together by an Andersen Consulting, for example, the "design and build" budget typically runs $80,000 per class hour... so a three-credit, 45-clock-hour course might have a development and marketing budget of $4 million. Who might invest in such a course? Publishers such as International Thomson, AWL, McGraw-Hill, John Wiley, and Simon & Schuster, who are angling to become content providers for Web-based courseware. One unit of an Ivy League university is looking toward Wall Street for the $15 million in start-up funds it would take to put its core courses online competitively.

Another part of the emergent industry looks to provide cost-effective delivery channels for distance education. All the major telecommunication companies are in the business. Connecticut-based Campus Televideo and Toner Cable claim to serve 85 universities nationwide. Want to broadcast abroad? Washington-based World Space is creating a global satellite-digital radio network... a medium of choice for reaching Third World learners.

Academic leaders are keeping an eye on industry ventures springing up in the K–12 arena. Knowledge Universe, for example, founded by the Milken brothers and Oracle's Larry Ellison, is a $600 million venture that's been snapping up software, IT-training, and consulting businesses. Last October it signed a deal with cable giant TCI to position itself as an online content provider, potentially to include a virtual university. In March, "global multiple-media publisher" Harcourt General hired Massachusetts's high-profile education commissioner

Robert Antonucci to head its ICS Learning Systems division, which serves 400,000 students worldwide. A NationsBanc Montgomery Securities publication describes at least three dozen well-financed K-12 competitors (labeled "education management organizations," "specialty service providers," and "content providers"), more than a few of which could become postsecondary players.

Not to be overlooked, too, is the explosion of distance learning programs within industry. It already spends $58 billion a year on employee training and development and sees distance technologies as a way to save time and cut costs (by 15% to 50%); an estimated 85% of the Fortune 500 now deploy some form of remote training. Health giant Kaiser Permanente is doubling its distance learning sites from 150 to 300, eating into "university business" by offering bachelor's and master's degrees for nurses and continuing education for physicians. MetLife, on the other hand, teamed with Drexel to bring its employees a master's degree in information systems.

How big is this new industry overall? TeleCon East is an annual trade show cosponsored by the United States Distance Learning Association and GE Spacenet. In 1994, its 65 exhibits drew 1,386 attendees; in 1997, 200 exhibits drew 6,595 viewers; 1998 attendance will surpass 10,000.

Competitors from Abroad?

The developments recounted here are hardly confined to the United States. Most of the Australian universities now have for-profit enterprises to market their courses and degrees, at home and abroad. A quick tour of the Web turns up virtual universities from Peru to Malaysia. Britain's much-admired, 168,000-student Open University, already a major player in Eastern Europe and the Far East, will enter the U.S. market in partnership with domestic universities (so far Florida State, CSU campuses, and WGU); it soon will announce the Open University of the United States, a nonprofit entity that will incorporate in Delaware and seek Middle States accreditation.

To track and sort through the maze of regulatory and quality issues raised by the worldwide spread of distance offerings, a Global Alliance for Transnational Education has formed. Australia's Monash University and United States-based International University recently completed GATE's "certification" process.

In Canada, with its long history of distance education, several universities are deeply into extending their reach, among them Simon Fraser, UBC, Athabasca, Laval, and Cape Breton. Several universities are partners in Theme Seven, an infrastructure that provides teacher professional development in the use of information technologies... a need that hardly stops at the border. On April 16th [1998], TVOntario, which sells educational programming in 136 countries, signed a deal with Israel's Arel Communications and Software to provide satellite-based interactive classrooms at 400 sites across the province. (Arel has opened an office in Atlanta to market its Integrated Distance Education and Learning system in the United States.) Canadian presidents (like their U.S. counterparts) fret privately that their existing distance learning initiatives will not be able to withstand well-heeled competitors operating across national borders.

For established colleges and universities, the competitive threat is four-fold. First, all face threats to their continuing education, degree-completion, or extension arm... which in more than a few cases is a key financial base for the institution. Second, in the convenience part of the market, less-selective colleges will feel real pressure on their base enrollments at the associate's, bachelor's, and master's levels. Third, most institutions and their faculties will confront difficult, market- and quality-based questions about whether to replace existing, home-grown courses with nationally produced courseware. Fourth, all institutions, Ivies and medallions included, may see their undergraduate franchise eroded as enrolled students appear in the registrar's office with brand-name course credits taken over the Web.

More broadly, an essence of distance learning is that it knows no boundaries of time or place; it is inherently transnational. A big fear among U.S. university leaders and postsecondary start-ups alike is that—just as happened in banking and health care—major international combines will emerge to quash today's smaller-time competitors. What would the postsecondary marketplace look like if (say) Microsoft, Deutsche Telekom, International Thomson, and the University of California combined to offer UC courses and degrees worldwide? In time, its only competitor could be a combine of like standing and deep pockets: an IBM-Elsevier-NEC-Oxford combine, for example. We shall see.

David F. Noble  **NO**

Digital Diploma Mills: The Automation of Higher Education

Recent events at two large North American universities signal dramatically that we have entered a new era in higher education, one which is rapidly drawing the halls of academe into the age of automation. In mid-summer the UCLA administration launched its historic "Instructional Enhancement Initiative" requiring computer Web sites for all of its arts and sciences courses by the start of the Fall term, the first time that a major university has made mandatory the use of computer telecommunications technology in the delivery of higher education. In partnership with several private corporations (including the Times Mirror Company, parent of the Los Angeles Times), moreover, UCLA has spawned its own for-profit company, headed by a former UCLA vice chancellor, to peddle online education (the Home Education Network).

This past spring in Toronto, meanwhile, the full-time faculty of York University, Canada's third largest, ended an historic two-month strike having secured for the first time anywhere formal contractual protection against precisely the kind of administrative action being taken by UCLA. The unprecedented faculty job action, the longest university strike in English Canadian history, was taken partly in response to unilateral administrative initiatives in the implementation of instructional technology, the most egregious example of which was an official solicitation to private corporations inviting them to permanently place their logo on a university online course in return for a $10,000 contribution to courseware development. As at UCLA, the York University administration has spawned its own subsidiary (Cultech), directed by the vice president for research and several deans and dedicated, in collaboration with a consortium of private sector firms, to the commercial development and exploitation of online education.

Significantly, at both UCLA and York, the presumably cyber-happy students have given clear indication that they are not exactly enthusiastic about the prospect of a high-tech academic future, recommending against the Initiative at UCLA and at York lending their support to striking faculty and launching their own independent investigation of the commercial, pedagogical, and ethical

From David F. Noble, "Digital Diploma Mills: The Automation of Higher Education," *First Monday: Peer-Reviewed Journal on the Internet,* <http://www.firstmonday.dk/issues/issue3_1/noble/index.html> (January 5, 1998). Copyright © 1998 by David F. Noble. Reprinted by permission.

implications of online educational technology. [Recently] the student hand-book distributed annually to all students by the York Federation of Students contained a warning about the dangers of online education.

The Classroom vs. The Boardroom

Thus, at the very outset of this new age of higher education, the lines have already been drawn in the struggle which will ultimately determine its shape. On the one side university administrators and their myriad commercial part-ners, on the other those who constitute the core relation of education: students and teachers. (The chief slogan of the York faculty during the strike was "the classroom vs the boardroom"). It is no accident, then, that the high-tech trans-formation of higher education is being initiated and implemented from the top down, either without any student and faculty involvement in the decision-making or despite it. At UCLA the administration launched their Initiative dur-ing the summer when many faculty are away and there was little possibility of faculty oversight or governance; faculty were thus left out of the loop and kept in the dark about the new web requirement until the last moment.

And UCLA administrators also went ahead with its Initiative, which is funded by a new compulsory student fee, despite the formal student recom-mendation against it. Similarly the initiatives of the York administration in the deployment of computer technology in education were taken without faculty oversight and deliberation much less student involvement. What is driving this headlong rush to implement new technology with so little regard for delib-eration of the pedagogical and economic costs and at the risk of student and faculty alienation and opposition? A short answer might be the fear of getting left behind, the incessant pressures of "progress". But there is more to it. For the universities are not simply undergoing a technological transformation. Be-neath that change, and camouflaged by it, lies another: the commercialization of higher education. For here as elsewhere technology is but a vehicle and a disarming disguise.

The major change to befall the universities over the last two decades has been the identification of the campus as a significant site of capital ac-cumulation, a change in social perception which has resulted in the systematic conversion of intellectual activity into intellectual capital and, hence, intellec-tual property. There have been two general phases of this transformation. The first, which began twenty years ago and is still underway, entailed the com-moditization of the research function of the university, transforming scientific and engineering knowledge into commercially viable proprietary products that could be owned and bought and sold in the market. The second, which we are now witnessing, entails the commoditization of the educational function of the university, transforming courses into courseware, the activity of instruc-tion itself into commercially viable proprietary products that can be owned and bought and sold in the market. In the first phase the universities became the site of production and sale of patents and exclusive licenses. In the second, they are becoming the site of production of—as well as the chief market for—copyrighted videos, courseware, CD-ROMs, and Web sites.

The first phase began in the mid-1970's when, in the wake of the oil crisis and intensifying international competition, corporate and political leaders of the major industrialized countries of the world recognized that they were losing their monopoly over the world's heavy industries and that, in the future, their supremacy would depend upon their monopoly over the knowledge which had become the lifeblood of the new so-called "knowledge-based" industries (space, electronics, computers, materials, telecommunications, and bioengineering). This focus upon "intellectual capital" turned their attention to the universities as its chief source, implicating the universities as never before in the economic machinery. In the view of capital, the universities had become too important to be left to the universities. Within a decade there was a proliferation of industrial partnerships and new proprietary arrangements, as industrialists and their campus counterparts invented ways to socialize the risks and costs of creating this knowledge while privatizing the benefits. This unprecedented collaboration gave rise to an elaborate web of interlocking directorates between corporate and academic boardrooms and the foundation of joint lobbying efforts epitomized by the work of the Business-Higher Education Forum. The chief accomplishment of the combined effort, in addition to a relaxation of anti-trust regulations and greater tax incentives for corporate funding of university research, was the 1980 reform of the patent law which for the first time gave the universities automatic ownership of patents resulting from federal government grants. Laboratory knowledge now became patents, that is intellectual capital and intellectual property. As patent holding companies, the universities set about at once to codify their intellectual property policies, develop the infrastructure for the conduct of commercially-viable research, cultivate their corporate ties, and create the mechanisms for marketing their new commodity, exclusive licenses to their patents. The result of this first phase of university commoditization was a wholesale reallocation of university resources toward its research function at the expense of its educational function.

Class sizes swelled, teaching staffs and instructional resources were reduced, salaries were frozen, and curricular offerings were cut to the bone. At the same time, tuition soared to subsidize the creation and maintenance of the commercial infrastructure (and correspondingly bloated administration) that has never really paid off. In the end students were paying more for their education and getting less, and the campuses were in crisis[1].

The second phase of the commercialization of academia, the commoditization of instruction, is touted as the solution to the crisis engendered by the first. Ignoring the true sources of the financial debacle—an expensive and low-yielding commercial infrastructure and greatly expanded administrative costs—the champions of computer-based instruction focus their attention rather upon increasing the efficiencies of already overextended teachers. And they ignore as well the fact that their high-tech remedies are bound only to compound the problem, increasing further, rather then reducing, the costs of higher education. (Experience to date demonstrates clearly that computer-based teaching, with its limitless demands upon instructor time and vastly expanded overhead requirements—equipment, upgrades, maintenance, and technical and administrative support staff—costs more not less than traditional education, whatever the reductions in direct labor, hence the need for outside funding and student technology fees). Little wonder, then, that teachers and students are reluctant to embrace this new panacea. Their hesitation reflects not fear but wisdom [2].

The Birth of Educational Maintenance Organizations

But this second transformation of higher education is not the work of teachers or students, the presumed beneficiaries of improved education, because it is not really about education at all. That's just the name of the market. The foremost promoters of this transformation are rather the vendors of the network hardware, software, and "content"—Apple, IBM, Bell, the cable companies, Microsoft, and the edutainment and publishing companies Disney, Simon and Schuster, Prentice-Hall, et al.—who view education as a market for their wares, a market estimated by the Lehman Brothers investment firm potentially to be worth several hundred billion dollars. "Investment opportunity in the education industry has never been better," one of their reports proclaimed, indicating that this will be "the focus industry" for lucrative investment in the future, replacing the health care industry. (The report also forecasts that the educational market will eventually become dominated by EMOs—education maintenance organizations—just like HMOs in the health care market). It is important to emphasize that, for all the democratic rhetoric about extending educational access to those unable to get to the campus, the campus remains the real market for these products, where students outnumber their distance learning counterparts six-to-one.

In addition to the vendors, corporate training advocates view online education as yet another way of bringing their problem-solving, information-processing, "just-in-time" educated employees up to profit-making speed. Beyond their ambitious in-house training programs, which have incorporated computer-based instructional methods pioneered by the military, they envision the transformation of the delivery of higher education as a means of supplying their properly-prepared personnel at public expense.

The third major promoters of this transformation are the university administrators, who see it as a way of giving their institutions a fashionably forward-looking image. More importantly, they view computer-based instruction as a means of reducing their direct labor and plant maintenance costs—fewer teachers and classrooms—while at the same time undermining the autonomy and independence of faculty. At the same time, they are hoping to get a piece of the commercial action for their institutions or themselves, as vendors in their own right of software and content. University administrators are supported in this enterprise by a number of private foundations, trade associations, and academic-corporate consortia which are promoting the use of the new technologies with increasing intensity. Among these are the Sloan, Mellon, Pew, and Culpeper Foundations, the American Council on Education, and, above all, Educom, a consortium representing the management of 600 colleges and universities and a hundred private corporations.

Last but not least, behind this effort are the ubiquitous technozealots who simply view computers as the panacea for everything, because they like to play with them. With the avid encouragement of their private sector and university patrons, they forge ahead, without support for their pedagogical claims about the alleged enhancement of education, without any real evidence of productivity improvement, and without any effective demand from either students or teachers.

In addition to York and UCLA, universities throughout North America are rapidly being overtaken by this second phase of commercialization. There are the stand-alone virtual institutions like University of Phoenix, the wired private institutions like the New School for Social Research, the campuses of state universities like the University of Maryland and the new Gulf-Coast campus of the University of Florida (which boasts no tenure). On the state level, the states of Arizona and California have initiated their own state-wide virtual university projects, while a consortia of western "Smart States" have launched their own ambitious effort to wire all of their campuses into an online educational network. In Canada, a national effort has been undertaken, spearheaded by the Telelearning Research Network centered at Simon Fraser University in Vancouver, to bring most of the nation's higher education institutions into a "Virtual U" network.

The overriding commercial intent and market orientation behind these initiatives is explicit, as is illustrated by the most ambitious U. S. effort to date, the Western Governors' Virtual University Project, whose stated goals are to "expand the marketplace for instructional materials, courseware, and programs utilizing advanced technology," "expand the marketplace for demonstrated competence," and "identify and remove barriers to the free functioning of these markets, particularly barriers posed by statutes, policies, and administrative rules and regulations."

"In the future," Utah governor Mike Leavitt proclaimed, "an institution of higher education will become a little like a local television station." Start up funds for the project come from the private sector, specifically from Educational Management Group, the educational arm of the world's largest educational publisher Simon and Schuster and the proprietary impulse behind their largesse is made clear by Simon and Schuster CEO Jonathan Newcomb: "The use of interactive technology is causing a fundamental shift away from the physical classroom toward anytime, anywhere learning—the model for post secondary education in the twenty-first century." This transformation is being made possible by "advances in digital technology, coupled with the protection of copyright in cyberspace."

Similarly, the national effort to develop the "Virtual U" customized educational software platform in Canada is directed by an industrial consortium which includes Kodak, IBM, Microsoft, McGraw-Hill, Prentice-Hall, Rogers Cablesystems, Unitel, Novasys, Nortel, Bell Canada, and MPR Teltech, a research subsidiary of GTE. The commercial thrust behind the project is explicit here too. Predicting a potential fifty billion dollar Canadian market, the project proposal emphasizes the adoption of "an intellectual property policy that will encourage researchers and industry to commercialize their innovations" and anticipates the development of "a number of commercially marketable hardware and software products and services," including "courseware and other learning products." The two directors of the project, Simon Fraser University professors, have formed their own company to peddle these products in collaboration with the university. At the same time, the nearby University of British Columbia has recently spun off the private WEB-CT company to peddle its own educational Web site software, WEB-CT, the software designed by one of its computer science professors and now being used by UCLA. In recent months, WEB-CT has entered into production and distribution relationships with Silicon Graphics and Prentice-Hall and is fast becoming a major player in the American as well as Canadian higher education market. As of the beginning of the Fall term, WEB-CT licensees now include, in addition to UCLA and California State University, the Universities of Georgia, Minnesota, Illinois, North Carolina, and Indiana, as well as such private institutions as Syracuse, Brandeis, and Duquesne.

Education As a Commodity

The implications of the commoditization of university instruction are two-fold in nature, those relating to the university as a site of the production of the commodities and those relating to the university as a market for them. The first raises for the faculty traditional labor issues about the introduction of new technologies of production. The second raises for students major questions about costs, coercion, privacy, equity, and the quality of education.

With the commoditization of instruction, teachers as labor are drawn into a production process designed for the efficient creation of instructional commodities, and hence become subject to all the pressures that have befallen production workers in other industries undergoing rapid technological transformation from above. In this context faculty have much more in common with the historic plight of other skilled workers than they care to acknowledge. Like these others, their activity is being restructured, via the technology, in order to reduce their autonomy, independence, and control over their work and to place workplace knowledge and control as much as possible into the hands of the administration. As in other industries, the technology is being deployed by management primarily to discipline, de-skill, and displace labor.

Once faculty and courses go online, administrators gain much greater direct control over faculty performance and course content than ever before and the potential for administrative scrutiny, supervision, regimentation, discipline and even censorship increase dramatically. At the same time, the use of the technology entails an inevitable extension of working time and an intensification of work as faculty struggle at all hours of the day and night to stay on top of the technology and respond, via chat rooms, virtual office hours, and e-mail, to both students and administrators to whom they have now become instantly and continuously accessible. The technology also allows for much more careful administrative monitoring of faculty availability, activities, and responsiveness.

Once faculty put their course material online, moreover, the knowledge and course design skill embodied in that material is taken out of their possession, transferred to the machinery and placed in the hands of the administration. The administration is now in a position to hire less skilled, and hence cheaper, workers to deliver the technologically prepackaged course. It also allows the administration, which claims ownership of this commodity, to peddle the course elsewhere without the original designer's involvement or even knowledge, much less financial interest. The buyers of this packaged commodity, meanwhile, other academic institutions, are able thereby to contract out, and hence outsource, the work of their own employees and thus reduce their reliance upon their in-house teaching staff.

Redundant Faculty in the Virtual University

Most important, once the faculty converts its courses to courseware, their services are in the long run no longer required. They become redundant, and when they leave, their work remains behind. In Kurt Vonnegut's classic novel *Player Piano* the ace machinist Rudy Hertz is flattered by the automation engineers who tell him his genius will be immortalized. They buy him a beer. They capture his skills on tape. Then they fire him. Today faculty are falling for the same tired line, that their brilliance will be broadcast online to millions. Perhaps, but without their further participation. Some skeptical faculty insist that what they do cannot possibly be automated, and they are right. But it will be automated anyway, whatever the loss in educational quality. Because education, again, is not what all this is about; it's about making money. In short, the new technology of education, like the automation of other industries, robs faculty of their knowledge and skills, their control over their working lives, the product of their labor, and, ultimately, their means of livelihood.

None of this is speculation. [Recently] the UCLA faculty, at administration request, have dutifully or grudgingly (it doesn't really matter which) placed their course work—ranging from just syllabi and assignments to the entire body of course lectures and notes—at the disposal of their administration, to be used online, without asking who will own it much less how it will eventually be used and with what consequences. At York University, untenured faculty have been required to put their courses on video, CD-ROM or the Internet or lose their job. They have then been hired to teach their own now automated course at a fraction of their former compensation. The New School in New York now routinely hires outside contractors from around the country, mostly unemployed PhDs, to design online courses. The designers are not hired as employees but are simply paid a modest flat fee and are required to surrender to the university all rights to their course. The New School then offers the course without having to employ anyone. And this is just the beginning.

Educom, the academic-corporate consortium, has recently established their Learning Infrastructure Initiative which includes the detailed study of what professors do, breaking the faculty job down in classic Tayloristic fashion into discrete tasks, and determining what parts can be automated or outsourced. Educom believes that course design, lectures, and even evaluation can all be standardized, mechanized, and consigned to outside commercial vendors. "Today you're looking at a highly personal human-mediated environment," Educom president Robert Heterich observed. "The potential to remove the human mediation in some areas and replace it with automation—smart, computer-based, network-based systems—is tremendous. It's gotta happen."

Toward this end, university administrators are coercing or enticing faculty into compliance, placing the greatest pressures on the most vulnerable —untenured and part-time faculty, and entry-level and prospective employees. They are using the academic incentive and promotion structure to reward cooperation and discourage dissent. At the same time they are mounting an intensifying propaganda campaign to portray faculty as incompetent, hidebound, recalcitrant, inefficient, ineffective, and expensive—in short, in need of improvement or replacement through instructional technologies. Faculty are portrayed above all as obstructionist, as standing in the way of progress and forestalling the panacea of virtual education allegedly demanded by students, their parents, and the public.

The York University faculty had heard it all. Yet still they fought vigorously and ultimately successfully to preserve quality education and protect themselves from administrative assault. During their long strike they countered such administration propaganda with the truth about what was happening to higher education and eventually won the support of students, the media, and the public. Most important, they secured a new contract containing unique and unprecedented provisions which, if effectively enforced, give faculty members direct and unambiguous control over all decisions relating to the automation of instruction, including veto power. According to the contract, all decisions regarding the use of technology as a supplement to classroom instruction or as a means of alternative delivery (including the use of video, CD-ROMs, Internet Web sites, computer-mediated conferencing, etc.) "shall be consistent with the pedagogic and academic judgments and principles of the faculty member employee as to the appropriateness of the use of technology in the circumstances." The contract also guarantees that "a faculty member will not be required to convert a course without his or her agreement." Thus, the York faculty will be able to ensure that the new technology, if and when used, will contribute to a genuine enhancement rather than a degradation of the quality of education, while at the same time preserving their positions, their autonomy, and their academic freedom. The battle is far from won, but it is a start.

Student Reactions

The second set of implications stemming from the commoditization of instruction involve the transformation of the university into a market for the commodities being produced. Administrative propaganda routinely alludes to an alleged student demand for the new instructional products. At UCLA officials are betting that their high-tech agenda will be "student driven", as students insist that faculty make fuller use of the Web site technology in their courses. To date, however, there has been no such demand on the part of students, no serious study of it, and no evidence for it. Indeed, the few times students have been given a voice, they have rejected the initiatives hands down, especially when they were required to pay for it (the definition of effective demand, i.e. a market).

At UCLA, students recommended against the Instructional Enhancement Initiative. At the University of British Columbia, home of the WEB-CT software being used at UCLA, students voted in a referendum four-to-one against a similar initiative, despite a lengthy administration campaign promising them a more secure place in the high tech future. Administrators at both institutions have tended to dismiss, ignore, or explain away these negative student decisions, but there is a message here: students want the genuine face-to-face education they paid for not a cyber-counterfeit. Nevertheless, administrators at both UCLA and UBC decided to proceed with the their agenda anyway, desperate to create a market and secure some return on their investment in the information technology infrastructure. Thus, they are creating a market by fiat, compelling students (and faculty) to become users and hence consumers of the hardware, software, and content products as a condition of getting an education, whatever their interest or ability to pay. Can all students equally afford this capital-intensive education?

Another key ethical issue relates to the use of student online activities. Few students realize that their computer-based courses are often thinly-veiled field trials for product and market development, that while they are studying their courses, their courses are studying them. In Canada, for example, universities have been given royalty-free licenses to Virtual U software in return for providing data on its use to the vendors. Thus, all online activity including communications between students and professors and among students are monitored, automatically logged and archived by the system for use by the vendor. Students enrolled in courses using Virtual U software are in fact formally designated "experimental subjects." Because federal monies were used to develop the software and underwrite the field trials, vendors were compelled to comply with ethical guidelines on the experimental use of human subjects. Thus, all students once enrolled are required to sign forms releasing ownership and control of their online activities to the vendors. The form states "as a student using Virtual U in a course, I give my permission to have the computer-generated usage data, conference transcript data, and virtual artifacts data collected by the Virtual U software . . . used for research, development, and demonstration purposes."

According to UCLA's Home Education Network president John Korbara, all of their distance learning courses are likewise monitored and archived for use by company officials. On the UCLA campus, according to Harlan Lebo of the Provost's office, student use of the course Web sites will be routinely audited and evaluated by the administration. Marvin Goldberg, designer of the UCLA WEB-CT software acknowledges that the system allows for "lurking" and automatic storage and retrieval of all online activities. How this capability will be used and by whom is not altogether clear, especially since Web sites are typically being constructed by people other than the instructors. What third parties (besides students and faculty in the course) will have access to the student's communications? Who will own student online contributions? What rights, if any, do students have to privacy and proprietary control of their work? Are they given prior notification as to the ultimate status of their online activities, so that they might be in a position to give, or withhold, their informed consent? If students are taking courses which are just experiments, and hence of unproven pedagogical value, should students be paying full tuition for them? And if students are being used as guinea pigs in product trials masquerading as courses, should they be paying for these courses or be paid to take them? More to the point, should students be content with a degraded, shadow cyber-education? In Canada student organizations have begun to confront these issues head on, and there are some signs of similar student concern emerging also in the U.S.

Conclusion

In his classic 1959 study of diploma mills for the American Council on Education, Robert Reid described the typical diploma mill as having the following characteristics: "no classrooms," "faculties are often untrained or nonexistent," and "the officers are unethical self-seekers whose qualifications are no better than their offerings." It is an apt description of the digital diploma mills now in the making. Quality higher education will not disappear entirely, but it will soon become the exclusive preserve of the privileged, available only to children of the rich and the powerful. For the rest of us a dismal new era of higher education has dawned. In ten years, we will look upon the wired remains of our once great democratic higher education system and wonder how we let it happen. That is, unless we decide now not to let it happen.

Notes

1. Tuition began to outpace inflation in the early 1980's, at precisely the moment when changes in the patent system enabled the universities to become major vendors of patent licenses. According to data compiled by the National Center for Educational Statistics, between 1976 and 1994 expenditures on research increased 21.7% at public research universities while expenditure on instruction decreased 9.5%. Faculty salaries, which had peaked in 1972, fell precipitously during the next decade and have since recovered only half the loss.

2. Recent surveys of the instructional use of information technology in higher education clearly indicate that there have been no significant gains in either productivity improvement or pedagogical enhancement. Kenneth C. Green , Director of the Campus Computing Project, which conducts annual surveys of information technology use in higher education, noted that "the campus experience over the past decade reveals that the dollars can be daunting, the return on investment highly uncertain." "We have yet to hear of an instance where the total costs (including all realistically amortized capital investments and development expenses, plus reasonable estimates for faculty and support staff time) associated with teaching some unit to some group of students actually decline while maintaining the quality of learning," Green wrote. On the matter of pedagogical effectiveness, Green noted that "the research literature offers, at best, a mixed review of often inconclusive results, at least when searching for traditional measures of statistical significance in learning outcomes."

POSTSCRIPT

Is the Marketing of Online Degree Programs a Threat to Traditional Education?

M anagement messiah" Peter Drucker predicts that in 30 years "the big university campuses will be relics and that the residential university is destined to yield to the virtual university." In March 1999 Colorado-based Jones University became the first fully accredited, actively online university, and the list has been growing rapidly ever since. Over 1,500 educational institutions currently offer courses through distance learning. In the United States alone, more than 300 fully accredited major colleges and universities offer degrees in over 800 fields of study through distance learning. Approximately 80 educational institutions offer MBAs and doctorates. Even the American Marketing Association (AMA) has a partnership program with Cappella University in offering online MBA courses. However, the American Association of University Professors wrote the Jones University accrediting agency to voice its "shock and dismay." And, as one Georgetown University professor has suggested, Internet-based distance learning is "the new version of a trade school and joke of the twenty-first century."

Emerging companies like Pensure, Inc., based in Los Altos, California, develop and market programs to corporations with online courseware from schools such as the University of Pennsylvania's Wharton Direct Program, a division of the university's prestigious School of Business. Many view this as an innovative teaching tool, allowing students from all corners of the world to interact in this educational model of the new millennium. Executives from many companies believe that online education draws people together and opens doors for middle managers who need to train for the new economy. Furthermore, they believe that online discussion surpasses any other forms of discussion that can be simulated in a face-to-face classroom, where students can more easily escape participation. They maintain that students are forced to become active participants rather than classroom spectators who do not need to be mentally tuned in.

Online education is necessitated by two major factors—geography and modern social demands. The Internet has opened up vast opportunities for educational institutions, and many believe that the ones that do not adapt are in danger of becoming obsolete. The flexibility and convenience of this channel has obvious advantages. Recently, there has been a plan to offer free Ivy League education to anyone around the world. In what way can we better link people around the globe than with education?

On the other hand, there are critical questions that remain unanswered. Can virtual education substitute campus life experiences and "human moments" with charismatic professors? Is the lack of social contact with students' peers likely to have an adverse effect on group/team building skills? Can professors function well without the benefit of direct feedback from students? Are we ready for "virtual professors"?

Suggested Readings

Tom P. Abeles, "The Academy in a Wired World," *Futures* (September 1998)

John Daniel, *Mega-Universities and Knowledge Media: Technology Strategies for Higher Education* (Kogan Page, 1998)

Kristen Gerencher, "MBA Programs Go Online," *InfoWorld* (December 21, 1998)

Richard N. Katz, ed., *Dancing With the Devil: Information Technology and the New Competition in Higher Education* (Jossey-Bass, 1999)

Irene Kim and Deborah Hairston, "Remote Education: As the Virtual Classroom Becomes a Reality, More Engineering Courses Are Out of 'Site,'" *Chemical Engineering* (April 1998)

Robert H. Krapels, Cathy Ryan, and James Lane, "Education Initiatives Inside Business Today," *Business Communication Quarterly* (December 1998)

Nadalyn C. Larsen, "Distance Learning: Linking the Globe Through Education," *World Trade* (December 1999)

Rena M. Palloff and Keith Pratt, *Building Learning Communities in Cyberspace: Effective Strategies for the Online Classroom* (Jossey-Bass, 1999)

Lynnette R. Porter, *Creating the Virtual Classroom: Distance Learning With the Internet* (John Wiley, 1997)

Heidi Schweizer, *Designing and Teaching an On-L2ine Course: Spinning Your Web Classroom* (Allyn & Bacon, 1999)

Ken W. White and Bob H. Weight, eds., *The Online Teaching Guide: A Handbook of Attitudes, Strategies, and Techniques for the Virtual Classroom* (Allyn & Bacon, 1999)

National Universities Degree Consortium. http://www.nudc.com

American Marketing Association. http://www.ama.org

On the Internet ...

Research on Gun Violence and Gun Violence Prevention

The research department of the Center to Prevent Handgun Violence has produced a significant body of cutting-edge research measuring the effectiveness
of gun control laws and tracking independent studies of firearms deaths and
injuries.

http://www.cphv.org/research.htm

The Harvard School of Public Health College Alcohol Study 1998

Visitors to this Web site may download or view the 1998 college alcohol study
report by the Harvard School of Public Health.

http://www.hsph.harvard.edu/cas/1998_rpt.htm

State Lottery Revenues and Spending

This Web site offers a downloadable 1998 report on lottery revenues and
spending broken down by state.

http://www.census.gov/ftp/pub/govs/state/98lottery.xls

Grassroots.com

This Web site offers an extensive network of political action news and information.

http://www.grassroots.com

PART 5

Societal and Regulatory Influences

*D*oes it seem that all of society's ills and problems are blamed on marketing? Should the notions of freedom of speech, capitalism, and democracy be factored into the issues in this section? For example, people increasingly believe that media, music, video games, and Hollywood movies are responsible for the violence associated with America's youth. Are marketers responsible for the toxic culture of violence in the United States? Are marketers responsible for sustaining the icon of "gunocracy" that has come to depict firearms as the quintessential symbol of American life?

Recently, the practice of advertising distilled spirits on television has been reintroduced in several Sun Belt states, inviting a storm of criticism from advocacy and special interest groups. Should these liquor advertisers be denied access to media that affords the same opportunity to beer and wine marketers? A similar issue relates to the legitimacy of state lottery promotion. As a leisure industry, gambling is experiencing an astonishing growth. As casino gambling and gaming Web sites explode, will the lure of reaching state lottery consumers eventually spur politicians into using the Web as an advertising venue?

And finally, is the role of marketing dominating the electoral process for Congress and the presidency? How can voters become better informed about the patrons and special interest groups that some critics portray as "buying" the Congress and the presidency? Has the role of marketing become too powerful and pervasive in U.S. society?

- Are Marketers Culpable for America's Culture of Violence?

- Should Alcohol Advertising Be Regulated Further?

- Is It Appropriate for the Government to Market Lotteries?

- Is Political Marketing Essentially Buying Politicians?

ISSUE 17

Are Marketers Culpable for America's Culture of Violence?

YES: David Grossman, from "Trained to Kill," *Christianity Today* (August 10, 1998)

NO: Wendy Melillo, from "After Columbine, Legislators Attack Media Violence," *Adweek* (May 24, 1999)

ISSUE SUMMARY

YES: David Grossman, a military psychologist, offers theories and evidence correlating video games and the marketing of media violence with conditioning kids to kill.

NO: Wendy Melillo, a regular contributor to *Adweek,* provides an overview of legislative endeavors to halt the use of violence in marketing videos and general media appeals. She argues that this movement is largely politically motivated and that it ignores the importance of family influence and upbringing.

I n 1999 President Bill Clinton reported that over 300 studies show a link between sustained exposure to violent entertainment and violent behavior. Many feel that children are desensitized to violence because violent entertainment made for adults is marketed to children. And it seems logical that children who are desensitized to violence are more likely to commit acts of violence themselves.

How culpable are marketing and the media for America's culture of violence? The tragedy that occurred in 1999 at Columbine High School in Littleton, Colorado, and other unfathomable horrors of teen violence have forced national attention on guns and media violence. This heated debate is currently the embodiment of some of the most viscious accusations against marketing as a social institution. The areas of marketing in the forefront of attack with regard to America's culture of violence are products, promotion, and the pervasiveness of gratuitous violence. Guns are the products most scrutinized in terms of public concern. The controversy over gun control, gun safety locks, and the liability of firearms manufacturers are central challenges for marketers.

The other product arena deals with entertainment and media. David Grossman's selection serves as a call to action against violent videos; music with obscene lyrics; "splatter" movies, which are saturated with gratuitous violence; and sex and "trash" TV. Grossman introduces the term *killology*, which is the study of methods and psychology of training army recruits to circumvent their natural inhibition to killing fellow human beings. He analyzes how the same tactics used to train soldiers are embedded in American entertainment media and, more specifically, video games. Grossman's critics suggest that the latest horrific acts of violence are isolated events. They contend that crime rates are declining at the same time that video game sales are increasing. Grossman maintains that the increasing rate of imprisonment of violent offenders and the thousands of lives saved through advances in medical technology have kept the rate of aggravated assault down substantially. He presents evidence to show that the phenomenal growth in crime rates are indigenous to countries where media violence is presented as entertainment to children.

The promotion of violent material is a controversial issue. Critics accuse advertisers of interpreting violence as cool, effective, emotionally satisfying, and an acceptable part of American popular culture. The tremendous success of the wrestling industry exemplifies the pervasiveness of violence as being *normalized* in pop culture. Its popularity was recently reflected in a *Time* magazine cover story, reporting top ratings in TV, books, and videos. The Xtreme Football League (XFL) promises to spice up professional football with its glorification of violence to the demise of tradition and established rules.

The pervasiveness of violence is a major social concern. Research reveals that by the time the typical child is 18, he or she has seen 200,000 dramatized acts of violence and 40,000 dramatized murders. How pervasive is violent media? American households with teenagers reportedly watch 59 hours of TV a week. Teens watch 67 full-length movies a year, and they own an average of 42 musical compact disks, 16 game cartridges, and 7 computer games. Thirty-five percent even have their own TV.

Many feel that the entertainment industry feeds children a dependable daily dose of violence, which consistently desensitizes them to its consequences. Controversial talk shows like *Jerry Springer* and direct coverage of *real* news like *America's Most Wanted* and *Top-Cops* are replete with real violence. These programs are believed to validate the reality of actual violence as an integral part of American culture. Has the violence-saturated media desensitized children and created a fertile ground for continued aberrant behavior?

Wendy Melillo infers that the primary responsibility for halting the culture of violence lies with families and parental upbringing. She supports investigation of marketing practices but spurns some politicians' implications of directly linking marketing to tragedies like Columbine. In Melillo's overview of forthcoming bills and legislation, she quotes Dan Jaffe of the National Association of Advertisers, who believes that the power to protect the family belongs to parents. Others believe that the government must play the pivotal role (with products like the V-chip, which are now required in all TVs). Yet is it dangerous for the government to put itself in the role of parent?

David Grossman  **YES**

Trained to Kill

Virus of Violence

To understand the *why* behind Jonesboro and Springfield and Pearl and Paducah, and all the other outbreaks of this "virus of violence," we need to understand first the magnitude of the problem. The per capita murder rate doubled in this country between 1957—when the FBI started keeping track of the data—and 1992. A fuller picture of the problem, however, is indicated by the rate people are *attempting* to kill one another—the aggravated assault rate. That rate in America has gone from around 60 per 100,000 in 1957 to over 440 per 100,000 by the middle of this decade. As bad as this is, it would be much worse were it not for two major factors.

First is the increase in the imprisonment rate of violent offenders. The prison population in America nearly quadrupled between 1975 and 1992. According to criminologist John J. DiIulio, "dozens of credible empirical analyses... leave no doubt that the increased use of prisons averted millions of serious crimes." If it were not for our tremendous imprisonment rate (the highest of any industrialized nation), the aggravated assault rate and the murder rate would undoubtedly be even higher.

The second factor keeping the murder rate from being any worse is medical technology. According to the U.S. Army Medical Service Corps, a wound that would have killed nine out of ten soldiers in World War II, nine out of ten could have survived in Vietnam. Thus, by a very conservative estimate, if we had 1940-level medical technology today, the murder rate would be ten times higher than it is. The magnitude of the problem has been held down by the development of sophisticated lifesaving skills and techniques, such as helicopter medevacs, 911 operators, paramedics, CPR, trauma centers, and medicines.

However, the crime rate is still at a phenomenally high level, and this is true worldwide. In Canada, according to their Center for Justice, per capita assaults increased almost fivefold between 1964 and 1993, attempted murder increased nearly sevenfold, and murders doubled. Similar trends can be seen in other countries in the per capita violent crime rates reported to Interpol between 1977 and 1993. In Australia and New Zealand, the assault rate increased approximately fourfold, and the murder rate nearly doubled in both nations.

The assault rate tripled in Sweden, and approximately doubled in Belgium, Denmark, England-Wales, France, Hungary, Netherlands, and Scotland, while all these nations had an associated (but smaller) increase in murder.

This virus of violence is occurring worldwide. The explanation for it has to be some new factor that is occurring in all of these countries. There are many factors involved, and none should be discounted: for example, the prevalence of guns in our society. But violence is rising in many nations with draconian gun laws. And though we should never downplay child abuse, poverty, or racism, there is only one new variable present in each of these countries, bearing the exact same fruit: media violence presented as entertainment for children.

Killing Is Unnatural

Before retiring from the military, I spent almost a quarter of a century as an army infantry officer and a psychologist, learning and studying how to enable people to kill. Believe me, we are very good at it. But it does not come naturally; you have to be taught to kill. And just as the army is conditioning people to kill, we are indiscriminately doing the same thing to our children, but without the safeguards.

After the Jonesboro killings, the head of the American Academy of Pediatrics Task Force on Juvenile Violence came to town and said that children don't naturally kill. It is a learned skill. And they learn it from abuse and violence in the home and, most pervasively, from violence as entertainment in television, the movies, and interactive video games.

Killing requires training because there is a built-in aversion to killing one's own kind. I can best illustrate this from drawing on my own work in studying killing in the military.

We all know that you can't have an argument or a discussion with a frightened or angry human being. Vasoconstriction, the narrowing of the blood vessels, has literally closed down the forebrain—that great gob of gray matter that makes you a human being and distinguishes you from a dog. When those neurons close down, the midbrain takes over and your thought processes and reflexes are indistinguishable from your dog's. If you've worked with animals, you have some understanding of what happens to frightened human beings on the battlefield. The battlefield and violent crime are in the realm of midbrain responses.

Within the midbrain there is a powerful, God-given resistance to killing your own kind. Every species, with a few exceptions, has a hardwired resistance to killing its own kind in territorial and mating battles. When animals with antlers and horns fight one another, they head butt in a harmless fashion. But when they fight any other species, they go to the side to gut and gore. Piranhas will turn their fangs on anything, but they fight one another with flicks of the tail. Rattlesnakes will bite anything, but they wrestle one another. Almost every species has this hardwired resistance to killing its own kind.

When we human beings are overwhelmed with anger and fear, we slam head-on into that midbrain resistance that generally prevents us from killing.

Only sociopaths—who by definition don't have that resistance—lack this innate violence immune system.

Throughout human history, when humans fight each other, there is a lot of posturing. Adversaries make loud noises and puff themselves up, trying to daunt the enemy. There is a lot of fleeing and submission. Ancient battles were nothing more than great shoving matches. It was not until one side turned and ran that most of the killing happened, and most of that was stabbing people in the back. All of the ancient military historians report that the vast majority of killing happened in pursuit when one side was fleeing.

In more modern times, the average firing rate was incredibly low in Civil War battles. Patty Griffith demonstrates that the killing potential of the average Civil War regiment was anywhere from five hundred to a thousand men per minute. The actual killing rate was only one or two men per minute per regiment (*The Battle Tactics of the American Civil War*). At the Battle of Gettysburg, of the 27,000 muskets picked up from the dead and dying after the battle, 90 percent were loaded. This is an anomaly, because it took 95 percent of their time to load muskets and only 5 percent to fire. But even more amazingly, of the thousands of loaded muskets, over half had multiple loads in the barrel—one with 23 loads in the barrel.

In reality, the average man would load his musket and bring it to his shoulder, but he could not bring himself to kill. He would be brave, he would stand shoulder to shoulder, he would do what he was trained to do; but at the moment of truth, he could not bring himself to pull the trigger. And so he lowered the weapon and loaded it again. Of those who did fire, only a tiny percentage fired to hit. The vast majority fired over the enemy's head.

During World War II, U.S. Army Brig. Gen. S. L. A. Marshall had a team of researchers study what soldiers did in battle. For the first time in history, they asked individual soldiers what they did in battle. They discovered that only 15 to 20 percent of the individual riflemen could bring themselves to fire at an exposed enemy soldier.

That is the reality of the battlefield. Only a small percentage of soldiers are able and willing to participate. Men are willing to die, they are willing to sacrifice themselves for their nation; but they are not willing to kill. It is a phenomenal insight into human nature; but when the military became aware of that, they systematically went about the process of trying to fix this "problem." From the military perspective, a 15 percent firing rate among riflemen is like a 15 percent literacy rate among librarians. And fix it the military did. By the Korean War, around 55 percent of the soldiers were willing to fire to kill. And by Vietnam, the rate rose to over 90 percent.

The Methods in This Madness: Desensitization

How the military increases the killing rate of soldiers in combat is instructive, because our culture today is doing the same thing to our children. The training methods militaries use are brutalization, classical conditioning, operant conditioning, and role modeling. I will explain these in the military context and show how these same factors are contributing to the phenomenal increase of violence in our culture.

Brutalization and desensitization are what happens at boot camp. From the moment you step off the bus you are physically and verbally abused: countless pushups, endless hours at attention or running with heavy loads, while carefully trained professionals take turns screaming at you. Your head is shaved, you are herded together naked and dressed alike, losing all individuality. This brutalization is designed to break down your existing mores and norms and to accept a new set of values that embrace destruction, violence, and death as a way of life. In the end, you are desensitized to violence and accept it as a normal and essential survival skill in your brutal new world.

Something very similar to this desensitization toward violence is happening to our children through violence in the media—but instead of 18-year-olds, it begins at the age of 18 months when a child is first able to discern what is happening on television. At that age, a child can watch something happening on television and mimic that action. But it isn't until children are six or seven years old that the part of the brain kicks in that lets them understand where information comes from. Even though young children have some understanding of what it means to pretend, they are developmentally unable to distinguish clearly between fantasy and reality.

When young children see somebody shot, stabbed, raped, brutalized, degraded, or murdered on TV, to them it is as though it were actually happening. To have a child of three, four, or five watch a "splatter" movie, learning to relate to a character for the first 90 minutes and then in the last 30 minutes watch helplessly as that new friend is hunted and brutally murdered is the moral and psychological equivalent of introducing your child to a friend, letting her play with that friend, and then butchering that friend in front of your child's eyes. And this happens to our children hundreds upon hundreds of times.

Sure, they are told: "Hey, it's all for fun. Look, this isn't real, it's just TV." And they nod their little heads and say *okay*. But they can't tell the difference. Can you remember a point in your life or in your children's lives when dreams, reality, and television were all jumbled together? That's what it is like to be at that level of psychological development. That's what the media are doing to them.

The *Journal of the American Medical Association* published the definitive epidemiological study on the impact of TV violence. The research demonstrated what happened in numerous nations after television made its appearance as compared to nations and regions without TV. The two nations or regions being compared are demographically and ethnically identical; only one variable is different: the presence of television. In every nation, region, or city with television, there is an immediate explosion of violence on the playground, and within 15 years there is a doubling of the murder rate. Why 15 years? That is how long it takes for the brutalization of a three- to five-year-old to reach the "prime crime age." That is how long it takes for you to reap what you have sown when you brutalize and desensitize a three-year-old.

Today the data linking violence in the media to violence in society are superior to those linking cancer and tobacco. Hundreds of sound scientific studies demonstrate the social impact of brutalization by the media. The *Journal of the American Medical Association* concluded that "the introduction of television in the 1950's caused a subsequent doubling of the homicide rate, i.e., long-term childhood exposure to television is a causal factor behind approximately one half of the homicides committed in the United States, or approximately 10,000 homicides annually." The article went on to say that "... if, hypothetically, television technology had never been developed, there would today be 10,000 fewer homicides each year in the United States, 70,000 fewer rapes, and 700,000 fewer injurious assaults" (June 10, 1992).

Classical Conditioning

Classical conditioning is like the famous case of Pavlov's dogs you learned about in Psychology 101: The dogs learned to associate the ringing of the bell with food, and, once conditioned, the dogs could not hear the bell without salivating.

The Japanese were masters at using classical conditioning with their soldiers. Early in World War II, Chinese prisoners were placed in a ditch on their knees with their hands bound behind them. And one by one, a select few Japanese soldiers would go into the ditch and bayonet "their" prisoner to death. This is a horrific way to kill another human being. Up on the bank, countless other young soldiers would cheer them on in their violence. Comparatively few soldiers actually killed in these situations, but by making the others watch and cheer, the Japanese were able to use these kinds of atrocities to classically condition a very large audience to associate pleasure with human death and suffering. Immediately afterwards, the soldiers who had been spectators were treated to sake, the best meal they had had in months, and to so-called comfort girls. The result? They learned to associate committing violent acts with pleasure.

The Japanese found these kinds of techniques to be extraordinarily effective at quickly enabling very large numbers of soldiers to commit atrocities in the years to come. Operant conditioning (which we will look at shortly) teaches you to kill, but classical conditioning is a subtle but powerful mechanism that teaches you to *like it.*

This technique is so morally reprehensible that there are very few examples of it in modern U.S. military training; but there are some clear-cut examples of it being done by the media to our children. What is happening to our children is the reverse of the aversion therapy portrayed in the movie *A Clockwork Orange*. In *A Clockwork Orange*, a brutal sociopath, a mass murderer, is strapped to a chair and forced to watch violent movies while he is injected with a drug that nauseates him. So he sits and gags and retches as he watches the movies. After hundreds of repetitions of this, he associates violence with nausea, and it limits his ability to be violent.

We are doing the exact opposite: Our children watch vivid pictures of human suffering and death, and they learn to associate it with their favorite soft drink and candy bar, or their girlfriend's perfume.

After the Jonesboro shootings, one of the high-school teachers told me how her students reacted when she told them about the shootings at the middle school. "They laughed," she told me with dismay. A similar reaction happens all the time in movie theaters when there is bloody violence. The young people laugh and cheer and keep right on eating popcorn and drinking pop. We have raised a generation of barbarians who have learned to associate violence with pleasure, like the Romans cheering and snacking as the Christians were slaughtered in the Colosseum.

The result is a phenomenon that functions much like AIDS, which I call AVIDS—Acquired Violence Immune Deficiency Syndrome. AIDS has never killed anybody. It destroys your immune system, and then other diseases that shouldn't kill you become fatal. Television violence by itself does not kill you. It destroys your violence immune system and conditions you to derive pleasure from violence. And once you are at close range with another human being, and it's time for you to pull that trigger, Acquired Violence Immune Deficiency Syndrome can destroy your midbrain resistance.

Operant Conditioning

The third method the military uses is operant conditioning, a very powerful procedure of stimulus-response, stimulus-response. A benign example is the use of flight simulators to train pilots. An airline pilot in training sits in front of a flight simulator for endless hours; when a particular warning light goes on, he is taught to react in a certain way. When another warning light goes on, a different reaction is required. Stimulus-response, stimulus-response, stimulus-response. One day the pilot is actually flying a jumbo jet; the plane is going down, and 300 people are screaming behind him. He is wetting his seat cushion, and he is scared out of his wits; but he does the right thing. Why? Because he has been conditioned to respond reflexively to this particular crisis.

When people are frightened or angry, they will do what they have been conditioned to do. In fire drills, children learn to file out of the school in orderly fashion. One day there is a real fire, and they are frightened out of their wits; but they do exactly what they have been conditioned to do, and it saves their lives.

The military and law enforcement community have made killing a conditioned response. This has substantially raised the firing rate on the modern battlefield. Whereas infantry training in World War II used bull's-eye targets, now soldiers learn to fire at realistic, man-shaped silhouettes that pop into their field of view. That is the stimulus. The trainees have only a split second to engage the target. The conditioned response is to shoot the target, and then it drops. Stimulus-response, stimulus-response, stimulus-response—soldiers or police officers experience hundreds of repetitions. Later, when soldiers are on the battlefield or a police officer is walking a beat and somebody pops up with a gun, they will shoot reflexively and shoot to kill. We know that 75 to 80 percent of the shooting on the modern battlefield is the result of this kind of stimulus-response training.

Now, if you're a little troubled by that, how much more should we be troubled by the fact that every time a child plays an interactive point-and-shoot video game, he is learning the exact same conditioned reflex and motor skills. I was an expert witness in a murder case in South Carolina offering mitigation for a kid who was facing the death penalty. I tried to explain to the jury that interactive video games had conditioned him to shoot a gun to kill. He had spent hundreds of dollars on video games learning to point and shoot, point and shoot. One day he and his buddy decided it would be fun to rob the local convenience store. They walked in, and he pointed a snub-nosed .38 pistol at the clerk's head. The clerk turned to look at him, and the defendant shot reflexively from about six feet. The bullet hit the clerk right between the eyes— which is a pretty remarkable shot with that weapon at that range—and killed this father of two. Afterward, we asked the boy what happened and why he did it. It clearly was not part of the plan to kill the guy—it was being videotaped from six different directions. He said, "I don't know. It was a mistake. It wasn't supposed to happen."

In the military and law-enforcement worlds, the right option is often not to shoot. But you never, never put your quarter in that video machine with the intention of not shooting. There is always some stimulus that sets you off. And when he was excited, and his heart rate went up, and vasoconstriction closed his forebrain down, this young man did exactly what he was conditioned to do: he reflexively pulled the trigger, shooting accurately just like all those times he played video games.

This process is extraordinarily powerful and frightening. The result is ever more homemade pseudosociopaths who kill reflexively and show no remorse. Our children are learning to kill and learning to like it; and then we have the audacity to say, "Oh my goodness, what's wrong?"

One of the boys allegedly involved in the Jonesboro shootings (and they are just boys) had a fair amount of experience shooting real guns. The other one was a nonshooter and, to the best of our knowledge, had almost no experience shooting. Between them, those two boys fired 27 shots from a range of over 100 yards, and they hit 15 people. That's pretty remarkable shooting. We run into these situations often—kids who have never picked up a gun in their lives pick up a real gun and are incredibly accurate. Why? Video games.

Role Models

In the military, you are immediately confronted with a role model: your drill sergeant. He personifies violence and aggression. Along with military heroes, these violent role models have always been used to influence young, impressionable minds.

Today the media are providing our children with role models, and this can be seen not just in the lawless sociopaths in movies and TV shows, but it can also be seen in the media-inspired, copycat aspects of the Jonesboro murders. This is the part of these juvenile crimes that the TV networks would much rather not talk about.

Research in the 1970s demonstrated the existence of "cluster suicides" in which the local TV reporting of teen suicides directly caused numerous copycat suicides of impressionable teenagers. Somewhere in every population there are potentially suicidal kids who will say to themselves, "Well, I'll show all those people who have been mean to me. I know how to get my picture on TV, too." Because of this research, television stations today generally do not cover suicides. But when the pictures of teenage killers appear on TV, the effect is the same: Somewhere there is a potentially violent little boy who says to himself, "Well, I'll show all those people who have been mean to me. I know how to get my picture on TV, too."

Thus we get copycat, cluster murders that work their way across America like a virus spread by the six o'clock news. No matter what someone has done, if you put his picture on TV, you have made him a celebrity, and someone, somewhere, will emulate him.

The lineage of the Jonesboro shootings began at Pearl, Mississippi, fewer than six months before. In Pearl, a 16-year-old boy was accused of killing his mother and then going to his school and shooting nine students, two of whom died, including his ex-girlfriend. Two months later, this virus spread to Paducah, Kentucky, where a 14-year-old boy was arrested for killing three students and wounding five others.

A very important step in the spread of this copycat crime virus occurred in Stamps, Arkansas, 15 days after Pearl and just a little over 90 days before Jonesboro. In Stamps, a 14-year-old boy, who was angry at his schoolmates, hid in the woods and fired at children as they came out of school. Sound familiar? Only two children were injured in this crime, so most of the world didn't hear about it; but it got great regional coverage on TV, and two little boys in Jonesboro, Arkansas, probably did hear about it.

And then there was Springfield, Oregon, and so many others. Is this a reasonable price to pay for the TV networks' "right" to turn juvenile defendants into celebrities and role models by playing up their pictures on TV?

Our society needs to be informed about these crimes, but when the images of the young killers are broadcast on television, they become role models. The average preschooler in America watches 27 hours of television a week. The average child gets more one-on-one communication from TV than from all her parents and teachers combined. The ultimate achievement for our children is to get their picture on TV. The solution is simple, and it comes straight out of the suicidology literature: The media have every right and responsibility to tell the story, but they have no right to glorify the killers by presenting their images on TV.

Unlearning Violence

What is the road home from the dark and lonely place to which we have traveled? One route infringes on civil liberties. The city of New York has made remarkable progress in recent years in bringing down crime rates, but they may have done so at the expense of some civil liberties. People who are fearful say that is a price they are willing to pay.

Another route would be to "just turn it off"; if you don't like what is on television, use the "off" button. Yet, if all the parents of the 15 shooting victims in Jonesboro had protected their children from TV violence, it wouldn't have done a bit of good. Because somewhere there were two little boys whose parents didn't "just turn it off."

On the night of the Jonesboro shootings, clergy and counselors were working in small groups in the hospital waiting room, comforting the groups of relatives and friends of the victims. Then they noticed one woman sitting alone silently.

A counselor went over to the woman and discovered that she was the mother of one of the girls who had been killed. She had no friends, no husband, no family with her as she sat in the hospital, stunned by her loss. "I just came to find out how to get my little girl's body back," she said. But the body had been taken to Little Rock, 100 miles away, for an autopsy. Her very next concern was, "I just don't know how I'm going to pay for the funeral. I don't know how I can afford it." That little girl was truly all she had in all the world. Come to Jonesboro, friend, and tell this mother she should "just turn it off."

Another route to reduced violence is gun control. I don't want to downplay that option, but America is trapped in a vicious cycle when we talk about gun control. Americans don't trust the government; they believe that each of us should be responsible for taking care of ourselves and our families. That's one of our great strengths—but it is also a great weakness. When the media foster fear and perpetuate a milieu of violence, Americans arm themselves in order to deal with that violence. And the more guns there are out there, the more violence there is. And the more violence there is, the greater the desire for guns.

We are trapped in this spiral of self-dependence and lack of trust. Real progress will never be made until we reduce this level of fear. As a historian, I tell you it will take decades—maybe even a century—before we wean Americans off their guns. And until we reduce the level of fear and of violent crime, Americans would sooner die than give up their guns.

Fighting Back

We need to make progress in the fight against child abuse, racism, and poverty, and in rebuilding our families. No one is denying that the breakdown of the family is a factor. But nations without our divorce rates are also having increases in violence. Besides, research demonstrates that one major source of harm associated with single-parent families occurs when the TV becomes both the nanny and the second parent.

Work is needed in all these areas, but there is a new front—taking on the producers and purveyors of media violence. Simply put, we ought to work toward legislation that outlaws violent video games for children. There is *no* constitutional right for a child to play an interactive video game that teaches him weapons-handling skills or that simulates destruction of God's creatures.

The day may also be coming when we are able to seat juries in America who are willing to sock it to the networks in the only place they really understand—their wallets. After the Jonesboro shootings, *Time* magazine said: "As for media violence, the debate there is fast approaching the same point that discussions about the health impact of tobacco reached some time ago—it's over. Few researchers bother any longer to dispute that bloodshed on TV and in the movies has an effect on kids who witness it" (April 6, 1998).

Most of all, the American people need to learn the lesson of Jonesboro: Violence is not a game; it's not fun, it's not something that we do for entertainment. Violence kills.

⟨◉⟩

Every parent in America desperately needs to be warned of the impact of TV and other violent media on children, just as we would warn them of some widespread carcinogen. The problem is that the TV networks, which use the public airwaves we have licensed to them, are our key means of public education in America. And they are stonewalling.

In the days after the Jonesboro shootings, I was interviewed on Canadian national TV, the British Broadcasting Company, and many U.S. and international radio shows and newspapers. But the American television networks simply would not touch this aspect of the story. Never in my experience as a historian and a psychologist have I seen any institution in America so clearly responsible for so very many deaths, and so clearly abusing their publicly licensed authority and power to cover up their guilt.

Time after time, idealistic young network producers contacted me from one of the networks, fascinated by the irony that an expert in the field of violence and aggression was living in Jonesboro and was at the school almost from the beginning. But unlike all the other media, these network news stories always died a sudden, silent death when the network's powers-that-be said, "Yeah, we need this story like we need a hole in the head."

Many times since the shooting I have been asked, "Why weren't you on TV talking about the stuff in your book?" And every time my answer had to be, "The TV networks are burying this story. They know they are guilty, and they want to delay the retribution as long as they can."

As an author and expert on killing, I believe I have spoken on the subject at every Rotary, Kiwanis, and Lions Club in a 50-mile radius of Jonesboro. So when the plague of satellite dishes descended upon us like huge locusts, many people here were aware of the scientific data linking TV violence and violent crime.

The networks will stick their lenses anywhere and courageously expose anything. Like flies on open wounds, they find nothing too private or shameful for their probing lenses—except themselves, and their share of guilt in the terrible, tragic crime that happened here.

A CBS executive told me his plan. He knows all about the link between media and violence. His own in-house people have advised him to protect his child from the poison his industry is bringing to America's children. He is not going to expose his child to TV until she's old enough to learn how to read. And then he will select very carefully what she sees. He and his wife plan to send her to a daycare center that has no television, and he plans to show her only age-appropriate videos.

That should be the bare minimum with children: Show them only age-appropriate videos, and think hard about what is age-appropriate.

The most benign product you are going to get from the networks are 22-minute sitcoms or cartoons providing instant solutions for all of life's problems, interlaced with commercials telling you what a slug you are if you don't ingest the right sugary substances and don't wear the right shoes.

The worst product your child is going to get from the networks is represented by one TV commentator who told me, "Well, we only have one really violent show on our network, and that is *NYPD Blue.* I'll admit that that is bad, but it is only one night a week."

I wondered at the time how she would feel if someone said, "Well, I only beat my wife in front of the kids one night a week." The effect is the same.

"You're not supposed to know who I am!" said *NYPD Blue* star Kim Delaney, in response to young children who recognized her from her role on that show. According to *USA Weekend,* she was shocked that underage viewers watch her show, which is rated TV-14 for gruesome crimes, raw language, and explicit sex scenes. But they do watch, don't they?

Education about media and violence does make a difference. I was on a radio call-in show in San Antonio, Texas. A woman called and said, "I would never have had the courage to do this two years ago. But let me tell you what happened. You tell me if I was right.

"My 13-year-old boy spent the night with a neighbor boy. After that night, he started having nightmares. I got him to admit what the nightmares were about. While he was at the neighbor's house, they watched splatter movies all night: people cutting people up with chain saws and stuff like that.

"I called the neighbors and told them, 'Listen: you are sick people. I wouldn't feel any different about you if you had given my son pornography or alcohol. And I'm not going to have anything further to do with you or your son—and neither is anybody else in this neighborhood, if I have anything to do with it—until you stop what you're doing.' "

That's powerful. That's censure, not censorship. We ought to have the moral courage to censure people who think that violence is legitimate entertainment.

One of the most effective ways for Christians to be salt and light is by simply confronting the culture of violence as entertainment. A friend of mine, a retired army officer who teaches at a nearby middle school, uses the movie *Gettysburg* to teach his students about the Civil War. A scene in that movie very dramatically depicts the tragedy of Pickett's Charge. As the Confederate troops charge into the Union lines, the cannons fire into their masses at point-blank range, and there is nothing but a red mist that comes up from the smoke and flames. He told me that when he first showed this heart-wrenching, tragic scene to his students, they laughed.

He began to confront this behavior ahead of time by saying: "In the past, students have laughed at this scene, and I want to tell you that this is completely unacceptable behavior. This movie depicts a tragedy in American history, a tragedy that happened to our ancestors, and I will not tolerate any laughing." From then on, when he played that scene to his students, over the years, he says there was no laughter. Instead, many of them wept.

What the media teach is unnatural, and if confronted in love and assurance, the house they have built on the sand will crumble. But our house is built on the rock. If we don't actively present our values, then the media will most assuredly inflict theirs on our children, and the children, like those in that class watching *Gettysburg,* simply won't know any better.

There are many other things that the Christian community can do to help change our culture. Youth activities can provide alternatives to television, and churches can lead the way in providing alternative locations for latchkey children. Fellowship groups can provide guidance and support to young parents as they strive to raise their children without the destructive influences of the media. Mentoring programs can pair mature, educated adults with young parents to help them through the preschool ages without using the TV as a babysitter. And most of all, the churches can provide the clarion call of decency and love and peace as an alternative to death and destruction—not just for the sake of the church, but for the transformation of our culture.

Wendy Melillo

 **NO**

After Columbine, Legislators Attack Media Violence

Is our culture toxic? The Senate thinks so. It claims the makers of violent movies, videogames and music are peddling death to kids—and that their marketing practices should be investigated. Capitol Hill is turning the Columbine tragedy into political fortune. Sen. Orrin Hatch (R-Utah) cites ads in gaming magazines aimed at teenagers for videogames Destrega, which states, "Let the slaughter begin," and for Carmageddan, which boasts, "As easy as killing babies with axes." Hatch says ads for Resident Evil 2, a violent videogame rated for adults only, appeared in *Sports Illustrated for Kids.* Not to be outmaneuvered, Democrats exhibited gun ads in youth magazines. During debate on the Senate floor, Sen. Barbara Boxer (D-Calif.) held up gun ads and a catalog of colorful photos from gun maker Beretta's "Youth Collection" that touted "an exciting, bold designer look that's sure to make you stand out in a crowd." Boxer's proposal—to require an investigation of gun marketing practices along with the Federal Trade Commission study of violent entertainment aimed at children—was reluctantly accepted by Republicans.

Why are the parties likely to find the big bad wolf in opposite camps? Money. Republicans point to Hollywood because it's a big Democratic supporter. (Ironically, many GOP politicians who denounce Hollywood accept its lucre. Bob Dole's '95 anti-Hollywood speech did not include legislation.) Conversely, Democrats lay the Littleton, Colo., massacre at the feet of the National Rifle Association, which supports the wide availability of guns and the Republican Party, (although Hillary Clinton recently slammed filmmakers for debasing the culture). Did someone say elections?

"The issues are deeper than the media, advertising and products," says Paul Kurnit, president of New York-based Griffin Bacal, who agrees that advertisers should be sensitive to the audience videogames target. "It relates to what's going on in the family, in schools and what kind of communication we have with our kids."

Welcome to round two in Congress' war against media violence. Last time politicians traveled this road, we got the V-chip. Now, with national attention riveted on Littleton, legislative proposals are attempting to curtail commercial speech.

For instance: Several proposals have been attached to a massive juvenile justice bill called "The Violent and Repeat Juvenile Offender Accountability and Rehabilitation Act." One proposal requires the National Institute of Health to study whether violent videogames and music lyrics adversely affect a child's emotional and psychological development. Another allows the FTC [Federal Trade Commission] and the Department of Justice [DOJ] to subpoena entertainment-industry marketing plans and internal memos to determine who is marketing violence to children.

More telling, a joint probe by the FTC and DOJ would allow Congress to launch what ad lobbyists call "a fishing expedition" to determine the extent companies target violent and sexually explicit material to kids, and "whether such content is advertised or promoted in media outlets in which minors comprise a substantial percentage of the audience." The study would also include whether retailers honor voluntary industry codes and labeling systems.

"This is a modest but necessary first step toward encouraging a sense of corporate responsibility among some of the most powerful corporations in the world," says Sen. Sam Brownback (R-Kan.), who introduced the legislation along with Hatch, Joseph Lieberman (D-Conn.) and Wayne Allard (R-Colo.).

Advertisers, however, fear that the Republican thirst for revenge against Hollywood, combined with a political desire to create knee-jerk solutions to complex problems, has created enough momentum to get the bill passed. But first things first.

Lieberman and Sen. John McCain (R-Ariz.) recently introduced a separate bill that would create a national commission of experts to study youth violence. Lieberman said he and his colleagues will "push the entertainment industry to stop glorifying and romanticizing violence. In particular, to stop marketing murder and mayhem directly to kids." Ad lobbyists heatedly counter that there's no evidence that violent media content prompts kids to pick up a gun and kill.

"Before you talk about enforcing codes and censoring marketing, you need to know what the causes of violence are," says John Fithian, counsel to the Freedom to Advertise Coalition in Washington, D.C.

While research indicates that viewing violence can cause aggression, studies conclude that the leading determinant of violent behavior is upbringing. Predictably, politicians have been silent on this finding. Poor parenting, after all, is not a traditional vote-getter.

So what's the responsible thing to do? Sen. Robert Byrd (D-W. Va.), a moderate, says Hollywood and the NRA alike "bear some responsibility to end the madness." Byrd's nonpartisan plea hopes to transcend political backbiting, a notion Edgar Bronfman Jr., CEO of Seagram, Universal Studio's parent company, seconds. "Violence is not an entertainment problem, it's a societal problem. The government [should] deal with it . . . rather than create a quick fix that may be popular but is ultimately a disservice to constituents," says Bronfman, one of the first Hollywood CEOs to speak out. Until now, moguls have been reluctant to discuss the issue with lawmakers or testify.

They may change their mind after the Senate's violence study, which will try to determine whether any of their companies' current marketing practices violate federal law. This raises a thorny problem for the FTC because, unlike tobacco, there is no federal law that says marketing violent media content to those under 18 is illegal.

To bring a case under its unfair trade practices statute, as it did with Joe Camel, the FTC would have to prove that entertainment companies deliberately target violent content to kids—and that it caused harm. The irony, as advertisers know, is that Hollywood reduced smoking in movies and ads so kids didn't get the wrong idea. But glamorizing weapons, which is equally dangerous, continues unabated. "There is no statute that says you can't advertise an R-rated movie to 15-year-olds," says Douglas J. Wood of the New York-based law firm Hall Dickler Kent Friedman & Wood. "They would have to show that not only was there intent to do something wrong, but that 15-year-olds didn't know any better and were harmed by improper enticement." Meanwhile, Sen. Ernest Hollings (D-S.C.) has resurrected an unwelcome idea advertisers thought was dead. His proposal would give the Federal Communications Commission power to decide which TV shows are violent. Any show deemed unsuitable for kids would be banished to late-night hours. Though Hollings' proposal was defeated, he vows to win approval.

Republicans were reluctant to include it at this time because of a previous agreement with the entertainment industry that gives the V-chip three years to work before imposing content restrictions. By 2000, all new TV sets 13 inches or larger must include it. Still, a number of shows do not carry a "V" rating for violence. One expert testified last week that even with the V-chip ratings, four out of five shows would still carry violent scenes.

Dan Jaffe, executive vice president of the National Association of Advertisers, has another worry: The Senate has forgotten the First Amendment. He wonders how far Congress will go to curb media violence. "We are not concerned about giving parents power to protect their families," Jaffe says, "but now the government is putting itself in the role of parent—and that's dangerous. A national nanny is not the solution to these problems."

POSTSCRIPT

Are Marketers Culpable for America's Culture of Violence?

America's culture of violence is an extremely complex problem with many contributing factors. While many argue that responsibility rests predominantly with parents, society is also profoundly responsible—and largely failing—as evidenced by the steady stream of injuries and deaths horribly illustrated in U.S. schools and streets. In James T. Hamilton's book *Channeling Violence* (Princeton University Press, 1998), he contends, "If it bleeds, it leads." This refers to the trend of news programs to open with the most violent stories first. While this practice attracts both viewers and sponsors, it does not create a favorable atmosphere for violence.

Marketers point to other factors to bear responsibility. Some cite deteriorating soundness, effectiveness, and vitality of public schools in the United States. Others look toward the demographics of single-parent households, the impermanence of marriage, and the lack of quality-time supervision as factors that create a volatile and insecure environment for American children. Of paramount importance to many is the availability of guns and their access to children. The gun manufacturer Smith and Wesson recently agreed to ensure gun-owner security measures. But the mandate for self-regulation is clear. Marketers who fail to respond by acting as responsible corporate citizens will face serious regulatory measures, as outlined by Melillo.

Suggested Readings

Kelly Anders, "Marketing and Policy Considerations for Violent Video Games," *Journal of Public Policy and Marketing* (Fall 1999)

Sissela Bok, *Mayhem: Violence As Public Entertainment* (Perseus Books, 1999)

Joanne Cantor, *Mommy, I'm Scared: How TV and Movies Frighten Children and What We Can Do to Protect Them* (Harcourt Brace, 1998)

Mark Del Franco, "Mailers Still Packing the Heat," *Catalog Age* (July 1999)

Jeffrey H. Goldstein, ed., *Why We Watch: The Attractions of Violent Entertainment* (Oxford University Press, 1998)

James T. Hamilton, ed., *Television Violence and Public Policy* (University of Michigan Press, 1998)

Lisa M. Keefe, "Too Much Sex and Violence on the Net," *Marketing News* (July 5, 1999)

ISSUE 18

Should Alcohol Advertising Be Regulated Further?

YES: Laurie Leiber, from "Should the Government Restrict Advertising of Alcoholic Beverages? Yes," *Priorities for Long Life and Good Health* (vol. 9, no. 3, 1997)

NO: Federal Trade Commission, from *FTC Reports on Industry Efforts to Avoid Promoting Alcohol to Underage Consumers* (September 9, 1999)

ISSUE SUMMARY

YES: Laurie Leiber, director of the Center on Alcohol Advertising, contends that the increased awareness of beer commercials on TV leads to favorable beliefs about underage drinking and increases the likelihood of youngsters' intentions to drink as adults. She asserts that Americans are becoming favorably disposed toward restricting or eliminating broadcast advertising of alcohol.

NO: The Federal Trade Commission (FTC) addresses the needs and benefits of self-regulation to prevent alcohol advertising from influencing underage drinkers. The FTC examines the problems and guidelines for ad placement, ad content, product placement in movies, college marketing, and online advertising.

$\mathbf{M}$any contend that the alcohol industry creates favorable beliefs about underage drinking and portrays alcohol as an integral part of sports, holidays, and American culture through the use of TV commercials. Many believe that children are more likely to drink alcohol earlier in life than they would if they were not exposed to such a barrage of positive images of alcohol consumption. Research has shown that junior high school kids can name more brands of beer than they can U.S. presidents. Beer appears to be the beverage of choice—and many consider it a "gateway" drug—for teenagers. Experts say that consuming beer as a teenager will likely lead later in life to products with a higher alcohol content. The pipeline of new products that are low-alcohol but packaged similarly to tasty fruit drinks—such as "Alco pops," refreshers, and wine coolers— are a source of criticism. These are considered by many to be "bridge drinks," with particular appeal to youthful new consumers who do not like the taste of alcohol but enjoy fruit/juice drinks.

The liquor industry, having honored a pledge not to advertise distilled spirits for 50 years on broadcast media, shocked the nation by breaking its voluntary ban in 1996. Most notably, Seagram's placed a series of ads for Crown Royal Canadian whiskey. After two decades of declining sales (consumption fell almost 30 percent from 1980 to 1995), Seagram's turned to television for a short period. But a negative public reaction, an outcry from special interest groups, and the threat of regulation has halted broadcast advertising of alcohol products, at least for the time being. In contrast, beer consumption has increased by 20 percent per capita since it has dominated television advertising, representing 94 percent of alcoholic beverage spending in 1996. Do broadcasters who refuse to run their ads but who are amenable to beer and wine advertising discriminate against distilled liquor companies?

The question of advertising effectiveness with regard to alcohol consumption is central to this debate. Critics contend that beer ads influence the perceptions of millions of children, exaggerating positive associations with alcohol while "whitewashing" its potentially negative effects. They illustrate common themes in beer ads, which sell their brands as "tickets to friendship, success, happiness, athletic accomplishment, and sexual conquest." Critics also suggest that marketing influences the manner, style, and meaning of drinking in society. Many agree that advertising is not the sole, nor the most important, influence on alcohol consumption for youth or adults. But beer marketers contend that they are simply trying to promote and differentiate their specific brands and that advertising has no effect on the total consumption of their products. Critics consider this argument disingenuous at best, and they point to the hundreds of millions of dollars the industry spends on advertising as proof that such heavy investments surely must be made only to bring in new consumers and cause existing ones to drink more.

Laurie Leiber and others feel that self-regulation by the alcohol industry is inadequate, and they challenge the assertion that public service announcements (PSAs) sponsoring "responsible drinking" are sufficient. The practice of promoting malt liquor on MTV, which has an audience of almost 70 percent below the legal drinking age of 21 (according to *Advertising Age*), has been called a travesty. Competition for the share of the burgeoning "generation Y" market is not expected to end the aggressive marketing of alcohol products on a voluntary, self-regulatory basis. Many feel that *all* broadcast advertising of alcoholic products should be banned.

The FTC favors self-regulation because it contends that it is a realistic and responsive approach to the problem of blatant appeals and advertising to underage consumers. The agency sees self-regulation as a quicker, more flexible solution than government intervention. Since alcohol is illegal for those under age 21, and freedom of speech protects advertisers in marketing their products, the FTC has made recommendations concerning specific standards and advertising codes it wants the industry to enforce. In the second of the following selections, the FTC presents a series of recommendations concerning third-party reviews, advertising placements, and "best practices."

Laurie Leiber

Should the Government Restrict Advertising of Alcoholic Beverages?—Yes

For nearly two decades, two U.S. Surgeon Generals—C. Everett Koop and Antonia Novello—and numerous public health organizations—including the American Academy of Pediatrics, the National Parent Teachers Association, the American Medical Association, and Mothers Against Drunk Driving—have called upon manufacturers of alcoholic beverages to advertise more responsibly. National polls show that Americans increasingly favor either restricting or banning broadcast alcohol advertising.

But despite this widespread support for advertising reform, the alcohol industry—using its considerable political clout and such preemptive PR strategies as public-service campaigns and voluntary advertising codes—has averted government limits. During the same 20 years, public health advocates working at local, state, and national levels began implementing a new approach to preventing alcohol-related problems. This new public health response is based on a substantial and growing body of evidence that limiting both alcohol advertising and alcohol availability and raising alcohol taxes decreases alcohol-related problems.

Alcohol-industry representatives often cite the incompleteness of the research record on alcohol advertising as proof that alcohol promotion has no impact on consumption. However, to clarify the impact of promotional efforts—efforts on which the industry spends $2 billion annually—independent researchers have begun to frame questions and pursue studies on the relationship between alcohol advertising and behavior and health.

Although more research is needed, there is strong scientific evidence that the effects of alcohol advertising, like the effects of tobacco advertising, are not limited to brand selection by adults. Research conducted by Joel W. Grube and Lawrence Wallack suggests that awareness of TV beer commercials leads to favorable beliefs about drinking in children 10 to 12 years old and increases their intention to drink as adults. Henry Saffer compared motor-vehicle deaths with quarterly measures for broadcast advertising in 75 media markets over a three-year period. He concluded that a ban on broadcast alcohol advertising would save 2,000 to 3,000 people annually from death due to alcohol-related motor-vehicle crashes.

In the past, alcoholic-beverage producers have argued that their voluntary public-service campaigns are more effective at decreasing alcohol-related problems than are government-imposed limits on alcohol advertising. But while public-service messages may engender goodwill for the companies sponsoring them, researchers DeJong, Atkin, and Wallack have described these "responsible drinking" spots as thinly disguised drinking promotions. The longest-running campaign, Anheuser-Busch's "Know When to Say When," omits that sometimes it is not safe to imbibe at all. The campaign also leaves "when" undefined. At a recent Anheuser-Busch board meeting, officers opposed a shareholder request to add the U.S. Dietary Guidelines definition of moderation to the company's alcohol awareness materials.

Manufacturers of alcoholic beverages also assert that, because responsible advertising is advantageous to the industry, government-imposed restrictions are unnecessary. Trade groups representing the three branches of the alcohol industry (wine, beer, and distilled spirits) have adopted voluntary advertising codes. But these voluntary standards have not prevented the brewers from turning Halloween into a beer festival, marketing malt liquor on MTV, or using cute cartoon animals in commercials aired on TV during peak viewing times for young people.

Neither did the industry's standards prevent liquor producers from ending their decades-long voluntary ban on broadcast liquor commercials. After Seagram broke the ban in June 1996, the Distilled Spirits Council of the United States (DISCUS) simply rewrote its Code of Good Practice.

Since then, commercials for Seagram's Crown Royale whiskey that feature dogs, ducks, and peacocks have appeared during weekend telecasts of college and professional sports events, broadcasts of ABC's *Monday Night Football*, and a 7:00 P.M. *Cosby Show* rerun. Print ads for liquor—a magazine mainstay—appear in periodicals such as *Spin,* nearly half of whose readers are under 21, and *Allure,* 44 percent of whose readers are underage. Billboard and print ads for Gordon's gin feature a cartoon boar. Quirky cutout characters populate Tanqueray vodka ads.

In terms of both content and placement, manufacturers of alcoholic beverages find few real limitations in the industry's voluntary advertising guidelines. Research conducted in spring 1996 by the Center on Alcohol Advertising showed that children aged 9 to 11 are more familiar with the Budweiser frogs than they are with Smokey Bear or Tony the Tiger.

Anheuser-Busch, the maker of Budweiser, responded to widespread criticism of the frog commercials by citing the adult appeal of the croaking amphibians. According to the Beer Institute ad code, if a symbol or character appeals to persons over 21, beer makers are free to use that image in their promotions no matter how much the image appeals to children.

The industry's voluntary standards also address settings in which alcohol ads should not appear. According to the Beer Institute's code, beer advertising is inappropriate for TV programs most of whose audience is "reasonably expected to be below the legal purchase age." However, both *Advertising Age* and *The Wall*

Street Journal have reported that beer ads on MTV reached viewers 69 percent of whom were below the legal drinking age of 21.

The pertinent section of the Beer Institute's Advertising and Marketing Code reads: "Beer advertising and marketing materials should not be placed in magazines, newspapers, television programs, radio programs, or other media where most of the audience is reasonably expected to be below the legal purchase age." This means that the Institute does not consider an ad placement questionable unless at least half the audience is underage. In December 1996, possibly because it foresaw the *AdAge* and *WSJ* reports, Anheuser-Busch moved its ads from MTV to VH-1, a cable station whose proportion of adult viewers is higher. Five months later, Miller, the number-two brewing company, announced that it would follow suit.

While broadcasters and advertisers routinely use detailed reports of audience demographics to develop marketing strategies, this information is not generally available to people concerned about the impact of broadcast advertising on the welfare of children or of the public. The "sentinel effect" of the *AdAge* and *WSJ* reports is temporary and narrow, affecting only a handful of cable stations.

Our government should mandate monitoring the reach of alcohol commercials and should hold broadcasters responsible for limiting young people's exposure to such advertising. By law, television and radio stations licensed to broadcast on the public airwaves must do so in the public interest. The Federal Communications Commission (FCC) does not collect information on the frequency of alcohol commercials; nor does it gather age information on the viewers of such ads. The FCC could use such information to set goals for decreasing youth exposure. The agency could also require broadcasters to provide equal time for health-and-safety messages when alcohol commercials air during primetime or sports programs that reach large numbers of underage viewers.

While broadcast ads probably constitute their most powerful marketing tool, producers of alcoholic beverages use various other media to reach young consumers. Control of unethical alcohol advertising in these other media will require different strategies: An ordinance in Baltimore restricts billboard ads for alcoholic beverages to certain areas of the city. Citizens of Marin County, California, petitioned to eliminate prizes "decorated" with beer logos from the midway at their county fair. In 1996 groups in several states asked their alcoholic-beverage control agencies to ban Halloween-theme displays for beer in convenience stores and groceries. And the Federal Trade Commission's vote to restrict the use of R. J. Reynolds' Joe Camel character may open the door to similar action against "unfair" alcohol ads.

Advocates of public health and safety should press for mandatory limits on alcohol promotions that reach underage consumers, as manufacturers of alcoholic beverages have demonstrated that they cannot be trusted to market their products responsibly. The manufacturers are well aware that maintaining industry profits depends on "recruiting" young drinkers. Most Americans "mature out" of heavy drinking by their mid to late 20s, but an analysis of American alcohol consumption shows that heavy drinkers dominate the market: A mere 5 percent of the population drinks 53 percent of all the alcohol consumed in this country. Because nearly half of all young people in the U.S. begin drinking before they have graduated from junior high school, competition for market share among the next group of heavy drinkers means attracting people well below the legal drinking age. And people who begin drinking when they are very young are the likeliest lifelong heavy drinkers.

No one should expect alcoholic-beverage manufacturers to end their aggressive targeting of young people voluntarily. The industry is fiercely competitive and thus far has not placed children's welfare above profits. The costs to the United States of alcohol consumption are tremendous, with recent estimates approaching $100 billion per year. Our government has a legitimate interest in reducing both these costs and the human costs of alcohol-related illness, injury, and death. Restricting the promotion of alcoholic beverages, and particularly their promotion to children, should be part of a comprehensive strategy to abate alcohol-related problems through policy reform.

FTC Reports on Industry Efforts to Avoid Promoting Alcohol to Underage Consumers

Although the alcohol industry generally complies with existing self-regulatory standards intended to prevent alcohol advertising that appeals to underage consumers, industry self-regulatory efforts should be improved, a report by the Federal Trade Commission [FTC] released [September 9, 1999] states. The report, "Self-Regulation in the Alcohol Industry," reviews voluntary efforts by alcohol companies and trade associations to engage in self-regulation to avoid promoting alcohol to teenagers and young adults. It examines alcohol ad placement and content, product placement, online advertising and college marketing, and highlights "best practices" currently followed by some companies, which if more widely adopted, would improve overall self-regulation efforts. The report recommends that industry improve enforcement by adopting third-party review of compliance, and reduce underage exposure to alcohol ads by changing the current placement standards that allow advertising in media when as much as 50 percent of the audience is under 21.

"Underage alcohol use and abuse are significant national concerns," said FTC Chairman Robert Pitofsky. "Last year, a third of twelfth graders reported binge drinking. Finding ways to deter alcohol use by those under 21 is a challenge for government agencies, consumer organizations and the beverage alcohol industry."

"This report offers insights into the self-regulatory system the industry uses to reduce the likelihood that alcohol advertising will reach and appeal to underage consumers," Pitofsky said. "Self-regulation can deal quickly and flexibly with a wide range of advertising issues and brings the accumulated experience and judgment of an industry to bear. While we found that the alcohol industry, for the most part, complies with its existing codes, our review also identified steps the industry can and should take in this area."

From Federal Trade Commission, *FTC Reports on Industry Efforts to Avoid Promoting Alcohol to Underage Consumers* (September 9, 1999). Washington, DC: U.S. Government Printing Office, 1999.

The report, prepared in response to a joint request from the House and Senate Committees on Appropriations, is based on "special reports" filed with the Commission by eight key alcohol industry members, discussions with industry trade associations, a review of alcohol company web sites, and information provided by interested government agencies and consumer groups. It describes key provisions of the industry's voluntary advertising codes and identifies strengths and weaknesses in the current system.

The report recommends that all industry members adopt and build upon the industry's current best practices—enforcement policies that go beyond minimum code requirements. The best practices identified by the report are as follows:

- *For ad placement:* Reduce the percentage of the underage audience, bar placement on television series and in other media with the largest underage audiences, and conduct regular audits of previous product placements.
- *For ad content:* Prohibit ads with substantial underage appeal, even if they also appeal to adults; or target ads to persons 25 and older.
- *For product placement in movies and television:* Restrict the promotional placement of alcohol products to "R" and "NC-17" rated films (or, if unrated, to films with similarly mature themes) and apply the standards for placing traditional advertising to product placement on television.
- *For online advertising:* Use available mechanisms to reduce underage access and avoid content that would attract underage consumers.
- *For college marketing:* Curb on-campus and spring break sponsorships and advertising.

The special reports were filed by the beverage alcohol companies in response to Commission orders issued in August 1998. The eight companies are: Anheuser-Busch, Inc.; Bacardi-Martini USA, Inc.; Brown-Forman Corporation; Coors Brewing Company, Inc.; Diageo plc; Miller Brewing Company, Inc.; Stroh Brewery Company, Inc.; and Joseph E. Seagram & Sons, Inc.

The three trade associations are: The Beer Institute, which represents the interests of more than 200 brewers that produce more than 90 percent of the beer brewed in the U.S. and comprises a majority of the imported beer consumed here; the Distilled Spirits Council of the United States, which represents most of the major U.S. distilled spirits marketers—its members produce over 85 percent of the distilled spirits sold here; and the Wine Institute, which represents over 300 California vintners—its members market over 75 percent of the wine sold in the United States, as well as most of the American wines sold abroad.

Advertising Codes

All three associations have voluntary codes with similar provisions about the placement and content of ads designed to prevent the marketing of alcohol to underage consumers. Some companies also have individual guides that, in most cases, parallel those of the trade associations.

Advertising Placement

In general, the codes currently require that more than 50 percent of the audience for their advertising be over 21.

The report reflects mixed compliance with the codes' requirement. "Half of the companies were able to show that nearly all of their ads were shown to a majority legal-age audience," the report notes. The other four companies did not fare as well. Two companies' data showed weeks when many ads (as high as 25 percent) were shown to majority underage audiences. Two others failed to provide reliable information showing the audience for their ads, and thus could not demonstrate whether or not they complied with the codes' placement provisions.

In addition to reporting on the industry's compliance, the report points out that only 30 percent of the U.S. population is under the age of 21, and only 10 percent is age 11 to 17. "The 50 percent standard, therefore, permits placement of ads on programs where the underage population far exceeds its representation in the population."

The report recommends that the industry raise the current standard to reduce underage alcohol ad exposure. For example, it notes that some companies restrict advertising to shows in which underage consumers represent not more than 40, 30 or even 25 percent of the audience. To ensure compliance with the higher placement standard, companies should measure their compliance against the most reliable up-to-date audience composition data available, according to the report's recommendations.

Advertising Content

The codes prohibit alcohol advertisers from using advertising content that is *more* appealing to underage consumers than to adults, including 21 year olds. Each of the three codes also expressly prohibits the use of certain characters or people in alcohol ads such as: actors under 25 (Beer); children (Spirits); Santa Claus (Beer and Spirits); and sports celebrities or "current or traditional heros of the young" (Wine).

The report notes that industry members appear to make significant efforts to comply with the codes' standards, instructing their staffs and ad agencies to avoid content with greater appeal to kids than to adults. At the same time, it notes that the standard permits ads targeted at 21-year-olds, although they might also have "overflow" appeal to younger consumers, and that existing research raises the question whether some recent campaigns indeed have high underage appeal. Again, the report identifies best practices that some companies follow that reduce the likelihood that an ad will have substantial appeal to underage consumers.

Product Placement

Product placement is the practice of getting an alcohol beverage brand used as a prop in a film or television show. Many alcohol companies hire an agent or use internal staff to seek product placements. According to the report, in 1997–98 the eight reporting companies placed products in 233 motion pictures and in one or more episodes of 181 different television series.

The report states that "alcohol placement has occurred in 'PG' and 'PG-13' films with significant appeal to teens and children; in films where the advertiser knew that the primary target market included a sizeable underage market; and on eight of the 15 television shows most popular with teens." The report notes that a few companies have taken steps to reduce the likelihood that a substantial underage audience will see their products promoted in movies and on television.

Online Advertising

"Members of the beverage alcohol industry have created over 100 commercial web sites to promote their products," the report states. While the Wine Institute's code does not address online advertising, the Beer code and Spirits code do, and most companies comply with the provisions of these two codes.

"There are, of course, no foolproof measures to prevent underage access to inappropriate web sites," the report states. "Companies therefore need to give special attention not only to restricting access, but to ensuring that web site content is not attractive to underage consumers."

The report outlines the best practices that some companies have taken to attempt to address concerns about online alcohol sites. For example, it notes that some have discontinued the use of content that may appeal to underage users.

College Marketing

"Advertising on campuses remains a source of concern given the presence of a significant underage audience on most campuses and the high incidence of abusive college drinking," the report states. The Distilled Spirits Council of the United States and a growing number of colleges and universities prohibit marketing activities on campus, and most companies have stopped sponsoring special spring break activities, although not mandated by the code. The report urges more alcohol companies to curb campus advertising and marketing.

Code Enforcement

While the report notes that most industry members seek to comply with current code requirements, compliance is not universal. Currently, complaints regarding alcohol advertising practices are considered by the company itself, in the case of beer and wine industries; and by a review board within the trade association, in the case of the distilled spirits industry. The report recommends that the industry should provide for third-party review by creating independent external review boards with responsibility and authority to address complaints from the public or other industry members. "Experience in other industries suggests that independent mechanisms for evaluating compliance, particularly in the face of complaints from the public or competitors, ensure that industry members are held to reasonably consistent standards," the report points out.

According to the report, "the recommended changes would promote the goals underlying the codes, as well as improve public confidence in industry's efforts to self-police."

The Commission vote to authorize release of the report was 4-0.

POSTSCRIPT

Should Alcohol Advertising Be Regulated Further?

In light of recent developments in the tobacco and firearm industries, with government controls devastating the tobacco industry and product safety and marketing restrictions looming for the firearms industry, advocates and attorneys have "tasted blood." Many believe that marketers of alcoholic beverages place profits before concerns related to influencing underage drinkers. Many of the same ingredients for inviting public wrath are present. Will self-regulation alone stem the tide of public displeasure toward alcohol advertising?

A number of European countries have already faced this issue. Sweden has banned *all* advertisements targeted to children under 12 years of age, and efforts are being made to get the entire European bloc to do the same. There have been many recent attempts to get Congress to further regulate and even bar alcohol advertising targeted to children. Proponents of the industry contend that this is an issue of freedom of speech. They point to the increase in PSAs as evidence of their efforts to promote responsible drinking.

A key issue extends beyond the boundaries of alcohol advertising. It is the visible trend, the collective momentum, that society can build and bring to bear against a product category that falls into public disfavor. Advocates, lawyers, and special interest groups have the power to sway national sentiment and cripple marketing efforts through advertising regulations, taxes, safety requirements, and class action suits. Is this merely democracy at work or something more insidious? For example, the use of cell phones in vehicles is alleged by some sources to cause as many accidents as drunken drivers do. For this reason, should cell phones be restricted or outlawed entirely?

Suggested Readings

Sally Beatty, "Seagram Baits the Ad Hook for Television," *The Wall Street Journal* (September 15, 1996)

George A. Hacker, "Liquor Advertisements on Television: Just Say No," *Journal of Public Policy and Marketing* (Spring 1998)

Laurie Leiber, *Commercial and Character Slogan Recall by Children Aged 9 to 11 Years: Budweiser Frogs Versus Bugs Bunny* (Center on Alcohol Advertising, 1996)

Joseph C. Fisher and Peter A. Cook, *Advertising, Alcohol Consumption, and Morality* (Greenwood Press, 1995)

The Beer Institute. http://www.beerinst.org

ISSUE 19

Is It Appropriate for the Government to Market Lotteries?

YES: Edward J. Stanek, from "Take the High Road and Keep the Upper Hand," Speech Delivered to the North American Association of State and Provincial Lotteries at its Twenty-Third Annual Meeting in Boston, Massachusetts (September 29, 1997)

NO: National Gambling Impact Study Commission, from *Lotteries* (May 29, 1998)

ISSUE SUMMARY

YES: Edward J. Stanek, president of the North American Association of State and Provincial Lotteries, argues for the benefits derived from state-promoted lotteries and against time-worn criticisms of state-sanctioned lotteries.

NO: The National Gambling Impact Study Commission, based on a two-year study of the social and economic impact of gambling in the United States, outlines criticisms of lotteries, such as offering the worst odds, misleading allocation of funds, and deceptive, inappropriate advertising.

The gambling industry in America has taken off. Revenues from all legal state-sponsored lotteries now exceed over $33 billion a year. This is more than revenues from movies, books, recorded music, and park and arcade attractions combined. Now referred to as the "gaming" industry, it includes casinos and all categories of legal gambling. Critics consider it unethical for the state to be marketing a vice, and successful marketing it is, indeed. In 1998 state lotteries spent close to $2 billion in advertising and the administration of lotteries.

State lotteries are distinct from other gaming products in that players risk small amounts of money against very large odds to win a large prize, with net proceeds going to the public good. While lotteries can be traced to antiquity and were common throughout the American Revolution, they were established in their current form in New Hampshire in 1964. Now they are operating in 37 states and the District of Columbia. The principal argument in each state for promoting the adoption of state lotteries has centered on its value as a "painless" form of revenue, voluntary as opposed to a generally imposed tax. Tax relief is the main motivator for the public's acceptance. Politicians are favorably disposed on this issue because they like the tax revenue and are loath to challenge the government's promotion of lotteries due to voter popularity. Another reason for support of government lottery promotion is to suppress illegal "numbers rackets" and gambling, which would siphon potentially public money into criminal hands.

The National Gambling Impact Study Commission believes that the benefits of state lottery promotions are more than offset by the expanding numbers of people drawn into gambling. The commission charges that lotteries allegedly promote addictive gambling behavior. Furthermore, it is considered a form of regressive taxation on lower-income groups, which leads to other abuses. The central issue rests on the criticism of the state's "inherent conflict" in responsibility—its desire to increase revenues and its duty to protect the public welfare. Not only does the state condone what might otherwise be illegal activity, but it endorses and promotes a highly addictive form of behavior.

The commission contends that the growth of lotteries fits a similar pattern. As states actually legislate a "controlled monopoly," they begin with a moderate number of simple games but eventually face traditional *lifecycle* problems as revenues eventually level off and decline. This boredom of lottery consumers leads to a constant pipeline of new product games as the lotteries expand in terms of cost and marketing complexities. Innovations such as "scratch tickets" and "instant games" provide immediate gratification, increasing the excitement value dramatically.

The relentless pressure for revenue is evidenced by a bevy of new marketing techniques, such as computerized vending and video lottery terminals. Even slot machines are adapted to lottery programs as innovative games continue to convert inactive or moderate players into more active participants. Most controversial of marketing practices relates to the advent of the Internet. While state lotteries are currently not utilizing the Internet, this promises to be a major future issue. Questions of privacy, appeals to children, competition from casino gambling, and the enabling features of the Internet are now issues to be considered. The Lotto, with its enormous jackpots and publicity, has become the lottery form played most by the general public. Multistate consortia have generated tremendous publicity and profile stories about winners and have transformed the lottery into an integral part of American culture.

How harmful are lotteries to society? Most arguments focus on the exploitation of the poor. Some studies suggest that a small segment of lottery players generate an overwhelming percentage of the revenues. Critics suggest that these are the "mathematically challenged" and vulnerable people who become "lottery junkies."

Edward J. Stanek dispels many of the myths about the lottery and neutralizes many of its perceived risks to society. He suggests that for a small cost, consumers can enjoy the arousal, suspense, and excitement that come from the possibility of winning. Stanek addresses the criticism of targeting and taking advantage of the poor, the low probabilities of winning, Federal Trade Commission (FTC) regulation, and other controversial aspects of lotteries.

Edward J. Stanek

 **YES**

A Critique of Lottery Critics

The cornerstone of the lottery business is honesty. It is particularly distressing for those of us in the lottery business who try to practice this virtue to be attacked by those less virtuous from institutions that profess to be the public conscience. Most journalists are honest and hardworking. For example, National Public Radio's recent feature of lottery opponent Robyn Gearey and lottery proponent David Gale on its "Talk of the Nation" program was balanced. However, there is no licensing or review board to ferret out prejudice, incompetence, bias and malintent on the part of the media as there is with virtually every other respected profession. Some of the media seem to take an attitude best described by Mark Twain: "I like the truth sometimes, but I don't care enough for it to hanker after it."

Obviously, most journalists do care for the truth, but their perspective may not be representative of the public as a whole. According to the Prothman-Lichter study done in 1979 and 1980, 95% of leading journalists are white, 60 percent are male, and 50 percent profess no religion at all. According to Understanding the Press, in the 1972 general election, 61 percent of the American electorate voted for one presidential candidate, and 81 percent of the media voted for the other. Such a difference could imply that journalists as a group are leaders among the public or it could imply that they "lead" the public—an act devoid of the objectivity that the public expects and journalists profess. As a group, journalists have difficulty relating to business and that lack of understanding leads to slanted reporting. Lotteries are a unique hybrid of business and government in which even veterans can get confused. The tenets of good business remain unflinching while the perspectives of good government sway with the party in power and the public mood.

Lotteries don't take advantage of the poor   Poor people are allowed to vote, get married, and sign contracts. Society in the U.S. and Canada does not usurp rights and privileges based on socioeconomic status. Why then, do those less prosperous needs to be protected from making a one-dollar decision?

Being born is a lottery. No one had the ability to establish the qualifications for his or her parents. No one examined the pool of available genes and chromosomes and selectively chose his or her own physical, emotional, and intellectual characteristics. Therefore, through no accomplishment of our own, all of us have unique attributes that are lacking in others. It is true that work is an essential element to create success, but most of us, no matter how hard we try, will never have the looks of a supermodel, the voice of an opera singer, be the high scorer in the NBA or derive the general theory of relativity. Why? The luck of the draw! That same luck governs who has a name like Kennedy or Rockefeller and is a millionaire at birth. Big jackpot games are equalizers. Those who were not fortunate in the drawing of genes and inheritance can venture a chance equal to everyone else to benefit financially. No promises—just a chance. Just like life.

There are those zealots who want to deprive others of a chance to prosper —because they think they know what's best for others. Despite the pretense, they don't.

Lotteries don't discriminate among their customers. They sell to tall, short, rich and poor. If there is something inherently wrong with allowing less prosperous people the choice to buy a ticket, then the protectionists should seek legislation to prohibit low-income citizens from taking a chance. Why haven't they? Because the folly of their self-righteous protectionism would be exposed.

For a lottery to take "advantage" of the poor would imply that the poor have a "disadvantage." Obviously they have less money, which means that lotteries can benefit them more relative to helping those of greater means. The only way that the poor can be at a disadvantage is if they don't have the same mental capacity to make $1 decisions as those who are wealthier. It follows that those who make such claims are assuming that the poor have a diminished intellectual capacity. But economic status is not a measure of intelligence. Saying that the poor are taken advantage of in this context is an insult to the intelligence of those who play lottery games.

It has been alleged that lower-income people spend a higher percentage of their income on lottery products. Obviously such is true for any product with a fixed price, whether it is bread, clothing, shampoo or a movie ticket. Whatever price is chosen for a product, divide it by a lower income and you get a higher percentage. If this issue were really socially significant, government could issue gaming stamps like food stamps to low income customers and give a discount on tickets that would negate the issue... but it would not negate the critics. Obviously, a person making $10,000 a year will spend a higher percentage of his or her salary on a $1 ticket than a person making $100,000 per year. That fact, however, does not support the hypothesis that low-income persons are lottery customers or that they are targets of marketing campaigns. The logic is faulty and numerous studies have concluded that middle-income persons are the lottery's principal customers.

In certain instances where "daily numbers" games are sold in large metropolitan areas from St. Louis east, there exists a cultural anomaly where lower-income blue-collar workers play the game in distinctly higher proportions than their white-collar counterparts. Data will show that this particular game has a lower-income following. The game was sold by organized crime for generations. Government lotteries in Washington D.C., Boston, Baltimore,

New York, and elsewhere took almost all of that business away from organized crime. Proving that this phenomenon is a cultural rather than an economic bias is the fact that the same game, sold by lotteries to the same economic demographic west of St. Louis, has resulted in relative consumer rejection and virtual failure. Cities west of St. Louis developed into urban areas later and were devoid of the criminal numbers running tradition. The game is a cultural preference.

If lotteries were to remove this game with such significant demand from eastern metropolitan areas, organized crime would again fill the void. Since experiments with prohibition have failed, government has but one choice—sell the game and capture the profits or let crime bosses have the income.

Lotteries do have more retail outlets in lower-income neighborhoods   Why? Lotteries don't discriminate on income but do try to service their customers. More $75,000 homes can fit into a square mile than $500,000 estates can fit into the same space. More one-bedroom apartments can fit into a square mile than $125,000 houses can fit in the same space. With more homes there are more people. If lotteries don't discriminate based on income, they must have more outlets where there are more people in order to provide equal service.

How about those studies that have shown more lottery outlets per capita in poorer neighborhoods in some states? I live in a neighborhood called "South of Grand" in Des Moines. It's an old established neighborhood where the wealthiest lawyers, doctors and business people live. Despite the large size of the neighborhood, there are no lottery outlets there—not one. There are no stores in "South of Grand." Zoning doesn't allow stores. When doctors and lawyers who live South of Grand want to buy a lottery ticket, they have to go to a less prosperous neighborhood—not for reasons of social consequence, but because they can only shop in a neighborhood with stores. Yes, it is true that there are more lottery outlets in neighborhoods that have more stores.

In some cases the stores are located in industrial or commercial areas which have a very large middle class population of workers by day who buy their tickets while the sun shines and leave the neighborhood to a different demographic group, the census takers, and tabloid journalists by night.

Lotteries don't target advertising to the poor   It would be both a bad business decision and a bad political decision. It would be bad business, because attracting customers with less money doesn't add to the bottom line. It would be bad politics because lotteries are public entities. There was a billboard in one neighborhood cited over and over last year as alleged proof of targeting the underprivileged. That particular billboard was one in a campaign involving hundreds of billboards in every class of neighborhood. There was no targeting. Even so, it was one billboard over ten years ago and not another billboard example in any state or province out of thousands of possibilities has been cited as corroboration.

Why do lotteries advertise? Because players have a right to know the rules, what the prizes are, where to buy tickets, and other information. State lotteries are public, not secret enterprises. The advertising money does not come from taxpayers—it comes from lottery players. So it is the players, the customers, the people who earned their money and the right to spend it, that should have the loudest voice in determining advertising policy. The next loudest voice should be given to retailers—they provide a service to the state for a low commission, and all the products that they sell deserve support from the companies that provide the products. Why should lotteries shortchange retailers with inadequate advertising support? Yet some policy makers keep trying to arrange it. If the public were asked which ads are more honest and more essential, most lottery ads or most political campaign ads—what do you think would be the answer.

Lottery advertising should be regulated by the Federal Trade Commission   I received 26 direct mail pieces from private sweepstakes companies in the course of a few weeks. Many of them made outrageous proclamations that assured me that I was the winner of millions of dollars when I wasn't. Some said that all I needed to do was fill in the forms and follow instructions to claim the prize. The instructions are cumbersome and lead the respondent to decide on making a purchase several times along the way to completion. In one multimillion-dollar giveaway in which I was a definite winner, I claimed the unspecified prize and received a packet of seeds several weeks later.

These mailings come in envelopes that look like they contain legal documents or express delivery to feign importance—but they are usually sent bulk rate. No North American lottery would tolerate the misleading marketing used by these companies. Yet all of the companies sending these notices are regulated by the Federal Trade Commission. So much for the FTC's ability to keep advertising forthright. It's a good thing that government lotteries hold themselves to a higher advertising standard than is required of the private sweepstakes companies.

Lotteries don't advertise the odds of winning all prizes in all ads   It's hard to get every message into a 30-second TV spot. But all lotteries make all of those odds available in print just like food companies list their ingredients. Except for the famous "two all-beef patties, special sauce, lettuce, cheese, pickles, onions on a sesame seed bun" ad, I don't know of any food company that uses TV to list every ingredient.

Do lotteries foster the notion of something for nothing?   Inheritance, interest on idle cash, capital gain—they are all financial gain for no work. The first due to luck and the other two the result of risk-taking and usury, which until the 20th century meant charging any amount of interest on a loan. In the Bible, usury is a sin. " ... thou hast taken usury and increase and thou hast greedily gained of thy neighbors by extortion, and forgotten me, saith the Lord God." Eze 22:12. "If thou lend money to any of my people that is poor by thee, thou shalt not be to him as a usurer, neither shall thou lay upon him usury." Exd 22:25. And there is more about this subject in the Good Book. Shakespeare said, "Neither a Borrower nor a Lender be." Why? Because charging interest is the wealthy who have money taking advantage of the poor who don't. How many bankers do you see lined up at confessionals after work every day? Banks in the U.S. made over $59 billion last year by charging interest on loans of other people's idle money. Lotteries made $11.8 billion. Yet the principles of banking are seldom the target of tabloid journalism.

Should we spend money to take a chance?   Think carefully about insurance companies. They sell chances. State lotteries would prefer that their customers think something good might happen to them if they buy lottery products. Insurance companies count on customers thinking something bad might happen to them so that they feel compelled to buy insurance products. Lotteries use optimism to make a sale. Insurance companies use fear to make a sale. Both count on statistics and take calculated risks to make a profit. [In 1996] the U.S. insurance companies made $39.9 billion for themselves. Lotteries made $11.8 billion for the public good.

Banks and insurance companies play valuable roles in today's society. Despite their dependence on risk, usury, and fear, they should be tolerated—and so should lotteries. Lotteries don't depend on usury and fear. Besides, with lotteries the risk is much lower and players don't have to be rich to participate.

History has documented relatively few people who have risked so much on lotteries that they lost house and home. History has documented relatively many people who have risked so much on the stock market, commodities, and farming that they did lose house and home. There is only one medicine to prevent these afflictions. It's called moderation. Obviously the risk on lottery tickets is lower than the risk on most other gambles, even though the potential reward with the lottery could be higher. Still, moderation in all things—"play with your head not over your head." Don't bet the farm and don't buy lottery tickets on credit, even though credit is commonly used when gambling on stocks and pork bellies (margin).

Lotteries have a positive impact on the economy   Some economists have asserted that the money wagered on lotteries is taken out of the economy and isn't used for goods and services that support employment or meaningful activity. Their analysis is shallow. Money spent on lottery tickets gets parceled several ways:

- Commissions to retailers
- Fees to companies for services
- Advertising
- Satellite uplinks, television studios, rents, vehicle fleets, accounting firms, data processing, drawing machines, ticket printers. Lottery revenues are channeled into the economy the same as the revenues of an average business.
- There are profits that go to the government. Those profits take the place of higher taxes and are used to deliver goods and services like other money circulating through the economy.
- What's left? Only prize money. It does get redistributed to those who win from those who don't. Those who don't win can't buy chocolate

bars, gum, or rent movies but the winners can buy toasters, scholarships, new cars, and houses, or start their own businesses. So the real economic drawback must be the really big winner who can't spend money fast enough and must stuff it into a mattress or keep it in the basement, where it does no one any good. I do know of those big winners who have spent money on lawyers and accountants. I know that some idle winnings go into the bank or into a brokerage account— economists must say that's okay. Where are the overstuffed mattresses?

Lotteries are not an expenditure of money lacking a useful purpose Lotteries are entertainment—a little bit of fun for a small prize or a fantasy about a big prize. Each ticket costs about a dollar. Have the same critics thought about expenditures on spectator sports? Sports in general are fabulous creations. Those who participate in them learn teamwork, self-discipline, and other social skills. They get stronger, faster, or at least minimally keep their bodies in shape. But as a spectator, not one of these benefits accrues to the ticket buyer. Fun—yes. Entertainment—yes. Even some hope. But real value—no.

What do those sports tickets cost? It depends on whether the event is collegiate or professional—$15 to $75 or maybe even $2,200 if it's the Super Bowl. How about the two-minute prize fight that took a small bite out of the boxer's ear and a big bite out of spectators' wallets! It should be difficult to rationalize taking $75 from the poor and giving it to the rich (pro athletes and owners) especially when taxpayers are asked to use tax dollars to build the stadiums where the rich get richer. (Tax dollars are not used to build lotteries.) With the lottery, for one buck if a player wishes, he or she can fantasize for a day or two, as opposed to being entertained for an hour or two by a sporting event. Lottery tickets on average return over 50% of the price to the players. Not so with pro sports—when the money's spent there's no hope of ever getting any of it back.

How about movies or television? Admittedly there are some educational productions that leave the public a little wiser. But do most movie theaters, cassette rentals, or TV shows really enrich human lives, make people smarter or stronger? How about Hollywood's reliance on a preponderance of sex and violence? State lotteries don't rely on sex and violence to make a sale. Lottery tickets contain no tars or nicotine, no caffeine, sodium, calories, cholesterol, saturated fats, carcinogens, preservatives, or alcohol. They don't impair driving, cause cancer, or clog arteries. As an entertainment mechanism with no poisons, they should be more socially acceptable than television, spectator sports, or a quarter-pounder with cheese.

Lottery tickets can be addictive The degree of addiction is different for various games. Video lottery problems, although confined to only a few states, are the most pronounced. The problems must be acknowledged. The lottery industry must support treatment and keeping the problems in perspective. *Every* human being that frequents heroin will become an addict. Between 2% and 4% of the general population has a propensity to become compulsive gamblers.

Some new research suggests that compulsive behavior is the result of a chemical or biological problem that manifests itself by excessive gambling, drinking, drug use, sex, fanatical religion, or something else, implying that gambling itself is not the problem. More conventional thinking suggests that if lottery tickets are the only available gambling product, 20% to 40% of the 4% with a propensity for problem gambling could become lottery addicts. But cards, sports betting (legal or illegal) and commodity markets are available everywhere. In a state like Iowa, where other forms of gaming are available, there are good statistics on the contributions of the lottery to problem gambling. Last year nearly 3,700 urgent calls were placed to the Iowa Department of Public Health on the Gambling Treatment Helpline. It's an 800-toll free number. It is printed on every Iowa lottery ticket, lottery terminal, lottery vending machine, play station and brochure. It does not appear on every slot machine or blackjack table—although it can be found on a poster somewhere in a 50,000 square foot casino. Last year 6% of all the calls on these lines were from people who had played lottery games. That means that 94 % of the callers did not have a problem with lottery games. Also remember that the 6% who did account for 0.12% of the adult population. There is a credo that dictates even one problem is too many. But is it fair to restrict the activities of 99.7% of the adult population to shield the other 0.3%? Since the leading cause of death other than by disease is vehicle accidents, should cars, trucks, and buses be outlawed? Lottery tickets don't cause death! Restrictions may need to be enacted to protect people from other people. Assistance should be provided to people who may otherwise hurt themselves—but there should be moderation in protectionism lest the living be buried in a coffin of fear and overreaction.

Lotteries must be proponents for problem gambling treatment and for reform of the methods used to diagnose it   The South Oaks Gambling Screen, the best detection tool so far developed, has been shown to diagnose more false positives than true positives. In New Zealand, it classified non-pathological gamblers as pathological nearly three times as frequently as it correctly classified pathological gamblers. It has classified 64.6% of sports card collectors as probable pathological gamblers. Using current methods of data tabulation, problem gambling behavior is assumed to be permanent and it is eternal. Rates can only increase—never decrease for a given population—not because of measured problems, but "by definition." Using a screwdriver because it is the only tool available to pound a nail does not justify its use. Relying on aspirin because it is the only medicine available as a cure for cancer is false pretense. The old diagnostics provide consistency only for its own sake and have become the hobgoblins of small and large minds alike. It is time to develop new tools that work, rather than waste time using old tools that don't work.

Compulsive gamblers and white-collar crime   In January of 1997 *The Economist* ventured that "American Insurance Institute estimates that 40% of white collar crime has its roots in gambling." Congressman, professors, authors and the *Harvard Mental Health Letter* have all used the conclusion from the American Insurance Institute. However, there is no American Insurance

Institute or any study documenting the above conclusion. It's a hoax. After exhaustively using all of the directories, contacts, and computer tools available, the Institute cannot be found and those who have quoted its conclusions cannot find it or produce the study either. Joseph M. Kelly has published a detailed treatise in the *Gambling Law Review* (Volume 1, Number 2, 1997) documenting the unwitting use of this farce by prestigious persons and institutions.

Lotteries are not self-regulating   Earlier this year, I read that other forms of gaming shouldn't pose much work for the national commission because they are highly regulated, but state lotteries are not subject to such scrutiny. All Lottery board meetings are public meetings. Lottery files are public records. What companies must produce for the press any record requested—only lotteries and the U.S. Postal Service that I know of. Each legislative session, with few exceptions, each state lottery is subjected to legislative scrutiny both for budgets and for operations. Detractors have the power to examine the minutest lottery details, voicing opinions, and voting on the lottery's business operations. Which other gaming enterprises present their operations to a group of detractors for approval and open their files for the press? Which other businesses give a vote on their operations to those opposed to their existence? The regulation in Nevada and Atlantic City doesn't even come close.

[Recently], a question has been posed in many different forums. "For generations we were taught that gambling was evil. Now the government is promoting it. If it was wrong before, isn't it wrong now and how can the government be so immoral?" Morality can't be legislated but governments try to do it all of the time.

Our ideas on right and wrong come from religious roots and social norms, which vary from culture to culture and time to time. Religion is not a topic in this treatise. However, rightness and wrongness as a matter of law or social acceptability offer some insights. Something should not be labeled right or wrong just because it is so labeled at another place or time. In Afghanistan today, sanctions are applied to men who trim their beards and women who don't cover their faces or who seek education or employment. In America's past, women were burned alive if suspected of witchcraft. Dancing was forbidden. Galileo was excommunicated from the Church because he would not accept that the sun revolves around the earth, which was believed to be the center of the universe. It was illegal to own gold bullion in the U.S. from 1934 until 1971. It was illegal for women to vote in the U.S. until 1920. Should these things be wrong here and now just because they were there and then? . . .

Lotteries are also not charities and to pretend that they are for purposes of efficiency comparisons is also the product of a confused mentality. One can't pull an oxcart with a hamster. The charity may be warm and fuzzy, but who in their right mind would expect that the public would give $13.5 trillion a year to their government voluntarily? Because government could never function under such a scheme, we have taxes and lotteries. Lotteries are products that must return value to the customer. If not, there's no sale and no penalty. There is a penalty for not paying taxes—prison. Which is more in keeping with the Land of the Free, lotteries or taxes?

Odds of winning   Lottery critics often say the odds of winning are "slim and none" or about the same as getting killed by lightning. On the *Arts & Entertainment* cable channel last year a coin was thrown off a skyscraper and just missed a paper cup far below on the street. The mathematician doing the demonstration said, "Like state lotteries, close doesn't count." Close *does* count. The highest jackpot odds game in the country is Powerball. But being less than precise in picking numbers can result in $100,000, $5,000, $100, $5, $2 or maybe just a buck. Being "not even close" counts in most lottery jackpot games and odds of 1 in 5 are common in scratch games. Last year in North America, lotteries awarded $52 million in prizes everyday—that's $36,000 every minute, 24 hours a day. Maybe the "performances" of critics would be more credible if they first learned to play the games that they're critiquing. A lot of smart people vote to have lottery games with every dollar that they spend on tickets. Last year over 40 billion of those one-dollar votes were cast in North America in favor of lotteries. By the way—in 1995, lightning in the U.S. and Canada killed 91 people and 1,136 people won $1,000,000 or more playing lotteries in the U.S. and Canada. (4,520 won $100,000 or more playing lotto.)

I will make a couple of concessions, though. The odds of getting killed by lightning are better than the odds of winning Powerball—in Utah (where there is no lottery). The odds of getting killed by lightning are better than the odds of winning a Powerball jackpot—but only on Monday, Tuesday, Thursday, Friday and Sunday. (Drawings are only on Wednesday and Saturday.) Remember, when calculating these odds, that anyone can be struck by lightning any time, any day. You can only win Powerball if you buy a ticket and then only on drawing days. One should ask, "What are the odds of getting killed by lightning on a Wednesday or Saturday in a state that sells Powerball?'

Using data from the National Safety Council, I have calculated that the odds of an average American being killed by lightning on any particular day are one in 1,178,989,420. Therefore you are 21.44 times more likely to win Powerball on Wednesday or Saturday with only one ticket than you are to be killed by lightning. You are 224 times more likely to win a Lotto 6/42 than to be killed by lightning. Here's something to think about. Of the people struck by lightning in 1995, some were golfing, some were picnicking, fishing, boating, or hiking—not one was playing lotto at the time....

Benefits   North American lotteries provide funding for education, economic development, natural resource protection, elder care programs, and more. They have contributed over $100 billion for worthy causes over the years. With only 8% of North America's $500 billion in annual wagering, lotteries directly or indirectly provide over 250,000 jobs. Over 240,000 retailers sell lottery products in North America. Last year they were paid over $3 billion in commissions.

Conclusion   Lotteries raise money for good causes. They don't target the poor. They have no more influence on the work ethic than inheritance, interest payments, and capital gains. Their fund raising is fairer and more American that taxation. Their games contribute to the economy as much as any other business activity does. Their odds are reasonable for a $1 risk. They have maintained a reputation of honesty and have earned the public trust and confidence. A clear majority of citizens in lottery states have for decades given their support. Despite the media myths and the crusades of social vigilantes, the honest and secure lotteries of the U.S. and Canada have prospered. Common sense among common men and women has spoken louder than the prejudice, the politics, and the uninformed emotionalism of egalitarian cynics.

Lotteries

In the words of one lottery director: "Lotteries are different from any other gaming product. Lottery players risk a small amount of money against very long odds to win a large prize, with the net proceeds going to the public good."

The lottery industry stands out in the gambling industry by virtue of several unique features. It is the most widespread form of gambling in the U.S.: currently, lotteries operate in 37 states and the District of Columbia. It is the only form of commercial gambling which a majority of adults report having played. It is also the only form of gambling in the U.S. that is a virtual government monopoly. State lotteries have the worst odds of any common form of gambling (a chance of approximately 1 in 12–14 million for most existing lotto games), but they also promise the greatest potential payoff to the winner in absolute terms, with prizes regularly amounting to tens of millions of dollars.

Lotteries rank first among the various forms of gambling in terms of gross revenues: total lottery sales in 1996 totaled $42.9 billion. 1982 gross revenues were $4 billion, representing an increase of 950% over the preceding 15 years, 1982–1996.

Lotteries have the highest profit rates in gambling in the U.S.: in 1996, net revenues (sales minus payouts, but not including costs) totaled $16.2 billion, or almost 38% of sales. They are also the largest source government revenue from gambling, in 1996 netting $13.8 billion, or 32% of money wagered, for governments at all levels....

Reestablishing the Industry

The revival of lotteries began in New Hampshire in 1964 with its establishment of a state lottery. Inspired by New Hampshire's positive experience, New York followed in 1966. New Jersey introduced its lottery in 1970, and was followed by 10 other states by 1975. Currently, 37 states and the District of Columbia have operating lotteries.

In virtually every state, the introduction of lotteries has followed remarkably uniform patterns: the arguments for and against adoption, the structure of the resulting state lottery, and the evolution of the lottery's operations all demonstrate considerable uniformity.

From National Gambling Impact Study Commission, *Lotteries* (May 29, 1998). Washington, DC: U.S. Government Printing Office, 1998. Notes omitted.

The principal argument used in every state to promote the adoption of a lottery has focused on its value as a source of "painless" revenue: players voluntarily spending their money (as opposed to the general public being taxed) for the benefit of the public good. According to one expert, the dynamic is as follows: "Voters want states to spend more, and politicians look at lotteries as a way to get tax money for free." A key element in winning and retaining public approval is the degree to which the proceeds of the lottery are seen as benefiting a specific public good, such as education. This argument is particularly effective in times of economic stress, especially given the prospect of tax increases or cuts in public programs. But studies have also shown that the popularity of lotteries is not necessarily connected to the state government's actual financial health, as lotteries have consistently won broad public approval even when the state's fiscal condition is good. As [Charles T.] Clotfelter and [Philip J.] Cook report, "the objective fiscal circumstances of the state do not appear to have much influence on whether or when states adopt lotteries." In this sense it appears that the public's approval of lotteries rests more on the *idea* of lotteries reducing the potential tax burden on the general public than it is on any specific instance of relief.

That being the case, lotteries have proven to be remarkably popular: in authorizing the lottery, virtually every state has required approval by both the legislature and the public in a referendum on the subject. Yet in only one state —North Dakota—has the public consistently voted against a lottery.

Once established, lotteries retain their broad public support: in states with lotteries, 60% of adults report playing at least once a year. In addition to the general public, lotteries also develop extensive specific constituencies, including convenience store operators (the usual vendors for lotteries); lottery suppliers (heavy contributions by suppliers to state political campaigns are regularly reported); teachers (in those states in which revenues are earmarked for education); state legislators (who quickly become accustomed to the extra revenue), etc. Since New Hampshire initiated the modern era of state lotteries in 1964, no state lottery has been abolished.

A second argument made by lottery promoters is that because illegal gambling already exists, a state-run lottery is an effective device both for capturing money for public purposes that otherwise would disappear into criminal hands and also for suppressing illegal gambling. The evidence suggests that this may be partially true for the so-called "numbers" games. Some lotteries have explicitly designed their games toward this public policy goal. New York's lottery, for example, reports that as a result, "illegal numbers activities have been eliminated for the most part in most areas of the State with the exception of New York City."

Critics counter, however, that whatever the impact on revenue and illegal gambling may be, the benefits of the lottery are more than offset by its expanding the number of people who are drawn into gambling. Worse, lotteries are alleged to promote addictive gambling behavior, are characterized as a major regressive tax on lower-income groups, and are said to lead to other abuses. Even more troubling, however, is the general criticism that the state faces an inherent conflict in its desire to increase revenues and its duty to protect the public welfare. These criticisms will be discussed further below. . . .

The Evolution of Debate

Once the lottery has been established, debate and criticism change focus from the general desirability of a lottery to more specific features of its operations, including the problem of compulsive gamblers, alleged regressive impact on lower-income groups, and other problems of public policy. These criticisms both are reactions to, and drivers of, the continuing evolution of the industry.

Promoters of state-run lotteries usually invoke the concept that, regardless of one's views about the morality of gambling, a lottery can be used to support the general welfare, either as a means of increasing funding for public works or by reducing the necessity to raise taxes. In recent years, however, there has been increasing criticism that the public's perception of where the money generated by the lottery is going is incorrect, or even that the public is being deliberately misled. In a minority of states, the proceeds of the lottery are sent directly to the general fund for the legislature to appropriate as it sees fit. Far more common is the "earmarking" of lottery money for identified programs. Currently, 10 states earmark lottery money exclusively for education; in 15 others, it is directed toward uses as varied as tourism, parks and recreation, economic development, construction of public buildings, etc. Colorado targets revenues to environmental protection programs; the Virgin Islands uses part of its earnings to help fund a local children's hospital. In Massachusetts, lottery revenues are redistributed to local governments, amounting to over $500 million in FY 1997 and acounting for 3/4 of the state's aid to cities and towns.

Critics charge, however, that the "earmarking" of funds is misleading: lottery proceeds used for a specific program, such as public education, in fact simply allow the legislature to reduce by the same amount the appropriations it would otherwise have had to allot for that purpose from the general fund. The money "saved" remains in the general fund, to be spent on whatever purpose the legislature chooses. Critics add that, as there is little or no evidence that overall funding has increased for the targeted recipients of lottery revenues, the only result has been to increase the discretionary funds available to the legislature, which may be a key reason for the popularity of lotteries in the state houses. . . .

Pressures for Revenue

Despite the extensive praise [some] states have received for their innovative programs, it is uncertain how widely their example can or will be copied, as to do so in states with existing lotteries would force legislatures to cover the resulting deficit in the general fund with politically unpopular spending cuts or tax increases. The most basic fact driving all lottery operations is the pressure for revenue: "To judge from their public statements and their actions, all lottery directors feel pressure to maintain, if not to increase, existing levels of revenues," a pressure that is "relentless."

This has produced a second set of issues stemming from the fact that the growth in revenue from traditional forms of lotteries has plateaued, prompting expansion into new games such as keno and video poker, along with a more aggressive effort at promotion, especially through advertising.

Although strong sales growth for lotteries has continued—totaling 11.7%, 12.9%, and 11.7% in 1994, 1995, and 1996 respectively—these figures obscure an important shift in the sources of revenue in recent years. As the traditional lottery industry has matured and fully penetrated its various markets, sales growth has leveled off. Most of the recent growth has come from the introduction of new forms of wagering, such as machine keno and video lottery devices, revenues from which grew by 41.8% in 1996 alone. These machines are commonly licensed to bars, convenience stores, etc., thus dramatically increasing their presence in public life. They also have prompted concerns that these new games exacerbate existing alleged negative impacts of the lottery, such as the targeting of poorer individuals, increased opportunities for problem gamblers, presenting the latter with far more addictive games, etc.

The evolution of the Massachusetts lottery is instructive: the lottery began operations in 1975 with a 50-cent ticket and a once-a-week drawing. Scratch tickets with instant payoffs were introduced in 1974. In 1993, the lottery introduced keno games and currently there are nearly 1600 keno vendors in Massachusetts, most of them in stores open to the general public. Lottery revenues have risen from $71 million in 1975 to more than $3 billion in 1997.

There have been several controversies regarding these issues in Massachusetts and elsewhere, as well as several attempts to deal with them. The legislature passed the Keno Reform Act in 1996 to address some of the more prominent complaints, reforms which included allowing communities to ban keno or restrict without suffering a fiscal penalty (money from the lottery is distributed to local communities on a complicated formula that is based on how much money each community generates for the lottery), capping the number of keno licenses statewide, etc. However, neither opponents or proponents have indicated any satisfaction with the existing situation.

Advertising

Lotteries have also come under increasing criticism in the area of advertising, especially regarding alleged aggressive advertising practices aimed at lower-income groups. Many critics have long been uncomfortable in general with state governments promoting what they see as a vice. The federal government banned lottery advertising until 1975; once this prohibition was lifted, increasingly larger sums have been devoted to the promotion of lotteries: in fiscal year 1997, state lotteries spent over $400 million on advertising and promotion.

Because the lotteries are run as a business with a focus on maximizing revenues, advertising necessarily focuses on persuading target groups to spend their money on the lottery. The questions are 1) does this promotion of gambling lead to negative consequences for the poor, problem gamblers, etc.?; and 2) even if these problems are minimal, is this an appropriate function for the state? Is running a lottery at cross-purposes with the larger public interest?

Critics charge that lottery advertising seeks "to stimulate rather than merely accommodate demand," a role for the state that "may be inconsistent with other functions of government... Lottery advertisements must either encourage existing players to buy more tickets or entice non-players into becoming players." These and other opponents allege that lottery advertising is targeted to appeal to the irrational elements in the public's imagination, seeking to persuade potential players that they can influence their odds through the choices of numbers they pick and also that it attempts to convince the individual player that his chance is winning is far greater than the odds would suggest. In the words of one, lottery play depends on encouraging people's "magical thinking," which advertising must target. According to New Jersey's lottery director, the purpose of advertising is to "tak[e] an infrequent user and [try] to convert him into a more frequent user."

To this end, lotteries use traditional marketing methods, such as identifying likely players, compiling extensive socio-economic profiles, conducting focus group research, test marketing new products, etc. The media plan for the Iowa lottery stated its strategy as "to target our message demographically against those that we know to be heavy users, while encouraging purchases among light or non-users." The research leaves few areas untouched: the Colorado state lottery reportedly "spent $25,000 for a study called Mindsort to analyze the left and right sides of the human brain to understand how to manipulate player behavior."

Critics charge that much lottery advertising is deceptive, commonly presenting misleading information about the odds of winning the jackpot, inflating the value of the money won (lotto jackpot prizes are usually paid in equal annual installments over 20 years, with inflation and taxes dramatically eroding the current value); and so forth.

Growing criticism has helped to persuade some legislatures to mandate restrictions on lottery advertising. In Massachusetts, the legislature imposed a significant reduction in the money allotted for lottery advertising, from $12 million in 1993 to $400,000 in 1997. Lottery advocates claim that the Massachusetts lottery spent no money on advertising in 1997 outside of point-of-purchase sites (i.e., no television, radio, newspaper, or billboard advertising). As a direct result, there was an absolute decline in lottery revenue for the first time. Despite the increasing salience of the issue, only three states—Minnesota, Virginia, and Wisconsin—have imposed significant restrictions on lottery advertising (Massachusetts' legislature did the same by means of its virtual elimination of the advertising budget; other states have similarly reduced the advertising budget, but for a variety of reasons). But many state lottery organizations claim to have significantly reduced their overall advertising on their own initiative, or to have changed it in ways to make it more "socially responsible."

Criticism of the advertising practices of lotteries is not confined to critics outside of the industry. Speaking to a meeting of his fellow lottery directors,

Jeff Perlee, Director of the New York State Lottery, warned that although most lottery advertising was responsible in its claims, lottery officials:

> must confront the fact that the product they market is a vice that is not universally accepted... [Some state lottery advertisements] are so far-fetched and so fanciful that they would not stand up to the same "truth-in-advertising" standards to which advertising conducted by private industry is held. Add to that the fact that our advertising is often relentless in its frequency, and lottery critics and even supporters are left wondering what public purpose is served when a state's primary message to its constituents is a frequent and enticing appeal to the gambling instinct. The answer is none. No legitimate public purpose justifies the excesses to which some lottery advertising has resorted.

A Maryland state budget examiner's report on that state's lottery advertising stated that it contained "misleading gimmickry" that exaggerated the benefits to the public from lottery revenues. In fact, state lotteries are exempt from the Federal Trade Commission's truth-in-advertising standards because they are state entities and, in terms of their advertising, can in fact operate in a manner that true commercial businesses cannot.

Regressivity

The focus on convincing non-players or infrequent players to utilize the lottery, as well as persuading frequent players to play even more, is the source of an additional array of criticisms. Giving force to this concern is the widespread conception that the lottery is a regressive tax because it draws a disproportionate amount of its revenues from lower-income groups. The image of the state promoting a highly regressive scheme among its poorest citizens by playing on their unrealistic hopes is a highly evocative one. The most frequently cited, and most egregious, example of this was a billboard in one of Chicago's poorest neighborhoods that touted the lottery as: "How to go from Washington Boulevard to Easy Street—Play the Illinois State Lottery." ...

Income aside, there are clear differences in lottery play by socio-economic group and other factors. Men tend to play more than women; blacks and Hispanics more than whites; the old and the young play less than those in the middle age ranges; and Catholics tend to play more than Protestants. Interestingly, "lottery play falls with formal education" even though non-lottery gambling in general tends to increase.

Other Criticisms

Compulsive Gambling

There is growing evidence that the new games the lotteries have introduced to increase sales are more addictive, and are compounding the problem of compulsive gamblers. Dr. Lance Dodes, Director of the Center for Problem Gambling at Mt. Auburn Hospital in Cambridge Massachusetts, estimates that 40% of his patients are lottery players. A 1996 survey in New York found that 9% of lottery players, and 14% of keno players, have been compulsive gamblers at some point in their lives. The study also concluded that keno in particular fosters addiction. One study of the effect of VLTs [Video Lottery Terminals] on compulsive gamblers found that the number of individuals in South Dakota seeking treatment for problem gambling declined significantly during a temporary downtime for the lottery's VLTs and rose sharply once they were returned to service.

This link is widely recognized, even by those in the industry. In the words of one lottery director: "[G]ambling, including playing the lottery, is ... potentially addictive and can be dangerous and destructive for some people, some of the time." The new games "have created what was once an almost unthinkable link between lotteries and compulsive behavior."

Despite significant annual revenues from the lottery, however, treatment of compulsive gambling receives relatively little money from the state. In Massachusetts, for example, the state budgeted only $450,000 in FY 1996 on compulsive gamblers, including only $120,000 for actual treatment, even though the lottery revenues for the state amounted to $720 million. The Ohio lottery is one of only a few that operates a compulsive gambling treatment operation as part of its regular operations, employing six problem gambling experts. Five states require a telephone number for help for problem gamblers be printed on its lottery tickets.

Underage Gambling

The sale of lottery games to minors is illegal in every state. However, by all measures, it is commonplace. A survey in Minnesota of 15- to 18-year-olds found that 27% had purchased lottery tickets for themselves. Even higher levels of 32%, 34%, and 35% were recorded in Louisiana, Texas, and Connecticut, respectively. In Massachusetts, Connecticut, and other states, lottery tickets are available to the general public through self-service vending machines. When one store owner in Boston was asked if minors purchased tickets from the lottery ticket dispenser in his lobby, he replied: "How would I know? No one's watching it." Thus, it is not surprising that a survey conducted by the Massachusetts Attorney General's office found that minors as young as 9 years old were able to purchase lottery tickets on 80% of their attempts, and that 66% of minors were able to place bets on keno games. 75% of Massachusetts high school seniors report having played the lottery.

Charitable Gambling

The lottery has also apparently had a negative impact on charitable gambling. In 1984, charitable gaming in Massachusetts, such as church bingo, had revenues of $250 million. By 1995, those figures had declined to $200 million. Competition from the lottery is usually blamed, especially following the introduction of keno.

"We're getting slaughtered by Keno," said one local rabbi.

Impact on State Politics

The negative impact on state politics of money connected with the lotteries is often cited by critics, with the commercial suppliers and operators commonly used as examples. GTech and Automated Wagering International (AWI) are the two companies that dominate the lottery supply and lottery operations businesses. In 1997, of the 38 lotteries, GTech had contracts to operate 29; AWI had 7; Massachusetts and Virginia run their own systems. These two companies have contributed heavily to state races. When GTech won the contract to operate the California lottery in 1986, it had been the 6th largest contributor to state campaigns that year, having donated a total of $300,000 to individual state races. In addition, both companies devote substantial sums to lobbying state legislatures and officials. GTech is alleged to have spent $11 million on lobbyists in 1993 alone.

Public Policy

It needs to be emphasized that although lottery officials are often lightning rods for criticism, they are not free agents operating on their own; they must respond to directions from state officials, which often contain conflicting goals. Thus, they may be told to reduce advertising even as their performance is measured by their ability to increase lottery revenues.

This schizophrenic approach can lead to many problems. For example, in Massachusetts, the pressure on the lottery to produce additional revenue remained even after the legislature dramatically reduced the funding for advertising. One result was that the lottery began using its "free play" coupons as money, reportedly using $8 million of them to pay for advertising (although the budget had been cut, no prohibition was made against advertising per se). This in turn generated an investigation by the Massachusetts Attorney General's office, but also prompted the IRS to investigate the alleged non-reporting of income (in its eyes, the coupons were being used as money).

The most important issue regarding lotteries is the ability of government at any level to manage an activity from which it profits. In an anti-tax era, many state governments have become dependent on "painless" lottery revenues, and pressures are always there to increase them. A study done in Oregon found that one result common to every state financial crisis over the past couple of decades was that a new form of gambling had been legalized for the state to profit from. As a consequence, Oregon currently has more forms of legal gambling than any other state outside of Nevada. Clearly there are conflicting goals which can only be prioritized by political officials, be they in the executive or legislative branch. There have been surprisingly few attempts to grapple with this problem.

The evolution of state lotteries is a classic case of public policy being made piecemeal and incrementally, with little or no general overview. Authority—and thus pressures on the lottery officials—is divided between the legislative and executive branches and further fragmented within each, with the result that the general public welfare is taken into consideration only intermittently, if at all.

Few, if any states, have a coherent "gambling policy" or even a "lottery policy." Policy decisions taken in the establishment of a lottery are soon overcome by the ongoing evolution of the industry. It is often the case that public officials inherit policies and a dependency on revenues that they can do little or nothing about.

Many public officials, including some charged with overseeing the lottery, have expressed public and private discomfort about many aspects of their state's lottery or even about the wisdom in general of the state's running a lottery, and often add that they and their colleagues are powerless to change the system. This raises the troubling question of whether the state itself has become addicted to lottery revenues. In the words of Harvard University professor Michael Sandel:

> "No politician, however troubled by the lottery's harmful effects, would dare raise taxes or cut spending sufficiently to offset the revenues a lottery brings in. With state hooked on the money, they have no choice but to continue to bombard their citizens, especially the more vulnerable ones, with a message at odds with the ethic of work, sacrifice, and moral responsibility that sustains democratic life."

POSTSCRIPT

Is It Appropriate for the Government to Market Lotteries?

The tremendous success of state lotteries is largely attributed to marketing, which has played a central role in creating public acceptance of the practice as a viable way for states to generate income. Lotteries frequently lead the gaming industry in terms of growth. Marketing has successfully increased customer-based per capita spending, dispelled stereotypes about typical lobby consumers, and stimulated public interest through creative advertising. It has provided a consistent pipeline of innovative games.

Most recently, the impact of lottery critics has stimulated controversy and resulted in some dramatic changes and developments in the marketing of state lotteries. Some recent studies have questioned whether or not lotteries indeed represent a form of regressive revenue production. In a bold move, Massachusetts is no longer advertising the lottery, and some states, such as New Hampshire, are running ads to discourage compulsive gambling and informing the public about the low probabilities of winning. Conversely, Texas, for the first time, has established a separate advertising account to target minority communities. In Colorado lottery players have the option of choosing from a series of funds supported by lottery revenues. Rather than appealing to winning and greed, the advertising appeals to the humanitarian side of consumers by allowing them to provide the state with help for a specific project, like protecting parks and nature trails. Is the use of creative, cause-related lottery marketing the panacea to this problem? Does this technique benefit all the stakeholders involved?

Suggested Readings

Glen Fest, "Lottery Lineups in Texas," *Adweek* (May 24, 1999)

David Gianatasio, "Mass. Lottery Ads Scratched Again," *Adweek* (June 14, 1999)

David Nibert, *Hitting the Lottery Jackpot: State Governments and the Taxing of Dreams* (Monthly Review Press, 2000)

Anthony Miyazaki, Jeff Langenderfer, and David Sprott, "Government-Sponsored Lotteries: Exploring Purchase and Nonpurchase Motivations," *Psychology and Marketing* (January 1999)

"Trailblazing Approach: Colorado Lottery Considers Ad Change," *Marketing News* (March 29, 1999)

ISSUE 20

Is Political Marketing Essentially Buying Politicians?

YES: Charles Lewis and the Center for Public Integrity, from *The Buying of the President 2000* (Avon Books, 2000)

NO: Russell Roberts, from "Will Campaign Finance Reform Enhance the Power of the People?" *Ideas on Liberty* (September 2000)

ISSUE SUMMARY

YES: Investigative reporter Charles Lewis provides a portrait based on documented research of the sources and financial power behind the marketing of U.S. presidential candidates, focusing on "the most obscenely expensive race in history." He argues that special (and often secret) interest groups heavily invest in politicians who, in turn, become beholden to their political patrons.

NO: Professor of labor economics and public policy Russell Roberts deems absurd the idea of purging special interest money from politics. He is concerned that banning soft money may conflict with the First Amendment and suggests alternative means for making politicians accountable.

M any would agree that in the past decade infusion of marketing and money into the electoral process has had the most impact on the American political system. Entering the new millennium, campaign finance reform is the top issue in American presidential politics, and the preponderance of evidence supports the contention that the amount and quality of the candidate's marketing correlate highly to the candidate's successful election. Special interest groups are allegedly "buying" the Congress and presidency while mitigating the power of the populace in the electoral process.

Marketing first became highly visible in the early 1950s when the Eisenhower administration originally booked TV broadcast ads with the classic slogan "I like Ike." The Democratic candidate Adalai Stevenson refused to run ads. He stated that such practices "were below the integrity of the presidency." The floodgates have since opened to the point where marketing is the most crucial component of the American political process, many say. Charles Lewis consistently illustrates that the "dirty secret" of American presidential politics is that the nation's wealthiest interests largely determine the next president of the United States.

Lewis asks, What is the price of power? Moreover, what is the cost to the nation? He offers a litany of examples of relationship marketing in its purest form, as well as examples of how obscenely expensive politics has become. Special interest groups and wealthy campaign contributors are invariably rewarded with legislative favors from elected officials. Consistently, the linkage between candidates, patrons, and political favors is clearly evidenced. Yet the issue of campaign finance is one of the least popular among American voters. This is despite the fact that special interest groups influence Capitol Hill lawmakers, who in turn protect polluters, food producers, and insurance and pharmaceutical companies. Consumers cannot shop, buy drugs, or breathe the air without being directly affected by decisions that Congress makes. Choosing a president has moved "from the voting booth to the auction block." With only 1 percent of the U.S. population controlling 40 percent of the nation's assets, the problem of political marketing has become insidious and systemic. The problems are many, but the main focus is that politicians and their political parties can collect limitless amounts of money. The lack of enforcement of campaign funding policies by the Federal Election Committee (FEC) has been widely criticized. Recent publicity has focused on obvious abuses in both the Clinton and Dole presidential campaigns in 1995–1996, which were totally dismissed by the FEC. How can this accountability issue be resolved?

Russell Roberts uses the examples of the car companies of Ford and General Motors (GM) in his marketing metaphor. He contends that the fact that $1.7 trillion is at the discretion of about 533 congressmen and the president creates an incredibly volatile situation for competing special interest groups. Is it realistic to assume industrial stakeholders and interest groups would not exercise their constitutional rights to lobby for their candidate's favor and legislative agenda? The argument is that the limits on soft money support incumbents who benefit because they are already known "brand names." New candidates need mammoth amounts of advertising and promotional dollars to get their "brand awareness" and to differentiate their political platforms.

The question of soft money limits is also compromised by the many alternatives for "influence peddling." Issue advertising is not supposed to advocate election or defeat of a candidate; rather, it should vividly illustrate and explain a candidate's position. Such advertising can be critical of a candidate and often convey a powerfully damaging message with memorable imagery. In 1998, $260 million was spent on such ads, with the promise of record-breaking growth for the presidential election. More and more groups are taking advantage of issue ads and the new election loopholes, such as unlimited contributions and the fact that they do not need to reveal their successes. Another controversial new loophole is section 527 of the Tax Code, which allows outside groups—called 527 committees—to become political nonprofit groups that pay no taxes and are not required to disclose donors' names to the FEC or the Internal Revenue Service.

 **YES**

The Buying of the President 2000

Introduction

It was a moment that exquisitely captured the state of American politics today.

[In] August, nearly half a year before the Iowa caucuses on January 24, 2000, the state's Republican Party staged its quadrennial fund-raising event. This peculiar political carnival—featuring live presidential candidates—fattened the state party's coffers by at least $1 million. Approximately 650 reporters swarmed around defenseless Ames, Iowa, to cover what veteran journalist David Broder of the *Washington Post* branded "the totally unofficial but historically significant straw pull." All of the 23,685 votes cast were paid for, legally. The two candidates who bought the most votes won, and their "victories" were front-page news nationwide.

Nine Republican presidential candidates set up operation outside the Hilton Coliseum at Iowa State University. The campaign of Texas Governor George W. Bush outbid the others and ended up paying $43,500 to rent the prime location—60,000 square feet of grass—for the event. What transpired on August 14 was an orgy of free food, entertainment, walk-around celebrities, and gifts, with each campaign flying to outdo the others. Utah Senator Orrin Hatch's tent had singer Vic Damone and Utah Jazz pro basketball star Karl Malone. Bush had former Dallas Cowboys quarterback Roger Staubach and singers Tracy Byrd and Linda Davis. Malcolm "Steve" Forbes, Jr., had singers Debby Boone and Ronnie Milsap crooning away in a huge, air-conditioned tent with French doors, which one wag from a rival campaign dubbed "Chateau Malcolm." The multimillionaire publisher also served up 3,100 pounds of pork and set up a miniature amusement park, complete with an inflatable mountain for children to rappel down. Bush and Forbes were the only candidates to have their tents next to the coliseum's entrances.

Candidates were judged in part by the goodies they lavished on caucus-goers. Every campaign had T-shirts. Elizabeth Dole's campaign offered up balloon hats, while Pat Buchanan gave away pot holders. The Bush folks also offered a free lunch and dinner. Hatch provided chicken, Alan Keyes free ice cream. Former Vice President Dan Quayle's low-budget campaign was criticized for passing out bundles of corn.

The Iowa Republicans who were hauled in for the event were pretty much props, too, like the singers and the barbecued pork. The Bush and Forbes campaigns each rented a hundred or so buses to fetch their supporters throughout Iowa. In the evening, inside the Hilton Coliseum, the only people allowed entry were the voters whose $25 entry fees had been paid for by the candidates. Each of the presidential candidates was permitted to speak for ten minutes, and their supporters were then allowed to demonstrate for up to three minutes. Forbes put on the most elaborate show of the night, with thousands of balloons dropped onto the crowd. Because the candidates had bought so many tickets, ordinary, nonpaying citizens who just wanted to listen to the speeches were turned away at the door.

The winner of the Iowa straw poll was Bush, whose campaign had shelled out $825,000 for 7,418 votes—about $111 a vote. "I am proud to be here," Bush told the crowd that night, "for this grassroots exercise in democracy." Broder breathlessly praised his triumph as a "combination of broad public appeal and skillful organization." Forbes finished second, at an even steeper cost: He spent nearly $2 million for 4,921 votes—about $400 a vote.

Welcome to the 2000 presidential campaign. It is disconcerting to behold a political process that so matter-of-factly rewards unabashed, competitive gluttony, a process so utterly devoid of substantive discourse, a process so disdainful of the very people it is supposed to serve. But the lack of self-awareness and independence by the participants themselves is even more stupefying.

Of course, there's much more to electing the most powerful leader on earth than straw votes and sound bites, primaries and party conventions and commercials. Fact is, it takes mammoth sums of money to obtain power. Precisely *how* that all evolves is not always apparent, but one thing is quite clear. As we noted in 1996 in *The Buying of the President*, "Before the first vote is cast in a presidential primary, a private referendum has already been conducted among the nation's financial elites as to which candidate shall earn his party's nomination." Certain candidates are winnowed out, either choosing not to enter the fray at all or attempting it unsuccessfully. And a fundamental determinant in their decision—and in our choices at the polls—is money.

The dirty secret of American presidential politics is that the nation's wealthiest interests largely determine who will be the next President of the United States, in the year *before* the election. As political fund-raising consultant Stan Huckaby has noted, without exception, in every election since 1976, the candidate who has raised the most money by the end of the year preceding the election, and who has been eligible for federal matching funds, has become his party's nominee for President.

The most recent case in point: The two presidential candidates who raised the most money in 1995 and were eligible for matching funds—Clinton and Dole—won their parties' nominations. Both men raised more than $20 million in the year before the election. Of the 16,200 donors who contributed $1,000 to the Clinton-Gore reelection campaign, 15,200, or 94 percent, gave their money early, in 1995. Of the 48,000 donors who contributed the legal maximum of $1,000 to GOP presidential candidates in the 1995–96 election cycle, 39,800, or 83 percent, gave in 1995.

It is the *price* of power that interests us the most in *The Buying of the President 2000*. What accommodations have been made to achieve that power, and with whom? What is the cost to the nation? Who are these presidential candidates, really, and what powerful interests are aligned with them?

For more than a year roughly two dozen researchers, writers, and editors have been analyzing thousands of primary and secondary sources of information, including campaign finance data from the Federal Election Commission and the Center for Responsive Politics, personal financial disclosure forms, and congressional voting records, in some cases going back twenty years. We have interviewed hundreds of individuals. The book has chapters on all major presidential candidates who were active contenders as of September 1999, which explains why we write about Elizabeth Dole and Dan Quayle but not Lamar Alexander or John Kasich. Once again, each candidate chapter contains a list of the Top Ten Career Patrons, those most steadfastly generous, important donors who have helped to underwrite the candidate's political career. And, for the first time, we also list the Top 50 Patrons since 1991 (measured in "soft money" contributions) for each of the two major political parties.

"The saddest life is that of a political aspirant under democracy," H. L. Mencken once wrote. "His failure is ignominious and his success is disgraceful." We respect the ideal of public service in the public interest, and we fully recognize that on a personal level, politics can be a brutal exercise. We have tried to be fair to the men and woman who aspire to hold the highest office in the land. For example, every reasonable effort to interview the candidates has been made, over many months. Unfortunately, the candidates *all* declined our repeated requests for interviews. (By way of comparison, for the 1996 book, half of the candidates consented to interviews.)

It should be clear that, simply stated, *The Buying of the President 2000* highlights areas of interest to us, vital information that we believe the American people want—and need—to know. We did not seek to provide *every* detail of the candidates' interactions with their contributors. Nor did we see it as our role to present slick, swooning profiles of the candidates—readers can get that stuff from their authorized campaign biographies or Web sites (which we reference in [the book's] pages and on the Center's Web site). Indeed, the book does *not* contain full biographies of the candidates or personal financial disclosure reports, including investments, speaking fees, and all-expenses-paid trips, or specific details about many of the public policy decisions they have made in the past. This kind of information, plus each candidate's "Top 25 Career Patrons" and capsule profiles of those patrons, is at *www.publicintegrity.org.*

We do not live in an inspiring time of candor or contrition when it comes to politics, and to the role of money in politics. Our politicians seem to have become increasingly shameless, arrogant, and loose with the truth. Unfortunately, after the decades of deceit since Vietnam and Watergate, the American people are no longer surprised when government officials ignore or mislead them. It's gotten harder and harder to get straight answers from politicians and those who work for them. Lying is now called spin or "damage control," and it's studied, taught, and even admired by many people in Washington today as an effective public relations technique.

We spoke with Archibald Cox, the enormously respected former Watergate independent prosecutor whom President Nixon fired in October 1973, in the opening salvo of the infamous "Saturday Night Massacre." Cox believes there is much less trust in government today than there was during the Watergate years. And he said that campaign finance abuses are "far worse today" than during Watergate, when many unlawful corporate contributions were discovered and prosecuted.

Cox believes that today the threat to the democratic process is even graver. "The abuses are worse partly because there's much more money and ... there's much more pressure on those who receive the money to yield to the wishes of those who give it," Cox told the Center. "I'm speaking of a lot of elected officials across the board, but particularly in Congress."

Of course, what happens *after* public officials leave government is also troubling, a subject the Center for Public Integrity has investigated frequently over the years. The Washington mercenary culture, absorbing former government decision makers who triple or quadruple their salaries as lobbyists or consultants, grows each year. Thirty years ago there were fewer than 100 registered lobbyists in the nation's capital; today there are approximately 14,000. But we also are seeing more garish profiteering from public service. Some of the nation's most respected political leaders now unabashedly cash in personally as soon as they're off the public payroll. Some, such as former Governors Ann Richards and Mario Cuomo, have done Doritos commercials. Robert Dole does TV ads about penile erection dysfunction for Viagra (you don't see too many television ads about election dysfunction). Former Senate Majority Leaders George Mitchell and Howard Baker, Jr., recently have made money the old-fashioned Washington way, by lobbying for the tobacco companies.

More broadly, in the three years since the 1996 election we have seen a steady deterioration in tolerable standards of political conduct. What was outrageous yesterday merely seems to be accepted reality today.

In late 1996 and throughout 1997, for example, we learned that President Clinton was personally involved in raising and channeling millions of dollars in Democratic Party contributions to his own reelection campaign, with the money spent on television commercials that he personally approved and that were aired more than a year before the 1996 election. The Democratic Party accepted millions of dollars in illegal contributions from foreign nationals, many of whom met personally with the President. Vice President Albert Gore, Jr., spoke at a fund-raising event at a Buddhist monastery in Los Angeles, and everyone from a Colombian drug trafficker to Chinese arms dealers passed through the White House, obtaining access for cash. Separately, from January 1995 to August 1996, the White House hosted 103 coffees—attended by 1,544 people seeking "face time" with the President, the Vice President, and their spouses —who collectively contributed at least $26.4 million to the Democratic Party for the 1996 election. Besides being rewarded with overnight stays at the White House and at Camp David, in 1995 and 1996, major Democratic Party donors and fund-raisers rode on Air Force One, Marine One, Air Force Two, and Marine Two (the latter two are the Vice President's aircraft) more than 300 times. In addition, both the President and Vice President solicited campaign contributions by telephone from the White House, Clinton from his residential quarters and Gore from his office. At first Gore said that he dialed for dollars "on a few occasions"; he later acknowledged that he did it fifty-six times. This was the potentially criminal matter that produced the now infamous statement by the Vice President: "My counsel advises me that there is *no controlling legal authority* or case that says that there was any violation of law whatsoever in the manner in which I asked people to contribute to our reelection campaign." [emphasis added]

Sadly, Gore was right. None of this unprecedented activity, which certainly had the stench of misconduct and impropriety, was seriously prosecuted by the Justice Department. Only the small fry were pursued. Attorney General Janet Reno steadfastly refused to name an independent counsel to investigate the various 1996 campaign-finance allegations. And when the Senate Governmental Affairs Committee attempted to investigate the 1996 election abuses, more than forty-five potential witnesses fled the United States or invoked the Fifth Amendment. Months of public hearings were held, but it was painfully obvious that the committee was severely hamstrung by both the White House and the Senate Republican leadership. And there was the hypocrisy of virtually ignoring *congressional* campaign-finance issues, even though, over the years, five of the committee's sixteen members had themselves, through their campaigns, violated federal election laws.

To add insult to injury, the following year, Americans suffered through Monica Mania, ending with the first impeachment of an elected President in U.S. history. Whatever your opinion of Bill Clinton, former White House intern Monica Lewinsky, Independent Counsel Kenneth Starr, or Congress, one thing is clear: In 1998, we reached the lowest point in our nation's political discourse and decorum, including the most blatant, look-you-in-the-eye-with-a-straight-face lying by a sitting President ever. And let us not forget that this whole sordid episode got its start with campaign contributions: Lewinsky became a White House intern in the first place because a friend of her family had given more than $330,000 to the Democratic Party.

In 1999 the presidential election season began with further evidence that the post-Watergate campaign finance system is broken. The son of former President George Bush, George W. Bush, leading all prospective presidential candidates in public opinion polls, set the political world on its ear. Without any detailed policy positions, federal government experience, or stated vision for the future, and while hardly leaving his home in Austin, he raised $37 million in four months. That is more money at that early point in a presidential campaign than any previous White House contender, more than the ten other Republican contenders combined, and more than either Clinton or Dole raised for their respective campaigns in the entire 1995–96 election cycle. Bush's campaign took in the astonishing sum of $310,748 a day—that's $12,947 an hour—in contributions. The previous record had been set in 1995, when Clinton raised $26 million in seven months.

This kind of money isn't raised at backyard barbecues or from neighborhood bake sales, of course. It comes from thousands of the wealthiest Americans, many of whom want something from the government. To be sure, significant cash is, by itself, certainly not sufficient to ensure future residence at 1600 Pennsylvania Avenue. Just ask John Connally (1980), Ross Perot (1992 and 1996), or Steve Forbes (1996), to name three well-financed, unsuccessful aspirants. But without question, money is a *necessary* ingredient for a candidate, along with a timely, articulate message; credible professional credentials; confident, attractive presentation; and an effective campaign organization.

Weeks after his campaign's dramatic disclosure that it had raised $37 million in the first half of 1999, Bush announced that he would forgo federal matching funds and the spending limits that accompany them. In so doing, he can ignore the spending ceiling of nearly $50 million in the preconvention phase of the election cycle as well as state-by-state spending caps. Forbes, who also will forgo matching funds, as he did in 1996, vowed to match Bush dollar for dollar. Bush put his family's extensive network of political money-raisers under the charge of his best friend, Donald Evans, who told a reporter for the *New York Times* that he regards his work as a form of public service. "Behind every check, there's a willing heart," Evans said. "To me, its not a check, it's a person, someone who cares about this great country."

Bush's calculation that Americans won't mind how much money he raises, or what rules he plays by, is telling. Simply put, it marks a new level of political audacity. Heretofore, it would have been completely unthinkable for a popular candidate with serious hopes of landing a major party nomination to forsake the public subsidies established in the wake of the worst political scandal of the twentieth century. But this largely anointed GOP presidential candidate with the famous last name is willing to do it because he thinks he *can* do it. The nation's political establishment even seems to canonize candidates with the Midas touch. The unfortunate wretches who are unable to amass sizable political war chests give off the fetid odor of dead meat, going nowhere fast. The actual merits of the candidates' ideas and backgrounds are largely irrelevant. And meanwhile, there is little public consideration of precisely where the political money has come from or what the donors seek in return.

Certainly, the mutual dependency between politicians and their patrons is nothing new. But one can't help wondering how Abraham Lincoln or Harry Truman would fare in todays political, mega-fund-raising milieu. Would they be willing to dial for dollars for several hours each day and, with frozen smiles, shake thousands upon thousands of strangers' hands at hundreds of fund-raising events throughout the country, a full *year* before the election? It frankly is difficult to fathom.

The stark fact today is that, increasingly, good people are not entering politics for a host of reasons, financial ones chief among them. In 1998 there were more than ninety *uncontested* elections for the U.S. House of Representatives, and the states of Arkansas, Florida, and Louisiana didn't bother to even count votes. In Florida the names of those lucky candidates in uncontested House races didn't even appear on the ballot.

In the past two election cycles we have seen record-shattering sums of private, special-interest money pouring into the political process. We have seen the worst campaign-finance scandals since Watergate. And, at the same time, we have witnessed the worst voter disillusionment in more than half a century.

How did things get so bad?

The short answer is that politicians have become so deeply enmeshed in the money chase and personally tied to powerful economic interests that they have lost the esteem and trust of the American people.

Confidence in government has waned to historic lows. In 1996, 100 million eligible voters declined to participate in this democracy, the lowest turnout (49 percent) in a presidential election year since 1924, and the second lowest since 1824. Only 36 percent of eligible voters went to the polls in 1998, the lowest turnout since 1942.

Meanwhile, the ruling class of politicians and patrons has not felt compelled to open democracy to greater citizen participation. The 1996 presidential election revealed what moneyed interests have done to the political process. "The abuses of the campaign finance system, as practiced by both parties in 1996 ... destroyed what was left of this country's campaign-finance laws," journalist Elizabeth Drew observed in her 1999 book, *The Corruption of American Politics.* "There were now effectively no limits on how much money could be raised and spent in a campaign, and the limits on how it could be raised were rendered meaningless. Powerful people had undermined the law...."

The reckless orgy in 1996 between politicians and their deep-pocketed patrons came at the same time the rich were getting richer. More people have become billionaires in the past fifteen years than at any other time in U.S. history, and the 189 American billionaires today (more than twelve times the number in 1982) have well over a trillion dollars in wealth. In Silicon Valley alone, sixty-four new millionaires are made each day. One percent of the population controls 40 percent of the nation's assets, and the United States now has the widest gap between rich and poor of any industrialized country.

Meanwhile, the number of bankruptcy cases has risen almost 70 percent since 1995. One in five American children—a total of 14.5 million children—live in poverty. Every day, 1,827 babies are born in the United States without health-care coverage; 11.3 million children from coast to coast are without health care.

Wall Street bestowed $11 billion in bonuses in 1998, up from $2 billion in 1990. In this new Gilded Age of twenty-something millionaires and ostentatious materialism, from Manhattan to Silicon Valley, we are witnessing almost incomprehensible wealth wash over the political system as well, further transforming it. The same 535 Members of Congress, two political parties, and presidential candidates who raised $2 billion in 1992 and $2.4 billion in 1996 are well on their way to amassing more than $3 billion in this election cycle. And that's just the money we know about.

This game is too rich for ordinary folks. In 1996, for example, only four percent of the American people gave money to candidates for any political office. Only one-fourth of one percent gave $200 or more to candidates for federal office. Our electoral process is now so besotted by big money that millionaires now make up more than a third of the U.S. Senate, even though fewer than one percent of Americans are so fortunate. And while practically no one has noticed, at least ten of the presidential candidates in 1999—Lamar Alexander, Bill Bradley, Pat Buchanan, George W. Bush, Elizabeth Dole, Steve Forbes, Al

Gore, Orrin Hatch, John McCain, and Dan Quayle—are millionaires. The richest candidate by far is Forbes, who will tap his personal wealth of more than $400 million to bankroll his own campaign, as he did in 1996. Among other things, he favors eliminating the tax on capital gains.

It is hardly coincidental that over the years, Congress has substantially reduced both the top income-tax rate and the tax on capital gains. Or that Congress and its banking patrons killed legislation that would have eliminated bank ATM fees. Or that Congress has failed to pass legislation that would have required employers to help pay for health-care insurance. Or that Congress has passed special "cheap labor" immigration-exemption laws and Y2K liability exemption laws at the request of Silicon Valley companies. The list of special favors for the privileged few is quite, quite long. As political scientist Louise Overacker wrote in 1932, "Even a dog will not bite the hand that feeds it, and a political party will hardly 'sell out' the person whose money it accepts." And every public policy dispensation for political donors—no matter how crass or narrow the economic interest—is invariably cloaked under some kind of broader, nobler pretext.

At various times in the past century, the American people have expressed their outrage over the deterioration of their political process into a mercenary, pay-to-play culture, and insisted that system be reformed. The most recent eruption of public will was a quarter century ago, in 1974. After two years and hundreds of stories (including many of major campaign contributors getting special government favors), Americans were completely fed up with the widespread corruption and lying of Washington officials. "Watergate" was shorthand for cash contributions in paper bags, illegal corporate donations, secret slush funds, and the like. Just weeks after Richard Nixon's resignation, the new President, Republican Gerald Ford, signed historic campaign finance-reform legislation. "The times," he said, "demand this legislation."

The law created a new regulatory agency, the Federal Election Commission (FEC); contribution and expenditure disclosure requirements for all federal elections; and specific limits on what individuals, political committees, and party organizations could give to federal campaigns. It also set up a system of partial public financing of presidential campaigns—voluntary public matching funds during the primaries and full public financing during the general election. The idea behind the matching funds was to reduce potentially corrosive fund-raising pressures during the late stages of the campaign and encourage small donations in the early going.

No one disputes that the new disclosure requirements dramatically opened up the political process, and the contribution limits prevented the kind of huge donations to candidates that had badly stained the presidential election of 1972. Indeed, for many years, presidential campaigns seemed relatively free of the taint of scandal.

But the authority of this new regulatory system was soon undermined. In 1976, in a landmark case, *Buckley v. Valeo,* the Supreme Court framed campaign spending as a First Amendment, free-speech issue. In other words, wealthy individuals can spend as much of their own money as they want on their own campaigns. At the same time, the controversial decision recognized the importance of "the primary purpose" of the 1974 reform law, "to limit the actuality and appearance of corruption, resulting from large individual financial contributions." The Court also held that while advertisements expressly advocating the election or defeat of a candidate for federal office could be regulated, advertisements about issues could not be restricted under the Constitution.

Separately, it soon became obvious that the FEC was incapable of independently regulating the politicians and the political industry. The agency became an easy mark for the aggressive tactics of party lawyers, accountants, and candidates. For example, because of several FEC advisory opinions, approved without hearings or public comment, beginning in the 1980s, the two major political parties were permitted to raise back-door, unlimited contributions known as "soft money." In 1995–96 the two parties raised $262 million in soft money— three times the 1991–92 total. It was mostly raised through large contributions from corporations and labor unions, which are prohibited from making direct contributions to federal candidates and committees.

What is the significance of all this? The post-Watergate reforms have been eroded and trivialized, with debilitating repercussions. Today's unvarnished political realities are:

1. Politicians and their parties can collect and spend as much money they want.

It's not only soft money that's exploding. In 1995–96, twenty-nine organizations spent $135 million to $150 million on "issue-advocacy" advertising in the presidential and congressional elections; in 1997–98, seventy-seven groups spent roughly $300 million. Those soft-money and issue-ad numbers are expected to go through the roof in 2000. Mel Sembler, the finance chairman of the Republican National Committee, plans to raise a special, new $30 million fund "to support the most aggressive issue-advocacy program in GOP history."

2. Candidates and their campaigns are raising and spending secret money.

Presidential candidates this time around have raised millions of dollars in nonfederal accounts that aren't subject to public disclosure requirements. Their other techniques for hiding money include creating nonprofit organizations. These undisclosed revenue streams render the traditional reporting system a relic.

3. The enforcement of election laws is almost always too little, too late.

After the biggest political scandal since Watergate, not a single White House or Democratic National Committee official was indicted. The FEC is completely captive to the politicians, and would be regarded as a national embarrassment if anyone cared. A case in point: After the 1996 election scandal, even though FEC auditors and FBI agents found that the Clinton and Dole campaigns had misspent tens of millions of dollars, the FEC's six commissioners—

three Democrats and three Republicans—ultimately declined to impose fines or other sanctions on either side.

4. Political accountability itself is in danger of becoming a lost virtue.

With voter participation and trust at historic lows, the American people have come to expect and accept the worst from their politicians. Public interest and news media interest in politics generally have declined; so has the inclination of citizens to get involved in political causes. Increasingly, the disengagement is making government the exclusive province of vested economic interests and the politicians they support. Politicians do not take responsibility for this reality, nor are they asked to. And as long as no one is marching in the streets, prodigious amounts of money will be sloshing through the system, sometimes secretly, sometimes illegally, sometimes directly influencing life-and-death public policy decisions. We also will continue to have mock sincerity and epidemic equivocation by our elected officials.

All in all, the potential for corruption is enormous, and the immediate prospects for reform are not auspicious. It is against this sobering backdrop that we have produced *The Buying of the President 2000*. We present not only chapters about the major candidates, but also the fascinating milieu in which they exist, the political parties. Ironically, as historian Arthur Schlesinger, Jr., has observed, the Articles of Confederation and the Constitution contained no mention of political parties. And yet throughout the twentieth century no one has been elected President from *outside* the Democratic and Republican parties. The candidates' ideas, organizations, and campaign finances are deeply enmeshed in the culture and daily operations of their respective political parties. We examine some of the practical, grubby realities of the two major parties in Washington, which act as legal conduits between policy makers and the most powerful economic interests affected by their decisions. These special interests open the spigots of cash flowing to the party and its leading members holding public office. And they facilitate access to power by the captains of industry and labor, who have paid handsomely and expect special consideration. Private corporations with public stature and function, these quasi-public institutions are themselves as deeply mired in high-powered influence-peddling in Washington as any lobbying firm. It is long past time that we correct our vision of these American icons.

President Harry Truman once said, "1 never give them hell—I just tell the truth and they think it's hell." Over the years at the Center for Public Integrity, we have earned the enmity of a wide array of entrenched interests, and we were once dubbed "the scourge of lobbyists" by *National Journal....*

It might not surprise you, then, that we are not part of the Washington power circuit, or invited to dinners at the White House, regardless of occupant. Chances are, neither are you. Bu by reading *The Buying of the President 2000*, you will at least get a better idea about who is coziest with the next leader of the free world—and why.

Russell Roberts

 **NO**

Will Campaign Finance Reform Enhance the Power of the People?

A common cry among the reform set these days is that there is too much money in politics. Those who decry the role of money in politics imagine a world where the 535 members of Congress along with the President sit around in togas discussing the best way to serve the people and discharge their civic responsibility. Rather than being influenced by money or special interests, these modern-day Platos and Aristotles would be motivated by the public good and the voices of the people.

There are various policy reforms being proposed to achieve that utopia. The most common is a ban on soft money, the money that can be donated in unlimited amounts to the political parties. These proposals may violate the First Amendment. But ignoring constitutional issues, will these reforms enhance or reduce the power of the people?

Getting the money out of politics is like wanting to take the grinder out of the sausage factory. The federal government currently spends about $1.7 trillion dollars annually. With that much money up for grabs, it's awfully hard to stop people from trying to influence how it's spent. It's only a question of how that influence will manifest itself. Will it be out in the open or done in hidden ways? Is there a way to balance the will of the people against the power of the special interests?

Alas, if truth be told, in most cases there is no will of the people. There's my will and yours and the will of the other 275 million Americans. A lot of what we find ugly about politics is the attempt to compromise or balance the desires of one group against the desires of another. In your eyes, perhaps, my group of brave activists valiantly fighting to achieve a policy goal I cherish is nothing more than a group of sleazy lobbyists fighting for a special interest. When my preferred policy initiative fails, I decry the special interests that spent all that money to keep it from happening. When my policy initiative succeeds, you decry the influence of money that allowed such a travesty.

The political marketplace is adversarial. On most policy issues, there is money arrayed on both sides, jockeying for position. In other settings, we understand the beneficial role of this adversarial setting. We understand that while

Adapted from Russell Roberts, "Will Campaign Finance Reform Enhance the Power of the People?" *Ideas on Liberty* (September 2000). Copyright © 2000 by Russell Roberts. Reprinted by permission of the author and The Foundation for Economic Education, Irvington-on-Hudson, NY.

Ford spends money to tell us its cars are great, it's a healthy thing that GM can spend money letting us know about their cars as well. We also understand the importance of letting Toyota and Honda and others enter the fray. Competition is good for the consumer.

Banning soft money closes off one way for special interests to influence policy. It encourages them to compete in less obvious ways that are harder to detect. At the same time, it reduces the ability of new entrants to challenge entrenched incumbents. That means a smaller voice for the voters.

If you want to see how competition would be affected by a ban on soft money, consider the following fable. Once upon a time, there were only two manufacturers of cars, Ford and GM, but cars could only be marketed and sold in a very unusual way. Each manufacturer was allowed to nominate one car that it would manufacture and sell for the next four years. While there were two manufacturers, only one was chosen to actually produce and sell the car. That was determined by a vote of the people.

To let the voters and consumers make an informed choice, the car manufacturers took the cars on tour to let the voters see them and kick the tires. Unfortunately, voters couldn't drive the cars. That made voting wisely a little tougher, so voters turned to various ways to get information about the candidates. I mean, cars. We did the best we could. We carefully watched the advertising campaigns of the manufacturers to gain information. Some of that information was GM knocking Ford's product or vice versa, but that was often very useful. People also relied on information from the media—the writers and reporters and talk show hosts who covered the car industry had specialized knowledge of the products.

In this weird car market, the two major manufacturers picked their cars very carefully. There was a lot of competition behind the scenes, as the designers of each brand within Ford and GM lobbied and cajoled to get their brand chosen. But Ford and GM had a tendency to choose cars that were familiar to the voters, because the voters already had an idea of their quality and how they would turn out.

Every once in a while, a manufacturer would introduce a radical new concept, a minivan or a convertible. For these new models to have a chance, a lot of money would have to be spent advertising the product and getting voters acquainted with the new models' characteristics and features. It took a lot of money for a new brand to beat an established brand. Brand name recognition was very powerful, especially when consumers could only kick the tires rather than actually drive the cars. But if the product was good enough, a good advertising campaign would help it succeed.

Even rarer than a new product from GM and Ford was a new party, er, manufacturer. On rare occasions, a new manufacturer would come along and try to get the voters to take a chance on a new offering from a new company. Voters were hesitant to take a chance on an untested brand. But if the product was of a sufficiently high quality and enough money spent on marketing to convince the voters, these new manufacturers could be successful from time to time.

Then one day, people decided that the car companies were spending too much money advertising their cars. Wouldn't it be better, someone suggested, to limit the total amount of money they could spend promoting their products? Less money would be wasted on advertising and there would be less influence by special interests, the families always lobbying and advertising for minivans and the young always pushing for convertibles. Those expenditures tilted the choices in their direction and unfairly persuaded some voters to vote against the best interests of the country.

A law was passed radically limiting the amount of advertising. To make up for the lost advertising, a number of debates were held, where representatives from GM and Ford stood in front of their nominated cars and argued over their relative merits.

There were many changes in the car market caused by the limits on advertising. First, brand name became even more important. A new manufacturer found it almost impossible to introduce a new model. Without the ability to use a substantial advertising budget to overcome the brand name advantage of incumbent cars, even high quality products were unable to get a foothold in the market. They were rarely invited to the debates. After all, explained the organizers, those no-name cars don't realty have a chance. So the power of the two major manufacturers increased even more.

Incumbent cars became very difficult to defeat. Ford and GM usually nominated the same cars over and over again because they were familiar to voters. Any product changes were mainly cosmetic.

Innovation in the industry came to a standstill. What was the advantage to Ford and GM of improving their cars? Such improvements came at a cost. To let voters know about the quality of the new product required advertising that was no longer possible.

In this new world of limited advertising, the automotive press became more powerful than ever. Because there was very little advertising, most voters learned about the cars running for election by turning to the media for information. Some found this to be an improvement over the rough and tumble campaigns of the past—surely it was good to rely on experts without the negative mud-slinging that used to take place. But others worried about the ability of experts to remain objective when so much was at stake. They were also a little uncomfortable that the press had been one of the biggest leaders of the movement to limit advertising. Maybe their advocacy of limited advertising had been self-interested rather than altruistic.

Those who defended the limits on advertising found the greatest solace in what appeared to be the reduction in the power of special interests. They were no longer able to give money to influence the advertising campaigns. But special interests found other ways to influence the process.

Unfortunately, because these methods were now behind the scenes, they were harder to detect. How did the special interests influence outcomes without the ability to donate money to the manufacturers? They befriended people at Ford and GM to influence which cars were put forward by the manufacturers. They took reporters and TV anchors to dinner to tell them the virtues of their favorite cars. They placed people sympathetic to their outlook on the car company payroll and on newspaper staffs. They befriended talk show hosts. In this way, they insured sympathetic treatment of their views without looking heavy-handed.

But few noticed the corruption. And while some complained that the cars seemed to get duller and duller every year, few attributed the state of the market to the limits on advertising. Instead people looked for new reforms and new regulations to reduce the role of money even further. They didn't realize that each step in that direction made the market less competitive.

Most of the reforms of the political marketplace are taking us in the same direction. While they appear to enhance the power of the people relative to the special interests, they do so by reducing competition, the consumer and voter's best friend.

With less competition, the biggest beneficiaries of a ban on soft money will be incumbents. They will find it easier to use their already powerful brand-name recognition to overcome challengers who can no longer expect party money to help them establish their name and ideas.

Ironically, the best way to reduce the power of special interests is to allow hard money to flow without limitations—remove the limits on how much individuals and organizations can give directly to candidates. This appears to increase the potential influence of special interests. But the real impact is to increase competition. It allows new candidates to enter the political marketplace at lower cost than they can enter now. Instead of having to garner funds $1000 at a lime, unlimited hard money expands the field of potential candidates.

If wealthy individuals could give unlimited amounts to candidates, candidates could focus on campaigning and thinking and breathing instead of being non-stop fund-raisers. In today's world, the limits on hard money produce candidates who can stomach rubber chicken night after night. We would be better off choosing from a wider field. The major complaint against unlimited hard money is that the rich would have too much influence. But this fear ignores the power of the ballot box. Having a great deal of money to spend does not guarantee victory as Steve Forbes and Ross Perot can attest. Besides, plenty of rich folks want politicians to redistribute wealth to the poor. That's presumably the reason why millionaire Stuart Mon financed George McGovern in the 1972 presidential race, before the limits on hard money were in place that we live under today. And our choices have become a lot less interesting and a lot less diverse since those limits were put in place.

The ultimate arbiter is always the ballot box. Unlimited hard money allows voters to have more choices. Promptly post all contributions on the Internet. Candidates who are in the pocket of special interests can be reviled by the media and then by the voters. When the government spends almost $2 trillion dollars and writes a myriad of regulations, keeping the political marketplace competitive remains our best hope for enhancing the power of the people.

POSTSCRIPT

Is Political Marketing Essentially Buying Politicians?

Surprisingly, many consider campaign finance to be a political issue dealing with laws about finance. Both Lewis and Roberts agree that campaign finance is squarely a *marketing* issue, and the ever-increasing encroachment of political marketing in the American electoral process is the subject of intense debate. It is crucial to recognize that political marketing draws from the entire spectrum of marketing tools and techniques. Campaign strategy, voter research, positioning the candidates to various voter segments, building strategic alliances with special interest groups, and media and message choices are all marketing-driven decisions.

The public seems largely desensitized and apathetic toward the issue of campign finance reform because of its complexity and the sense of futility concerning foreseeable change and meaningful results. Certainly candidates are "brands" managed by some of the keenest marketing strategists, who bring to bear the best available research and communication technologies. More money was spent selling U.S. presidential candidates in 2000 than any other product marketing campaign in world history.

Votes are taken through the entire purchase decision process, from unawareness to the product disposal. In the end, when going to the presidential polls, voters only buy once, and the choice is mostly between two brands of the same product. This is a dangerously competitive situation whereby the negative ads and "astroturf" strategies (creating and developing crisis-type issues) find fertile ground.

Roberts acknowledges the problems of secrecy and suggests that all donors and their support activities should be published on the Internet. But with the opportunities to conceal donor identity, such as 527 committees, and other behind-the-scenes promotions, can these contributors be truly exposed? Do 527 committees deserve special treatment? The reality is the systemic nature of American politics, which invites the talents of marketing strategists to accomplish their communication goals. The values may change, but the game will basically remain the same.

Two explosive marketing developments deal with issue advertising and the impact of the Internet on political marketing. According to media consultants, "issue" ads constituted 40.6 percent of all political advertising in 1996, up from 15.7 percent in 1992. The national expenditure on political commercials is $600 million.

From eContributor.com to eCommercial.com (recently renamed MindArrow Systems, Inc.), electronic commerce (e-commerce) is rapidly emerging as political marketers' new favorite tool. Mike McCurry, President Clinton's previous White House spokeman states, "The Era of the imagemaker is giving way to the Era of the webmaster." Political campaign donations made online have increased tenfold in the last two years.

What is the future of fund-raising—big money raised through relationships or marketing through the Internet? Will restricting amounts of "soft money" restore power to the people?

Suggested Readings

Elizabeth Drew, *The Corruption of American Politics: What Went Wrong and Why* (Birch Lane, 1999)

Nick Higham, "Exposing the 'Millbank Myth' of Political Marketing Success," *Marketing Week* (May 27, 1999)

Steven Kates, "A Qualitative Exploration into Voters' Ethical Perceptions of Political Advertising: Discourse, Disinformation and Moral Boundaries," *Journal of Business Ethics* (December 1998)

Bruce Newman, *The Mass Marketing of Politics: Democracy in an Age of Manufactured Images* (Sage Publications, 1999)

Wayne Rash, "Politics and Marketing Team on the Internet," *Internetweek* (September 13, 1999)

Jules Whitcover, *No Way to Pick a President: How Money and Hired Guns Have Debased American Elections* (Farrar, Straus & Giroux, 1999)

The Southern Party. http://www.southernparty.org

eContributor.com. http://www.econtributor.com

MindArrow Systems. http://www.mindarrow.com

Today's Voter.com. http://www.voter.com

Contributors to This Volume

EDITORS

BART MACCHIETTE is a professor and the coordinator of marketing at Plymouth State College of the University System of New Hampshire. He received his B.S. from Nasson College in 1965, his M.B.A. from American University in 1970, and his Ph.D. from the Union Institute in 1980. He has close to 30 years of teaching experience, including 8 years at Towson State University and 21 years at Plymouth State, with strong participation in their M.B.A. programs. His area of expertise lies in marketing to minorities, affinity marketing, and consumer behavior. His papers have been published in the *Journal of Consumer Marketing, Journal of Direct Marketing, Journal of Services Marketing,* and the *Journal of Product and Brand Management.* He has been on the editorial review boards for the *Journal of Consumer Marketing* and the *Journal of Services Marketing* for several years, and he has reviewed many books in marketing and consumer behavior. Dr. Macchiette is faculty adviser to the student chapter of the American Marketing Association. He can be reached at bartm@oz.plymouth.edu.

ABHIJIT ROY is a doctoral student in marketing at Boston University. He has an M.B.A. and an M.S. from the University of Arizona, and his undergraduate degree in mechanical engineering is from the University of Allahabad in India. He has over 16 years of teaching experience—as a lecturer at Boston University and the University of Arizona and as a full-time faculty member at Plymouth State College. His papers have been published in the *Journal of Consumer Marketing, Journal of Direct Marketing, Journal of Services Marketing, Encyclopedia of Advertising,* and the *Encyclopedia of Popular Culture.* Mr. Roy has served as director of the Small Business Development Program at Plymouth State College. He may be contacted at abhijitr@bu.edu.

STAFF

Theodore Knight   List Manager
David Brackley   Senior Developmental Editor
Juliana Poggio   Developmental Editor
Rose Gleich   Administrative Assistant
Brenda S. Filley   Director of Production/Design
Juliana Arbo   Typesetting Supervisor
Diane Barker   Proofreader
Richard Tietjen   Publishing Systems Manager
Larry Killian   Copier Coordinator

AUTHORS

STEPHEN BARRETT, a retired psychiatrist, is a nationally renowned author, editor, and consumer advocate. An expert in medical communications, he is medical editor of Prometheus Books and consulting editor of *Nutrition Forum,* a newsletter emphasizing the exposure of fads, fallacies, and quackery. His 47 books include *The Health Robbers: A Close Look at Quackery in America,* rev. ed., coauthored with William Jarvis (Prometheus Books, 1993). He is also a board member of the National Council Against Health Fraud, a scientific adviser to the American Council on Science and Health, and a fellow of the Committee for the Scientific Investigation of Claims of the Paranormal (CSICOP).

BETH BELTON, a writer for *USA Today,* specializes in world business and technology news.

JAMES T. BENNETT is a professor of economics at George Mason University in Fairfax, Virginia. He received his Ph.D. from Case Western Reserve University in 1970 and has specialized in research related to public policy issues, the economics of government and bureaucracy, labor unions, and health charities.

MARK S. BONCHEK is director of research at the Strategos Institute, a knowledge-creating community of executives, consultants, and academics learning how to embed an ongoing capacity for strategy innovation in organizations. He has contributed several articles to *Management Review.*

JENNIFER BRESNAHAN, a former senior writer for *CIO Enterprise Magazine,* is a student of law and a contributing writer.

DALE D. BUSS writes on marketing topics for *Nations Business* and *Advertising Age.* He has also written several articles on distribution management.

ANN CLURMAN is coauthor, with J. Walker Smith, of the book *Rocking the Ages: The Yankelovich Report on Generational Marketing* (HarperInformation, 1997). She is a Yankelovich partner and has worked on the Monitor project for more than 20 years.

D. KIRK DAVIDSON began a second career in academia after more than 30 years as a marketing and retailing executive in San Francisco and Carmel, California. He is an assistant professor in the Department of Business, Accounting, and Economics at Mount Saint Mary's College in Emmitsburg, Maryland, and the author of *Selling Sin: The Marketing of Socially Unacceptable Products* (Quorum Books, 1996). He regularly contributes articles on ethical issues in marketing to *Marketing News.*

THOMAS J. DiLORENZO is a professor of economics at the Sellinger School of Business and Management at Loyola College in Baltimore, Maryland.

PEGGY J. FARBER is an educator and a radio and print reporter. She holds the Prudential Fellowship at the Columbia Graduate School of Journalism, and she is writing a book on for-profit education in the classroom. She has also written and produced radio programs that deal with historical subjects and current affairs.

PETER FERRARA is general counsel and chief economist for Americans for Tax Reform.

MARCY GORDON is a business writer for the Associated Press.

KARL TARO GREENFELD writes about business issues for *Time* magazine.

DAVID GROSSMAN, a retired lieutenant colonel in the U.S. Army, is director of the Killology Research Group and a professor of psychology at West Point. He is coauthor, with Gloria DeGaetano, of *Teaching Our Kids to Kill: A Call to Action Against TV, Movie and Video Game Violence* (Crown, 1999), an internationally acclaimed book on the impact of media violence, and the author of *On Killing: The Psychological Cost of Learning to Kill in War and Society* (DIANE, 1998), a Pulitzer-nominated book and a standard text in universities, military academies, and police academies worldwide.

MARY BETH GROVER is an editor at *Forbes* magazine, where she is known for her enlightening articles on new trends in business.

EDWARD M. HALLOWELL is a psychiatrist who practices in Concord, Massachusetts, and an instructor of psychiatry at Harvard Medical School. He is the author of the best-seller *Connect: Twelve Vital Ties That Open Your Heart, Lengthen Your Life, and Deepen Your Soul* (Pantheon Books, 1999) and *Driven to Distraction: Recognizing and Coping With Attention Deficit Disorder from Childhood Through Adulthood* (Simon & Schuster, 1995).

REBECCA PIIRTO HEATH is a regular contributor to *American Demographics* and *Marketing Tools*.

PAUL HOLMES is the editor of *Reputation Management* and *Inside PR*.

MICHAEL F. JACOBSON is cofounder of the Center for the Study of Commercialism and executive director of the Center for Science in the Public Interest. He is the author or coauthor of many books, including *What Are We Feeding Our Kids?* (Workman, 1994) and *Marketing Disease to Hispanics*, coauthored with Bruce Maxwell (Center for Science in the Public Interest, 1989).

LUCETTE LAGNADO is a writer for the *Wall Street Journal*, particularly on the drug and health care industry.

CHARLES LEWIS was an investigative reporter for *ABC News* as well as a producer for *60 minutes*. He received a McArthur Fellowship in 1998, and he is the founder and executive director of the Center for Public Integrity, a nonpartisan, nonprofit organization located in Washington, D.C., that examines public service and ethics-related issues.

LAURIE LEIBER is director of the Center on Alcohol Advertising.

PIERRE M. LOEWE is a founding director of Strategos, a global strategy innovation firm based in Menlo Park, California, that helps companies reinvent themselves and their industries. He is also executive director of the Strategos Institute, and he has contributed several articles to *Management Review*.

LAURIE ANN MAZUR is a writer and a consultant to nonprofit organizations who has written widely on environmental and social justice issues.

TED MARCHESE is vice president of the American Association of Higher Education (AAHE). He holds degrees from Rutgers University (English), Georgetown University (law), and the University of Michigan (Ph.D. in Higher Education). He has also worked in Washington, D.C., as a staff aide to U.S. Senator Clifford P. Case and for the American Council on Education's Commission on Academic Affairs. He edits the *AAHE Bulletin,* a monthly periodical, and he is the executive editor of *Change,* one of higher education's most widely read magazines.

REGIS McKENNA is chairman of the the McKenna Group, a management and marketing consulting firm in Palo Alto, California, that specializes in the development and application of information and telecommunications technologies. He lectures and conducts seminars on technology marketing and competitiveness issues throughout the United States, Europe, and Asia.

WENDY MELILLO is a regular contributor to *Adweek* magazine.

GEOFFREY E. MEREDITH is founder of Lifestage Matrix Marketing, a marketing consulting firm based in Lafayette, California.

MARY MODAHL is vice president of research at Forrester Research, Inc., in Cambridge, Massachusetts, the leading provider of primary research, market analysis, and strategic guidance in the area of electronic commerce. She has been profiled in the *Wall Street Journal* and *Wired* magazine, and she has appeared as a guest on CBS, National Public Radio, CNN, and CNBC. She was recently named one of the 25 most influential people in electronic business by *Business Week.*

DAVID F. NOBLE is a historian and cofounder of the national coalition for Universities in the Public Interest. He is also a professor at York University and the author of *The Religion of Technology: The Divinity of Man and the Spirit of Invention* (Penguin Putnam, 1999).

GEORGE RITZER is a professor of sociology at the University of Maryland. He is known worldwide for coining the term *McDonaldization of society* and for his publications on the subject.

STEVE RIVKIN, who teaches in the Department of Economics at Amherst College in Massachusetts, has a special expertise in public finance and neoclassical cost-benefit analysis.

RUSSELL ROBERTS is the John M. Olin Senior Fellow at the Center for the Study of American Business at Washington University in St. Louis. His research and writing centers on the interaction between economics and public policy. He is the author of *The Choice: A Fable of Free Trade and Protectionism* (Prentice Hall, 1993), which was named one of the top 10 books of 1994 by *Business Week.* His latest book, *The Invisible Heart: An Economic Romance* (MIT Press, 2001), is a defense of capitalism and free markets and is written as a novel. His articles have been published in the *Wall Street Journal* and the *New York Times.* He is also a frequent contributor to National Public Radio's Morning Edition.

JAMES R. ROSENFIELD is chairman/CEO of San Diego–based Rosenfield & Associates and one of today's leading speakers and writers on marketing and direct marketing. A graduate of Columbia University, he has taught there as well as at the University of Colorado and Ohio State University. He serves on the editorial review board of the *Journal of Interactive Marketing,* and he has over 300 articles to his credit in publications ranging from *Direct Marketing* to the *Wall Street Journal.*

CHARLES D. SCHEWE is a professor of marketing at the University of Massachusetts at Amherst as well as principal in Lifestage Matrix Marketing, a marketing research and consulting firm located in Amherst. Dr. Schewe received his Ph.D. from the Kellogg Graduate School of Management at Northwestern University. He has published over 50 articles in such academic journals as *Journal of Marketing, Journal of Marketing Research, Business Horizons, Marketing Management,* and the *Journal of Consumer Marketing.* He is the author of *Marketing: Principles and Strategies* (McGraw-Hill, 1987) and coauthor, with Alexander Hiam, of *The Portable MBA in Marketing,* 2d ed. (John Wiley, 1998).

ERICK SCHONFELD, a graduate of Cornell University, is an investment writer for *Fortune* magazine.

EVAN I. SCHWARTZ is a contributor to *Wired* and the *New York Times* and a former editor for *Business Week.* He is the author of the best-seller *Digital Darwinism: Seven Breakthrough Business Strategies for Surviving in the Cultural Web Economy* (Broadway Books, 1999). His previous book, *Webonomics* (Broadway Books, 1998) was also a best-seller as well as a finalist for both the Booz Allen Global Business Book Award and the Computer Press Award.

J. WALKER SMITH is a managing partner and has been a member of the Yankelovich organization since 1991. He holds a Ph.D. in mass communications research from the University of North Carolina at Chapel Hill, and he is a frequent commentator on trends in American society in newspapers and network business news programs. Prior to joining Yankelovich, he was research director at Dow Brands. He is coauthor, with Ann S. Clurman, of *Rocking the Ages: The Yankelovich Report on Generational Marketing* (HarperInformation, 1997).

EDWARD J. STANEK is president of the North American Association of State and Provincial Lotteries.

MYRA STARK is director of knowledge management and consumer insight at Saatchi and Saatchi in New York City. She is a frequent contributor to *Brand Week.*

MARCIA STEPANEK is a regular contributor to *Business Week e.biz* magazine.

ELYSE TANOUYE is a writer for the *Wall Street Journal,* particularly on health and medical issues.

JACK TROUT is president of Trout & Partners, a marketing firm with headquarters in Greenwich, Connecticut, and offices in 13 countries. He manages and supervises a global network of experts that apply his concepts and develop his methodology around the world. He has published numerous publications on "positioning" with Al Reis.

Index